D1094503

SLAVERY
IN THE COURTROOM

THE
BOSTON SLAVE RIOT,
AND
TRIAL
OF
Anthony Burns,

CONTAINING THE

REPORT OF THE FANEUIL HALL MEETING; THE MURDER OF
BACHELDER; THEODORE PARKER'S LESSON FOR THE DAY;
SPEECHES OF COUNSEL ON BOTH SIDES, CORRECTED
BY THEMSELVES; VERBATIM REPORT OF JUDGE
LORING'S DECISION; AND, A DETAILED AC-
COUNT OF THE EMBARKATION.

BOSTON:
FETRIDGE AND COMPANY.
1854.

Press of J. S. Potter & Co., 2 Spring Lane and 130 Washington Street.

Title page from *The Boston Slave Riot, and Trial of Anthony Burns* (Boston, 1854), a pamphlet containing valuable primary source material about the trial of Anthony Burns and the events that surrounded it, events that demonstrated strong public reaction to the enforcement of the Fugitive Slave Act.

SLAVERY
IN THE COURTROOM

AN ANNOTATED
BIBLIOGRAPHY OF
AMERICAN CASES

by Paul Finkelman

Washington   Library of Congress   1985

Library of Congress Cataloging in Publication Data

Finkelman, Paul, 1949–
  Slavery in the courtroom.

  "Includes materials from the collections of the
Law Library, including its rare book collections, and
from the general collections and the Rare Book and
Special Collections Division of the Library of Congress"
—Introd.
  Bibliography: p.
  Includes index.
  Supt. of Docs. no.: LC 1.12/2:Sl,1/2
  1. Slavery—Law and legislation—United States—Cases
—Bibliography. 2. Slavery—United States—Legal status
of slaves in free states—Cases—Bibliography.
I. Library of Congress. II. Title.
KF4545.S5A123   1985   016.34273'0873   83–600166
ISBN 0–8444–0431–4   016.347302873

For sale by the Superintendent of Documents
U.S. Government Printing Office
Washington, D.C. 20402

For John Hope Franklin, scholar, teacher, and friend.

CONTENTS

Table of Cases	ix
List of Pamphlets	xiii
Illustrations	xxi
Key to Location Symbols	xxiii
Foreword	xxv
Preface	xxvii
Introduction	3
The Slave in a Free Jurisdiction	**19**
Fugitive Slaves	**59**
Abolition and Abolitionists in the North	**139**
Abolitionists in the South	**157**
Slave Revolts	**197**
The African Slave Trade	**211**
Miscellaneous Trials and Cases	**251**
Appendix: British Cases	271
Selected Bibliography of Secondary Sources	293
Index	301

TABLE OF CASES

Ableman v. Booth   119
Alberti, Commonwealth v.   83
Allen, People v.   103
L'Amistad, Gedney v.   222
The Amistad, United States v.   222
Armitage, Forbes and,
    Ohio v.   68
Arnold v. Booth   119
Aves, Commonwealth v.   25

Bates, In re   239
Birney v. State   29
Booth, Ableman v.   119
Booth, Arnold v.   119
Booth, Ex parte   119
Booth, In re   119
Booth and Rycraft, In re   119
Broad, People v.   253
Brown, Commonwealth v.   188
Brown, In re Isaac   77
Brown, In re Thomas   186
Burns, In re   107
Bushnell, Ex parte   123
Bushnell, United States v.   123

Chaplin, In re   182
Christiana Treason Trials;
    see United States v.
    Hanway
Cobb, United States v.   103
Commonwealth v. Alberti   83
Commonwealth v. Aves   25
Commonwealth v. Brown   188
Commonwealth v. Garner   177
Commonwealth v. Myers   127
Commonwealth v. Stratton   32
Commonwealth v. Tracy   64
Commonwealth v. Webster   175
Corrie, United States v.   246
Corse, People v.   263
Crandall, United States v.   164

Crandall v. State   139
Crocker, Norris v.   80
Curtis v. Mussey   88

Daggs v. Frazier   79
Deliesseline, Elkison v.   256
Denmark Vesey Conspiracy;
    see Vesey Conspirators
Drayton v. United States   179
Dred Scott v. Sandford   43
    see also Scott v. Emerson

Ela v. Smith   107
Elkison v. Deliesseline   256
Emerson v. Scott   43
Emerson, Scott v.   43

Forbes and Armitage,
    Ohio v.   68
Frazier, Daggs v.   79

Garland, United States
    ex rel. v. Morris   119
Garner, Commonwealth v.   177
Garrison, Todd v.   161
Gedney v. L'Amistad   222
Gilman, State v.   147
Gordon v. United States   135
Graham v. Strader   35
Graham, Strader v.   35
Groves v. Slaughter   33
Gruber, Maryland v.   158

Hamlet, In re   85
Hanway, United States v.   95
Hodge, King v.   290
Hossack, United States v.   128

Jackson v. Lively   283
La Jeune Eugénie, United
    States v.   217

Jones v. Van Zandt	70
Kimber, King v.	277
King v. de Zulueta	285
King v. Hodge	290
King v. Kimber	277
King v. Mark and Phillis, slaves	251
King v. Smith	272
Kirk, In re	75
Langston, Ex parte	123
Langston, United States v.	123
Latimer Case	64
Lemmon v. People	54
Lemmon, People ex rel, Napoleon v.	54
Lewis, Williamson v.	39
Lively, Jackson v.	283
Mark and Phillis, slaves, King v.	251
Maryland v. Gruber	158
Matilda, Case of	29
Morris, United States v.	86
Morris, United States ex rel, Garland v.	119
Mussey, Curtis v.	88
Myers, Commonwealth v.	127
Napoleon, People ex rel., v. Lemmon	54
Newton, Norris v.	80
New York Slave Conspirators, In re,	197
Norris v. Crocker	80
Norris v. Newton	80
Ohio v. Forbes and Armitage	68
Passmore Williamson, Case of	39
Pennsylvania, Prigg v.	60
People v. Allen	103
People v. Broad	253
People v. Corse	263
People ex rel. Napoleon v. Lemmon	54
People, Lemmon v.	54
Phillis, slaves, King v. Mark and	251
Post, State v.	150
Prigg v. Pennsylvania	60
Reed, United States v.	103
Ross v. Duncan	267
Ross v. Vertner	267
Rycraft, In re Booth and	119
Rycraft, United States v.	119
Sandford, Scott v.	43
Scott v. Emerson	43
Scott v. Sandford	43
Scott, Emerson v.	43
see also Dred Scott v. Sandford	
Scott, United States v.	86
Shadrach Case; see United States v. Morris and United States v. Scott	
Sims, In re	88
Slaughter, Groves v.	33
Smith, Ela v.	107
Smith, King v.	272
Somerset v. Stewart	19
State v. Gilman	147
State v. Post	150
State v. Storrs	143
State v. Van Beuren	150
State, Birney v.	29
State, Crandall v.	139
Stewart, Somerset v.	19
Storrs, State v.	143
Stout, United States v.	128
Stowell, United States v.	107
Strader v. Graham	35
Strader, Graham v.	35
Stratton, Commonwealth v.	32
Todd v. Garrison	161
Tracy, Commonwealth v.	64
United States v. The Amistad	222
United States v. Bushnell	123

United States v. *Cobb*	103	*Van Beuren, State* v.	150
United States v. *Corrie*	246	*Van Zandt, Jones* v.	70
United States v. *Crandall*	164	*Vertner, Ross* v.	267
United States v. *Gordon*	135	Vesey Conspirators	202
United States v. *Hanway*	95		
United States v. *Hossack*	128		
United States v. *The La Jeune*			
Eugénie	217	*Walker, In re*	170
United States v. *Langston*	123	*The Wanderer*	246
United States v. *Morris*	86	*Webster, Commonwealth* v.	175
United States v. *Reed*	103	*Wheeler, United States ex rel.*	
United States v. *Rycraft*	119	v. *Williamson*	39
United States v. *Scott*	86	Williamson's, Passmore,	
United States v. *Stout*	128	Case	39
United States v. *Stowell*	107	*Williamson* v. *Lewis*	39
United States ex rel. Garland		*Williamson, United States ex*	
v. *Morris*	119	*rel, Wheeler* v.	39
United States ex rel. Wheeler			
v. *Williamson*	39		
United States, Drayton v.	179		
United States, Gordon v.	135	*de Zulueta, King* v.	285

LIST OF
PAMPHLETS

Pamphlets annotated in the bibliography are listed here by case in the order in which they appear within each chapter. Short title and date of original publication are given, but reprints and later editions listed in the bibliography are not listed here.

THE SLAVE IN A FREE JURISDICTION

Somerset v. *Stewart*

Francis Hargrave, *An Argument in the Case of James Sommersett* (1772)   21

Edward Long, *Candid Reflections upon the Judgement Lately Awarded* (1772)   22

A Letter to Philo Africanus, upon Slavery (1788)   23

Commonwealth v. *Aves*

Case of the Slave Child, Med (1836)   28

The Case of Matilda

Salmon Portland Chase, *Speech of Salmon P. Chase* (1837)   31

Commonwealth v. *Stratton*

Report of the Holden Slave Case (1839)   33

Groves v. *Slaughter*

Robert J. Walker, *Argument of Robert J. Walker, Esq., before the Supreme Court of the United States* (1841)   34

Strader v. Graham

James Gillespie Birney, *Examination of the Decision of the Supreme Court* (1852)   37

United States ex rel. Wheeler v. *Williamson*

Case of Passmore Williamson (1856)   41

Narrative of the Facts in the Case of Passmore Williamson (1855)   42

Joseph J. Lewis, *Passmore Williamson vs. John K. Kane* (1857)   42

Dred Scott v. *Sandford*

U.S. Supreme Court, *Dred Scott vs. John F. A. Sandford; Additional Brief of M. Blair for Appellant* (1856)   48

U.S. Supreme Court, *A Report of the Decision of the Supreme Court* (New York, 1857)   49

U.S. Supreme Court, *Report of the Decision of the Supreme Court* (Washington, 1857)   49

U.S. Supreme Court, *The Case of Dred Scott in the United States Supreme Court* (1860)   50

Thomas Hart Benton, *Historical and Legal Examination of That Part of the Decision* (1857)   50

Horace Gray and John Lowell, Jr., *A Legal Review of the Case of Dred Scott* (1857)   51

A Review of the Decision of the Supreme Court (1857)   52

U.S. Supreme Court, *The Dred Scott Decision: Opinion of Chief Justice Taney* (1859)   52

Samuel Alfred Foot, *An Examination of the Case of Dred Scott* (1859)   53

Lemmon v. *The People*

New York Court of Appeals, *Report of the Lemmon Slave Case* (1860)   54

FUGITIVE SLAVES

Prigg v. *Pennsylvania*

U.S. Supreme Court, *Report of the Case of Edward Prigg* (1842)   61

Maryland General Assembly, House of Delegates, *Report of the Committee on Grievances and Courts of Justice* (1841)   63

The Latimer Case

An Article on the Latimer Case (1843)   65

Norfolk, Va., *Proceedings of the Citizens of the Borough of Norfolk, on the Boston Outrage* (1843)   67

Ohio v. *Forbes and Armitage*

William Johnston, *The State of Ohio vs. Forbes and Armitage* (1846)   69

Jones v. *Van Zandt*

Salmon Portland Chase, *Reclamation of Fugitives from Service* (1847)   73

William Henry Seward, *Argument of William H. Seward* (1847)   75

In re Kirk

Supplement to the New York Legal Observer, Containing the Report of the Case (1847)   76

In re Isaac Brown

Case of the Slave Isaac Brown (1847)   78

Daggs v. *Frazier*

> *Ruel Daggs vs. Elihu Frazier, et al., Trespass on the Case* (1850) 79

Norris v. *Newton*

> *The South Bend Fugitive Slave Case* (1851) 82

Commonwealth v. *Alberti*

> *A Review of the Trial, Conviction, and Sentence of George F. Alberti* (1851) 84

In re James Hamlet

> American and Foreign Anti-Slavery Society, *The Fugitive Slave Bill* (1850) 85

United States v. *Morris*

> *United States vs. Charles G. Davis* (1851) 87

In re Thomas Sims

> *Trial of Thomas Sims, on an Issue of Personal Liberty* (1851) 91

Charge to the Grand Jury

> U.S. District Court, Pennsylvania (Western District), *A Charge, to the Grand Jury* (1851) 94

United States v. *Hanway*

> *A Full and Correct Report of the Christiana Tragedy* (1851) 98

> *Report of the Trial of Castner Hanway for Treason* (1852) 99

> Maryland, Attorney General's Office, *Report of Attorney General Brent* (1852) 100

> *A History of the Trial of Castner Hanway and Others* (1852) 101

People v. *Allen*

> *Trial of Henry W. Allen, U.S. Deputy Marshal* (1852) 103

> Gerrit Smith, *Abstract of the Argument on the Fugitive Slave Law* (1852) 107

In re Anthony Burns

> *The Boston Slave Riot, and Trial of Anthony Burns* (1854) 112

> William I. Bowditch, *The Rendition of Anthony Burns* (1854) 113

> Theodore Parker, *The Trial of Theodore Parker* (1855) 115

> Wendell Phillips, *Argument of Wendell Phillips* (1855) 117

> Richard Henry Dana, *Remarks of Richard Henry Dana, Jr.* (1855) 118

In re Booth

> Wisconsin Supreme Court, *Unconstitutionality of the Fugitive Slave Act* (1855) 120

> *Unconstitutionality of the Fugitive Act; Argument of Byron Paine, Esq., and Opinion of Hon. A. D. Smith* (1854?) 121

Ex parte Bushnell

Jacob R. Shipherd, *History of the Oberlin-Wellington Rescue*
(1859)   125

Commonwealth v. *Myers*

The Trial of Emanuel Myers, of Maryland, for Kidnapping Certain Fugitive Slaves (1859)   127

United States v. *Hossack*

Report of the Trial of John Hossack Indicted for Rescuing a Fugitive Slave (1860)   129

John Hossack, *Speech of John Hossack, Convicted of a Violation of the Fugitive Slave Law* (1860)   131

H. S. Fitch, *Argument of H. S. Fitch, Esq., United States District Attorney, on the Trial of John Hossack* (1860)   132

United States v. *Gordon*

John Joliffe, *In the Matter of George Gordon's Petition for Pardon* (1862)   134

ABOLITION AND ABOLITIONISTS IN THE NORTH

Crandall v. *State*

Report of the Arguments of Counsel, in the Case of Prudence Crandall (1834)   141

State v. *Storrs*

George Storrs, *Mob, under Pretence of Law, or, The Arrest and Trial of Rev. George Storrs* (1835)   145

State v. *Gilman*

Alton Trials: of Winthrop S. Gilman (1838)   148

State v. *Post; State* v. *Van Beuren*

Alvan Stewart, *Legal Argument before the Supreme Court of the State of New Jersey* (1845)   152

ABOLITIONISTS IN THE SOUTH

Maryland v. *Gruber*

Trial of the Rev. Jacob Gruber (1819)   159

Todd v. *Garrison*

William Lloyd Garrison, *A Brief Sketch of the Trial* (1834)   163

United States v. *Crandall*

The Trial of Reuben Crandall, M.D. (Washington, 1836)   166

The Trial of Reuben Crandall, M.D. (New York, 1836)   168

Francis Scott Key, *A Part of a Speech* (1836)   169

In re Jonathan Walker

Jonathan Walker, *Trial and Imprisonment of Jonathan Walker* (1845)   173

Commonwealth v. *Webster*

Delia A. Webster, *Kentucky Jurisprudence: A History of the Trial of Miss Delia A. Webster* (1845)   176

Commonwealth v. *Garner*

Samuel Vinton, *Substance of an Argument of Samuel F. Vinton* (1846)   178

Drayton v. *United States*

Daniel Drayton, *Personal Memoir of Daniel Drayton* (1855)   181

In re William Chaplin

The Case of William L. Chaplin (1851)   185

In re Thomas Brown

Thomas Brown, *Brown's Three Years in the Kentucky Prisons* (1857)   187

Commonwealth v. *Brown*

The Life, Trial, and Conviction of Captain John Brown (1859)   192

SLAVE REVOLTS

In re New York Slave Conspirators

Daniel Horsmanden, *A Journal of the Proceedings in the Detection of the Conspiracy* (1744)   200

The Denmark Vesey Conspirators

An Official Report of the Trials of Sundry Negroes (1822)   204

James Hamilton, Jr., *An Account of the Late Intended Insurrection Among a Portion of the Blacks of This City* (1822)   208

THE AFRICAN SLAVE TRADE

Charge to the Grand Jury

Joseph Story, *A Charge, Delivered to the Grand Juries of the Circuit Court* (1819?)   214

United States v. *The La Jeune Eugénie*

A Report of the Case of the Jeune Eugénie (1822)   220

United States v. *The Amistad*

U.S. Circuit Court (2d Circuit), *The African Captives: Trial of the Prisoners of the Amistad* (1839)   229

John Quincy Adams, *Argument of John Quincy Adams, before the Supreme Court* (1841)   232

Roger S. Baldwin, *Argument of Roger S. Baldwin of New Haven before the Supreme Court of the United States* (1841)   237

In re Bates

Isaac William Hayne, *Argument before the United States Circuit Court* (1859)   240

Report of the Trials in the Echo Cases (1859)   244

The Wanderer

The United States of America, by Information, Versus the Schooner Wanderer (1860)   248

MISCELLANEOUS TRIALS AND CASES

King v. *Mark and Phillis, Slaves*

Abner Cheney Goodell, Jr., *The Trial and Execution for Petit Treason, of Mark and Phillis* (1883)   252

People v. *Amos Broad*

The Trial of Amos Broad and His Wife (1809)   254

Elkison v. *Deliesseline*

William Johnson, *The Opinion of the Hon. William Johnson* (1823?)   259

Benjamin Faneuil Hunt, *The Argument of Benj. Faneuil Hunt* (1823)   261

People v. *Corse*

Isaac Tatem Hopper, *Exposition of the Proceedings of John P. Darg, Henry W. Merritt, and Others* (1840)   265

Ross v. *Vertner*

John Ker, *A Brief History of an Attempt during the Last Session of the Legislature, in 1841, to Interfere with the Judgments of the Courts* (1842)   268

APPENDIX: BRITISH CASES

The King v. *Rev. John Smith*

The London Missionary Society's Report of the Proceedings against the Late Rev. J. Smith (1824)   275

The Missionary Smith: Substance of the Debate in the House of Commons (1824)   276

The King v. *Kimber*

The Trial of Captain John Kimber, for the Supposed Murder of an African Girl (1792)   279

The Trial of Captain John Kimber, for the Murder of Two Female Negro Slaves (1792)   280

Jackson v. *Livesly*

    The Remarkable Case of Potter Jackson (1807?)   284

The King v. *Pedro de Zulueta*

    Trial of Pedro de Zulueta, Jun., on a Charge of Slave Trading (1844)   287

    Trial of Pedro de Zulueta, Jun., in the Central Criminal Court of the City of London (1844)   288

The King v. *Hodge*

    A Report of the Trial of Arthur Hodge, Esquire (1812)   290

ILLUSTRATIONS

The Boston Slave Riot, and Trial of Anthony Burns (1854)   ii

Handbill for an Escaped Slave (1825)   2

An Argument in the Case of James Sommersett (1722)   18

Lemuel Shaw   26

Benjamin Robbins Curtis   27

Rufus Choate   28

Salmon P. Chase   30

James G. Birney   36

Passmore Williamson   40

Roger Brooke Taney   44

Charles O'Conor   55

"100 Dollars Reward" Broadside (1834)   58

Levi Woodbury   71

William Henry Seward   72

Wendell Phillips   89

Thaddeus Stevens   96

Robert C. Grier   97

Samuel Joseph May   104

Marshal's Posse with Anthony Burns   108

Theodore Parker Lecturing   109

John Hale   110

John Albion Andrew   111

"$200 Reward" Broadside (1847)   137

Prudence Crandall   138

Alvan Stewart   151

John Brown   156

William Lloyd Garrison   162

"The Author Confined in the Pillory," from *Trial and Imprisonment of Jonathan Walker* (1845)   171

"Common Mode of Whipping," from *Trial and Imprisonment of Jonathan Walker* (1845)   171

"United States Marshal Branding the Author," from *Trial and Imprisonment of Jonathan Walker* (1845)   172

Robert Toombs   183

Alexander Hamilton Stephens   184

"Bringing the Prisoners Out of the Engine House," from *The Life, Trials, and Execution of Capt. John Brown* (1859)   188

"Attack on the Insurgents at the Bridge," from *The Life, Trials, and Execution of Capt. John Brown* (1859)   189

Samuel Gridley Howe   190

A Journal of the Proceedings in the Detection of the Conspiracy (1744)   196

Argument of John Quincy Adams before the Supreme Court of the United States (1841)   210

Joseph Story   213

John Quincy Adams   223

Lewis Tappan   224

Roger S. Baldwin   225

James Moore Wayne   240

Isaac Hayne   241

"Negroes for Sale," Spring Hill, Arkansas (1842)   250

William Johnson   257

The Remarkable Case of Potter Jackson (1807?)   270

KEY TO LOCATION SYMBOLS

Law Library	Trials Collection, Law Library, Library of Congress
LLRBR	Rare Book Collection, Law Library, Library of Congress
Rare Book Room	Rare Book and Special Collections Division, Library of Congress
Class numbers	In the general collections of the Library of Congress unless otherwise specified
AC 901-995	Pamphlet collections.
E 441-453	History—United States—Revolution to the Civil War—Slavery
F 1-975	United States local history
HV 40-696	Social sciences—Social pathology, social and public welfare, criminology—Charities
JX 2001-5810	Political science—International law. Law Library
KF	Law of the United States—Federal Law. Common and collective state law. Law Library

F O R E W O R D

In its role as a national library and a center for scholars, the Library of Congress endeavors to go beyond serving merely as a huge book repository, a lending library for government agencies, or a museum that displays rare books. Like other parts of the Library, the Law Library is all of these things. It also strives, however, to make its collections as accessible as possible to the public so that the heritage its holdings contain can be passed on to all levels of readership and can actively inspire further learning and research.

In many corners of this vast institution, there are constant discoveries of collections that enrich and deepen our knowledge of ourselves and our past. This bibliography brings to light one such collection. Its appearance should be useful not only to legal historians but to students and researchers in many other disciplines as well. In 1979, during his work on the enforcement of the fugitive slave laws as the J. Franklin Jameson Fellow at the Library of Congress, Prof. Paul Finkelman uncovered the existence of a vast number of uncataloged pamphlets dealing with the law of slavery. It is to his credit that he undertook the task of compiling these materials, which record—often quite dramatically—such a critical phase of America's past.

Carleton W. Kenyon
The Law Librarian

PREFACE

In 1979 while conducting research in American legal history on the enforcement of the Fugitive Slave Acts of 1793 and 1850, I discovered that the Law Library of the Library of Congress had a large number of pamphlets dealing with fugitive slave cases. These were mingled with pamphlets about thousands of other cases, on all sorts of subjects. Indeed, the Trials Collection at the Library of Congress may be the best collection of literature relating to trials in the United States.

Unfortunately, this valuable collection is not fully cataloged. About thirty thousand cards record the cases by names of litigants, but there is no subject access to the collection. To search thoroughly for fugitive slave cases, I read through all thirty thousand cards. In the process I discovered cases dealing with other aspects of slavery. This eventually led me to a full search for materials on all trials dealing with slavery, not only in the Law Library but throughout the Library of Congress.

I began this project during the time I was fortunate enough to hold the J. Franklin Jameson Fellowship, a fellowship jointly administered by the Library of Congress and the American Historical Association, which was inaugurated under the leadership of Librarian of Congress Daniel J. Boorstin. Marlene C. McGuirl, Chief of the American-British Law Division of the Law Library, encouraged this project from the start. Without her commitment to scholarship and publishing, this bibliography would not have been undertaken.

In working on this book I was aided by a number of friends and librarians. Byrgen Pickering Finkelman generously took time away from her own research and writing to help with the laborious process of reading proofs. Her keen sense of good writing and clear style made this a far better book. Virginia Heamstreet, Kim Horney, and Susan Spicer also helped proofread. Abraham and Carol Wagner kindly lent me their apartment in Washington and allowed me to use their office for typing. Margaret Thomas helped me search through card files. I am especially grateful to Richard Holland, history bibliographer, Perry Castaneda Library, University of Texas, who read much of the manuscript for this book and made many valuable suggestions. Roy Mersky and his reference staff, Tarlton Law Library, University of Texas, were very helpful to me, as were Harry F. Martin, director, Harvard Law Library, and Joan Shear and Terry Swanlund of the reference department there.

At the Library of Congress, Bruce Martin of the General Reading Rooms Division showed me around the Library, provided me with a study desk, and helped find missing materials. Thomas D. Burney was a great help in the Rare Book and Special Collections Division. Evelyn Sinclair, Joan O'Callaghan, and Natalie Gawdiak helped edit this book. Robert Nay and Mary Ann Ellery of the Law Library staff and Warren Rosmarin, a Library of Congress intern, reviewed the entire manuscript.

Finally, I owe a special debt to Larry M. Boyer, who at the time I was working on this material helped me with the Law Library's rare books and trials collections. Resourceful and always helpful, Larry took time to search out obscure pamphlets and books. He often stayed late so he could help me find and photocopy rare materials to annotate later. Above all, Larry is a friend and compatriot who understands the importance of historians and librarians working together.

SLAVERY
IN THE COURTROOM

$50 REWARD.

NEGRO WASHINGTON eloped from my farm, the 31st of October, living in St. Mary's county, near Charlotte Hall Post Office. Said negro is about 19 years of age; yellow complexion; much freckled; he has a scar over one of his eyebrows, which not recollected; large coarse features; about five feet high; bulky made. Has taken with him several suits of clothing, both summer and winter; a snuff colored frock coat and pantaloons; a light colored short grey coat and pantaloons. His summer clothing, check domestic cotton, linen and domestic cotton shirts; bell crown furred hat, about half worn. He has been used to house work, from ten years of age. He was brought from the State of Tennessee about the month of May, and remained at Mr. Brown's Hotel during that month. He may possibly attempt to return to Winchester in Tennessee, where he lived for four or five years.

GEORGE G. ASHCOM.

November 3, 1825.

Many of the ironies and inhumanities of slavery are found in this handbill for an escaped slave. The slave was named after George Washington, the man who led the American colonies in their struggle for freedom from British rule. This slave has now sought his own kind of freedom. Like many slaves, Washington may have wanted to return to his friends and family. The amount of clothing he took with him and his job as a house servant suggest that Washington was materially better off than most slaves. But nice clothing, decent working conditions, and perhaps better food were no substitute for freedom and the right to live among one's friends and family.

Broadside Collection, Rare Book and Special Collections Division.

Introduction

In January 1620, John Rolfe, the secretary and recorder for the Virginia Colony, wrote to Sir Edwin Sandys in London to report on conditions and events in the colony. In an offhand manner Rolfe noted, "About the latter end of August, a Dutch man of Warr . . . arrived. . . . He brought not anything but 20. and odd Negroes, which the Governor and Cape Marchand bought for victualle."[1] Thus, in this casual way, the beginnings of American slavery were recorded.

These twenty Negroes were not immediately treated as slaves. Rather, they were probably considered indentured servants, or servants for a term of years. Some of these first twenty may well have gained their freedom in a few years. By the 1630s and 1640s, in fact, Virginia records indicate that some blacks were property owners and, ironically, the masters of other indentured servants.

Other records from this period, however, show that black servants were gradually being reduced to a status below that of white servants. In 1640, for example, three indentured servants—two whites and one black— ran away from their master but were recaptured. All three were sentenced to "the punishment of whipping and to have thirty stripes apiece."[2] The two white servants were also required to serve their master an extra year after completing their original indentures. They were further sentenced to serve the colony for three years after they had completed all service to their master. This was surely harsh punishment for simply having run away.

But compared with that of their black companion, the white servants' sentence of four additional years of servitude was light. The court declared "that the third being a negro named John Punch shall serve his said master or his assigns for the time of his natural life here or elsewhere."[3] In such ways African servants in Virginia and Maryland became slaves. The process in the first half of the seventeenth century was haphazard, inconsistent, and unsystematic. Some African servants completed their indentures, became free men and women, and even hired other servants, both black and white. A few of these ex-servants ultimately became the owners of African slaves. By midcentury, however, such African slaveholders were the exception.

The process of enslavement that began in the seventeenth century was not planned. Indeed, it was what historian Winthrop Jordan has aptly called an "unthinking decision."[4] The reasons for the enslavement of blacks are not entirely clear, but it appears that several factors were at work. Human greed may have been the strongest motivation. By the 1630s and 1640s it simply became more profitable to own slaves than to control indentured servants. Racism was also a factor. Africans were clearly different from Europeans, and so it was perhaps easier to view them as property or things rather than persons. That they were not Christian also helped. Enslaving heathens was surely more acceptable than enslaving fellow Christians. Indeed, very early on some masters argued that the enslavement of heathen Africans was really a blessing to the slaves because, under English tutelage, the heathens could learn Christianity. That Africans did not know about or understand English custom and law also facilitated the growth of slavery. Unaware of the ''rights of Englishmen'' and separated from their own cultures, Africans were particularly vulnerable to enslavement. Finally, many Africans in this early period came to the English colonies *as slaves*. These Africans had been enslaved in Africa or had been made slaves by Spanish, Portuguese, Dutch, or English slave traders. African slavery was a factor in the New World for more than a century before English colonists became owners of human chattel.

From the first statutes concerning slavery in the English colonies one may deduce the system's unplanned nature. There are no early Virginia or Maryland laws creating slavery per se. Rather, there are laws acknowledging that slavery exists. Thus a Virginia statute of 1660-61 declares: *''Bee it enacted* That in case any English servant shall run away in company with any negroes who are incapable of making satisfaction by addition of time, *Bee it enacted* that the English so running away in company with them shall serve for the time of the said negroes absence as they are to do for their owne by a former act.'' Only one type of Negro would be ''incapable of making satisfaction by addition of time''—a Negro slave.[5]

A Maryland act of 1663 was titled ''An act concerning negroes and other slaves.'' It declared that ''All negroes or other slaves within the province, and all negroes and other slaves to be hereafter imported into the province, shall serve *durante vita;* and all children born of any negro or other slave, shall be slaves as their fathers were for the term of their lives.''[6] While ensuring that future generations of Africans and their Afro-American children would be slaves, this statute began with the assumption that slavery and slaves already existed in Maryland.

Thus, without the benefit of statutes or other legislation, slavery came to exist in the British colonies of North America, and colonists simply began to assume that slavery existed. In drafting a constitution for the proposed colony of South Carolina, Sir Anthony Ashley Cooper and his protégé John Locke included the following provision: ''Every Freeman of Carolina shall have absolute power and authority over Negro Slaves, of what opinion or Religion soever.''[7] Other colonies, and later the American states, also began with slavery as an accepted and established institution. Legislatures passed slave codes and other legislation to control and protect the "peculiar institution," but throughout the American colonies slavery came into being without any particular legislative forethought.

The evolution of slavery and of a law of slavery resembles the classic development of common law. First there was a need for laborers. Africans were used, and soon, by custom and through usage, they were thought of and treated as slaves, unless designated otherwise. Along with this status, a set of customs developed for dealing with slaves. Gradually these customs were institutionalized into customary rules, or customary law. Eventually the customary law was applied in the courts and became common law. Much of this law was incorporated into statutes, casebooks, court decisions, or common law rules.

Oliver Wendell Holmes's description of the development of the common law also applies to the origin of slave law: "The life of the law has not been logic; it has been experience. The felt necessities of the time, the prevalent moral and political theories, intuitions of public policy, avowed or unconscious, even the prejudices which judges share with their fellow-men, have had a good deal more to do than the syllogism in determining the rules by which men should be governed."[8] The necessity for cheap and pliable labor, the moral theories of the English settlers, the public policy of the colonies and the English government, and, of course, the prejudices of the colonial ruling class all led to Afro-American slavery, first as custom and later as law.

By the end of the seventeenth century, slavery was well entrenched in much of British North America. It would remain a strong and economically important institution until 1865. Throughout much of that period, the law connected to that institution expanded with the institution itself. By the time of the American Revolution, slavery was part of the unwritten constitution of the English colonists who were about to assert their independence. The institution had been around so long that Americans no longer wondered or worried about how slavery began.

There is of course something profoundly ironic about this haphazard development of slavery in America. The New World was to have been a place where human society could develop and energies be released without the constraints of European class and caste systems. It was John Locke's ideal state of nature.

In legal terms there was also an irony. Although the law of slavery and the common law developed similarly, the result was quite the opposite. William Blackstone found that English law was based on "three principal or primary articles: the right of personal security, the right of personal liberty, and the right of private property."[9] He declared:

"Next to personal security, the law of England regards, asserts, and preserves the personal liberty of individuals. This personal liberty consists in the power of loco-motion, of changing situation, or removing one's person to whatsoever place one's own inclination may direct; without imprisonment or restraint, unless by due course of law."[10]

Such rights, of course, were incompatible with chattel slavery. Even as early as 1765 Blackstone himself recognized this. At that time many Englishmen, including the royal family and government officials, participated in the African slave trade (with the encouragement of Parliament). Many English citizens and colonists owned and kept slaves. Nevertheless, Blackstone believed "this spirit of liberty is so deeply implanted in our constitution, and rooted even in our very soil, that a slave or a negro, the moment he lands in England, falls under the protection of the laws, and with regard to all natural rights becomes *eo instanti* a freeman."[11] Seven years later, Lord Mansfield, chief justice of the Court of the King's Bench, would reach precisely this conclusion in the famous case of *Somerset* v. *Stewart*.

Although decided by an English judge, *Somerset* v. *Stewart* has been included in the main body of this book, rather than in the appendix with other English cases. The reason for this is two-fold. First, *Somerset* v. *Stewart* was decided in 1772, four years before American independence was declared. Thus, Lord Mansfield's decision was part of that body of statutes, decisions, compilations, treatises, and opinions known as the English common law at the time the American colonies broke from their mother country. The new American states adopted the common law of England as their own, except where it conflicted with their recently written republican constitutions or with new laws they had passed. *Somerset* v. *Stewart* therefore became part of the newly developing American common law. Not surprisingly, then, the case was widely discussed in America both before and after the Revolution. The various American reports of the case, including a 1774 Boston imprint annotated below, attest to its importance in America.

The second reason for including *Somerset,* and indeed beginning this bibliography with it, is that *Somerset* was the most important English case dealing with slavery. It is rivaled by few American cases in its renown or its impact on the law of slavery. *Somerset* did not end all slavery in England, but the case did indicate what legal status slavery had there. Moreover, *Somerset* underscored the great tension created by slavery in Anglo-American law. This tension—between the common law and constitutional rights of freedom and liberty and the denial of that liberty under slavery—is a major theme that runs throughout the history of the law of slavery. In nearly all of the cases discussed in this bibliography there is a conflict between liberty and tyranny—between freedom and slavery.[12]

For the most part, the books and pamphlets annotated in this bibliography are found in the magnificent Trials Collection in the Law Library of the Library of Congress. There are more than ten thousand separate items in the Trials Collection. Most are cataloged only by the name of the case or the litigants involved. Thus, it is difficult for those interested in the law of slavery to make use of this invaluable collection. It is hoped that this bibliography will make the collection more accessible to scholars and researchers interested in the legal history of slavery, race relations, and Afro-Americans.

All of the pamphlets and books presenting primary source accounts of trials involving slaves are not, however, found in the Trials Collection or even in the Law Library. Important and rare works are scattered throughout the Library of Congress. Thus, this bibliography includes materials from the collections of the Law Library, including its rare book collections, and from the general collections and the Rare Book and Special Collections Division of the Library of Congress. Taken together, the materials annotated here provide a guide for the printed trial materials on the law of slavery in our national library.

Most of the pamphlets annotated here date from the period 1772 to 1861. Thus, they do not represent a complete history of the law of slavery. They touch, nevertheless, on most of the important subjects connected to slavery and law. Moreover, they often present materials that can be found nowhere except in pamphlet form. It is not surprising that we have pamphlets giving the arguments of counsel, the opinions of judges, or even the trial transcripts for significant or famous cases, such as *Somerset* v. *Stewart*.[13] *Dred Scott* v. *Sandford*,[14] or the trial of John Brown (1859). But many trials discussed here were not well known, even at the time they took place. Pamphlets describing them record what happened in trial courts (which are not always courts of record) in obscure jurisdictions. Indeed, the only existing record of some of these trials is found in these pamphlets. Thus, these materials give us a view of eighteenth- and nineteenth-century courts that is unavailable elsewhere.

The materials annotated here vary greatly in extent and depth. For some cases, there is little more than a few pages describing the cases and their outcomes. For other cases, there are word-for-word transcripts, taking up hundreds of pages. Such transcripts are often supplemented by reproductions of evidence, descriptions of pretrial activities, and illuminating discussions of the cases by participants.

The section on fugitive slaves and the fugitive slave laws, for instance, illustrates the range of these pamphlets and books. *Prigg* v. *Pennsylvania* was a major case heard by the U. S. Supreme Court.[15] The pamphlet report is simply a reprinting of the official published report. It adds little to our knowledge from the easily accessible *United States Reports*. A second pamphlet, however, contains an obscure Maryland House of Delegates report on the case.

The case of Castner Hanway,[16] tried for treason for opposing the Fugitive Slave Act of 1850,[17] was reported in the *Federal Cases.* That report briefly summarizes the case and the opinion of Justice Robert Grier. The four items about the case annotated here contain much more— records of pretrial hearings before local judges, a history of the case by one of Hanway's attorneys, a report by the Maryland attorney general, and a 275-page transcript of the trial record.

After reading through this mass of material, one quickly realizes how much is left out of most official reports of cases. In this same section on fugitive slaves is an eight-page account of the *Case of the Slave Isaac Brown.* Although an obscure proceeding with a report that is hardly as extensive as it could be, it is the only record we have of the case, which apparently never went beyond a Pennsylvania court of quarter sessions. There are also many pamphlets describing cases before irregular courts, such as the hearings held by commissioners under the Fugitive Slave Act of 1850. These cases were not officially reported. But, through the books and pamphlets annotated here, we nevertheless have excellent records of some of them.

Perhaps the most dramatic example of how important these pamphlets are can be seen in the case of *United States* v. *Hossack.*[18] This case was argued before the U. S. District Court for Northern Illinois. But in the late nineteenth century when all known cases in the lower federal courts were compiled into the set of volumes known as the *Federal Cases*, the compiler could find no report for the *Hossack* case. Only the docket number and name of the case still existed. The compiler thus inserted into the *Federal Cases* the following statement about *United States* v. *Hossack:* ''Nowhere reported; opinion not now accessible.'' Despite this notation, in the Law Library of the Library of Congress there is a 265-page transcript of the case. Not only is the opinion of the judge available, but so are the testimony, evidence, and arguments of counsel.

The materials annotated here have been organized by general topic rather than by title or author. This method and the rather extensive annotations are designed to make the bibliography a more useful tool. There are, of course, some cases that do not easily fit into one category. Thus, for some subjects it will be necessary to examine all of the annotations in a number of areas, rather than simply one. There is, for example, a section on slave riots and rebellions, but a number of trials involving riots or rebellions are also discussed in the sections on fugitive slaves or abolitionists. Similarly, some of the cases described in the section on slave transit may easily fit into other categories. Extensive annotations are provided to aid scholars who will not have immediate access to these rare pamphlets, which are unavailable in most libraries.

Understanding why these pamphlets were originally published

helps us to understand the legal dilemmas and the human passions created by slavery. Some of them were published simply to make money. The black sailor Potter Jackson hoped that the description of his beatings would arouse public sympathy. Sales of the history of his case would bring in some money, and he hoped that more would come through donations. As a sailor on a slave-trading ship, he had been beaten nearly to death and desperately needed this money for his very survival.

The needs of other publishers were less pressing. Richard Peters, an official reporter for the U. S. Supreme Court, believed that a pamphlet version of *Prigg* v. *Pennsylvania* would be popular enough to turn a profit.[19] Similarly, Benjamin Howard, another Supreme Court reporter, and other publishers as well tried to make money from the *Dred Scott* case.

That these publishers thought profits could be made, or donations received, through publishing pamphlets about slave cases suggests the level of interest in such cases. In the nineteenth century, this interest was hardly confined to lawyers or politicians. Abolitionists and others opposed to slavery undoubtedly bought and read many of these pamphlets. So, no doubt, did slave owners interested in the value and protection of their property. But many of these pamphlets were also directed at a larger audience—the educated and reading public of the late eighteenth and the nineteenth centuries.

Not all of these pamphlets were published with profit in mind. Indeed, the majority were part of propaganda campaigns or political actions by abolitionists and politicians. Some of these activists no doubt hoped to combine politics and profit. Horace Greeley, the publisher of the *New York Tribune*, was a shrewd and successful businessman as well as a Republican party leader. In publishing the *Report of the Lemmon Slave Case*, he looked to both his conscience and his pocketbook. The pamphlet went through two editions (1860 and 1861), which suggests that it sold well. Even if he had not expected it to sell well, Greeley might have supported the report's publication. The case involved the attempt of a Virginia couple, the Lemmons, to bring eight slaves into New York while they awaited passage by ship to Texas. For Greeley the case was not one of interstate comity or the privileges and immunities of the two citizens of Virginia to travel with their property. Rather, it was a case involving an attempt to introduce slavery into the Empire State and perhaps to force slavery on the North. Thus, when the New York Court of Appeals upheld a lower court decision freeing the eight slaves, Greeley was delighted. The case appeared to be looming as a political issue that might go to the U. S. Supreme Court. Some called it ''the next *Dred Scott* case.'' By publishing his report, Greeley was educating the public to the political issues raised by the case. Here, good politics also ended up being good economics. Greeley's 1860 publication of *The Case of*

Dred Scott . . . with an Analysis of the Points Ruled, and Some Concluding Observations no doubt complemented his *Report of the Lemmon Slave Case*. Both pamphlets kept the Supreme Court and the issue of slavery in the public eye in the critical election year of 1860.

The political motivations of other pamphleteers were not always as broad as Greeley's. Nor were their pamphlets as profitable. Dr. John Ker, of Natchez, Mississippi, published *A Brief History of an Attempt during the Last Session of the Legislature, in 1841, to Interfere with the Judgments of the Courts* simply to explain to his constituents why he voted a particular way in the legislature. Salmon P. Chase needed to have printed copies of his argument before the Supreme Court in *Jones* v. *Van Zandt* to distribute to the members of the court and the other attorneys involved in the case.[20] In a successful attempt at self-promotion, and because he truly believed his argument was important to the antislavery cause, Chase had about a thousand copies of his argument printed. These were sent around the nation to politicians, lawyers, judges, antislavery activists, and friends. A few were sent for distribution or for sale, but most were sent as gifts. Between February 10, 1847, and July 29, 1847, Chase sent out more than 450 copies of his argument, *Reclamation of Fugitives from Service*.[21] Earlier in his career Chase had sent numerous people his *Speech . . . in the Case of the Colored Woman, Matilda*. This self-promotion helped make Chase nationally known as "The Attorney General for Fugitive Slaves" and spread his theories on slavery and constitutional law throughout the North.

Men like Salmon P. Chase, William F. Seward, and Gerrit Smith combined their personal desire for fame with their desire to oppose slavery. Not surprisingly, many pamphlets annotated in this bibliography contain the arguments of attorneys in cases involving slaves. Such pamphlets were useful to other lawyers arguing similar cases.

One example of the utility of publishing the arguments made in slave cases can be seen in the Connecticut case of *Jackson* v. *Bulloch*.[22] This case involved the right of a Georgia slave owner to bring slaves into Connecticut while visiting that state. It was argued a year after a similar case in Massachusetts, *Commonwealth* v. *Aves*, led to the freedom of a slave brought into the Bay State.[23] Theodore Dwight Weld, an abolitionist organizer, was visiting Connecticut when *Jackson* v. *Bulloch* was about to come to trial.[24] Weld wrote to the New York abolitionist Lewis Tappan to ask for a copy of Ellis Gray Loring's argument before the Massachusetts Supreme Judicial Court.[25] Weld had already given attorneys for the slave Nancy Jackson a copy of Chief Justice Lemuel Shaw's opinion, but he thought the Loring argument would also help this case. That argument was published in the pamphlet *Case of the Slave-Child Med*, and may well have aided Jackson's lawyers in their successful effort to free her.

To be successful throughout the nation, the antislavery movement required widespread communication of ideas and facts. The published arguments of attorneys helped facilitate that communication. These pamphlets also helped make the general public aware of the legal, constitutional, moral, and political issues involved in the slavery question. Many of the arguments presented in these pamphlets went well beyond the legal citations found in a normal brief. They were often eloquent discussions of what was as much a political and moral issue as a legal one.

Although some of the arguments of counsel were published by the lawyers themselves, many of the arguments, as well as the reports of the cases, were published by antislavery societies. Such societies devoted much of their energies and finances to pamphleteering and propagandizing. They also devoted some time and money to legal cases. Thus, publishing and distributing a pamphlet about a legal case was practical for a number of reasons.

If the case written about was an antislavery victory, the society involved probably wanted to publicize this turn of events. A publication about the trial would bring favorable notice to the society. People who might wonder why they should actively support the antislavery movement would now have an answer: because antislavery organizations could use their money to win suits and legal cases. These cases showed that such organizations could be practical and constructive and could undertake such positive actions as winning a legal case. Instead of simply condemning slavery and slaveholders in another state, antislavery activists could show they were capable of action that would gain someone's freedom. In fact, these were the only cases in which antislavery organizations could alter the status of slaves through legal and constitutional means and thus successfully assault slavery. Slavery was too often an abstraction. These cases helped to make it a reality that could be fought face to face. Finally, the antislavery societies that supported legal actions could be portrayed as defending their free states from the intrusion of slavery.

Many of these ideas were expressed by the Holden (Massachusetts) Anti-Slavery Society, in the *Report of the Holden Slave Case*. The authors of the account of this trial noted that "Abstract Slavery everyone abhors; but of slavery, as it exists, so little is even yet known that most seem to regard it as mainly a nominal evil, and therefore, experience very little sympathy with those who are called slaves." This pamphlet was published to "dissipate this darkness and overcome this apathy" by showing how a woman tried to introduce slavery into the town of Holden, Massachusetts.[26]

Besides showing how effective antislavery societies could be and helping lawyers involved in similar cases, these pamphlets educated the public about the evils and dangers of slavery. Throughout the pamphlets are descriptions of slavery, accounts of the barbaric treatment of slaves and blacks, and assertions that slavery might soon encroach on free territory or free states. Many of the pamphlets involving fugitive slaves, slave transit, or the African slave trade focused on the need to prevent the moral decay that slavery brought with it and to protect the rights of whites, as well as blacks, from the harsh law of slavery.

The pamphlets suggest a desire to show that slavery would adversely affect whites. One section of this bibliography is devoted to cases involving whites who were accused of helping slaves and suffered for their humanity and charity. The most striking example of this is the case of Jonathan Walker, the "Man with the Branded Hand." Walker helped some slaves escape from the Florida Territory. After he and the slaves were captured, Walker was imprisoned for a long time, put in a pillory, and "branded on the right hand with the letters SS [for slave stealer]."[27] This barbaric punishment was exploited by antislavery societies. Accounts of Walker's trial and punishment were published, complete with pictures of his branded hand. Abolitionists proclaimed slavery to be inhuman and barbaric, and Walker was living proof of this. Because his punishment was meted out in the Florida Territory, which was then under control of the U. S. government, Walker's case was also proof of the corrosive effects of slavery. Although the U. S. Constitution prohibited "cruel and unusual punishment," the "demands" of slavery were so great that the Constitution was ignored and Walker was cruelly and unusually punished. The threat to whites and to constitutional rights and liberties was clear from Walker's case.

What emerges from these pamphlets is a notion of how the antislavery movement used the legal system to further its cause. Legal cases served many functions. They could free from bondage one or more individuals. Although freeing isolated individuals would not quickly end slavery, many abolitionists believed that such a humanitarian effort, especially if successful, justified any time or money spent on the case. From a larger political perspective they were probably correct. Freeing even one slave, by whatever means, publicized the strength of antislavery in the North. Such cases also angered the South. There are no easy and simple explanations for secession, the Civil War, or the ultimate end of slavery. To some extent, however, the cases described in these pamphlets played a critical role. They helped lead to Southern anger and the rise of "fire-eating" politicians in the South, which in turn led to secession, the Civil War, and ultimately emancipation.

From this analysis follows a formulation of two other uses of these cases by abolitionists. Even if a case did not free a slave—even if it in fact led to the reenslavement of a black or the incarceration of a white abolitionist—it could at least serve as a propaganda device.

Northern readers could be educated about the dangers of slavery by reading about cases involving the system. In addition, the trials, and the pamphlets connected with them, were organizing tools. Not only did antislavery organizations want to educate their Northern neighbors, they also hoped to use the legal system as a forum for bringing people into the movement. The rescue of a fugitive slave from a jail or a courtroom required a community effort. Once that effort was made, it was easier to gain more members for the antislavery movement.

Abolitionists were not the only publishers of pamphlets detailing what happened at trials involving slaves. Such pamphlets were also published by those who supported slavery, or at least did not oppose it. Officials in New York City and Charleston, South Carolina, for example, wanted to explain to the world how they had handled abortive conspiracies in their cities. Similarly, the Christiana Slave Riot stimulated two proslavery pamphlets. The first was written by Lancaster County alderman J. Franklin Reigart, who wanted to defend his acts (and publicize his role) in the pretrial hearings. The second was written by Maryland Attorney General Robert J. Brent as a report to the governor of Maryland. In this report Brent attempts to explain why Castner Hanway, the first person tried under a charge of treason for his part in the riot, was acquitted. Brent's report is primarily an attack on Pennsylvania and the officials in that state and an attempt to justify his role in the failed prosecution. The complete reports of the Hanway trial and the trial of another Pennsylvania abolitionist, Passmore Williamson, were taken down by a court reporter named Arthur Cannon. Although these pamphlets—*Case of Passmore Williamson* and the *Report of the Trial of Castner Hanway for Treason*—were not official reports, they were published most probably with the knowledge and agreement of the jurists involved—U. S. District Judge John K. Kane and U. S. Supreme Court Justice Robert C. Grier.

There are also two pamphlets annotated in this volume published in the North that are blatantly proslavery. The first is *A Review of the Trial, Conviction, and Sentence of Georgia F. Alberti, for Kidnapping,* probably published in Philadelphia in 1851. Alberti was a notorious slave catcher who was often accused of kidnapping free blacks, a crime for which he was convicted in 1851. In this case, the pamphlet was designed to win sympathy for Alberti and gain support for his release. It is impossible to know how influential the pamphlet was, but Alberti was released in 1852 after serving only a small part of his ten-year sentence. Exploiting the emotional issues and the threat to the freedom of whites usually associated with antislavery, this pamphlet's author used these issues to support his proslavery stand. *The Dred Scott Decision . . . with an Introduction by Dr. J. H. Van Evrie* is one of the few Northern defenses of Taney's infamous opinion. The volume also contains an essay by Dr. S. A. Cartwright of New Orleans, who argued that blacks were racially inferior to whites. This proslavery and racist pamphlet was designed to heighten the anxieties and fears of white workers in the North. It reminds readers that not all Northerners sympathized with the slave.

The legal issues surrounding slavery and antislavery were part of the larger questions of the place of human bondage and the role of the Afro-American in the United States. These questions were debated by politicians, ministers, scientists, philosophers, and reformers, as well as by lawyers and judges. The law of slavery—and attempts to create a law of freedom—must be viewed as a part of the history of slavery and race relations in the United States. For a number of reasons the law, the legal issues, and the legal cases bear careful examination. The pamphlets annotated here, and the cases from which they are derived, must be part of this examination.

Americans have always been peculiarly legalistic. From the time of the drafting of the Mayflower Compact to give colonists a "legal" basis for settlement to the current debates over constitutional amendments, Americans have placed great faith in the law as a vehicle for social control or social change. Slavery must be understood not only as a social, economic, or political institution but also as a legal institution. Indeed, at the foundation of slavery was the legal right to own another human being. That right was always in opposition to the great Anglo-American right of human liberty. The cases and pamphlets discussed here allow scholars interested in the issues of slavery and freedom to see how law affected these issues in the United States.

In addition, cases can be seen as a useful tool for studying the political or social history of slavery. The law is a political instrument, and its very enforcement may be seen as *political* in the broadest sense of the term. In many of the pamphlets annotated here there is as much political rhetoric, analysis, argument, and discussion as there is legal argument. The political ideas and concepts that surrounded slavery were debated in the courtrooms with as much skill and persistence as they were debated in Congress. These cases can thus be used as an additional source for understanding the political issues of the eighteenth and nineteenth centuries, where these issues touched on the question of slavery. Finally, many of the cases—and the pamphlets published about them—became political issues themselves. Indeed, the debates of the 1850s over slavery, slave expansion, fugitive slaves, the *Dred Scott* decision, and the role of the Supreme Court in American politics can only be understood in the context of the legal cases discussed here. The pamphlet literature published at the time made information about these cases available to all interested citizens.

As a resource for social historians, these case reports are also useful. "Slaves" and "free blacks" cease to be abstract concepts in many of these pamphlets. Through court testimony, we see flesh-and-blood individuals—litigants, defendants, and seekers of justice. The *Official Report of the Trials of Sundry Negroes,* for example, contains the testimony of numerous slaves and free blacks arrested after the abortive Denmark Vesey conspiracy. Although the slaves examined in these trials are unusual in that they were involved in the conspiracy, many of them nevertheless are ordinary individuals—they were not all leaders. Some were simply followers, and some, who were acquitted of any wrongdoing, may not in fact have been involved in the conspiracy at all. Their collective testimony, found in the *Official Report,* provides a useful and rare insight into the ideas, beliefs, fears, goals, and desires of slaves in South Carolina. Here, as in much of the other material discussed in this bibliography, we can observe individual lives caught up in the institution of slavery. This view helps Americans to understand not only their legal and political history but also a part of their social and cultural heritage.

NOTES

1. John Rolfe to Sir Edwin Sandys, January 1619-20, *The Records of the Virginia Company of London,* ed. Susan M. Kingsbury, 4 vols. (Washington: U. S. Government Printing Office, 1933), 3:24-25.

2. *Minutes of the Council and General Court of Colonial Virginia, 1622-1632, 1670-1676 . . .,* ed. H. R. McIlwaine (Richmond: Colonial Press, 1924), p. 466.

3. Ibid.

4. Winthrop Jordan, *White over Black: American Attitudes toward the Negro, 1550-1812* (Chapel Hill: University of North Carolina Press, 1968).

5. Act of October 1660, ch. 22, 2 Hening's *Statutes of Virginia* 26 (1810).

6. Act of October 3, 1663, ch. 30, Bacon's *Laws of Maryland* (1765).

7. John Locke, "The Fundamental Constitutions of Carolina," art. 110, 1 *Statutes at Large of South Carolina* 55 (1836).

8. Oliver Wendell Holmes, *The Common Law* (Boston: Little, Brown and Co., 1881), p. 1.

9. William Blackstone, *Commentaries on the Laws of England,* 4 vols. (Oxford: Clarendon Press, 1765-69), 1:125.

10. Ibid., 1:130.

11. Ibid., 1:123.

12. Although the tension between slavery and freedom is obvious to Americans of the late twentieth century, it was not as clear at the time of the American Revolution. It was a slaveholder, after all, who wrote in the Declaration of Independence that "all men are created equal," and all are "endowed by their Creator with certain unalienable Rights, that among these are Life, Liberty and the pursuit of Happiness." More interesting still is the use of the word *slave* during the revolutionary period. As Donald Robinson has shown in *Slavery in the Structure of American Politics, 1765-1820* (New York: Harcourt Brace Jovanovich, 1971), Americans of the 1770s often portrayed themselves as slaves to Great Britain. John Dickinson, in his "Letters from a Farmer in Pennsylvania" asserted that *"Those* who are *taxed* without their own consent expressed by themselves or their representatives, are *slaves. We are taxed* without our consent. . . . We are therefore *slaves"* (Robinson, p. 63). A Virginia slave owner, Richard Bland, predicted in 1764 that Americans would soon be no better off than "galley slaves in Turkey or Israelites under an Egyptian bondage" (ibid.,

p. 64). For a leading Virginia planter and politician to use such an analogy suggests that Americans of the revolutionary period were not fully attuned to the notion that chattel slavery conflicted with liberty. The irony of this was not lost on Samuel Johnson, an English intellectual who had little regard for the American independence movement. He asked, ''How is it that we hear the loudest *yelps* for liberty among the drivers of negroes?'' (ibid., p. 80).

13. 98 Eng. Rep. 499 (K.B. 1772).

14. 60 U. S. (19 How.) 393 (1857).

15. 41 U. S. (16 Pet.) 539 (1842).

16. *United States* v. *Hanway*, 26 F. Cas. 405 (C.C.E. Pa. 1851)(No. 15, 299).

17. Act of Sept. 18, 1850, ch. 60, 9 Stat. 462.

18. 26 F. Cas. 378 (N.D. Ill. 1860)(No. 15.395).

19. 41 U. S. (16 Pet.) 539 (1842).

20. 46 U. S. (5 How.) 66 (1847).

21. Salmon P. Chase Letterbook, Chase Papers. Manuscript Division, Library of Congress.

22. 12 Day (Conn.) 38 (1837).

23. 35 Mass. (18 Pick.) 193 (1836).

24. *Jackson* v. *Bulloch*, 12 Day (Conn.) 38 (1837).

25. Weld to Tappan, June 8, 1837, *Letters of Theodore Dwight Weld, Angela Grimke Weld, and Sarah Grimke, 1822-1844*, ed. Gilbert H. Barnes and Dwight L. Dumond, 2 vols. (New York: Appleton-Century-Crofts, 1934), 1:397-400.

26. *Report of the Holden Slave Case* (Worcester: Printed by Colton & Howland, 1839), p. 3.

27. Jonathan Walker, *Trial and Imprisonment of Jonathan Walker* (Boston: Pub. at the Anti-Slavery Office, 1845), p. 39.

SLAVERY

IN THE COURTROOM

A N

ARGUMENT

IN THE CASE OF

JAMES SOMMERSETT

A N E G R O,

LATELY DETERMINED BY

THE COURT OF KING's BENCH:

Wherein it is attempted to demonstrate

THE PRESENT UNLAWFULNESS

O F

DOMESTIC SLAVERY IN ENGLAND.

TO WHICH IS PREFIXED

A STATE OF THE CASE.

By Mr. HARGRAVE,

One of the COUNSEL for the NEGRO.

L O N D O N:

Printed for the AUTHOR:

And fold by W. OTRIDGE, oppofite the New
Church, in the Strand.

M. DCC. LXXII.

Title page from *An Argument in the Case of James Sommersett* (London, 1772), the first edition of a pamphlet later reprinted in Boston in 1774, that addressed issues of direct importance to slaveholders in America. *Somerset* v. *Stewart* is, along with *Dred Scott* v. *Sandford*, one of the two most important slave cases in Anglo-American law.

The Slave in a Free Jurisdiction

One of the most difficult issues slavery created for lawyers, judges, and politicians was the problem of what to do with slaves brought into free jurisdictions. The status of a slave in a free state or country raised important questions about comity, international law, and the inviolability of freedom. In the United States this issue also raised important questions about comity in a union of free and slave states.

Slaves could enter a free jurisdiction in two ways. First, they could be brought in by their master—as transients or sojourners. Here the legal question was, at what point did the *lex fori* (law of the forum state) attach to a slave from another jurisdiction? Second, slaves could flee to a free jurisdiction—and in the process become fugitive slaves. Here the legal question was, could the free state or nation change the status of fugitive slaves?

In the United States both of these issues were extremely important to the development of slavery and to the legal and constitutional arguments leading up to the Civil War. Many pamphlets were published about cases concerning these issues. The fugitive slave cases attracted great attention—in part because of the drama they created and also because of their sheer number. The comity cases, although fewer in number, appear to be even more constitutionally significant, and at least as significant politically. The two most important slave cases in Anglo-American law, *Somerset* v. *Stewart* and *Dred Scott* v. *Sandford*, involved issues of comity and the status of slaves in free jurisdictions.

This chapter discusses the case and pamphlet material dealing with issues of comity and conflicts of law. The next chapter presents a short introduction to the issue of fugitive slaves in the United States, followed by annotations of the material dealing with that question.

Somerset v. Stewart

98 Eng. Rep. 499 (K. B. 1772)

Although this case was tried before the Court of King's Bench in England, it involved issues of direct importance to slaveholders in

America. James Somerset was the slave of Charles Stewart, a British customs officer living in the American colonies. In 1769 Stewart went to England on business and took Somerset with him. In 1771 Somerset ran away from Stewart. He was captured, however, and consigned to a ship captain named John Knowles, who was to take him to Jamaica to sell him. The great English abolitionist Granville Sharp convinced William Murray, Lord Chief Justice Mansfield, to issue a writ of habeas corpus. This writ removed Somerset from Knowles's ship and brought the question of slavery in England before the King's Bench.

Somerset v. *Stewart* became a major test case for the West Indian interests in London and the abolitionists led by Sharp. Mansfield repeatedly suggested that Stewart voluntarily manumit Somerset and thus moot the case. After a fifth hearing in the matter, Stewart still refused to take Mansfield's advice. The chief justice then declared, "If the parties will have judgement, *'fiat justitia, ruat coelum'"* ("Let Justice be done though the heavens fall") (1 Lofft 17).

No longer able to avoid the case, Justice Mansfield reached a narrow holding. He stated, "Contract for sale of a slave is good here [in England]; the sale is a matter to which the law properly and readily attaches." Such a ruling would preserve both slavery in the colonies and the African slave trade. The only issue before Mansfield was "whether any dominion, authority or coercion can be exercised in this country, on a slave according to the American laws" (1 Lofft 17).

Mansfield thought it would be impossible to accept the enslavement of one person in England without accepting the entire system of slavery. "The difficulty of adopting the relation, without adopting it in all its consequences, is indeed extreme; and yet, many of those consequences are absolutely contrary to the municipal law of England" (1 Lofft 17). Thus, Mansfield concluded, "The state of slavery is of such a nature, that it is incapable of being introduced on any reasons, moral or political; but only positive law, which preserves its force long after the reasons, occasion, and times itself from whence it was created, is erased from memory; it's so odious, that nothing can be suffered to support it, but positive law" (1, Lofft 19). Therefore, Somerset was freed, and by implication so were all other slaves brought to England.

Mansfield was at pains to point out, however, that all his decision did was to declare that no slave could be forced out of England against his will, and any slave under threat of coercive transportation could receive the benefits of a habeas corpus action. Indeed, masters continued to hold slaves in Britain until Parliament formally abolished the institution throughout the Empire (Slavery Abolition Act, 1833, 3 & 4 Will. 4, ch. 73). Nevertheless, many people in Britain and America believed that Mansfield had ended slavery in England because they believed that he had declared that "the air of England is too pure for a slave to breathe."

Historically, *Somerset* is one of the most misunderstood cases in Anglo-American law. It is also the most quoted slave case in Anglo-American law and the most important.

■ Hargrave, Francis. An argument in the case of James Sommersett a Negro, lately determined by the Court of King's Bench: wherein it is attempted to demonstrate the present unlawfulness of domestic slavery in England. To which is prefixed a state of the case. London, W. Otridge and G. Kearsly, 1772. 82 p.

Law Library

——London, printed; Boston, reprinted and sold by E. Russel, 1774. 56 p.

Law Library

——2d ed. London, W. Otridge and G. Kearsly, 1775. 82 p.

Law Library

Somerset's case was argued by four lawyers, serjeants William Davy and John Glynn and barristers James Mansfield and Francis Hargrave. Hargrave, a relatively young man at this time, made his initial reputation from this case. Much of this reputation was based on his pamphlet *An Argument in the Case of James Sommersett*. It briefly discusses the circumstances of Somerset's application for a writ of habeas corpus and the return made by John Knowles. Charles Stewart, through Knowles's return, argued that Somerset was a slave under the laws of the American colonies and that that was sufficient reason to restrain Somerset and forcibly return him to the New World.

Hargrave's essay is based on his notes from his oral presentation. But it is embellished with massive citations and is clearly better written than his original presentation to the Court of King's Bench. Many of the arguments found in it were later incorporated into Lord Mansfield's opinion in the case.

Hargrave asserts that American slavery could not be partly introduced into England. Either the entire system of servitude had to be accepted or there could be no slavery at all. Hargrave points out, in great detail, how many aspects of American slavery are contrary to English law and custom. He argues that the only type of slavery that was ever legal in England was villenage, "now expired." He later asserts that even if villenage were still practiced, that system of servitude would "not permit that high act of dominion [of sending Somerset out of the realm] which Mr. Steuart has exercised; for they restrained the lord from forcing the villein out of England" (p. 79).

In his opinion freeing Somerset, Lord Mansfield used language very similar to this to declare that Stewart could not send Somerset to Jamaica. Mansfield also accepted the argument that slavery must be either completely accepted or completely rejected. Although Hargrave was opposed to all slavery, he shrewdly did not attempt to make *Somerset* into something it could not be. Thus, he argued that there is no inconsistency between allowing slavery in the colonies and the African slave trade and yet not allowing slavery in England. Again, Mansfield accepted these arguments. Finally, Hargrave cites cases from Scotland, Holland, and France to show that England need not—indeed could not—enforce the lex loci of slavery when it was incompatible with the lex fori of England.

Hargrave's pamphlet is important for many reasons. First, as already noted, it helped launch his legal career. More importantly, it allowed lawyers, abolitionists, politicians, and publicists to read a clear, well-reasoned, and carefully documented attack on the legality of slavery in a free jurisdiction. The 1774 Boston reprint of this pamphlet is particularly significant in this way. It shows that Americans not only knew of *Somerset* at the time of the Revolution and the framing of the Constitution but also had access to the legal arguments surrounding the case.

■ Long, Edward. Candid reflections upon the judgement lately awarded by the Court of King's Bench, in Westminister-Hall on what is commonly called the Negroe-cause, by a planter. London, T. Lowndes, 1772. 76 p.

This pamphlet was written in reaction to the decision in *Somerset* v. *Stewart,* which it attacks on a number of grounds. The author, a spokesman for the West Indian planters, declares that "the art of *washing the Black-a-moor white* was happily reserved for a *lawyer:* the thing that *Solomon* thought impossible when he said, 'Can the *Aethiop* change his skin?' What the wife of *Aesop* esteemed a prodigy in nature, has, in the present wonder-working age, ceased any longer to be *miraculous* . . . . The name of **** M———shall henceforth become more popular among all the *Quacoes* and *Quashebas* of *America,* than that of patriot *Wilkes* once was among the porter-swilling swains of *St. Giles''* (pp. iii-iv).

The author argues on the basis of legal, historical, economic, racial, and public policy reasons that *Somerset* was incorrectly decided. First, he declares that the law of England would support Somerset's slave status while he was in England because villenage is still legal in England. A master has the common law right of caption and rendition of his fugitive slave, just as a master has the right to seize a fugitive villein. English recognition of the African slave trade provided further support for his position. This trade, the author declares, ''has been carried on by this nation from time immemorial. King, Lords, and Commons, have shared in its profits, and concurred in various laws for supporting, regulating, and firmly establishing it'' (p. 39). Since these laws declared ''that Negroes are chattels, saleable and convertable like any other goods'' (p. 39), it seemed logical that slavery was a status approved by England and enforceable under English law. Numerous statutes are cited in support of this position. Finally, the author notes that there is no law in England freeing slaves brought into the metropolis. Therefore, he thought it a clear rule of law and policy that the colonial law creating the slave status should follow the slave. This was because the property of a subject of the king ought to be recognized and protected by law. And, since Negroes were not subjects of the king, they should remain the slaves of English subjects when brought to England.

This historical and legal argument is buttressed by a discussion of the economic and social implications of *Somerset*. The author asserts that the West Indian colonies can only be cultivated by slave labor, and that free blacks are too lazy, too ignorant, and too inferior to work. He takes *Somerset* to its logical conclusion and declares that if slavery is repugnant to the law of England, then it must also be repugnant to the law of the colonies. This would lead to a general emancipation and an economic disaster. But, even if this general emancipation does not occur, the author predicts thousands of slaves will escape to England and become free. This, he says, will disrupt the economy, put many new people on the public dole, put honest Englishmen out of work, increase the crime rate, and lead to miscegenation.

This pamphlet is significant as an example of the fame of *Somerset* and the fear it created among some planters. *Candid Reflections* gives the broadest and most extreme reading to *Somerset* and its implications. It also contains blatantly racist arguments designed to heighten fears of a black invasion of Britain. Thus, as early as 1772 we find racism and economic exploitation being used to argue for a legal position that would favor slavery.

■ A letter to Philo Africanus, upon slavery; in answer to his of the 22d of November, in the General Evening Post, together with the opinions of Sir John Strange, and other eminent lawyers upon this subject, with the sentence of Lord Mansfield, in the case of Somerset and Knowles, 1772, with his Lordship's explanation of that opinion in 1786. London, Printed for W. Brown, 1788. 40 p.

——London, printed; Newport (Rhode-Island), reprinted by Peter Edes [1788] 23 p.

The first part of this pamphlet is an attack on Thomas Clarkson and other English abolitionists for their opposition to the African slave trade. The anonymous author supports slavery through biblical citations and a discussion of slavery in antiquity, arguing that Africans sold as slaves were captives in battle who were legitimately enslaved under the rules of their own society.

The second part contains "Cases Respecting Negro Slaves with Opinions Thereon" (pp. 18-23). This section includes the opinion of Lord Chief Justice Mansfield in *Somerset* v. *Stewart*. Another Mansfield opinion is presented from what this pamphlet calls *Parish of Thames Ditton* v. *St. Luke's Chelsea*, and which in fact appears to be the opinion from *The King* v. *Inhabitants of Thames Ditton*, 99 Eng. Rep. 891 (K.B. 1785). The pamphlet summarizes Mansfield's decision in that case as follows:

> In this case Lord Mansfield very particularly took occasion to declare, that the public were generally mistaken in the determination of the court of King's Bench, on case of Somerset the negroe, which had been often quoted, for nothing more was then determined, than that there was no right in the master forcibly to take the slave and carry him abroad. That the general question, whether the master might not sue any one who entertained him in his service, or for wages, was not before the court, nor was it held that the baptizing such slave made any alteration in his freedom, or that on setting foot in this country he instantly became emancipated. Therefore the only question on the habeas corpus in that case was, whether the master might forcibly compel the slave to go out of this kingdom? when it was determined he could not. [pp. 22-23]

The pamphlet also quotes a section from Blackstone's *Commentaries on the Law of England* (1 Blackstone 425) on slavery in England, and the "Opinion of Sir Philip Yorke, then Attorney-General, and Mr. Talbot, Solicitor-General," 33 Mor. (Dic.) 15547 (Ct. Sess. 1729), which supporters of slavery had used to show that the institution had been allowed in Great Britain (p. 20). Finally, the pamphlet relates the decisions, rulings, or opinions of legal experts in three unreported cases that took place between 1749 and 1763. The interpretation of the law on these cases is from the statements of various attorneys, including Edmund Hoskins, P. Ellers, and John Strange.

The purpose of this pamphlet is to provide biblical, historical, political, economic, and legal support for allowing the slave trade to continue and allowing slavery to exist in Great Britain. That the pamphlet was reprinted in Rhode Island indicates the strong American interest in slavery and British law even after the Revolution. By the time this pamphlet was written, Rhode Island, and indeed all states north of the Carolinas, had abolished the African slave trade. In addition, Rhode Island, Connecticut, and Pennsylvania had passed gradual emancipation statutes that accepted the ideology of *Somerset* but went beyond the case to end slavery in those jurisdictions. Massachusetts, New Hampshire, and the fourteenth state, Vermont, had already ended slavery through their state constitutions and state court decisions. Nevertheless, there remained some sympathy for slavery and the slave trade in the North. This was particularly true for the city of Newport (where this pamphlet was reprinted) because many great fortunes in that city had been built through the African slave trade.

Commonwealth v. *Aves*

35 Mass. (18 Pick.) 193 (1836)

In 1836 Mrs. Mary Aves Slater of New Orleans came to Boston to visit her father, Thomas Aves. Mrs. Slater brought with her a six-year-old slave girl named Med. At the instigation of the Boston Female Anti-Slavery Society, a writ of habeas corpus was served on Mr. Aves, who allegedly restrained Med against her will. Aves responded that Med was the slave of Mr. Samuel Slater of New Orleans, and that he held Med under Slater's authority.

The case was then brought before Chief Justice Lemuel Shaw of the Massachusetts Supreme Judicial Court. Benjamin R. Curtis (who would later serve on the U.S. Supreme Court and write a stinging antislavery dissent in the *Dred Scott* case) and his cousin Charles P. Curtis argued in favor of Aves's right to retain Med. Ellis Gray Loring, Samuel E. Sewall, and Rufus Choate argued on behalf of those seeking to free Med. In a precedent-setting decision, Chief Justice Shaw ruled that slaves brought into Massachusetts with the consent of their owner became free the moment they arrived in the state.

Lemuel Shaw (1781-1861). Chief justice of the Massachusetts Supreme Judicial Court from 1830 to 1860, Shaw was the most important and influential state jurist in the United States during his tenure on the bench. He wrote precedent-setting decisions in labor law, tort law, railroad law, criminal law, and the law of slavery and freedom. His decision in *Commonwealth* v. *Aves* (1836) was the first by an American court to apply the implications of *Somerset* to the interstate transit and sojourn of slaves. Shaw's decision in *Aves* was ultimately adopted by almost every free state court. Portrait by William M. Hunt. LC-USZ62-52119

Benjamin Robbins Curtis (1809-1874). A conservative Boston lawyer, Curtis defended the right of a slaveholder to bring human chattel into Massachusetts in *Commonwealth* v. *Aves* (1836). A supporter of the Fugitive Slave Law of 1850, Curtis was appointed to the Supreme Court in 1851 through the influence of Daniel Webster. Despite his proslavery record, Curtis became something of a hero in the North after 1857 because of his vigorous dissent in the *Dred Scott* case. This painting by Francis Alexander shows Curtis as a relatively young man; Curtis was twenty-five when he argued *Aves*. LC-USZ62-38483

Rufus Choate (1799-1859) was a conservative Massachusetts lawyer. During the 1850s he was one of the commonwealth's most prominent defenders of the fugitive slave law and advocates of accommodation with the South at any cost. In 1836, however, he argued on behalf of the Boston Female Antislavery Society in *Commonwealth* v. *Aves*. Although styled as a state prosecution, *Commonwealth* v. *Aves* was actually a private action initiated by antislavery activists to gain the freedom of the young slave girl Med. Choate appeared with two abolitionist attorneys, Ellis Gray Loring and Samuel Sewall.
Portrait by W. G. Doles, copyright 1898. LC-USZ62-59096

■ Case of the slave child, Med. Report of the arguments of counsel and of the opinion of the court, in the case of Commonwealth vs. Aves; tried and determined in the Supreme Judicial Court of Massachusetts. Boston, Isacc Knapp, 1836. 40 p

Law Library; E450.A94

This pamphlet contains the initial petition for the writ of habeas corpus, the returns made in response to the writ, the arguments of counsel for both sides that were made before the Massachusetts Supreme Judicial Court, and the complete opinion of Chief Justice Lemuel Shaw. The arguments made by Benjamin R. Curtis and Ellis Gray Loring contain some of the most sophisticated and thorough examinations of the problem presented by a union of slave and free states that were made in the antebellum period. Upon receiving a copy of these arguments, U.S. Supreme Court Justice Joseph Story told Loring, "I have rarely seen so thorough and exact arguments as those made by Mr. B. R. Curtis and yourself. They exhibit learning, research and ability of which any man may be proud" (W. W. Story, *Life and Letters of Joseph Story*, 2 vols. [1851], 2:235).

Curtis essentially argued that by comity Massachusetts ought to recognize the limited right of a master to visit the Bay State with a slave. Thus, Massachusetts, by comity, ought to enforce the laws of Louisiana that made Med a slave. Loring responded that slavery could not exist except by positive law, and it was such an immoral institution that it could not be enforced or supported through interstate comity. Chief Justice Shaw accepted Loring's argument and declared that all persons within the jurisdiction of Massachusetts were free, except fugitive slaves, because their status was controlled by the U.S. Constitution. Shaw's opinion and the argument first laid out by Loring were eventually incorporated into the law of most of the North. Shaw's opinion was cited throughout the North when state courts dealt with the problems of slave transit and comity.

The Case of Matilda

(Hamilton Cty. [Ohio] C. P. 1837) (Unreported)

Associated case: *Birney* v. *State*, 8 Ohio 230 (1837)

Matilda was the slave of Larkin Lawrence of Missouri. In 1836 Lawrence and Matilda were traveling to Missouri on a steamboat that stopped at Cincinnati. During this layover Matilda left Lawrence and disappeared into the city. Lawrence continued on without Matilda, and she was subsequently employed as a maid by the abolitionist publicist and politician James Gillespie Birney. About nine months later John W. Riley, a professional slave catcher, had Matilda arrested and placed in the custody of the sheriff until she could be sent to Lawrence.

At Birney's behest, Salmon P. Chase and Samuel Eells secured a writ of habeas corpus on behalf of Matilda and argued for her freedom

Salmon P. Chase (1808-1873). Known as the ''Attorney General for Fugitive Slaves,'' Salmon Chase was one of the leading political abolitionists of the antebellum period. He served as U.S. senator and governor of Ohio, and then as secretary of the treasury under Lincoln, who appointed him chief justice of the U.S. Supreme Court in 1864. Chase was involved in many antislavery cases, either as the attorney for a fugitive slave or an abolitionist or as the adviser to other antislavery lawyers. *Jones* v. *Van Zandt* and the case of Matilda are the two most famous of the fugitive slave cases he argued. LC-USZ62-19326

before the county court of common pleas. This was Chase's first major case in a long career as an abolitionist attorney and politician. Despite Chase's forensic skills, the writ was quashed and Matilda was quickly returned to slavery.

Riley then secured an indictment against Birney for harboring a slave in violation of Ohio law. Chase unsuccessfully defended Birney before the county court in this case. However, unlike Matilda, Birney remained in the state and could appeal this adverse decision. Before the Ohio Supreme Court, Chase was more successful, and Birney's conviction was reversed.

■   Chase, Salmon Portland. Speech of Salmon P. Chase, in the case of the colored woman, Matilda, who was brought before the Court of Common Pleas of Hamilton County, Ohio, by writ of habeus corpus; March 11, 1837. Cincinnati, Pugh & Dodd, printers, 1837. 40 p.

E450.C48

There is no report of the case against Matilda. Chase's pamphlet supplies copies of the writ of habeas corpus and returns by the sheriff and Riley, however. Following these is the argument made by Chase.

Throughout, Chase's argument is ambiguous about the nature of the legal question before the court. He fails to emphatically assert that Matilda was voluntarily brought into Ohio by her master and thus is free under the doctrine set down by Chief Justice Shaw in the Massachusetts case of *Commonwealth* v. *Aves*, 35 Mass. (18 Pick.) 193 (1836). This ambiguity may have resulted from Shaw's dictum that the only possible exception to the *Aves* (and *Somerset*) precedents might be masters in transit from one slave state to another.

This of course was precisely the situation in Matilda's case. Matilda's master had in fact been in transit from one slave state to another. Chase avoids Chief Justice Shaw's dictum (unsuccessfully, as it turned out) by citing *Somerset* v. *Stewart*, 98 Eng. Rep. 499 (K.B. 1772) and other cases to support his assertion that ''the moment the slave comes within such a [free] state, he acquires a legal right to freedom'' (p. 8). But, instead of tying this to the circumstances of Matilda's arrival in Ohio, Chase concentrates on the legality of Matilda's arrest and incarceration, the applicability of the Fugitive Slave Act, Feb. 12, 1793, ch. 7, 1 Stat. 302, to Ohio, and the constitutionality of that act. Chase makes a number of technical arguments against the validity of the warrant for Matilda's arrest. He then asserts that (1) Congress had no power to pass the Fugitive Slave Act, because the relevant clause in the Constitution is directed at the states, and no such power is authorized to Congress; (2) the act as passed violates various other provisions of the Constitution, including the Fourth and Fifth Amendments found in the Bill of Rights; (3) Congress has no power to authorize or compel state officials to enforce its acts, so even if the Fugitive Slave Act were constitutional, it could not be enforced by Ohio state officials; and (4) under the Northwest Ordinance, Ohio need return only fugitive slaves from the *original* states and not from Kentucky or Missouri.

All of these arguments were rejected by the county court, and Matilda was returned to slavery. The pamphlet, however, was widely circulated and brought some attention to Chase, who later revised and refined the same arguments and used them in other cases. Perhaps the most important aspect of this case and the pamphlet is their connection to Chase, who would ultimately gain the unofficial title of "Attorney General for Fugitive Slaves."

Commonwealth v. Stratton

(Worcester Cty. [Mass.] C.P. 1839) (Unreported)*

In 1839 Mrs. Olivia Eames returned to her native Massachusetts after residing in New Orleans for a number of years. Mrs. Eames brought with her a thirteen-year-old black girl named Anne, who had been her slave in Louisiana.

After they had spent five months in Holden, Massachusetts, a group of citizens led by a man named Samuel Stratton procured a writ of personal replevin in Anne's behalf and served this writ on Eames. The writ asserted that Anne was illegally held as a slave and that Eames intended to sell her. The writ would allow Anne's status to be determined by a jury. Mrs. Eames resisted the men who served her the writ. After they left with Anne, she complained to the county grand jury that these men had conspired to take Anne away from her against Anne's will. The men were indicted and prosecuted by the district attorney.

At the trial the prosecution asserted that Anne was free the moment she entered Massachusetts—under the doctrine laid out in *Commonwealth* v. *Aves*, 35 Mass. (18 Pick.) 193 (1836)—and thus had a right to work for whomever she wished. The defense called a number of witnesses to prove that Anne was in fact held as a slave. These witnesses testified that Anne had not been sent to school or to church; that she did not know her age until Eames recently told her; and that Eames beat her, forced her to carry buckets of water on her head, and treated her as a slave. Under cross-examination Mrs. Eames admitted that she might someday take Anne back to Louisiana. Anne was reluctant to testify against her mistress but ultimately admitted that she wished to be free and that Eames had beaten her for telling neighbors of this wish.

Much of this damaging information came out in cross-examination because the defense called only two witnesses. After this testimony the district attorney declared that he believed the defendants were justified in procuring the writ of personal replevin and were "fully entitled to a

---

*The Holden Slave Case

verdict of acquittal'' (Stratton, *Report of the Holden Slave Case*, p. 21). The question of Anne's freedom was not settled by this case but was later brought into the same court in the case of *Anne* v. *Eames*. ''The defendant appeared by her attorney, but afterwards was defaulted by consent'' and paid Anne nominal damages (ibid., p. 29). Anne thus gained her freedom.

■ Stratton, Samuel, *defendant*. Report of the Holden Slave Case, tried at the Court of Common Pleas, for the County of Worcester, A.D. 1839. Publ. by the Board of Directors of the Holden Anti-Slavery Society. Worcester, Printed by Colton & Howland, 1839. 32 p.

Law Library; E450.S92

The Holden Anti-Slavery Society published this pamphlet to show Northerners that slavery could exist in their communities and that it must be opposed. The pamphlet contains an introduction by the Anti-Slavery Society, a report of the prosecution of Stratton, which includes most of the testimony, and a number of the depositions of people who were going to testify on behalf of the defendants but were never called. The pamphlet ends with a copy of the indictment of Stratton, a copy of the statute allowing for a writ of personal replevin to test a person's status, and a transcript of the discussion between counsel and bench during Stratton's trial over the meaning of this statute.

The pamphlet is a useful example of how abolitionists used the legal system both to free slaves and to provide propaganda for their cause. It also allows scholars to examine trial court testimony and procedure at the county court level in a case that would otherwise have gone unreported. Finally, this pamphlet indicates that constitutional rulings, such as that in *Commonwealth* v. *Aves*, filtered down to the lowest courts, where they were applied in unreported cases.

Groves v. *Slaughter*

40 U.S. (15 Pet.) 449 (1841)

The Mississippi Constitution of 1832 prohibited the ''introduction of slaves'' into the state ''as merchandise or for sale'' after May 1, 1833. In 1836 Robert Slaughter imported slaves into Mississippi and sold them to citizens of that state. The slaves were not paid for at that time. Instead, promissory notes for various sums, totaling over seven thousand dollars, were signed by the purchaser and endorsed by Moses

Groves and others. When Slaughter sought to obtain the money owed him, Groves and the other sureties refused to honor their notes.

Groves and his codefendants argued that the importation and sale of the slaves violated the Mississippi Constitution. Thus, the notes were void because they were made for an illegal consideration. The U.S. District Court in New Orleans, however, held that the Mississippi constitutional provision did not become operative automatically. Rather, it had to be supported by legislation. Since there was no legislation, the sale was legal and the notes should be upheld. That court awarded Slaughter more than seven thousand dollars in damages. Groves appealed, but the lower court decision was upheld in a U.S. Supreme Court decision written by Justice Smith Thompson in 1841.

Thompson reviewed the lower court case and various Mississippi decisions. Upon concluding that the Mississippi constitutional provision needed legislative enforcement, Thompson declared it was "unnecessary to inquire whether this article in the constitution of Mississippi is repugnant to the Constitution of the United States." In separate concurrences, Chief Justice Roger B. Taney and Justices John McLean and Henry Baldwin asserted that the Commerce Clause of the Constitution did not prevent the states from regulating the introduction of slavery within their domain. Baldwin also asserted that the right of uninterrupted transit with slaves was protected by the Constitution, and that comity between states was implied by the Constitution and the union itself.

The importance of this case is suggested by the fame of the counsel for each side. Slaughter was represented by the "Ajax and Achilles" of the mid-nineteenth-century Supreme Court bar: Henry Clay and Daniel Webster. Groves retained former attorney general of the United States Henry D. Gilpin and U.S. senator from Mississippi Robert J. Walker.

■   Walker, Robert J. Argument of Robert J. Walker, esq., before the Supreme Court of the United States, on the Mississippi slave question, at January term, 1841. Involving the power of Congress and the states to prohibit the inter-state slave trade. Philadelphia, Printed by J.C. Clark, 1841. 88 p.

E445.M6W18

Argument in this case lasted seven days. Much of this time was taken by Senator Walker. The arguments of the other counsel were outlined, in some detail, in the printed report of the case. The case takes up sixty-eight pages in the *United States Reports*, of which forty-six are devoted to headnotes and the arguments of counsel. The arguments made by Walker, who opened and concluded for his client, were not printed with the case. Instead, the reporter placed them in an appendix to the report because they were "prepared with great ability and care" but "were found too large to be included in the body of the report, 40 U.S. (15 Pet.) 496 (1841). In addition, Walker's arguments were published separately by a Philadelphia printer, a version that appears to have been printed from the same plates as the appendix, since all pagination and wording, with one minor deletion, are the same.

Walker's argument is divided into two parts. In the first he argues that the Mississippi constitutional provision needs no enacting legislation. He further argues that the notes are void on the basis of this constitutional provision. This section is embellished with hundreds of case citations to English and American reports. In the second section Walker denies that the Mississippi constitutional ban on importing slaves as merchandise violates the Commerce Clause of the U.S. Constitution. He argues that slavery is exclusively a municipal institution, created solely by municipal law. Further, he declares that slaves are "persons" under the Constitution, and can not be regulated as commerce.

Both of these arguments had been used by abolitionists to free slaves in transit in the North. Yet, here Walker was protecting the constitution of Mississippi. He was also laying the groundwork for a defense of slavery in the states against federal interference. Walker's constitutional arguments would later be used to assert that Congress had no power to interfere with slavery in the territories.

Ironically, the Supreme Court majority in this case accepted the substance of Walker's second major argument: that a state prohibition on slave importation did not violate the U.S. Constitution. However, this acceptance came in concurring opinions. The opinion of the court, which the majority agreed to, rejected Walker's primary contention that the Mississippi constitutional prohibition was operative.

Strader v. *Graham*

51 U.S. (10 How.) 82 (1850)

Strader v. *Graham*

46 Ky. (7 B. Mon.) 633 (1847)

Graham v. *Strader*

44 Ky. (5 B. Mon.) 173 (1844)

Christopher Graham of Kentucky owned three slaves trained as musicians. Graham gave two of them, Henry and Reuben, permission to

James G. Birney (1792-1857). Birney was born and raised in Kentucky and inherited numerous slaves. He later moved to Alabama, where he had a successful law practice and was elected to the state legislature. His advocacy of colonization was tolerated in Alabama, but by 1834 he had become disenchanted with colonization and moved North, where he became a full-fledged abolitionist. In 1840 and 1844 he ran for president on the Liberty party ticket. LC-USZ62-15298 travel to Indiana and Ohio to perform. Both made numerous trips but always returned to Kentucky. In 1841, however, Henry, Reuben, and a third slave, George, boarded a steamboat owned by Jacob Strader and went to Cincinnati. There they disappeared, ultimately making their way to Canada.

Graham sued Strader for the value of the slaves, the value of the musical instruments they took with them, and the expenses connected with trying to recover them. Graham won his case in Kentucky's highest court, and Strader, a citizen of Ohio, appealed to the U.S. Supreme Court. Strader argued that the slaves had become free under the laws of Indiana and Ohio and the antislavery provision of the Northwest Ordinance.

In a unanimous decision, Chief Justice Roger Taney ruled the high court lacked jurisdiction for two reasons. First, "[e]very State has an undoubted right to determine the *status*, or domestic and social condition of the person domiciled within its territory, except in so far as the powers of the State in this respect are restrained, or duties and obligations imposed upon them by the Constitution of the United States." Therefore the status of the slaves was up to the courts of Kentucky to decide, and "could not be influenced by the laws of Ohio." Thus, the question of the slave's status under Ohio law could not come before the U.S. Supreme Court (Birney, *Examination of the Decision*, p. 12). Second, Chief Justice Taney declared that the Northwest Ordinance was no longer in force because the territories had become states. The Kentucky decision stood, and Strader was liable for the loss of Graham's slaves because he had allowed the slaves to board his steamboat in violation of Kentucky law.

■ Birney, James Gillespie. Examination of the decision of the Supreme Court of the United States, in the case of Strader, Gorman and Armstrong vs. Christopher Graham, delivered at its December term, 1850: concluding with an address to the free colored people, advising them to remove to Liberia. Cincinnati, Truman & Spofford, 1852. 46 p., and appendix.

E450.B57; AC901.W3 vol. 141 Rare Book Room

James G. Birney was an early opponent of the colonization movement and a leading political abolitionist. In 1840 and 1844 he was the Liberty party candidate for the presidency. By the time this pamphlet was written, Birney was in the twilight of his career and in some ways cut off from the mainstream of the antislavery movement. This isolation is reflected in Birney's advocacy of colonization for free blacks.

His pamphlet begins with an attack on the Supreme Court and a rambling essay on government. It is followed by a reprint of Chief Justice Taney's decision in *Strader* v. *Graham* and an extended, and highly critical, analysis of the decision. Birney argues that Graham's slaves were free the moment they entered Ohio with their master's consent. He further argues that the Northwest Ordinance remains in force in Ohio despite the change from territory to state. Finally, he asserts that the Constitution protects the free black citizens of the North, wherever they might travel, and that the Constitution recognizes the principle that slaves become free the moment they enter free jurisdictions with the consent of their master.

Despite these assertions, Birney realizes that the Supreme Court has reached precisely opposite conclusions. Birney ties the Supreme Court decisions in *Prigg* v. *Pennsylvania*, 41 U.S. (16 Pet.) 539 (1842) (see Fugitive Slaves chapter), and *Strader* v. *Graham* to the recent passage of the Fugitive Slave Act of Sept. 18, 1850, ch. 60, 9 Stat. 462. In so doing he reaches a startling and, for abolitionists, heretical conclusion: free blacks can no longer safely live in the United States and must migrate to Liberia for their own survival. Birney's analysis of these cases and statutes leads him to conclude that neither the state courts nor the federal courts will interfere with the kidnapping of free blacks. In *Prigg* the Court held that masters had a ''right of self-help'' to remove their alleged fugitives from free states without any court action. The 1850 Fugitive Slave Act made it possible to remove free blacks under the color of law because alleged fugitives could not testify on their own behalf before fugitive slave commissioners. Finally, *Strader* implied that the federal courts would not interfere with the status of a black in the slave states. Thus ''the free colored people can have no *feeling* of security any where in the Union'' (p. 20).

Although he despised the Colonizationists and had opposed them for most of his life, Birney believed that free blacks could survive only in Liberia, because ''the germs of civilization are there, and the white man does not rule'' (p. 45). Birney's article reflects his own pessimism over the state of abolition in the period following the Compromise of 1850. His analysis of the Court and the trend of constitutional decision making was perhaps more prophetic than he wished. Within five years of this pamphlet's publication, Chief Justice Taney would deliver his opinion in *Dred Scott* v. *Sandford*, 60 U.S. (19 How.) 393 (1857). In that opinion Taney essentially confirmed what Birney had feared, by declaring that Negroes ''had no rights which the white man was bound to respect,'' 60 U.S. (19 How.) 407 (1857).

United States ex rel. Wheeler v. Williamson

28 F. Cas. 682 (D.C.E.D. Pa. 1855) (No. 16,725)

United States ex rel. Wheeler v. Williamson

28 F. Cas. 686 (D.C.E.D. Pa. 1855) (No. 16,726)

Passmore Williamson's Case

26 Pa. 9 (1855)

Williamson v. Lewis

39 Pa. 9 (1861)

In July 1855 John H. Wheeler, U.S. minister to Nicaragua, visited Philadelphia on personal business. Wheeler, from North Carolina, was returning to Nicaragua and had with him three slaves—Jane and her two sons, Daniel and Isaiah.

While waiting for a boat to take them to New York, Jane was able to inform a Negro waiter that she wished to be free. This information was communicated to Passmore Williamson, the secretary of the acting committee of the Pennsylvania Abolition Society. When Wheeler's boat was about to depart, Williamson rushed aboard, in the company of a large number of free blacks. Williamson told Jane she was free under the laws of Pennsylvania and that she and her sons might leave with him if she wished. At this point the facts of the case are disputed. Witnesses for Williamson asserted that Jane and her sons voluntarily left the boat. This was later confirmed by Jane herself. Wheeler, on the other hand, asserted that Jane was forcibly removed from the boat against her will.

This event led to a series of cases in various courts. Wheeler immediately secured a writ of habeas corpus from Federal District Judge John K. Kane. The writ ordered Williamson to bring Jane to Kane's court. Wheeler also complained to local officials, and this resulted in indictments against Williamson and five blacks for riot, assault, battery, and robbery. In his return to the writ issued by Judge Kane, Williamson asserted that he did not have Jane in his custody and that he had never had her in his custody. Kane declared this was a false or evasive return and cited Williamson for contempt.

Williamson thus remained in prison from mid-July until early November. During this period he sought his freedom through a revised plea to Judge Kane and an action before the Pennsylvania Supreme Court. Neither was successful, and Kane allowed Williamson to leave

Passmore Williamson. An antislavery activist in Pennsylvania, Passmore Williamson gained fame for aiding the slaves of the U.S. ambassador to Nicaragua, John H. Wheeler, when he took them into Pennsylvania. Wheeler brought Williamson before U.S. District Judge John K. Kane, a Northerner notorious for his proslavery sympathies. When Williamson failed to produce Wheeler's slaves (so they could be returned to Wheeler), Judge Kane cited the abolitionist for contempt and sent him to jail. The longer Williamson languished in jail, the more Kane appeared a tyrant and the more Williamson seemed a martyr. Abolitionists made the most of the jailing of Williamson to show the proslavery bias of the federal courts.

"In Moyamensing Prison for alledged contempt of court." Engraving by E. Luders; lithograph by A. Kollner, 1855. LC-USZ62-16949

prison only when it became apparent (1) that Williamson did not have custody of the slaves, (2) that the slaves were safely in Boston (or beyond), and (3) that the further incarceration of Williamson would only bring him fame and sympathy.

Williamson did not appear before the state court in the criminal trial resulting from the rescue. The five blacks were tried. Three were acquitted of all charges, and two were fined $10 each and imprisoned for a week for threatening to kill Wheeler if he interfered with them.

Williamson's case raised a number of serious legal issues. In 1847 Pennsylvania enacted legislation that freed all slaves, except fugitives, in the state. Since Jane and her children were not fugitive slaves, it was quite likely that under Pennsylvania law they were free. This issue was not determined by any court. Nevertheless, Judge Kane emphatically asserted that there was a constitutional right of transit for person and property, and thus Jane was not free under Pennsylvania law.

Whatever Jane's status, it is not at all clear that Kane had any legitimate jurisdiction over the case. The Pennsylvania Supreme Court seemed to agree that Kane's jurisdiction was open to question, but that court nevertheless refused to interfere with Williamson's incarceration. This of course left Williamson in a legal no-man's-land: he was incarcerated by what he believed to be an arbitrary federal judge who had overstepped his jurisdictional bounds but could not turn to the state court for relief because that court did not believe it could interfere in a federal case.

Williamson's case was an important cause célèbre for the antislavery movement. It also strengthened the new Republican party. The case threatened to result in a major confrontation between the federal government and a state government. Officials in Washington anxiously awaited the result of Williamson's appeal to the Pennsylvania Supreme Court. Finally, this case must be viewed as another example of—and a contributor to—the legal crisis and the crisis in federalism that led to the Civil War.

■ Williamson, Passmore, *respondent*. Case of Passmore Williamson. Report of the proceedings on the writ of habeus corpus, issued by the Hon. John K. Kane, judge of the District Court of the United States for the Eastern District of Pennsylvania in the case of the United States of America ex rel. John H. Wheeler vs. Passmore Williamson, including the several opinions delivered; and the arguments of counsel, reported by Arthur Cannon, esq. Philadelphia, U. Hunt & Son, 1856. 191 p.

KF228.W45W5

This pamphlet contains the most complete record available of the proceedings before Judge Kane in the federal district court and the proceedings in this case before the Pennsylvania Supreme Court. Apparently all of the relevant legal documents are printed in it, along with arguments of counsel and opinions of the judges. Of particular interest is the dissent of Justice John C. Knox in Williamson's case before the Pennsylvania Supreme Court. This pamphlet is an important supplement to the official *Pennsylvania Reports*, which did not print Knox's dissent. In addition to the two published opinions of Judge Kane, it also includes Kane's opinions and remarks from various hearings not published in *Federal Cases*.

■ Narrative of the facts in the case of Passmore Williamson. Philadelphia, Merrihew & Thompson, 1855. 24 p.

E450.N23

Published by the Pennsylvania Anti-Slavery Society, the *Narrative of the Facts* was designed to tell Williamson's side of the case and to attack Judge Kane. Its most important contribution is its discussion of the criminal prosecution of Williamson and five blacks for the events surrounding Jane's rescue. Except for newspapers, there is no other source for this case, and news accounts do not give the details this pamphlet provides.

Besides Judge Kane, members of the Pennsylvania Supreme Court who refused Williamson's own petition for habeas corpus come under attack. The *Narrative* is designed to gain support for Williamson by showing the arbitrary nature of both the federal and state courts. It contains a plea to the "citizens of Pennsylvania" to beware of "the Slave power of this nation, which has been long and steadily encroaching upon the rights of the North," and, "emboldened by success, has evidently resolved to re-establish slavery on your soil" with the aid of the courts (pp. 21-22). At the end of the *Narrative* is a letter from Williamson, who was still in prison at the time the pamphlet went to press.

■ Lewis, Joseph J. Passmore Williamson vs. John K. Kane. Action for false imprisonment, before the Court of Common Pleas of Delaware County. Argument of Joseph J. Lewis, esq. of Westchester, on the part of the plaintiff. Delivered at Media, December 17th and 18th, 1856. Phonographically reported by David W. Brown. Philadelphia, Merrihew & Thompson, printers, 1857. 42 p.

Law Library

After his release from prison, Passmore Williamson initiated a civil suit against Judge Kane in which he sought to recover damages for the time he spent there. This pamphlet contains only the arguments of Williamson's counsel in that case, Joseph J. Lewis. Lewis was a prominent Philadelphia-area lawyer with antislavery sympathies. The bulk of Lewis's argument centers on the question of jurisdiction. He argues that Judge Kane had no jurisdiction over Williamson and thus the imprisonment was illegal. Kane's attorneys responded with a special plea based on Kane's position as a federal judge. The pamphlet does not give the outcome of the case, which was against Williamson.

The suit itself must be seen as an attempt to harass Kane and gain more publicity for Williamson and the antislavery cause. Williamson's suit had almost no chance of being successful. The pamphlet is the only printed record of it and provides a rare opportunity to view the workings of a court of common pleas in this period. It is unfortunate that Lewis chose to publish only his own arguments and not an in-depth report of the case. Because of the illness of one of Williamson's attorneys, the case was held over one term and hence was argued more than a year after Williamson's release. This chronology suggests that the pamphlet was designed to remind the public of Williamson's case and the dangerous precedents (from an antislavery perspective) set by Kane. It also served to provide lawyers with citations and arguments for future cases raising similar issues.

Dred Scott v. Sandford

60 U.S. (19 How.) 393 (1857)

Dred Scott v. Sandford

13 Am. St. Trials 243 (C.C.D. Mo. 1854)

Scott v. Emerson

15 Mo. 576 (1852)

Emerson v. Dred Scott

11 Mo. 413 (1848)

The *Dred Scott* case—or *Dred Scott* v. *Sandford*, 60 U.S. (19 How.) 393 (1857), as it is formally known—is the most famous legal case involving slavery. Indeed, with the possible exception of *Marbury* v. *Madison*, 5 U.S. (1 Cranch) 173 (1803), *Dred Scott* is the best known U.S. Supreme Court decision of the nineteenth century. Like *Marbury*, this case resulted in an act of Congress being declared unconstitutional, but here, unlike *Marbury*, the type of act and its importance was of major significance. In *Marbury* the Court voided a minor clause of an

Roger Brooke Taney (1777-1864). Roger B. Taney was chief justice of the U.S. Supreme Court from 1836 to his death in 1864. A Maryland slave owner, Taney was ambivalent about the peculiar institution. In 1819 he defended the Reverend Jacob Gruber, who was charged with inciting slaves to rebel. At about this time Taney joined the American Colonization Society and freed his own slaves, but by 1842 he had become a firm defender of slavery. In *Prigg* v. *Pennsylvania* he agreed with Justice Story's majority opinion, but wrote a bitter concurrence, attacking Story for what he perceived (correctly as it turned out) to be antislavery implications in the opinion. Taney is most remembered for his "Opinion of the Court" in *Dred Scott* v. *Sandford*. His opinion there was proslavery throughout, and replete with errors of fact. Taney hoped to end sectional squabbling over slavery by giving the South a complete victory on all constitutional issues relating to the subject. Instead, he exacerbated the sectional crisis and became the target of Northern policitians, editors, and, by 1860, the general public throughout the North.

Photograph by Anderson, New York, copyright 1891. LC-USZ62-20794 elaborate statute that had been in force only fourteen years. In *Dred Scott,* the Court declared that a major piece of legislation—a linchpin of the Compromise of 1820 (the Missouri Compromise)—was unconstitutional. This law had been in force for thirty-seven years and was the basis of numerous other federal statutes.

Dred Scott was the most controversial decision of the century, and perhaps in the history of the Supreme Court. All nine justices on the Court wrote opinions, but Chief Justice Roger B. Taney's fifty-four page opinion was designated the "Opinion of the Court." It was, with a few exceptions, vilified in the North and cheered in the South. Everywhere it was debated by politicians, journalists, and lawyers. The famous Lincoln-Douglas debates of 1858 and the political rhetoric of the 1860 presidential campaign centered largely on the meaning and importance of Taney's decision. The decision itself and various interpretations of it were widely circulated, read, and debated.

Dred Scott was the slave of Dr. John Emerson, a U.S. Army surgeon. In the 1830s and 1840s, Scott accompanied Emerson to a number of military posts. These included a post in the free state of Illinois and Fort Snelling, in the territory north of the State of Missouri, which had been declared "free" by Congress in the Compromise of 1820. In 1846 Dred Scott sued for his freedom in the St. Louis Circuit Court on the basis of his residence in these free jurisdictions. After a number of delays, hearings, trials, and retrials, a St. Louis jury declared Scott to be a free man in 1850.

This result was consistent with a long series of Missouri Supreme Court precedents, dating from *Winney* v. *Whitesides,* 1 Mo. 334 (1824), in which slaves who had resided in free states were determined to be free. In 1852, however, the Missouri Supreme Court reversed the decision in Scott's case—and nearly thirty years of precedents—and declared that Scott was still a slave. The motivation for this reversal of precedent was blatantly political. Chief Justice William Scott declared: "Times are not as they were when the former decisions on this subject were made. Since then not only individuals but States have been possessed with a dark and fell spirit in relation to slavery, whose gratification is sought in the pursuit of measures, whose inevitable consequence must be the overthrow and destruction of our government," *Scott* v. *Emerson,* 15 Mo. 576, 586 (1852). Under such conditions the Supreme Court of Missouri would no longer recognize the power of a free state to liberate a slave.

At this point the case should have ended. But, by 1852, Dr. Emerson's widow had remarried. The executor of Emerson's estate was now John F. A. Sanford, who lived in New York. (He did not spell his name *Sandford,* as U.S. Reporter Benjamin Howard thought he did, misspelling the name of the defendant in the official report.) On the pretense that he was a citizen of Missouri, Scott sued Sanford (a citizen of New York) under the diversity clause of the U.S. Constitution. In the U.S. Circuit Court for Missouri, Sanford entered a plea in abatement, asserting that, as a Negro, Scott could not be a citizen of the United States and thus could not sue in federal court. District Judge Robert Wells rejected this argument by ruling that *if* Scott were a free man, then he could sue in federal court under the diversity clause. Although Sanford lost on the procedural motion, he won the case on its merits, and Scott was once again declared to be a slave.

Scott then appealed to the U.S. Supreme Court, where the case was argued in February 1856. Scott's case was argued by Montgomery Blair, who would later become postmaster general in the Lincoln administration. Sanford was represented by U.S. Senator Henry S. Geyer of Missouri and Reverdy Johnson, a leading Maryland attorney and politician. The case was not decided during the presidential campaign of 1856, and in December 1856 the court heard reargument. The case was finally decided on March 6, 1857, the day after James Buchanan was inaugurated president.

There were four major questions before the Court when the case was decided. They were: (1) Was the plea in abatement before the court, or once that issue had been decided was it no longer subject to review? (2) Were Negroes citizens of the United States? (3) Was Scott free because he had lived in the free state of Illinois? (4) Was Scott free because he had lived in a territory made free by the Missouri Compromise?

Had Chief Justice Taney and his colleagues wished, they could have narrowly decided these issues and in so doing avoided a controversial decision. They could have ignored the questions of black citizenship and the plea in abatement and focused on the question of residence in Illinois and what would soon be the state of Minnesota. The Court could have relied on the recent decision in *Strader* v. *Graham*, 51 U.S. (10 How.) 82 (1850), which held that a slave state had a right to accept or reject free state law in these matters. Thus, Missouri had a right to ignore Illinois law.

As for the Missouri Compromise, a similar understanding of federal law might have been in order. The Court could have declared that Scott had a right to freedom while he lived in a free federal territory but lost that right when he left the territory. This could have been supported by an important British case, *The Slave, Grace*, 2 Hagg. 94, 166 Eng. Rep. 179 (1827).

But such a narrow decision would have displeased many people, including a number of slaveholders on the Court who wanted a stronger protection for slavery in the territories. Such a narrow decision was not what Taney wanted either. Taney thus wrote a long and complicated opinion in which he attempted to settle, at one stroke, the troubling issue of slavery and the federal territories, which had plagued the nation for a decade or more. This issue, and the question of black citizenship, were legitimately before the Court, and so Taney's comments on them, however wrong or impolitic, were not dicta.

In his controversial opinion, the chief justice ruled (1) that Congress did not have the power to prohibit slavery in the territories or, indeed, pass anything more than the most basic and general legislation for the territories; (2) that the Missouri Compromise was unconstitutional and thus void; (3) that slavery was legal in all the territories until such time as the territories became states and decided the slavery issue for themselves; and, (4) that Negroes could not become citizens of the United States and thus could not sue in federal court. This last point was based on a long, and largely false, historical argument that blacks had never been citizens of the United States or any of the states. In a bitter dissent, Justice Benjamin R. Curtis, of Massachusetts, showed many examples of blacks voting in states at the time of the Declaration of Independence and the ratification of the Constitution, as well as in 1857. Despite the dissents by Curtis and John McLean, a majority of the Court held that Scott was a slave.

One court opinion was not likely to end all the sectional problems of the nation. But Taney's opinion was particularly ill-suited to the task. It appeared to be an opinion that he desperately wanted to write. He worked behind the scenes in the Court to take the "opinion of the Court" away from Justice Samuel Nelson, of New York, who was going to write a narrow and moderate opinion, which became his concurrence. As a recent Pulitzer Prize-winning book on the case has shown, "Behind his mask of judicial propriety, the Chief Justice had become privately a bitter sectionalist, seething with anger at 'Northern insult and Northern aggression'" (Don E. Fehrenbacher, *The Dred Scott Case: Its Significance in American Law and Politics* [New York: Oxford University Press, 1978], p. 311).

As Justices Curtis and McLean demonstrated in their dissents, to settle the slavery issues in favor of the South, Taney ignored precedent, deliberately misread the Constitution, and rewrote history. Taking sides in the sectional crisis of the 1850s, Taney wrote a proslavery, pro-South decision that gave nothing to the North or freedom. "Taney's opinion," as Fehrenbacher has put it, "proves to be a work of unmitigated partisanship, polemical in spirit though judicial in its language, and more like an ultimatum than a formula for sectional accommodation. Peace on Taney's terms resembled the peace implicit in a demand for unconditional surrender" (Fehrenbacher, *Dred Scott Case*, p. 3).

This "surrender" required that all of the western territories be opened to slavery. In addition, it required that the North acknowledge, as Taney declared, that since the inception of the Declaration of

Independence, blacks were "altogether unfit to associate with the white race, either in social or political relations; and so far inferior, that they [Negroes] had no rights which the white man was bound to respect; and that the negro might justly and lawfully be reduced to slavery for his benefit," 60 U.S. (19 How.) 393, 407 (1857).

For many in the North, where slavery was outlawed and abhored and free blacks lived with some or all of the same rights as whites, the results of the decision were an anathema. Many of the publications presented below printed refutations of Taney's arguments, from the Curtis and McLean dissents and from other sources as well. Abraham Lincoln's popularity in the North in 1860 would be based, in part, on his critique of Taney and his decision.

Taney's decision settled little. Slavery in the territories remained an issue. The general question of slavery remained on the political agenda until it was resolved by the Civil War, Reconstruction, and three new amendments to the Constitution. One of these, the Fourteenth Amendment, was particularly aimed at the *Dred Scott* precedent, for it declared that blacks were indeed citizens of the United States. Even Dred Scott's own status was only marginally affected by the decision. A short time after the decision was announced, Scott was purchased by some white friends and freed.

■ U.S. Supreme Court. Dred Scott vs. John F. A. Sandford. Additional
    brief of M. Blair for appellant. Washington, Gideon, printer,
    1856. 8 p.

Law Library

——Dred Scott, pl'ff in er., v. John F. A. Sandford. In error to the
    U.S. Circuit Court for the District of Missouri. 15 p.

Law Library

These two items are bound together in the records and briefs of the U.S. Supreme Court. The first contains an outline of the case presented by Dred Scott's attorney, Montgomery Blair. Blair was a prominent Maryland politician who would later become postmaster general in the Lincoln administration. His brief contains the citations he used in oral arguments and indicates that he provided a great deal of evidence to refute many of Taney's contentions. The second contains records from the U.S. Circuit Court in Missouri, where Scott first brought his suit against Sanford. It includes the agreed-upon statement of facts that was presented to the Supreme Court, as well as other depositions and writs connected to the case. Both constitute an important primary source for scholars interested in the legal developments and arguments in this case.

■ U.S. Supreme Court. A report of the decision of the Supreme Court of the United States and the opinions of the judges thereof, in the case of Dred Scott versus John F. A. Sandford. December term, 1856. New York, D. Appleton & Co., 1857. pp. 393-633.

Law Library

This is an exact reprint of the original report of this case found in 60 U.S. (19 How.) 393 (1857). It was published by Benjamin C. Howard, the reporter for the U.S. Supreme Court, in an effort to profit from the case. This edition retains the original pagination and headnotes found in *United States Reports*. Howard's only addition is a table of contents and a prefatory advertisement. Its significance (other than demonstrating Howard's desire for profit) is best explained in the advertisement: ''In consequence of the general desire of the public to have access to these opinions, in a smaller book than the official volume of the Reports of the Supreme Court, I have determined to print that part of the volume which contains them in the following separate publication.''

■ U.S. Supreme Court. Report of the decision of the Supreme Court of the United States, and the opinions of the judges thereof, in the case of Dred Scott versus John F. A. Sandford. December term, 1856, Washington. Cornelius Wendell, printer, 1857. 239 p.

Law Library

——[Reprint] New York, DaCapo Press, 1970. 239 p.

KF4545.S5H64 1970

This report was not printed on behalf of Benjamin Howard and does not retain the original pagination or the headnotes found in the official report of the case. In all other respects, however, it is exactly the same as the official report.

Page 3 of this version is the same as part of page 396. Use of a small type size at the beginning of this volume allows the content to be completely synchronized with that of the official report by the beginning of page 6. Thus, page 6 is the same as 60 U.S. (19 How.) 400, and page 239 is the same as 60 U.S. (19 How.) 633.

Commissioned by the U.S. Senate for gratis distribution by senators, twenty thousand copies of this edition were printed at a cost of $6,150. An additional $1,500 was given to Benjamin Howard to compensate for the free distribution of this pamphlet undercutting the sales of the D. Appleton version authorized by Howard.

■ U.S. Supreme Court. The case of Dred Scott in the United States
Supreme Court. The full opinions of Chief Justice Taney and
Justice Curtis, abstracts of the opinions of the other judges; with
an analysis of the points ruled and some concluding observations.
New York, Horace Greeley & Co., 1860. 104 p.

E450.S398

——New York, Tribune Association, 1860. 104 p.

E450.S399

This pamphlet contains the two most important opinions in the
case—those of Chief Justice Taney and Associate Justice Benjamin
Robbins Curtis of Massachusetts. Greeley and McElrath, publishers,
first printed it in 1857. These two editions of it were reprinted in 1860
by Greeley and his newspaper, the *New York Tribune*.

The Curtis dissent is a stinging attack on Taney's opinion and
the assumptions underlying it. This dissent provided a great deal of
political ammunition for Northern politicians and editors who attacked
Taney's opinion. The last four pages of the pamphlet contain a report by
a joint committee of the New York State legislature attacking Taney's
opinion and a resolution passed by that body in support of the committee
report.

At twenty-five cents a copy, this pamphlet severely undercut the
sales of the D. Appleton version and allowed a large portion of the
population to read Taney's opinion and Curtis's attack on it. That three
separate editions were published between 1857 and 1860 underscores
the importance of the case to the politics of the period.

■ Benton, Thomas Hart. Historical and legal examination of that part of
the decision of the Supreme Court of the United States in the
Dred Scott Case, which declares the unconstitutionality of the
Missouri Compromise Act, and the self-extension of the
Constitution to territories, carrying slavery along with it. With
an appendix. . . . New York, D. Appleton and Co., 1857. 193 p.

Law Library

——[Reprint] New York, Johnson Reprint Corp., 1970. 193 p.

KF4545.S5B45 1970

Former U.S. Senator Thomas Hart Benton of Missouri was on
his deathbed at the time he wrote this book. It is the longest and most
elaborate attack on Chief Justice Taney's decision in *Dred Scott* written
before the Civil War. Benton was so incensed by Taney's opinion

that he hurriedly wrote this extended rebuttal, making three basic arguments. First, he asserts that the Constitution does not apply in toto to the territories—that it is designed only for the *states*. He supports this with references to numerous debates over territorial organization, showing that often Congress had explicitly denied the inhabitants of the territories basic constitutional rights (such as jury trials in civil cases where the amount in controversy was more than twenty dollars). Second, he argues that Congress has the power to legislate for any territory as it sees fit. Finally, he asserts that the laws of the states cannot follow the citizens of the states into the territories. Applying this to slavery, Benton notes that there are fifteen different slave states, with fifteen different slave codes. If the law of slavery followed the masters, then there would be fifteen separate slave codes in the territories.

Benton concludes that Taney is in error for declaring (1) that the Missouri Compromise is unconstitutional; (2) that the Constitution applies to the territories; and (3) that slavery was carried into the territories by the self-extension of the Constitution to the territories. His sixty-page appendix contains excerpts from various congressional debates and presidential messages dealing with slavery in the territories.

This volume exposed the political implications of Taney's decision and undercut its judicial authority. Benton tied Taney's decision to the doctrines of John C. Calhoun and to other political arguments that had never been accepted by a majority of Congress. Coming from an aged and respected statesman, who was also a former senator from a slave state, the attack on Taney took on added importance.

■ [Gray, Horace, and John Lowell, Jr.] A legal review of the case of Dred Scott, as decided by the Supreme Court of the United States. Boston, Crosby, Nichols and Co., 1857. 62 p.

Law Library

This was one of the earliest and best argued legalistic attacks on Chief Justice Taney's opinion in *Dred Scott*. It first appeared as an article in the June 1857 issue of the *Law Reporter*, which at the time was edited by Lowell. The authors made some alterations and corrections and reprinted the article as a pamphlet later the same year.

Both authors were bright young men rising in the legal profession. Lowell ultimately became a federal district judge, and Gray would spend twenty-one years as an associate justice of the U.S. Supreme Court. Although Gray and Lowell are quite mild in their criticism of Taney, the pamphlet is an excellent example of how conservative Northern lawyers were appalled by the partisan and unjudicial nature of

Taney's opinion. They suggest that his opinion ''is unworthy of the reputation of that great magistrate'' (p. 9).

In dissecting Taney's opinion, they present several arguments. (1) They argue that Negroes can be citizens of the United States. This is primarily a historical argument taken mostly from Justice Curtis's dissent. (2) If Taney is correct in his assertion that the Supreme Court has no jurisdiction in the case, because a black man cannot sue in federal court, then he also has no right to examine the merits of the case. (3) Congress has the right to regulate the territories. (4) The *Somerset* rule is good law in the United States, and thus any slave brought into a free jurisdiction by his master becomes free the moment that slave touches free soil. (5) The U.S. Supreme Court does not have to follow the ruling on Dred Scott's status as decided by the Missouri Supreme Court. Each of these propositions is supported by citations to numerous state, federal, and foreign cases, as well as the treatises of Joseph Story, Ulric Huber, and Lord Coke.

■   A review of the decision of the Supreme Court of the United States in the Dred Scott case. By a Kentucky lawyer. Louisville, Morton & Griswold, printers, 1857. 47 p.

E450.R45 Rare Book Room

The author of this pamphlet, an unknown Kentucky lawyer, believes that the Supreme Court should have delivered a very narrow decision in *Dred Scott*, denying jurisdiction on the grounds that Scott was not a citizen of Missouri and therefore not able to sue in federal court. He thinks the Court was incorrect in declaring the Missouri Compromise unconstitutional, making not only a legal error but a political one as well. Indeed, he thinks that the judges ''rendered a *political and sectional instead of a judicial decision*''—that they deserve a ''solemn rebuke, by way of protest, from Congress'' for their action, which did ''more to lower the moral tone and standing of our judiciary than any thing that has ever occurred'' (p. 44). This pamphlet appears to have had limited circulation, but it is a useful example of the moderate, border-state view of the decision, agreeing with the result but not with the political and controversial nature of Taney's decision.

■   U.S. Supreme Court. The Dred Scott decision. Opinion of Chief Justice Taney, with an introduction by Dr. J. H. Van Evrie also, an appendix, containing an essay on the natural history of the Prognathous race of mankind, originally written for the New

York Day-Book, by Dr. S. A. Cartwright, of New Orleans. New York, Van Evrie, Horton & Co., 1859. 48 p.

Law Library

One of the most controversial aspects of Chief Justice Taney's opinion was his assertion that Negroes could not be citizens of the United States, and that they were "a subordinate and inferior class of beings, who had been subjugated by the dominant race, and, whether emancipated or not, yet remained subject to their authority," 60 U.S. (19 How.) 404-405 (1857). Thus Taney concluded that blacks were "of an inferior order, and altogether unfit to associate with the white race, either in social or political relations; and so far inferior, that they had no rights which the white man was bound to respect," 60 U.S. (19 How.) 407 (1857). This position was supported by racialists in both the North and the South.

This pamphlet contains only Taney's opinion, supplemented by supporting arguments on race and racism. Van Evrie declares in his introduction that Taney's opinion is, with the exception of the Declaration of Independence, "the most momentous event that has ever occurred on this continent" (p. iii), and that it will uphold and preserve American freedom. He argues that emancipation would undermine the nation by freeing millions of inferior people. Furthermore, "this decision must be accepted and sustained by the northern masses, or there must be disunion and dismemberment of the Union" (p. ix).

In his essay, Cartwright, a noted physician from New Orleans who dabbled in anthropology and pseudoscientific investigations of the races of mankind, compares Negroes to "the ourang outang" and various monkeys (pp. 45-46). Much of his "scientific" evaluation is based on measurements of skulls and other visible physical differences between blacks and whites. He ends by suggesting that blacks are the descendants of both Cain and Noah's accursed grandson Canaan (pp. 47-48).

An indication of support for Taney and slavery in the North, this pamphlet shows how Northern racism affected popular understanding of Taney's opinion. By reprinting only Taney's opinion, Van Evrie was able to find legal support for his own racial theories and in turn give "scientific" support to Taney's legal position, without facing the embarassing arguments made in Curtis's dissent. Although this pamphlet represents a minority opinion in the North, it is nevertheless excellent evidence that the hostility towards Taney's opinion was not universal in that section of the country.

■ Foot, Samuel Alfred. An examination of the case of Dred Scott against Sandford, in the Supreme Court of the United States, and a full and fair exposition of the decision of the Court, and of the opinions of the majority of the Judges. New York, Wm. C. Bryant & Co., 1859. 19 p.

E450.F68 Rare Book Room

The contents of this pamphlet were originally presented in a speech before the Geneva Literary and Scientific Association in December 1858. The author was a distinguished attorney and former judge of the New York Court of Appeals, the state's highest court. While claiming to be impartial, Foot offers a critique of Taney's opinion that was prepared for informed laymen rather than attorneys. He argues that Taney's opinions on the territories and the rights of blacks were obiter dicta "and have no judicial authority." He suggests that Taney's erroneous notions will be "engrafted on our Constitution and laws by judicial legislation" (p. 18), unless there is a change in the makeup of the Supreme Court.

This pamphlet is a useful example of how Northerners viewed the decision and how they feared the Supreme Court would "give us a new constitutional and legal system on the subject of slavery and our territories" (p. 19). The publisher of this pamphlet, William Cullen Bryant, was one of the leading literary figures of the mid-nineteenth century and an active abolitionist.

Lemmon v. The People

20 N.Y. 562 (1860)

Lemmon v. The People

20 Barb. 270 (N.Y. Sup. Ct. 1858)

The People ex rel. Napoleon v. Lemmon

5 Sand. 681 (N.Y. Super. Ct. 1852)

Until 1841, New York allowed slave owners from other states to bring slaves into New York for periods of up to nine months. In 1841 this "nine months transit law" was unconditionally repealed.

In 1852 Jonathan and Juliet Lemmon left their home in Virginia to move to Texas, carrying eight slaves with them. At that time the most efficient way to get from Virginia to Texas was to take a steamer to New York and then a second ship directly to New Orleans. With this in mind,

Charles O'Conor (1804-1884). O'Conor was a conservative New Yorker and an active member of the Democratic party, even though he was never elected to any public office. In 1860 he argued the *Lemmon* case on behalf of the state of Virginia. After the Civil War he was counsel for Jefferson Davis when the former Confederate president was charged with treason.

Brady-Handy Collection. LC-BH82-5234

the Lemmons and their eight slaves went to New York, where they rented rooms while awaiting the departure of a ship for the Gulf Coast.

Immediately after their arrival they were discovered by a black named Louis Napoleon, who secured a writ of habeas corpus on behalf of the slaves. Seven days later Judge Elijah Paine of the New York Superior Court released the slaves from the custody of the Lemmons and declared them to be free persons under New York law. The Lemmons were indemnified for their loss by a group of New York businessmen, and they then returned to Virginia.

The state of Virginia, however, hired counsel and appealed this decision to the New York Supreme Court. In 1857 that court upheld Paine's decision. The state of Virginia then appealed to the New York Court of Appeals, the state's highest court. In 1860, by a vote of five to three, the justices of that court upheld the original decision in the case. An appeal to the U.S. Supreme Court was expected, but the election of Lincoln and the subsequent secession of Virginia foreclosed any further legal action in the case.

■ New York. Court of Appeals. Report of the Lemmon slave case; containing points and arguments of counsel on both sides, and opinions of all the judges. New York, H. Greeley & Co., 1860. 140 p.

Law Library

——New York, W. H. Tinson, printer, 1860. 146 p.
Law Library; E450.N56 1860

——New York, H. Greeley & Co., 1861. 140 p.
E450.N56 1861 Rare Book Room

This pamphlet contains the original petition for the writ of habeas corpus, the opinion of Judge Paine in the Superior Court, the opinion of Justice William Mitchell in the New York Supreme Court, the arguments of Charles O'Conor on behalf of the Lemmons and those of William M. Evarts for the state before the New York Court of Appeals, and the complete report of the New York Court of Appeals, including the opinion of the court, the concurring opinion, and all three dissents. Thus, it brings together most of the printed material available on this case. The only reported materials not here are the arguments of counsel before New York's intermediary appellate court, the New York Supreme Court.

The arguments of O'Conor and Evarts represent the fullest legal examination of slave transit and comity before the Civil War. The decision represents the most complete application of the pro-freedom doctrines initially laid out in *Somerset* v. *Stewart*, 98 Eng. Rep. 499 (K.B. 1772), and *Commonwealth* v. *Aves*, 35 Mass. (18 Pick.) 193 (1836). In *Commonwealth* v. *Aves*, Chief Justice Lemuel Shaw suggested that there might be some exemptions to slaves gaining their freedom the moment they set foot on free soil. One of those exemptions might be for travelers who must pass through a free state on their way from one slave state to another. This was not at issue in *Commonwealth* v. *Aves*, and thus Shaw gave no definitive opinion on the subject.

In *Lemmon* v. *The People*, however, this was precisely the issue. The *Lemmon* case is one of the most extreme examples of hostility to slavery in Northern courts. In dissent, Justice Clerke of the New York Court of Appeals warned that ''the violation of the right yielded by what is termed comity, under the law of nations, would, under certain circumstances, be a just cause of war,'' and thus New York ought to grant the minimal right of unhindered transit with slaves to citizens of the slave states, 20 N.Y. 643 (1860). The majority did not accept this position and in the process pushed the nation one step closer to Civil War.

This case was discussed by both Northern and Southern politicians in the late 1850s. The various printings of this pamphlet during the election of 1860 and the secession crisis of 1861 underscore the importance of the case to the politics and law of slavery.

100 Dollars REWARD.

RAN AWAY from the subscriber, living near Charlestown, Jefferson County, Virginia, on the night of the 4th instant, two Negro Men,

ROBERT & LEWIS.

ROBERT is about 22 years of age, about six feet high, black complexion, good features, pleasant countenance, very straight made, and has a good carriage. He has behind one of his ears, (thought to be his right,) a small scar, upon which there is no hair growing. He had on, when he absconded, a steel-mixed cassinet coat, a black fur hat, and a pair of calfskin shoes. **LEWIS** is about 24 years of age, 5 feet nine or ten inches high, yellow complexion, good features, stout made and somewhat fleshy. Had on, when he absconded, a steel-mixed cassinet coat, black fur hat; supposed to have had on a pair of fine shoes, linen or cassimere pantaloons.

I will give 20 dollars for each of said negroes, if taken in the county, and returned to me; and 50 dollars for each if taken in Maryland or Pennsylvania, and secured so that I get them again.

JOHN LOCK.

October 6, 1834.

PRINTED AT THE VIRGINIA FREE PRESS OFFICE, CHARLESTOWN.

This 1834 handbill is quite typical of those advertising for escaped slaves. The descriptions of the slaves are general and might apply to numerous blacks in the area. Although the owner is unsure of the location of scars on his slaves, he is fairly certain about the kind of clothing they wore. The owner also realizes that if his slaves escape to Maryland or Pennsylvania it will be harder (and thus more expensive) to recover them. It is also worth noting that the handbill is somewhat misleading as to the amount of reward offered. The "100 Dollars Reward" can be earned only if both slaves are captured and brought back from a neighboring state.

Broadside Collection, Rare Book and Special Collections Division.

Fugitive Slaves

The Northwest Ordinance of 1787 prohibited slavery in the area north of the Ohio River. It contained, however, the following exception: "*Provided, always,* That any person escaping into the same, from whom labor or service is lawfully claimed in any one of the original States, such fugitive may be lawfully reclaimed and conveyed to the person claiming his or her labor or service as aforesaid," *Northwest Ordinance,* July 13, 1787, Art. 6 (1 Stat. 51n).

This provision was repeated in a modified form in the U.S. Constitution. Late in the Convention of 1787, at the behest of Pierce Butler of South Carolina, the following clause was added: "No Person held to Service or Labour in one State, under the Laws thereof, escaping into another, shall, in Consequence of any Law or Regulation therein, be discharged from such Service or Labour, but shall be delivered up on Claim of the Party to whom such Service or Labour may be due" (U.S. Const., art. 4, sec. 2, cl. 3). There was virtually no debate over this clause at the Constitutional Convention, and it is unclear how the delegates to the convention expected it to work. Because it was placed in the same section of the Constitution as the "Privileges and Immunities Clause," it is reasonable to believe that this clause was directed at the states and that it was up to the states to enforce it.

This question was mooted, however, when Congress passed the first Fugitive Slave Act, Feb. 12, 1793, ch. 7, 1 Stat. 302. The 1793 act provided for an orderly return of runaway slaves. Under this law a master or his agent was empowered to seize or arrest a fugitive slave and take that fugitive before "any judge of the circuit or district courts of the United States, residing or being within the state, or before any magistrate of a county, city or town" where the arrest took place. Upon satisfactory proof, the judge or magistrate was to issue a certificate of removal, allowing the master to return home with the slave. Any person interfering with the rendition of a fugitive slave could be fined $500, which would be paid to the master. In addition, the master retained a "right of action for or on account of the said injuries or either of them." The act did not specify what kind of evidence was necessary to secure a claim to a fugitive slave. Nor did it prevent an investigation of the alleged slave's status by state authorities.

In 1850 this act was supplemented by a series of amendments, commonly known as the Fugitive Slave Act of Sept. 18, 1850, ch. 60, 9 Stat. 462. This law was part of the Compromise of 1850 and was designed to placate Southerners who felt the 1793 act was not being enforced by Northern jurists. Under the 1850 act, federal commissioners were appointed in each county in the United States to enforce the law. They were empowered to issue arrest warrants and appoint deputies and posse comitatus for capturing fugitives. Alleged fugitives could be brought before the commissioners, who would determine their status. At these hearings the alleged fugitives were explicitly prohibited from testifying in their own behalf; jury trials were also proscribed. Federal marshals and military officers were obligated to enforce the law, and "all good citizens" were "hereby commanded to aid and assist in the prompt and efficient execution of this law, whenever their services may be required." Federal marshals who failed to safeguard an alleged fugitive could be fined $1,000 and face civil suits for the value of any slaves rescued. Any person convicted of interfering with the rendition of a fugitive slave could be fined $1,000 and face up to $1,000 in civil damages for each slave lost. In addition, a person convicted of interfering with the law could be sentenced to six months in prison. Finally, the 1850 law provided for a $10 fee for the commissioner (to be paid by the claimant) if the commissioner found in favor of the claimant, but only a $5 fee if the commissioner decided the person before him was not a slave.

Both of these statutes led to a great amount of litigation in state and federal courts. The extensive pamphlet literature annotated here suggests the importance of the issue to antebellum Americans. The successful and unsuccessful renditions provided much propaganda, particularly for the antislavery cause. Many of these pamphlets give in-depth reports of trials that are available in no other form. Others reprint Supreme Court and lower court opinions. They were designed to make legal arguments and issues available to the American people as a whole and were often used to further the antislavery cause.

Prigg v. *Pennsylvania*

41 U.S. (16 Pet.) 539 (1842)

In 1837 Edward Prigg, a professional slave catcher from Maryland, seized Margaret Morgan, a fugitive slave residing in Pennsylvania. Under a Pennsylvania act of 1826, no alleged fugitive slave could be removed from the state without a certificate of removal issued by a state official. This state certification was required in addition to a similar certificate required by the federal Fugitive Slave Act of Feb. 12, 1793, ch. 7, 1 Stat. 302.

When Prigg brought Margaret Morgan before a state judge, he was unable to obtain a certificate. He then acted unilaterally and, in contravention of Pennsylvania law, took Morgan back to Maryland without any state process. He was subsequently indicted for kidnapping. After much negotiation between Pensylvania and Maryland authorities, Prigg was extradited to Pennsylvania. There he was tried and convicted. In a pro forma hearing, the Pennsylvania Supreme Court affirmed this conviction, and the case was then taken to the U.S. Supreme Court.

The overriding constitutional issue centered on the jurisdiction of Congress and the states over fugitive slaves. Writing for the Court, Justice Joseph Story held (1) that the power to regulate the rendition of fugitive slaves was exclusively within the prerogative of Congress, and thus the Pennsylvania statute requiring a separate certificate of removal was unconstitutional; (2) that despite the requirement in the Fugitive Slave Act of 1793 that a claimant take an alleged fugitive before some judicial authority, a "right of self-help" existed which allowed masters to remove fugitive slaves without any judicial superintendence—however, Story declared this was legal only if done without violence or breach of the peace—and (3) that the fedcral government could not force or require state officials to help enforce the Fugitive Slave Act or any other federal statute. Story went to great lengths, however, to assert that state officials *ought* to enforce the Fugitive Slave Act. With one justice, John McLean, dissenting, the Court held the Pennsylvania Act of 1826 unconstitutional as an interference with congressional power. The conviction of Prigg was reversed.

Although *Prigg* v. *Pennsylvania* decisively settled the jurisdictional issue resulting from the Fugitive Slave Clause, it did not lead to harmonious and smooth relations on this question, either between the North and the South or between the North and the federal government. Before *Prigg*, most putative masters had relied on state officials to issue certificates of removal. After *Prigg*, a number of Northern legislatures and courts used the decision to·support their refusal to aid in the rendition of fugitive slaves. Because there were few federal judges and magistrates in the free states, after 1842 it became extremely difficult for masters to obtain certificates of removal under the 1793 act. The right of self-help was only useful when fugitives could be captured quietly, without any breach of the peace.

The decision in *Prigg* ultimately became an antislavery weapon. It also led to increased demands for a new fugitive slave law. These demands were satisfied with the passage of the Fugitive Slave Act of 1850.

■ U.S. Supreme Court. Report of the case of Edward Prigg against the Commonwealth of Pennsylvania. Argued and adjudged in the

Supreme Court of the United States at January term, 1842. In which it was decided that all the laws of the several states relative to fugitive slaves are unconstitutional and void; and that Congress have the exclusive power of legislation on the subject of fugitive slaves escaping into other states. By Richard Peters, Reporter of the decisions of the Supreme Court of the United States. Philadelphia, Stereotyped by L. Johnson, 1842. 140 p.

KF4545.S5P73 1970; E450.P95 Rare Book Room

With the exception of the pagination, the title page, and a one-page preface by Richard Peters, this report of the case appears exactly as it did in volume 16 of Peters's *United States Reports*. Peters, the official Court reporter, authorized the publishing of this case as a pamphlet before the volume of *United States Reports* that it would appear in was available. This was done, according to his preface, because of ''the general and deep interest of all the citizens of the United States in the case'' (p. 3).

Peters does not exaggerate the interest in the case. Northerners and Southerners of all political viewpoints realized its importance. It affected all of the ''personal liberty laws'' of the North, which had been passed to protect free blacks from kidnapping and which were often used to hinder the return of fugitive slaves. The case was extremely complicated and easily misunderstood.

Although concurring in the result, Chief Justice Roger B. Taney complained that Justice Story's opinion would prohibit state officials from enforcing the federal law and that it would invalidate the laws of all the Southern and some of the Northern states that were designed to aid in the rendition of fugitive slaves. In his opinion, Story said that state officials could, and should, enforce the 1793 act. He furthermore declared that state legislation was void only if it added to the 1793 act and made the rendition process more difficult. Story explicitly allowed states to pass legislation ''to arrest and restrain runaway slaves, and remove them from their [the states'] borders,'' as long as such legislation was not designed to ''interfere with or to obstruct the just rights of the owner to reclaim his slave'' (p. 91).

Taney's differences with Story were actually quite small. His exaggeration of these differences may be attributed to Court politics and a desire on the part of the chief justice to emphasize the importance of state participation in the rendition process.

Less explicable are Peters's errors in his title, preface, and headnotes. The title of the pamphlet declares this was a decision ''In Which It Was Decided That All the Laws of the Several States Relative to Fugitive Slaves are Unconstitutional.'' This was clearly not so. In his preface Peters erroneously asserts that ''no state judicial officer, under the authority of state laws, can act in the matter.'' This error is repeated in the headnotes (pp. 3, 8). We can only assume that Peters misunderstood Story's complicated opinion, or that he assumed Taney's concurrence was an accurate reflection of the contents of Story's opinion.

The fame and importance of *Prigg* was in part a function of the availability of the decision almost immediately after it was announced. This pamphlet thus represents an unusually rare instance of ''instant'' mass communication in the mid-nineteenth century.

■ Maryland. General Assembly. House of Delegates. Committee on Grievances and Courts of Justice. Report of the Committee on Grievances and Courts of Justice relative to the surrender of fugitives from justice, made to the House of Delegates of Maryland. December session, 1841. [Annapolis?] 1841. 15 p.
E450.M4

The *Prigg* case raised an important issue for slave states: should they return alleged criminals, like Prigg, to free states when the alleged crime affected slavery? Prigg had, after all, done nothing that would have been deemed a violation of the law in Maryland. Only through a series of negotiations between Pennsylvania and Maryland officials was it possible to have Prigg returned for trial and the issue of Pennsylvania's ''personal liberty laws'' settled by the U.S. Supreme Court.

Pennsylvania and Maryland successfully negotiated their dispute, but New York and Virginia were unable to reach an accord in a similar case. In 1841 the governor of New York, William Henry Seward, refused to allow the extradition to Virginia of three free blacks charged in Virginia with stealing a slave. The three blacks had helped a slave from Norfolk escape on their boat. Governor Seward declared that slaves were not property in New York, and thus the three could not be extradited because they had committed no crime that New York recognized.

This led to a series of communications between the governors of the two states. These communications were copied by Virginia authorities and sent to the Maryland legislature. For Maryland, the two issues— *Prigg* and the New York-Virginia controversy—were similar. Both involved the extradition of people accused of a crime involving slavery, in which one state did not recognize the criminality of the alleged act committed in the other state.

This publication was a report to the Maryland House of Delegates on these two issues. Maryland compares its accommodation with Pennsylvania to the refusal of New York to act similarly. The pamphlet ends with two resolutions on the issue. One declares that stealing slaves is a crime. In such cases the slave and the thief should be returned to the state where the crime originated. The other asserts ''that it is the exclusive right of each State in this Union to define for itself what is felony or crime within the meaning of the Constitution . . . and that when a person who is charged in any State with the commission of an act which by the laws of that State is felonious or criminal, absconds from justice and flies to another State, it is the duty of the authorities of that State to surrender him for trial, on the demand of the State where the offence was committed'' (p. 15). The governor of Maryland was authorized to send copies of these resolutions to all other state governors in the nation.

The Latimer Case

5 Month. L. Rep. 481 (Mass. Cir. Ct. 1842)

Associated case: *Commonwealth* v. *Tracy*, 46 Mass. (5 Met.) 536 (1843)

On October 19, 1842, George Latimer, a Negro, was arrested for larceny by a policeman under a warrant issued by the Boston Police Court. The larceny charge was actually a pretext for seizing Latimer, who was, in fact, a fugitive slave. A crowd of blacks attempted to rescue Latimer before any hearing could be held to determine his status, but this effort failed. Abolitionists then petitioned Chief Justice Lemuel Shaw of the Massachusetts Supreme Judicial Court for a writ of habeas corpus. Shaw granted the writ, but at a hearing it became clear that Latimer was a fugitive slave owned by James B. Gray of Norfolk, Virginia.

Acting under the *Prigg* v. *Pennsylvania,* 41 U.S. (16 Pet.) 539 (1842), precedent, Shaw declared that he could not interfere with Gray's claim. Instead he ordered Latimer returned to Gray's custody, and Gray brought his claim to Latimer before U.S. Supreme Court Justice Joseph Story, who was in Boston at the time. Story gave Gray two weeks to obtain evidence of his ownership of Latimer. In the meantime Gray was allowed to maintain custody of Latimer. Gray knew that it would be impossible to hold a slave in Boston, and he turned Latimer over to the city jailer, who incarcerated Latimer. A second rescue attempt failed, and Chief Justice Shaw again refused to intercede on behalf of Latimer. Thus, Latimer remained in jail while Gray waited for proof of his ownership of Latimer to arrive from Virginia.

Latimer was not in jail under any court order or legal process. Rather, he was held by the jailer, Nathaniel Coolidge, who was paid by Gray for his services and the use of the jail. Although this act was perfectly legal and not considered corrupt by the standards of the time, abolitionists and their allies thought it was an improper and immoral use of state facilities.

Political pressure was soon put on the jailer and the sheriff to release Latimer or return him to Gray. Charles Sumner, Henry I. Bowditch, and others began circulating a petition calling for the removal of the county sheriff if he did not order Coolidge to remove Latimer from the jail. The sheriff himself had doubts about the propriety of holding a man in jail who was not indicted or under any warrant or writ. Good politics coincided with good conscience, and the sheriff ordered Coolidge to return Latimer to Gray.

Gray realized he could not hold Latimer privately, because a mob would free him. He thus agreed to sell Latimer to a group of Bostonians for $400, even though Gray claimed his slave was worth twice that much. Immediately after the sale, the Bostonians freed Latimer, and Gray returned to Virginia.

A few months later three free blacks in Boston were convicted of rioting for their abortive attempt to rescue Latimer. These convictions were sustained by Chief Justice Shaw in *Commonwealth* v. *Tracy.* Shortly after this, a petition of close to sixty-five thousand names was presented to the Massachusetts legislature demanding legislation to stop the enforcement of the Fugitive Slave Act in the Bay State. This resulted in the passage of "An Act Further to Protect Personal Liberty," ch. 69, 1843 Mass. Acts 33, commonly known as the "Latimer Law." This law prohibited state jurists and police officials from taking part in the rendition of fugitive slaves and banned the use of state facilities to hear fugitive slave cases or to incarcerate people seized under the federal law. This statute was deemed by some to be a legitimate implementation of the guidelines laid down by Justice Story in *Prigg* v. *Pennsylvania.*

■ An article on the Latimer case. Boston, Bradbury, Soden, and Co. 1843. 18 p.

Law Library

Like those for many other important fugitive slave cases, the proceedings in the *Latimer* case were not officially reported. However, a number of newspapers and periodicals carried information about the case.

While Latimer was in custody of the jailer, an ad hoc newspaper, the *Latimer Journal and North Star,* was published triweekly by Boston abolitionists. After the case was settled, the *Law Reporter,* a monthly conservative legal periodical published in Boston, devoted a long article to it in the March 1843 issue. The article showed great sympathy for

Justices Story and Shaw and mercilessly castigated the editors of the
Latimer Journal and North Star and the abolitionists who forced the
ultimate release of Latimer. The *Law Reporter*'s position was not
"proslavery" per se; rather, the editors argued for a strict and emphatic
enforcement of the U.S. Constitution and the Fugitive Slave Act of Feb.
12, 1793, ch. 7, 1 Stat. 302. Two months after this article appeared in
the *Law Reporter*, it was issued as a separate pamphlet, which, with the
exception of changes in pagination, is an exact reprint.

An Article on the Latimer Case contains the text of some of the
important writs and orders issued by Story and Shaw during the Latimer
controversy. It does not contain all of the pertinent writs and orders
connected to the case, but it is the most important existing source for
such material. The first pages of the pamphlet describe "the judicial
history of this case" (p. 4), giving a straightforward and useful summary
of the attempts by various lawyers to free Latimer through the use of a
writ of personal replevin or a writ of habeas corpus.

An extremely polemical "account of the contemporaneous doings
and events connected to it" (p. 4) follows. Most of it consists of a
rebuttal of the *Latimer Journal and North Star*, a defense of Justices
Story and Shaw, and attacks on all those who opposed enforcement of
the law. The abolitionists' speeches at a Faneuil Hall meeting called to
protest Latimer's arrest are analyzed and described as "exciting and
inflammatory" (p. 6). After describing and quoting from them, the
authors apologize for having "already disgusted the reader by these
quotations." But, the pamphlet "must wade into a still fouler mass of
violence, intemperance and folly," because at this meeting someone
"openly cursed the constitution of the United States" and actually had
his speech printed in the *Latimer Journal* (p. 6).

The Rev. John Pierpont is also berated in a four-page analysis of
his sermon "A Discourse on the Covenant with Judas," which he
preached while Latimer was in jail. In a rather pedantic and legalistic
approach to this sermon, the editors point out that Rev. Pierpont wrongly
quoted Sir William Blackstone to support the assertion "that a judge
may declare a law of the land void, if he supposes it to conflict with the
law of nature" (p. 15). Curiously, in applying their legal skills to refute
the legal scholarship of a minister, the authors of this pamphlet
undermined their own conservative position by suggesting an even more
drastic solution to the problems created by the Fugitive Slave Act of
1793. They assert that Blackstone did not believe laws could be
overturned by judges if they were in conflict with natural law. Rather,
"it is evident from a subsequent passage, that Blackstone here referred
to the moral right of revolution . . . to pronounce a law, made by the
supreme power of the state, void, as being against the law of nature" (p.

15). It is unlikely, however, that the editors of the *Law Reporter* wished for a revolution.

The editors claimed they did not immediately publish an article on the Latimer case because they "wished to wait until the immediate disturbance had subsided, meaning when we did speak, to speak to ears not filled with the din of public excitement." They wished to combat a "false morality, born from the sophistry of fanaticism" that was "seeking to take advantage of public and private sympathies, to impair the moral sense of the people in the obligations of the fundamental law of the nation, and to undermine their confidence in that judiciary who are bound by solemn oath to administer it" (p. 1).

This pamphlet in fact accomplished two things. It left a brief but detailed record of the proceedings in the case. It also presented a conservative argument in the fight to capture the "public and private sympathies" of the people of Boston and the North on an issue that continued to excite people and make them question their "moral sense . . . [and the] obligations of the fundamental law of the nation" (p. 2).

■ Norfolk, Va. Proceedings of the citizens of the borough of Norfolk, on the Boston outrage, in the case of the runaway slave George Latimer. Norfolk, T. G. Broughton & Son, printers, 1843. 20 p.
E450.L35N6 Rare Book Room

Latimer's case was one of the first to undermine interstate relations on the issue of fugitive slave rendition. When Latimer's owner, James B. Gray, returned to his home in Norfolk, Virginia, a town meeting was held to discuss and protest what had occurred in Boston. A committee was formed to investigate the issues. At a second town meeting the committee offered its official report. The report concluded that there was no defect in the U.S. Constitution but there was "a want of fidelity to the high and solemn behest of that instrument in a considerable portion of the population of Boston, and the inadequacy of the provisions of the act of Congress, passed on the 12th of February, 1793" (p. 4). The committee pointed out that the Fugitive Slave Act of 1793 made no provisions for the jailing or incarceration of alleged fugitives and that the rioters who threatened Gray had not actually violated the act. The committee report urged Congress to change the law to remove these defects.

Besides these recommendations, this pamphlet contains interesting and useful information about the process by which Latimer was freed. There are statements by James B. Gray, reprints from Boston and Norfolk newspapers, and some reprints of legal documents that had been published in newspapers.

The tone of this pamphlet is surprisingly mild, especially when compared to the fire-eating rhetoric of similar attacks on the North in the 1850s. At the time of the town meeting, Norfolk citizens believed that a new statute and stricter enforcement of the laws would solve the problems created by fugitive slave renditions.

Ohio v. Forbes and Armitage

(Franklin Cty. [Ky.] Cir. Ct. 1843)(Unreported)

Around 1830 the slave Jerry Phinney was rented to Mr. Allgaier of Kentucky, who took Phinney to Cincinnati and kept him there for six months. When Phinney's owner, a Mrs. Long, discovered that her slave had been taken out of the state, she immediately ordered Allgaier to return Phinney to Kentucky. Phinney was returned but persuaded his mistress to allow him to go back "to his last place of residence for his clothes" (pp. 9). With this permission Phinney went to Cincinnati and then he disappeared. Mrs. Long advertised him as a runaway on three different occasions, but Phinney was not found.

Finally, in 1846 Mrs. Long "executed regularly, according to law, a power of Attorney to Forbes" to capture Phinney and return him to her (pp. 9—10). With the aid of Armitage this was accomplished. The governor of Ohio then issued a warrant for the arrest of Armitage and Forbes for kidnapping Phinney and illegally removing him from Ohio. This warrant was delivered to the governor of Kentucky, who ordered the two slave catchers arrested as fugitives from justice.

Once arrested, Forbes and Armitage brought their cases before a county circuit court under a Kentucky statute of Jan. 27, 1820, ch. 490, 1820 Ky. Acts. That statute recognized that the captors of fugitive slaves might be indicted for kidnapping in other states. Under the 1820 law those arrested on such a charge had a right to a hearing before a circuit judge before they could be extradited to face kidnapping charges in another state.

In this hearing the judge was to determine (1) if the black seized actually was a slave, and (2) if the persons charged with kidnapping had a legal right to seize the fugitive. If a fugitive slave was captured by his owner or the bona fide agent of the owner, then those claimed as fugitives from justice would be released. If, however, it turned out the black was not a slave or that those charged with kidnapping had no legal authority to seize the person, then the alleged kidnappers would be returned to the state where they were charged with a crime. After examining the facts of the case and the law of 1820, Judge Mason

Brown concluded that the defendants should not be returned to Ohio. Forbes and Armitage were released.

■ Johnston, William. The State of Ohio vs. Forbes and Armitage, arrested upon the requisition of the government of Ohio on charge of kidnapping Jerry Phinney, and tried before the Franklin Circuit Court of Kentucky. N.p., 1846. 41 p.

E450.F69

This pamphlet, the only existing printed record of this case, contains a brief history of the case, the legal points made by counsel for both sides, the opinion of Judge Brown, and the complete text of William Johnston's speech to the court.

Johnston was sent to Kentucky by the governor of Ohio to argue this case, and his speech is extremely deferential and polite. He did not come "to quarrel with the domestic institutions of Kentucky, nor to add to the excitement unhappily too great on both sides of the water." Rather, he hopes "to promote peace and good will between citizens of sister States" (pp. 14−15).

Johnston argues that Phinney is a free man and therefore could not be captured as a fugitive slave. He asserts that Allgaier's act of bringing Phinney to Ohio freed the slave. Even if Allgaier did not have permission to take Phinney out of the state, he nevertheless did so, and as the agent of the owner, his act freed Phinney. But if this act did not free Phinney, he was nevertheless freed by the act of Mrs. Long when she voluntarily allowed him to return to Ohio. Johnston based this argument on a number of northern precedents, the most prominent of which is *Commonwealth* v. *Aves*, 35 Mass. (18 Pick.) 193 (1836). This pamphlet itself was printed by Johnston "to inform those who feel an interest in the matter, what was really done, both by the authorities of Ohio and Kentucky" (p. 1).

Despite the adverse outcome of the case, Johnston praises the Kentucky governor, Judge Brown, and the other court officials for their polite treatment of him and their "great kindness and cordiality" (p. 1). These statements in the preface suggest a desire on the part of Johnston (and perhaps other Ohio officials) to promote harmony between the two states, despite their differences on the issues of slavery and freedom.

Jones v. Van Zandt

46 U.S. (5 How.) 215 (1847)

Jones v. Van Zandt

13 F. Cas. 1040 (C.C.D. Ohio 1843)(No. 7,501)

Jones v. Van Zandt

13 F. Cas. 1047 (C.C.D. Ohio 1843)(No. 7,502)

Jones v. Van Zandt

13 F. Cas. 1054 (C.C.D. Ohio 1849)(No. 7,503)

Jones v. Van Zandt

13 F. Cas. 1056 (C.C.D. Ohio 1849)(No. 7,504)

Jones v. Van Zandt

13 F. Cas. 1057 (C.C.D. Ohio 1851)(No. 7,505)

John Van Zandt, an Ohio Quaker, was, according to his counsel, Salmon P. Chase, "an old man, of limited education and slender means, but distinguished by unquestioned integrity and benevolence of heart" (Chase, *Reclamation of Fugitives from Service*, p. 6).

In April 1842 Van Zandt went to Cincinnati to sell his farm produce. On returning from the city he encountered a group of nine blacks walking along the road about twelve miles north of the Ohio-Kentucky border and offered them a ride in his empty wagon. Although Van Zandt was opposed to slavery and had helped fugitive slaves in the past, there is no indication he knew these blacks were runaway slaves. Indeed, the fact that they were walking along the road in daylight may have led him to think they were free. Otherwise, Van Zandt might have attempted to conceal all the blacks in the back of his wagon, which he did not do.

Van Zandt and the nine blacks rode together for about four hours and covered fifteen miles. This rather leisurely pace also suggests that Van Zandt did not regard his traveling companions as desperate fugitives. At this point, Van Zandt was overtaken by two professional slave catchers from Kentucky. Without identifying themselves, "without any legal

Levi Woodbury (1789-1851). A New Hampshire lawyer and politician, Woodbury was an associate justice of the U. S. Supreme Court from 1845 until his death in 1851. There he wrote a proslavery opinion in *Jones* v. *Van Zandt*. There was speculation that Woodbury would be the Democratic party nominee for president or vice president in 1852, and his proslavery opinion was an appeal for Southern support. Woodbury died in 1851, but his New Hampshire neighbor Franklin Pierce did get the Democratic nomination for president.

Lithograph by J. H. Bufford after a daguerreotype copyright 1848 by Southworth & Hawes.

process, without any authority or request from any claimant or any other person, in broad day, in open breach of the laws of Ohio,'' the two men seized the blacks in order to ''carry them out of the state by force, on suspicion that they were fugitive slaves'' (Chase, *Reclamation*, p. 7). Eight of the blacks were seized, but the ninth, Andrew, escaped.

The owner of these slaves, Wharton Jones, had not authorized the slave catchers to retrieve his human chattel. Nevertheless, under

William Henry Seward (1801-1872). A Whig politician and lawyer, Seward was governor of New York, a U. S. senator, and secretary of state under Lincoln and Andrew Johnson. As governor, he refused to return to Virginia a group of free black sailors accused of helping a slave to escape. In 1847 he argued the case of *Jones* v. *Van Zandt* before the U. S. Supreme Court. Although considered a radical antislavery man in the 1850s because of his advocacy of a "higher law," he turned out to be one of the most conservative members of Lincoln's cabinet.
Brady-Handy Collection. LC-B8172-1431

Kentucky law he was obligated to pay the slave catchers $100 for each slave they brought back. Jones thus sued Van Zandt for the value of Andrew (who was not recovered), the reward he had to pay the slave catchers, and the $500 penalty allowed under the Fugitive Slave Act of Feb. 12, 1793, ch. 7, 1 Stat. 302.

Van Zandt's attorney, Salmon P. Chase, argued that his client could not know that a group of blacks, walking along the road in the free state of Ohio, were actually fugitive slaves. Thus, without ''notice'' he could not be charged with the crime of aiding fugitive slaves, nor be liable for their value or any other penalties. This argument was rejected by U.S. Supreme Court Justice John McLean, who heard the case while attending to his circuit court duties. A jury awarded Jones a judgment of $1,200.

Normally this case could not have been appealed to the U.S. Supreme Court because the amount in controversy was less than the $2,000 jurisdictional requirement for appeals to the nation's highest court. Because of its obvious importance, however, both sides and the Court wanted a definitive opinion. Thus, Justice McLean and District Judge H. H. Leavitt recorded a pro forma difference of opinion on the questions of law, which allowed the U.S. Supreme Court to rule on the constitutional issues.

There, in an uninspired opinion, Justice Levi Woodbury upheld the decision against Van Zandt. Many antislavery men thought the true motive for this opinion was not Woodbury's reading of the Constitution but his desire to placate Southern Democrats to gain their support for a spot on the national ticket in 1852. After this decision Van Zandt continued to appeal the case, and not until 1851 was his estate (Van Zandt died during the appeal) finally compelled to pay Jones the money initially awarded him.

■ Chase, Salmon Portland. Reclamation of fugitives from service. An argument for the defendant, submitted to the Supreme Court of the United States at the December term, 1846, in the case of Wharton Jones vs. John Van Zandt. Cincinnati, R. P. Donough & Co., 1847. 108 p.

E450.C481

——[Reprint] Freeport, N.Y., Books for Libraries Press, 1971. 108 p.
KF4545.S5C43 1971

Chase personally appeared before Justice McLean to argue Van Zandt's case before the circuit court. However, he was unable to travel to Washington to present his arguments on appeal to the U.S. Supreme Court. Instead, he sent a printed brief. William Henry Seward presented Chase's brief, along with his own brief and oral arguments.

In his printed brief Chase argues: (1) that Jones's declaration and other technical matters in the case are insufficient to uphold the verdict against Van Zandt; (2) that Van Zandt did not ''harbor'' or ''conceal'' the fugitive slaves within the meaning of the 1793 statute; (3) that the Northwest Ordinance of 1787, July 13, 1787, 1 Stat. 51n., is still in force in Ohio, and thus fugitive slaves can only be returned from the *original* states; and (4) that the act of 1793 is itself unconstitutional.

Chase's most important and influential arguments centered on points two and four. By raising these issues, Chase forced the Supreme Court to answer them. As the Court upheld the verdict against Van Zandt, this led to a harsh interpretation of the act of 1793, which provided fines and penalties for any person "who shall harbor or conceal such person [a fugitive slave] after notice that he or she was a fugitive."

Chase argues that "harbor" or "conceal" implies positive actions to avoid the master or his agent. Offering a ride to people walking along the road, does not, according to Chase, constitute such actions. Furthermore, Chase places great emphasis on the words "after notice." He says that "notice" had to be something more than "knowledge or belief" that someone was a fugitive slave (p. 29). He points out that all persons were presumed free in Ohio, and thus without some official or specific act by Jones or his agent, Van Zandt could not have had "notice" that the blacks in his wagon were fugitives.

In arguing for the unconstitutionality of the 1793 law, Chase acknowledges that the recent decision in *Prigg* v. *Pennsylvania*, 41 U.S. (16 Pet.) 539 (1842), has declared the law to be constitutional. But, he asserts that the court in *Prigg* had not been asked to consider certain important issues, and that the act of 1793, and particularly the right of recaption allowed in *Prigg*, violates the due process clause of the Fifth Amendment, the search-and-seizure provisions of the Fourth Amendment, and the jury trial provisions of the Seventh Amendment.

Finally, Chase argues that Congress has no power to require or allow state officials to enforce an act of Congress, and that in this case Congress has no power to legislate at all. Rather, Chase asserts that the Fugitive Slave Clause of Article IV is directed at the states.

Besides presenting these constitutional arguments, Chase attacks slavery as a violation of natural law and asserts the principal that "legislation against right" is void. He urges the Court to "rescue the Constitution from the undeserved opprobrium of lending its sanction to the idea that there may be property in men" (p. 108).

Although Chase lost this case, his argument had a significant impact on constitutional law and antislavery politics. In rejecting Chase's argument the Supreme Court was forced to expand on *Prigg* and construe the act of 1793 in a manner highly favorable to slaveholders. Chase sent out nearly five hundred copies of his argument to lawyers, politicians, judges, and antislavery activists. This brought him great fame and influence in the growing political movement against slavery. Indeed, Chase's constitutional arguments against slavery and federal support for it were ultimately adopted by the Republican party.

■ Seward, William Henry. Argument of William H. Seward on the law of Congress concerning the recapture of fugitive slaves. In the Supreme Court of the United States. John Van Zandt ad sectum Wharton Jones. Argument for the defendant. Albany, Weed and Parsons, 1847. 40 p.

Law Library

Seward's argument does not add a great deal to the more elaborate one given by Chase. Like Chase, Seward asserts that (1) "The Declaration [by Jones] is Insufficient" (p. 7); (2) the 1793 law is not applicable to the area governed by the Northwest Ordinance; (3) the act of 1793 is in violation of the U.S. Constitution; and (4) the evidence produced does not support the statutory requirement that "harboring" can take place only after "notice" has been given (p. 17). Seward's brief is almost devoid of the antislavery arguments offered by Chase. He is somewhat more legalistic and much briefer in his points and citations.

Unlike Chase, Seward did not have great quantities of his brief printed and sent to influential people around the country. This may be explained, in part, by the fact that Seward was already well known, having served as governor of New York and as a U.S. senator.

In re Kirk

1 Parker 67 (N.Y. Cir. Ct. 1846)

In re Kirk

9 Month. L. Rep. 355 (N.Y. Ct. Oyer & Term. 1846)

In re Kirk

9 Month. L. Rep. 361 (N.Y. Cir. Ct. 1846)

In re Kirk

4 N.Y. Leg. Obs. 456 (N.Y. Cir. Ct. 1846)

George Kirk was a slave from Georgia who stowed away on the brig *Mobile*, which was bound for New York. He was discovered when the *Mobile* was *"on the high seas"* hundreds of miles from Georgia (4 N.Y. Leg. Obs. 456 [1846]). Theodore Buckley, the master of the vessel, ordered Kirk bound and held until he could be returned to

Georgia. The *Mobile* then continued on to New York with its unwanted passenger.

When the *Mobile* docked in New York, a free black named Lewis Napolean secured a writ of habeas corpus on Kirk's behalf and brought the matter before a court of oyer and terminer headed by Circuit Judge John W. Edmonds. In his return to the writ, Buckley argued that Kirk was a slave under Georgia law, and a statute of that state required ship captains to return fugitive slaves who stowed away on their vessels. He also asserted a right under the Constitution and the Fugitive Slave Act of Feb 12, 1793, ch. 7, 1 Stat. 302, to return Kirk to Georgia.

In support of the writ of habeas corpus, the abolitionist attorney John Jay (son of Judge William Jay and grandson of U.S. Supreme Court Chief Justice John Jay) argued that the Fugitive Slave Act authorized only a master or his agent to seize a runaway. Buckley, Jay asserted, was neither. Furthermore, Jay argued that the Georgia law under which Buckley acted could have no force in New York. Finally, Jay cited *Somerset* v. *Stewart,* 98 Eng. Rep. 499 (K.B. 1772), *Commonwealth* v. *Aves,* 35 Mass. (18 Pick.) 193 (1836), and other cases to support the argument that slaves gained their freedom the moment they entered a free jurisdiction. Thus, he concluded, Kirk was free, at least until his master arrived from Georgia with adequate proof to make a claim under the act of 1793. Judge Edmonds accepted Jay's arguments and ordered Kirk released.

After this hearing, Kirk was seized by Buckley under an act of New York that allowed masters of vessels to incarcerate stowaway fugitive slaves until they could be returned to the place from which they escaped. Jay secured a second writ of habeas corpus, and the case was then argued before the recorder's court, which consisted of the mayor, the recorder for the city, and a circuit judge. That judge was none other than J. W. Edmonds. Speaking on behalf of the entire recorder's court, Edmonds again ordered Kirk released. His reasoning was based on his interpretation of *Prigg* v. *Pennsylvania,* 41 U.S. (16 Pet.) 539 (1842). Edmonds declared that the New York law that allowed the capture and return of stowaway fugitives was an unconstitutional interference with the federal act. Thus, for a second and final time, Kirk was released.

■ Supplement to the New York Legal Observer, containing the report of the case in the matter of George Kirk, a fugitive slave, heard before the Hon. J. W. Edmonds, Circuit Judge. Also the argument of John Jay of counsel for the slave. New York, Legal Observer Office, 1847. pp. 456-69, 10-20.

Law Library

This supplement contains the two articles about Kirk's case that first appeared at 4 N.Y. Leg. Obs. 456-69 (Dec. 1846) and 5 N.Y. Leg. Obs. 52-62 (Feb. 1847). The pagination for the first article is repeated in the supplement, but for some unknown reason, the pagination for the second was changed to number 10-20 in the supplement.

The first article contains the reports of Kirk's two cases before Judge Edmonds. With the exception of a few punctuation changes, this is exactly the same as the official report of the case, 1 Parker 67 (N.Y. Cir. Ct. 1846). The December publication of this report in the *New-York Legal Observer* undoubtedly preceded the official report, making this slave case immediately available to lawyers and abolitionists. A report of the case also appeared at this time in the *Monthly Law Reporter* published in Boston. It differed from the official report in its headnotes and certain details but was substantively the same.

The second article in this supplement contains the arguments of John Jay before the court of oyer and terminer. Parts of Jay's speech had been omitted from the original report for lack of space. The *Legal Observer's* editors state that "the entire speech of Mr. Jay . . . will be read by our readers with great interest," only regretting "that the arguments of the other learned counsel engaged in it . . . has not been fully reported and published in a volume" (p. 10). "So great an interest," the compiler observed, "attached to the case during its progress, and so important was the decision," that Jay's arguments deserved to be published as a supplement (p. 10).

Jay's arguments cite numerous statutes, treatises, cases, and other materials. Prominent among these are references to James Madison's *Debates, Somerset* v. *Stewart, Commonwealth* v. *Aves, Prigg* v. *Pennsylvania,* Kent's *Commentaries,* Blackstone's *Commentaries,* Story's *Conflict of Laws,* and the writings of the abolitionist Theodore Dwight Weld. The publishing of Jay's arguments and the reprinting of the case in this supplement underscore the interest of Northern lawyers and judges in slave cases.

In re Isaac Brown

(Philadelphia [Pa.] Ct. Quarter Sessions 1847) (Unreported)

Isaac Brown was born and raised as a slave in Maryland. In 1845 he was arrested, jailed, and severely whipped for allegedly attacking his master. Then, in contravention of Maryland law, the court ordered his sale to a slave trader. Brown was subsequently sold to a planter in Louisiana.

In 1846 Brown came to Pennsylvania under unknown circumstances. In May 1847 he was arrested as a fugitive from justice on a requisition signed by the governor of Maryland. A writ of habeas corpus was issued by Judge Parsons of the Philadelphia Court of Quarter Sessions, but this was discharged when the governor of Pennsylvania ordered Brown held as a fugitive from justice. Hearings began on this issue, but were suspended at the request of the governor. Finally, the Pennsylvania governor decided that his precept ordering Brown held was based on insufficient grounds, and so he informed Judge Parsons. The governor also informed Parsons that a second requisition from the governor of Maryland was expected but had not arrived.

Although the Pennsylvania governor revoked his first arrest order and had not yet issued a second one, Judge Parsons nevertheless ordered Brown committed. Chief Justice John Gibson of the Pennsylvania Supreme Court then issued a writ de homine replegiando, and the sheriff released Brown. When he discovered Brown had been released, Judge Parsons ordered the sheriff arrested and then held to bond for allowing Brown to "escape."

The outcome of this case is not known, but the sheriff had acted under the authority of a supreme court justice and this would probably have been an adequate defense against Judge Parson's petulant act. Parson's action indicates he may have had a proslavery bias and wished to keep Brown in jail as long as it was necessary so that Brown could be sent back to Maryland.

Once released from jail, Brown remained free. He then initiated an action for damages against the Marylanders who had contrived to have him arrested. The outcome of this suit is also not known.

■ Case of the slave Isaac Brown, An outrage exposed. N.p., 1847. 8 p.
E450.B875

This case was a clear attempt to kidnap Brown and bring him to Maryland where he could be either enslaved or sold. It is unclear if Brown actually was a fugitive slave while he was in Pennsylvania. However, if he was a fugitive slave, he was a fugitive from Louisiana, not Maryland. The agents who had him arrested avoided using the Fugitive Slave Act because they had no legal claim to Brown.

This pamphlet gives some of the testimony in the various cases concerning Brown. It is a useful example of lower court proceedings, the jealousies between jurists within a state, and the use of the courts by both proslavery and antislavery partisans. Supporters of Brown published the pamphlet to show the importance of the writ de homine replegiando and as *"a lesson to our Governor, our Courts, and our People"* (p. 8).

Daggs v. *Frazier*

6 F. Cas. 1112 (D. Iowa 1849)(No. 3,538)

In 1848 nine slaves owned by Ruel Daggs of Missouri escaped into Iowa. Daggs offered a reward for the capture of these slaves, and two men pursued them. The fugitives were discovered near Salem, Iowa, but the slave catchers were unable to remove them quickly and instead found themselves surrounded by some nineteen men led by Elihu Frazier. At the insistence of Frazier and his cohorts, the slaves were brought before a justice of the peace in Salem, who released them on the grounds that their captors did not have written authority from Daggs and thus could not be considered his agent under the Fugitive Slave Act of Feb. 12, 1793, ch. 7, 1 Stat. 302. Outnumbered and threatened with violence, the slave catchers returned to Missouri empty-handed.

Daggs then brought an action in trover against Frazier and others for $10,000. In 1849 the federal court in Iowa decided, that "[t]rover will not lie in this state to recover the value of slaves," 6 F. Cas. 1112, 1113. Daggs then was allowed to withdraw his action and sue the defendants for the value of the slaves under the act of 1793.

This suit was "continued from term to term, for cause shown" until the June 1850 term, when the court sustained "a motion by defendant's counsel to exclude all the plaintiff's depositions for irregularity" (*Ruel Daggs vs. Elihu Frazier . . . Reported by Geo. Frazee*, p. 3). The plaintiff then asked for a continuance, but this was overruled. Daggs then "entered a *nolle prosequi* as to several of the defendants and immediately subpoenaed them as witnesses to supply as far as it was possible the want of evidence occasioned by the exclusion of his depositions" (ibid., p. 3). The jury then heard arguments and testimony and found against six of the defendants, assessing damages of $2,900. Judgment was "entered upon the verdict" and the defendants "asked time to file their bill of exceptions, for the purpose of taking the case to the Supreme Court" (ibid., p. 40). This request was allowed, but the appeal was not made.

■ Daggs, Ruel, *plaintiff.* District Court of the United States for the Southern Division of Iowa, Burlington, June term, 1850. Ruel Daggs vs. Elihu Frazier, et al., trespass on the case reported by Geo. Frazee. Burlington, Printed by Morgan & M'Kenny, 1850. 40 p.

Law Library

This pamphlet appears to be the only known record of this trial in the federal district court. The *Federal Cases* contains a report of Daggs's suit in 1849 but does not give any information on this later case. This report of the case was originally prepared by George Frazee "solely for private use, but, upon the solicitation of the counsel engaged, as well as others," Frazee "consented to their publication" (title page). It contains transcripts of testimony and examinations of witnesses, speeches and arguments of counsel for both sides, the charge to the jury by Judge J. J. Dyer, the instructions asked for by each side and the instructions actually given by Judge Dyer, and the verdict.

Unlike most fugitive slave cases, in this case the defendants did not challenge the constitutionality of the 1793 act. Rather, they argued (1) that there was no proof that the alleged fugitive slaves had in fact *escaped* from Missouri; (2) that there was no proof that the men who seized these blacks in Iowa were in fact the authorized agents of Daggs; (3) that the defendants did not have "notice" that the blacks in question were fugitive slaves (the only "notice" they had was from the slave-catchers, who, if the jury accepted point two, did not have authority from Daggs and therefore did not know themselves if they had seized the right blacks); and (4) that no rescue took place, but rather the alleged fugitives were taken to a justice of the peace who released them. Frazier's attorney argued that there was little or no substantial evidence in this case to find the defendants responsible for any loss by Daggs. Despite this argument and the circumstantial nature of the testimony, the jury found against Frazier and five other defendants.

This was one of the last cases argued solely on the basis of the Fugitive Slave Act of 1793. It was also one of the few fugitive slave cases heard in Iowa. Because this case was not officially reported, this pamphlet presents unique information on the fugitive slave issue in this western border state.

Norris v. Newton

18 F. Cas. 322 (C.C.D. Ind. 1850) (No. 10,307)

Associated case: *Norris* v. *Crocker*, 54 U.S. (13 How.) 429 (1851)

John Norris, of Boone County, Kentucky, owned a family of six slaves. He allowed this family to cultivate a plot of land and sell the produce in Lawrenceburgh, Indiana. In October 1847, the family crossed the Ohio River into Indiana with the permission of Norris to sell their produce. Instead of returning to Kentucky however, the slaves continued north and settled in Cass County, Michigan, where they purchased a plot of land on time and began farming.

In September 1849, Norris and a party of eight other men broke into a house occupied by his former slaves, David and Lucy Powell and their four children. Mrs. Powell and three of her children were seized and taken away in a wagon. The other occupants of the house, including the wife of one of the Powell children, were forced to remain in their house and were guarded by some of the slave catchers to prevent them from giving the alarm. The four blacks were hurried south. However, a neighbor discovered what had happened and followed Norris, overtaking him in South Bend, Indiana. With the aid of a local attorney named E. B. Crocker, a writ of habeas corpus was procured and legal proceedings in the case began.

After examining the matter Judge Elisha Egbert of the probate court determined that Norris could not hold the alleged slaves under the Fugitive Slave Act of Feb. 12, 1793, ch. 7, 1 Stat. 302, because he had failed to get a certificate of removal as that statute required. Thus, Judge Egbert ordered the slaves released. Immediately after this E. B. Crocker announced the decision in a very loud voice, that all could hear. Norris and his friends responded to this decision by drawing their weapons and threatening to shoot anyone who tried to come near the blacks. This violent act took place inside the courtroom and before the court had adjourned. Norris ultimately released the blacks to the custody of the sheriff and then produced a writ under an Indiana statute concerning fugitives from labor, under which he claimed to hold them.

The next day warrants were issued for the arrest of Norris and his companions on various charges of assault, battery, and riot for their actions in the courtroom. Norris posted bond to appear in court on Monday. In the meantime, the Powells entered suits against Norris for trespass and false imprisonment. Lawyers for the Powells obtained writs of habeas corpus on their behalf, which were served on the sheriff.

All of these legal proceedings were initiated on Friday and Saturday and held over until Monday. Affidavits for the arrest of Norris and his party as fugitives from justice under Michigan and Indiana law were in the works. Meanwhile, a party of blacks estimated to number between seventy-five and two hundred people arrived from Cass County to aid their neighbors. On Monday Norris refused to appear in court, saying "he did not want the negroes, that he could make the citizens pay for them, which was all he wanted" (*The South Bend Fugitive Slave Case*, p. 7). The Powells then were released and returned to Michigan, where they continued to live.

Norris later sued Leander Newton, Crocker, and other citizens connected with the incident. Justice John McLean presided over this trial while riding circuit. He charged the jury that "Crocker acted as counsel. So far as his acts were limited to the duties of counsel he is not responsible. But if he exceeded the proper limits of a counselor of law, he is responsible for his acts the same as any other individual'' (ibid., p. 13). On the strength of this charge the jury found in favor of Norris, and damages were assessed at $2,856 (this case is reported as *Norris* v. *Newton*).

Norris later attempted to sue Crocker and others for the five-hundred-dollar penalty allowed under the act of 1793. He "intended to commence about twenty-five additional suits, for the penalty: and if successful in them all, they would have recovered judgments to the amount of about $15,000 to $20,000'' (ibid., p. 22). At the time this pamphlet was printed, the second series of suits was on appeal to the U.S. Supreme Court. That court, in *Norris* v. *Crocker,* ruled that the section of the 1793 act allowing for the $500 penalty had been repealed by the 1850 act.

■ The South Bend fugitive slave case, involving the right to a writ of habeas corpus. New York, Anti-slavery Office, 1851. 24 p.

E450.S72

This pamphlet contains detailed background information about the case. Various legal documents are printed in it, as well as a major portion of Justice John McLean's charge to the jury in *Norris* v. *Newton.*

The facts of the case given here differ in a number of ways from those presented by McLean in his charge to the jury. The authors of this pamphlet maintain that McLean misinterpreted a great deal of the evidence presented and failed to explain to the jury what a lawyer's role ought to be in a case such as this. Had the charge to the jury been correct, the authors believe the verdict would have been different. Finally, this pamphlet claims the trial took place in an emotionally charged atmosphere. Just before the trial began, the "Democratic Governor of Indiana, out of a superabundant courtesy, and an overflowing desire to bolster up the Union, which many seemed to think was tottering and falling into ruin, had invited the Whig Governor, Crittenden, of Kentucky, to pay him a friendly official visit; and a great Union Mass Meeting had been appointed at Indianapolis for the occasion to be held during the session of court'' (p. 10).

The court itself adjourned to attend this meeting, and Judge Elisha M. Huntington presided over the meeting. Huntington was the U.S. district judge in Indiana, and he had heard the initial arguments in the case and ruled against a number of the defense motions. Thus, the pamphlet implies that Huntington was biased against the defendants because he presided over the Union meeting at which a number of the speakers denounced those who interfered with the rendition of fugitive slaves. To make matters worse, the jurors in the trial also attended these meetings, "receiving these preliminary lectures upon their duties, and fully drinking in the idea, that it was all-important to sacrifice a few of these 'fanatical abolitionists,' for the good of this 'glorious Union' " (p. 11).

After this meeting Justice McLean arrived to preside over the trial. But the pamphlet also raises questions about McLean's ability to remain impartial. McLean

> had just left Washington City, where he had been listening to disunion threats all winter. With all the nervousness of a presidential aspirant, he, no doubt, felt sincerely desirous that the *Union* should be held together, *at any sacrifice*; and it is not strange, therefore, that, in his charge to a jury, where the claims of a slaveholder were in litigation, in which too, the argus eye of the Slave Power was upon him, he should so far forget himself, as to bring the *political agitations* of the country to bear upon a jury, who were called upon to decide a simple question of damages between private citizens [p. 21].

This pamphlet details the willingness of at least one local judge in Indiana to interfere in the rendition of fugitive slaves. It also shows the political nature of trials conducted under the acts of 1793 and 1850. By presenting all of the evidence and background material in this case, the authors undermine the notion of neutral justice, which McLean's charge to the jury appears to convey.

Commonwealth v. *Alberti*

2 Par. Eq. Cas. 495 (Philadelphia [Pa.] Ct. Common Pleas 1851)

On August 14, 1850, George F. Alberti, a professional slave catcher, seized a black woman named Mrs. Thompson and her twenty-one-month-old son, Joel Henry Thompson. He carried them to Maryland, claiming the woman was the slave of James Mitchel of Maryland. At the time Alberti seized the blacks, they were living in Philadelphia.

According to the official report of Alberti's case, "There was no legal proof that the woman was a slave, or that Mitchel was the owner, or that Alberti had any power of attorney or authority to arrest and remove the woman," 2 Par. Eq. Cas. 495, 497. There was no doubt, however, that the child Joel Thompson had been born in New Jersey and was thus born free. Alberti was convicted of kidnapping in violation of a

Pennsylvania statute of 1847. He was fined $1,000 and sentenced to ten years in prison, while his codefendant received a $700 fine and eight years in prison.

■ Alberti, George F., *defendant*. A review of the trial, conviction and sentence of George F. Alberti, for kidnapping. By P. A. Browne. [Philadelphia, 1851] 24 p.

Law Library

The author of this pamphlet, P. A. Browne, is extremely sympathetic to Alberti. He begins by noting that a citizen of Pennsylvania is under a harsh sentence. "Had his skin been *black*, considerable sympathy would have been excited in a certain portion of this community; but he is a *white man*, and very few, comparatively, appear to evince an interest in his fate." This appeal to racism is followed by the fact that Alberti is already sixty-six years old: "This sentence (for *ten years*) will terminate *with* his existence, if it does not *terminate* his existence" (p. 1).

The facts the author presents differ in a number of important ways from the facts presented in the official report of the case. The report claims that Mrs. Thompson begged Alberti to leave her child behind and to contact her husband so he could take the child before she was returned to Maryland. The *Review of the Trial,* on the other hand, asserts that Alberti did not want to take the child with him, but that Mrs. Thompson would not let go of the baby, which was ill and still being breast-fed. Similarly, the *Review* claims Alberti brought Mrs. Thompson to an alderman, while the official record asserts Alberti did not bring the alleged fugitive before any judicial authority. The *Review* claims that Judge Parsons, who heard the case, unfairly excluded defense testimony, while allowing the prosecution to use questionable evidence. It implies a conspiracy between the judge, the prosecution, and the governor of the state, by claiming that one of the chief prosecution witnesses was a convicted felon who was pardoned by the governor a day before the trial began, presumably so he could testify against Alberti. The *Review* further argues that the prosecution of Alberti was in violation of the U.S. Constitution and the Fugitive Slave Act of Feb. 12, 1793, ch. 7, 1 Stat. 302, as interpreted in *Prigg* v. *Pennsylvania,* 41 U.S. (16 Pet.) 539 (1842). Judge Parsons, however, interpreted *Prigg* to exclude the state authorities from cases involving only those who actually *were* fugitive slaves. Since the child Joel Thompson was not a fugitive slave, Judge Parsons upheld the right of the state to prosecute Alberti for kidnapping.

This pamphlet is very unusual. It gives useful details to supplement the official report of the case, though differing from it in a number of important and substantive ways. Furthermore, it is one of the very few pamphlets printed in the North at this time that supports slavery. However, this may be because the courts supported slavery in most cases involving fugitive slaves. In this case it is clear that Judge Parsons wanted to make an example of Alberti and hoped to deter others from engaging in his profession.

The sentencing of Alberti became an issue in the 1851 gubernatorial race in Pennsylvania. In 1852 the successful candidate, William Bigler, pardoned Alberti. Bigler, a Democrat, had campaigned against the Pennsylvania personal liberty law of 1847, under which Alberti was convicted. It is impossible to know how much influence this pamphlet had on Alberti's eventual release, but it is clear the sentiments expressed in it were shared by important Democratic politicians and their supporters.

In re James Hamlet

(U.S. Fugitive Slave Comm. N.Y. 1850) (Unreported)

James Hamlet was the first fugitive slave arrested and remanded under the Fugitive Slave Act of Sept. 18, 1850, ch. 60, 9 Stat. 462. Hamlet was seized just eight days after the law was passed. He was quickly brought before Alexander Gardiner, the clerk of the U.S. district court and a newly appointed commissioner under the act of 1850. Hamlet claimed to be a free man because his mother had been free. His testimony was not allowed, however, under the act of 1850. After a brief hearing, Hamlet was returned to Baltimore at the expense of the U.S. government.

Benjamin H. Tallmadge, a U.S. deputy marshal (and son of the U.S. marshal), accompanied Hamlet to Baltimore. Hamlet's "wife and two children, who had no knowledge of his doom till he was gone," remained in New York. They had been "deprived even the mournful consolation of bidding farewell to their husband and father" (American and Foreign Anti-Slavery Society, *The Fugitive Slave Bill*, p. 5). A subscription fund was quickly raised, and Hamlet was purchased from his master for $800. On October 5, Hamlet returned to New York where there was an integrated demonstration of four to five thousand people.

■ American and Foreign Anti-Slavery Society. The fugitive slave bill: its history and unconstitutionality; with an account of the seizure and enslavement of James Hamlet, and his subsequent restoration to liberty. 3d ed. New York, W. Harned, 1850. 36 p.

KF4545.S5A95

The main purpose of this pamphlet was to attack the newly enacted Fugitive Slave Act of 1850 and expose its workings to the American people. The pamphlet contains a four-page discussion of the arrest, trial, and rendition of Hamlet, followed by the text of the act of 1850, a "Synopsis of the Bill," an analysis of the voting on the law, and various speeches and protests against the law. The appendix contains the minutes and resolutions of a mass antislavery meeting. Finally, there is a short statement on the "Restoration of James Hamlet."

Throughout the pamphlet are attacks on the constitutionality of the Fugitive Slave Act. The preface, signed by Lewis Tappan, urges a wide circulation of the pamphlet. Tappan also urges people to help fugitive slaves and recommends the best methods of aiding slaves without detection.

The pamphlet itself provides the only printed record of Hamlet's case. In most hearings before the fugitive slave commissioners there were no published accounts or opinions of the commissioners. Only through ephemeral materials, such as this pamphlet, can scholars find records of the cases of these summary proceedings. The great public interest in the fugitive slave issue is demonstrated, in part, by the fact that this pamphlet went through three editions the year it was published.

United States v. Morris

26 F. Cas. 1323 (C.C.D. Mass. 1851) (No. 15,815)

United States v. Scott

27 F. Cas. 990 (D. Mass. 1851) (No. 16,240b)

Charge to the Grand Jury—Fugitive Slave Law

30 F. Cas. 1015 (D. Mass. 1851) (No. 18,263)*

On May 3, 1850, a slave known as Shadrach escaped from Norfolk, Virginia, to Boston, Massachusetts. On February 15, 1851, he was arrested by his master's agent under the Fugitive Slave Act of Sept. 18, 1850, ch. 60, 9 Stat. 462. This was the first attempt to enforce this law in Massachusetts.

Immediately after his arrest four lawyers—Samuel E. Sewell, Ellis Gray Loring, Charles List, and Charles G. Davis—volunteered to defend Shadrach's freedom. Other attorneys, including Richard Henry

---

*The Shadrach Case

Dana and the black lawyer Robert Morris, attended the hearing. Shadrach's lawyers asked for a postponement of the proceedings until February 18 so they might prepare for their case. George T. Curtis, the U.S. commissioner hearing this case, granted their request. Sewell, Loring, and List then left, while Davis and the abolitionist editor Elizur Wright remained with Shadrach.

In the meantime a crowd of some thirty blacks gathered outside the courtroom where Shadrach was talking to Davis and Wright. When these two men left the courtroom the blacks outside held the door open, and after a few minutes' struggle rushed in, overpowered the deputies in the room, and rescued Shadrach. Two days later Davis was arrested by federal marshals for his role in the rescue and brought before Commissioner Curtis. Davis was given bail, and a trial date was set for February 20.

This case lasted until February 26 when Curtis decided that there was not sufficient evidence to hold Davis for further trial. Thus, Davis was discharged. At this hearing Davis was represented by Richard Henry Dana and by himself. The U.S. district attorney, George Lunt, argued the case on behalf of the government.

■ Davis, Charles G., *defendant*. United States vs. Charles G. Davis. Report of the proceedings at the examination of Charles G. Davis, Esq., on a charge of aiding and abetting in the rescue of a fugitive slave, held in Boston, in February, 1851. Boston, White & Potter, 1851. 44 p.

Law Library

The attempted rendition of Shadrach was the first major test of the new Fugitive Slave Act. It was an embarrassing failure for the government. However, the arrest of Davis and the subsequent trials of others connected with the rescue indicated the Fillmore administration would attempt to punish severely those who interfered with the enforcement of the law.

This report was "published at the request of numerous persons who are of the opinion that all which is known of the operation of the Fugitive Slave Bill, should be spread before the public." It was published so the legal profession would "be able to judge of the constructions upon the Statute, and of the law of evidence, as laid down and applied by Government." It was also published so "the public, can judge of the temper, and manner, as to parties and witnesses" (p. 2).

This report is the only printed record of this case, which never went beyond the preliminary hearing before U.S. Commissioner George T. Curtis. It contains all pertinent legal documents, including the warrant for Shadrach's arrest, depositions, and the complaint against Davis. Besides these documents, the *Report* contains a transcript of the testimony at the hearing before Commissioner Curtis, the speeches of attorneys Dana and Lunt, the opinion of Curtis that led to Davis's release, and a copy of the Fugitive Slave Act of 1850.

The weakness of the evidence against Davis indicates that this attempt to prosecute him was based more on a desire for revenge than a desire for justice. Richard Henry Dana, in his argument before Curtis, suggests the political nature and absurdity of this preliminary hearing into the possible guilt of Davis:

> the law is violated—the outrage is done. This is a case of great political importance, and the deputy Marshal thinks it his duty, (I think in rather an extraordinary manner,) instantly, before any charge is made against him [for allowing the rescue of Shadrach], before any official inquiry is started, to issue a long affidavit, sent post haste to every newspaper, and hurried on to Washington— Congress in session—a delicate question there—Northern and Southern men arrayed against each other. Then comes an alarm. Then the Executive shrieks out a proclamation. A standing army is to be ordered to Boston. All good citizens are to be commanded to sustain the laws. The country thinks that mob law is rioting in Boston—that we all go armed to the teeth. The Chief Magistrate of fifteen millions of people must launch against us the thunders from his mighty hand. In the meantime, we poor, innocent citizens are just as quiet, just as peaceable, just as confident in our own laws, just as capable of taking care of ourselves on Saturday evening as on Friday morning. Only some frightened innocents, like the goose, the duck and the turkey in the fable, say the sky is falling, and they must go and tell the king [p. 25].

In re Thomas Sims

(U.S. Fugitive Slave Comm. Mass. 1851) (Unreported)

Associated cases: *Thomas Sims Case,* 61 Mass. (7 Cush.) 285 (1851)
Curtis v. *Mussey,* 72 Mass. (6 Gray) 261 (1856)

Thomas Sims was a slave in Savannah, Georgia. In February 1851 he stowed away on a ship bound for Massachusetts. In March he landed in Boston. Sims then wrote to his wife, a free black woman in Georgia, and through this letter his master discovered his whereabouts.

In April 1851 he was seized by his master's agent under the Fugitive Slave Act of Sept. 18, 1850, ch. 60, 9 Stat. 462. At the time of

· ANTI-SLAVERY MEETING ON THE COMMON.

Wendell Phillips (1811-1884). Although a Boston Brahman and a Harvard-trained lawyer, Phillips devoted his life to reform, especially the antislavery movement, women's rights, and, after the Civil War, the rights of freedmen and labor reform. In a golden age of oratory, Phillips was probably the best speaker in the nation. Even those opposed to his abolitionist beliefs were captivated by his speeches and lectures. Phillips was involved in most antislavery activities, including the protests over the arrest of Thomas Sims as a fugitive slave.

Wood engraving by Worcester of Phillips addressing a crowd during the trial of Thomas Sims, from *Gleason's Pictorial,* May 3, 1851. LC-USZ62-30792

his arrest, Boston was still recovering from the riot and rescue of the alleged slave Shadrach. Indeed, when Sims's case was being heard by the U.S. commissioner, a federal grand jury was investigating the alleged illegalities connected with the Shadrach rescue. To ensure that another Shadrach-type rescue did not occur, the city officials took extraordinary precautions. The courthouse was ringed with chains and ropes, and only people with pressing business were allowed to enter the building. An estimated five hundred policemen guarded the building, which was shared with state and local officials, so that even the venerated Chief Justice Lemuel Shaw had to stoop under chains to enter his courtroom. Some people thought this spectacle showed the willingness of the people of Massachusetts to submit to the law. Others saw it as a visible symbol of federal tyranny. For the abolitionist minister Theodore Parker, the courthouse in chains exposed the legal system, and Chief Justice Shaw, as ridiculous supporters of slavery. Parker wrote Charles Sumner, "think of old stiff-necked Lemuel visibly going under the chains! That was a spectacle!" (quoted in L. Levy, *The Law of the Commonwealth and*

Chief Justice Shaw [Cambridge, 1957], p. 102). The chains, however, served their purpose: Sims was not rescued, and the hearings in his case before Commissioner George T. Curtis were orderly and uneventful.

The arrest of Sims led to the first extensive examination of the meaning and constitutionality of the new law. Up to that time renditions had either proceeded smoothly, with little argument on behalf of the alleged slave, or, as in the case of Shadrach, had been interrupted by rescue. Here, however, the issues were fully argued. U.S. Senator Robert Rantoul, Jr., and Charles G. Loring argued Sims's case before Commissioner Curtis. Both men, along with Samuel E. Sewell and Richard Henry Dana, Jr., also argued on behalf of Sims in the state courts.

Before Chief Justice Lemuel Shaw these men argued that the act of 1850 was unconstitutional and that Shaw should grant them a writ of habeas corpus to test Sims's right to freedom in the state court. They also attempted to get a writ of habeas corpus or a writ of personal replevin from other state jurists. But these attempts failed, either because the jurists would not grant the writs or because, once they were granted, the U.S. marshal, Charles Devens, ignored the state process.

In desperation they even had Sims indicted for wounding a policeman when he resisted being arrested. They felt a few years in a Massachusetts prison were preferable to a lifetime of slavery on a Georgia rice plantation. Sims's lawyers argued that a criminal indictment under state law would take precedence over the civil process obtained under the Fugitive Slave Act. However, this stratagem failed when another U.S. commissioner, Benjamin F. Hallet, issued an arrest warrant for Sims on federal criminal charges, although he knew at the time that Sims had in fact not violated any federal laws.

Ultimately all legal attempts to free Sims failed. Commissioner Curtis rejected all arguments against the constitutionality of the 1850 act. U.S. District Judge Peleg Sprague and Massachusetts Chief Justice Shaw refused to interfere with the proceedings. Evidence that Sims might actually be free was supposed to be coming from Georgia, but Commissioner Curtis would not wait for it. He declared Sims to be a slave and gave his master's agent the proper papers. Sims pleaded for a knife to commit suicide with, but this request was not granted. At 4:15 a.m., under guard of more than one hundred policemen, Sims was removed from the courthouse and placed aboard a ship for Georgia. In arguing for his freedom, Rantoul had stressed that Sims would not be allowed to prove his right to freedom once he left Massachusetts. Curtis, however, declared that the rendition did not preclude a trial once he was returned. However, on his arrival in Georgia, Sims was given thirty-nine lashes and sent to labor.

During the Civil War Sims escaped from Georgia and made his

In re Thomas Sims   91

way to Union lines and then to Boston. In 1877 he became an employee of the U.S. Department of Justice. He gained this position through the influence of U.S. Attorney General Charles Devens. Ironically, Devens had been the U.S. marshal in Boston who arranged for Sims's arrest and rendition in 1851.

■ Sims, Thomas, *respondent*. Trial of Thomas Sims, on an issue of personal liberty, on the claim of James Potter, of Georgia, against him, as an alleged fugitive from service. Arguments of Robert Rantoul, Jr., and Charles G. Loring, with the decision of George T. Curtis. Boston, April 7-11, 1851. Boston, Wm. S. Damrell, 1851. 47 p.

LLRBR

Because hearings before U.S. commissioners were not regularly reported, this pamphlet provides the most complete printed record of this case. As the long title indicates, the pamphlet contains the arguments of Senator Rantoul and Charles Loring on behalf of Sims, as they were taken down during the hearings by a specially trained "phonographic reporter." A note on page 2 indicates that the opinion of Commissioner Curtis was provided by the commissioner, and thus it can be considered to be a reliable substitute for an official report. In addition to the arguments of Sims's counsel, this reporter took down conversations between the bench and Rantoul and Loring, as well as any other interruptions that took place during their presentation. During his argument, Rantoul presented for examination some, but not all, of the legal documents and affidavits connected to this case.

Because this was the first extensive examination of the Act of 1850, Rantoul presented a detailed attack on the constitutionality of the statute. He argued (1) that the commissioner exercised what was essentially a judicial power, yet was—as Rantoul thought—unconstitutionally selected so could not function in his position; (2) that the procedure was "a suit between the claimant and the captive, involving an alleged right of property on one hand, and the right of personal liberty on the other, and that either party therefore is entitled to a trial by jury," but since the law did not allow for such a trial, it was unconstitutional; (3) that the evidence of Sims's status taken down in Georgia before a state court was unacceptable in a federal hearing because "Congress having no power to confer upon State Courts or magistrates, judicial authority" could not pass such a law; (4) that the evidence collected in Georgia was "incompetent" because "the captive was not represented at the taking thereof, and had no opportunity for cross-examination"; and (5) that Congress was not authorized by the Constitution to pass the act of 1850 (p. 3).

Rantoul supported his assertions with a lengthy and detailed analysis of various sections of the Constitution, previous court decisions, various federal statutes, and numerous treatises, including Story's *Commentaries* and Coke's *Institutes*. His strongest arguments centered on the judicial nature of the hearing and the need for a jury trial. Citing *Prigg* v. *Pennsylvania*, 41 U.S. (16 Pet.) 539 (1842), Rantoul showed that U.S. Supreme Court Justice Joseph Story believed "that where *a claim* is made by the owner . . . capable of being recognized, and asserted by proceedings before a court of justice, between parties adverse to each other, it constitutes *in the strictest sense* a controversy between the parties, and is *a case* 'arising under the Constitution' of the United States; within the EXPRESS delegation of JUDICIAL POWER given by that instrument" (pp. 4-5, emphasis added by Rantoul in the pamphlet). From this declaration in *Prigg*, Rantoul argued that only a judge, appointed properly under Article III of the Constitution, could hear a case involving the rendition of a fugitive slave.

Rantoul also became involved in a heated argument with Curtis over the right of the fugitive to a trial either before or after rendition. He argued that the master could take Sims anywhere he chose, once he left Massachusetts, and thus deny him a trial on his right to freedom. Curtis, however, asserted that a certificate of removal required that the alleged slave be taken to the state from which he allegedly escaped, and in that state he could have a trial on the merits of his claim. Rantoul presented a long and elaborate argument on this issue, while Curtis often interrupted him to disagree. Clearly, despite the logic of his argument, Rantoul was unable to convince Curtis that the alleged slave could not expect to get a fair hearing elsewhere to his claim to freedom, and thus the hearing before the commissioner constituted a final decision on the matter. (The fact that when Sims arrived in Georgia he was immediately whipped in public and then sent to be a laborer suggested the factual strength of Rantoul's position.)

Rantoul's argument took up most of Monday and part of Tuesday. Despite his extensive references and citations, he complained that the twenty-four-hour period he was allowed was not enough time to adequately support his arguments. It seems clear from the nature of Rantoul's argument and the dialogue between Curtis and Rantoul that the commissioner was bent on ensuring that this hearing be summary.

Charles G. Loring began his closing argument with the same complaints enunciated by Rantoul:

> It must be, Sir, a matter of as much regret to the Court as to the Counsel, that so little time has been had for preparation in a case of this magnitude. Had I been applied to a civil suit, relating to property of any moment, involving an inquiry of so much intricacy and extent as this, I certainly should have declined being

retained. . . . But being called upon in behalf of a man arrested at midnight, and to be tried the next morning at nine o'clock, with my views of professional duty, and feeling that he had a right to call upon those who had some experience in the profession . . . I had no right to hesitate. And I am here, Sir, at his request, communicated to me to act as his counsel after the barricades had been erected around the court house, and within five minutes of the time I appeared before this tribunal. [p. 25]

Loring was absent from town when Sims was arrested and on the first day of the hearing, and he was annoyed and complains throughout his argument that Curtis would not delay the hearing in "a case of vast importance, involving the first principles of civil liberty and personal security under the laws and Constitution of the United States [and] . . . nothing else than a question of personal liberty between a man claiming to be a freeman, and another man claiming to seize and carry him away as his bound slave" (p. 23).

Many of the arguments presented by Loring were echoes of the ones introduced by Rantoul. But, unlike Rantoul, Loring seems to have explicitly attempted to draw Curtis into the argument and to personalize the issues. Loring presented "the idea that your hand-writing may consign that man to endless slavery!" Curtis responded, "That I cannot believe." Loring answered: "I submit to you with perfect confidence, that your decree to deliver the prisoner places his liberty for ever in the power of the claimant" (p. 30). Loring continued in great detail, with Curtis interrupting, asking questions, and at one point even asking Loring: "Will you pause for a moment? I want to get this point very distinctly" (p. 31). Loring attempted to show the rendition of an alleged fugitive is not the same as the extradition of an alleged criminal. His argument rested essentially on the unconstitutionality of the 1850 act and on the moral onus he attempted to place on Curtis.

Even though he allowed only limited time to Sims's attorneys to prepare their case, Commissioner Curtis himself took two days to prepare his opinion in the case and delivered it three days after closing arguments. In it he refused every objection raised by Rantoul and Loring. He also indicated his displeasure at their attempts to put him in a morally ambiguous position. During the arguments the difference in fees for the commissioner ($5 if he found against and $10 if he found in favor of the claimant) was declared to "be humiliating to this Court." Curtis noted in his opinion that "if the learned counsel supposed that the sum of five dollars was likely to influence my judgment upon any question in this case, he did right in reminding me that the Statute provides for a compensation," but Curtis declared he was not obligated to accept any compensation, and implying that he would not in fact do so, he saw "no cause for humiliation" (pp. 39-40). He also showed evident distaste for the attempt "to increase to the utmost intensity the responsibility of acting" in a manner that "will send this man to perpetual slavery" (p. 39). Curtis stated he would not be influenced by these considerations. In a long opinion he declared there was conclusive evidence that Sims was the slave of James Potter of Georgia, that the commissioner was not acting as a judge but was simply returning a claimed fugitive, and that the act of 1850 was constitutional. Seeing no reason not to, he then issued a certificate of removal to Potter's agent.

As the first important and intensive investigation of the meaning of the 1850 act, this case was extremely important and influential. This pamphlet allowed both antislavery lawyers and other federal commissioners to read the arguments and opinion in this case. The arguments of Rantoul and Loring would be copied, added to, and refined by other antislavery lawyers in the next decade. Similarly, various commissioners would borrow from Curtis to refute such arguments.

Charge to the Grand Jury

(U.S.D.C. W.D. Pa. 1851) (Unreported)

This charge does not appear to be connected to any reported case. In June 1851 U.S. District Judge Thomas Irwin "learned from the District Attorney of the United States, that bills will be presented to you [federal grand jurors] at this term, for the violation" of the Fugitive Slave Act of Sept. 18, 1850, ch. 60, 9 Stat. 462 (*A Charge, to the Grand Jury*, p. 5). Thus, Irwin charged the jury as to the meaning, interpretation, and importance of that law. It is unclear if any indictments resulted from this charge.

■ U.S. District Court. Pennsylvania (Western District). A charge, to the Grand jury, by the district judge of the United States, for the Western District of Pennsylvania. Delivered at June term, 1851. [Williamsport, Pa.] Printed by W.S. Haven, 1851. 20 p.
E450.U52 Toner Collection Rare Book Room

After receiving this charge, the foreman of the grand jury urged Judge Irwin to have his charge published because "in the present state of the public mind" the grand jurors unanimously believed "its publication will be beneficial" (p. 3). In his charge, Judge Irwin gives a brief history of the Fugitive Slave Clause of the Constitution and the Acts of Feb. 12, 1793, ch. 7, 1 Stat. 302 and Sept. 18, 1850, ch. 60, 9

Stat. 462. He declares that "this clause must not be regarded, as is often contended, as a concession to the Southern States, but as a security for a pre-existing right upon which their safety, social interests and property depended, recognised in this manner by all the States, and entitled to the same respect, and to be held as inviolable as any other the instrument contains" (p. 7). He points out that the parties to the Constitution were "sovereign States" that entered the Union only under certain conditions. He also asserts that no one objected to the clause at the time it was placed in the Constitution, and that it was approved by the states and the people of the North during the ratification process. Irwin regrets the "new discovery in ethics; that there are obligations and duties depending upon the dictates of conscience of a higher nature than the laws of our country, and to which obedience is due when in opposition to the laws" (p. 15). He declares that "Life, liberty and the pursuit of happiness, the vital objects for which men unite in society" are "the foundation of moral obligation to support laws" (p. 15). He urges the grand jurors to ignore the "erroneous opinions" that the act of 1850 is unconstitutional, "inexpedient, novel, oppressive and unjust in its features," and "that it is in opposition to a higher law, meaning it is supposed the law of God" (p. 5). Instead the grand jurors must do their duty and convict those who have violated the law.

Irwin's charge is unusually dispassionate, especially when compared with the charges and opinions on this subject by the other federal district judge in the state, John K. Kane. Irwin "forbear[s] to speak harshly of unseen motives and untried actions, and can only deeply deplore the influence of a pervading spirit that would sunder all these ties" of the Union and would "resist the law, excite to clamour, violence and tumult, and peril the safety of the Union." Thus, he urges the grand jurors to protect the law and the society with the "enduring consolation of knowing that you have discharged one of the most important duties you owe to your country" (p. 20).

United States v. *Hanway*

26 F. Cas. 105 (C.C.E.D. Pa. 1851) (No. 15,299)*

Charge to the Grand Jury—Treason

30 F. Cas. 1047 (C.C.E.D. Pa. 1851) (No. 18,276)

On September 11, 1851, a Maryland slave owner named Edward Gorsuch attempted to seize a group of fugitive slaves near Christiana,

---

*The Christiana Treason Trials of 1851

Thaddeus Stevens (1792-1868). Remembered most for his vigorous support of black rights during Reconstruction, Stevens was also a skilled antislavery lawyer and politician before the Civil War. His role in the Christiana treason trials was relatively low-key. He rarely spoke during the trial of Castner Hanway and did not give a summation for the defense, even though he was scheduled to present one. Nevertheless, Stevens's presence showed that Lancaster County's most important politician stood firmly with his neighbors and against the federal government and its attempt to enforce the Fugitive Slave Act of 1850.

Saylor Portraits, Lancaster, Pa. LC-USZ62-15441

Pennsylvania. Gorsuch led a predawn raiding party consisting of himself, his son, a nephew, a cousin, two neighbors, and U.S. Deputy Marshal Henry H. Kline. This group acted under a warrant issued by Edward D. Ingraham, the U.S. commissioner in Philadelphia.

When the party arrived at the home of William Parker, a runaway slave, Gorsuch was warned that the blacks inside were armed and ready

Robert C. Grier (1794-1870). As a U.S. Supreme Court justice, Robert Grier was known as a doughface—a Northern man with Southern principles. Yet even this conservative Democrat could not go along with the prosecution of Castner Hanway and others for treason because they had refused to help enforce the Fugitive Slave Law of 1850. Grier presided over Hanway's trial while riding circuit and, to the surprise of the prosecution, charged the jury that the evidence would not sustain a prosecution for treason. In *Dred Scott* v. *Sandford* (1857), Grier concurred with Taney's result, but not with the specifics of the chief justice's "opinion of the Court." Rather, Grier specifically concurred with the concurring opinion of Justice Samuel Nelson, another doughface from New York. Grier and Nelson would have upheld Dred Scott's slave status but not declared the Missouri Compromise unconstitutional.

Brady-Handy Collection. LC-BH82-32

to fight. While Parker and Gorsuch exchanged words, a number of blacks arrived to reinforce the fugitives in Parker's house. A few whites, including Castner Hanway and Elijah Lewis, also arrived. When Deputy Marshal Kline tried to deputize these two men, they refused and instead urged the outnumbered Gorsuch party to leave. This warning was ignored, and a skirmish soon ensued. When it was over Gorsuch was dead, his son was severely wounded, and other members of the party had either been hurt or fled the area.

Forty-one men—thirty-six blacks and five whites—were subsequently indicted for treason. These indictments were a function of President Millard Fillmore's desire to punish those who challenged the federal law and his hopes that this strong stand would gain him political support in the South. They were also urged by the governor of Maryland.

The political nature of the trial led to a curious array of counsel. Besides the U.S. district attorney for the Eastern District of Pennsylvania, John W. Ashmead, the prosecution team contained five lawyers hired by the federal government and the Gorsuch family. In addition, Robert Brent, the attorney general of Maryland, appeared in his official capacity as part of the federal prosecutor's staff. The defense consisted of five lawyers led by Congressman Thaddeus Stevens. U.S. Supreme Court Justice Robert C. Grier presided over the trial with the assistance of District Judge John K. Kane.

The first person tried was Castner Hanway. Hanway had taken no positive action against Gorsuch and his party. But he had refused to either join the posse or try to prevent the blacks from attacking the slave catchers. The prosecution in fact argued that Hanway urged the blacks to attack and in other ways gave them aid and leadership. The trial began on November 24, 1851, and lasted until December 8 of that year. On the last day of the trial, Justice Grier charged the jury that the act of refusing to aid in the rendition of a fugitive slave did not constitute treason. It took the jury just fifteen minutes to find Hanway innocent. Ultimately the other forty indictments were dropped.

These forty-one indictments represent the largest number of treason indictments in United States history (as of 1984) for a single incident or crime. The Christiana riot itself was the most violent episode in the struggle against the Fugitive Slave Act. The number of items annotated here indicates its national significance.

■ A full and correct report of the Christiana tragedy, in the county of Lancaster, state of Penna., Sept. 11, 1851, as reported verbatim et literatim, on the hearing and examination, as the same was presented in evidence, before Alderman Reigart, September 25th. Lancaster, Pa., John H. Pearsol. 1851. 24 p.

E450.F96 Toner Collection Rare Book Room

Alderman J. Franklin Reigart of Lancaster County was one of the most active local officials in the legal proceedings following the Christiana riot. On September 25, 1851, he presided over evidentiary hearings after the arrests of Castner Hanway, Elijah Lewis, and three other white men connected with the case. Statements from Federal Deputy Marshal Henry F. Kline taken on September 11, the day of the riot, were presented to Reigart. This was followed by testimony from Kline, a physician who treated some of the Gorsuch party, and numerous witnesses from the area. Those testifying were cross-examined by Thaddeus Stevens, who appeared on behalf of those arrested. Following these hearings, the five arrested men were sent to Philadelphia to be held for treason against the United States.

The hearings before Reigart came after more than a week's delay in the proceedings. During this period President Fillmore consulted with members of his Cabinet and other advisers about the case. The administration decided to seek treason indictments against Hanway and others connected with the incident. Reigart was apparently one of the few local officials willing to participate in this process. He supervised the taking of evidence and then turned those arrested over to federal authorities, even though they had been arrested by state process. Reigart later testified against Hanway at the trial, and the depositions printed here were entered in evidence against Hanway.

This pamphlet has no preface. It consists mostly of depositions and cross-examinations by Thaddeus Stevens. Although it is unclear why Reigart had it published, it is a useful supplement to the elaborate book published by the court reporter in the case, James J. Robbins. The Robbins book begins with the choosing of a jury in the case. This pamphlet provides an important body of evidence about the pretrial hearings.

■ Hanway, Castner, *defendant.* Report of the trial of Castner Hanway for treason, in the resistance of the execution of the Fugitive Slave Law of September 1850. Before Judges Grier and Kane, in the Circuit Court of the United States, for the Eastern District of Pennsylvania, held at Philadelphia in November and December, 1851. To which is added an appendix, containing the laws of the United States on the subject of fugitives from labor, the charges of Judge Kane to the grand juries in relation thereto, and a statement of the points of law decided by the court during the trial. By James J. Robbins, of the Philadelphia Bar; from the notes of Arthur Cannon and Samuel B. Dalrymple. Philadelphia, King & Baird, 1852. 275 p.

Law Library; E450.H25

——|Reprint| Westport, Conn., Negro Universities Press, 1970. 275 p.

KF223.H35R6 1970

This volume provides a complete transcript of the proceedings during the trial of Castner Hanway. It begins with the initial summoning of jurors and preliminary arguments by counsel for both sides. It ends with a hearing before Judge Kane after Hanway's acquittal, in which Hanway futilely attempted to have the U.S. government pay the costs connected with witnesses for the defense. An appendix at the end contains the texts of the Fugitive Slave Acts of Feb. 12, 1793, ch. 7, 1 Stat. 302 and Sept. 18, 1850, ch. 60, 9 Stat. 462; Judge Kane's charge to the grand jury, which led to the indictments for treason; lists of grand and petit jurors; and a summary of the legal points raised during the case.

The speeches, testimony, and arguments printed in this volume were taken down during the trial by two specially trained ''phonographic reporters.'' Two reporters were hired so that court sessions could be held all day and in the evening. Justice Grier did ''not feel disposed to hurry or drive either party,'' but he did wish to return to Washington for the opening of the Supreme Court term (p. 12). The importance of the case led to the use of specially trained reporters ''who, by the valuable art of Phonography, were enabled to transfer to paper every expression'' (preface, unpaginated).

This book thus contains as complete a record as possible of any trial in the nineteenth century. Besides providing legal arguments, it contains the testimony, examinations and cross-examinations, discussions between bar and bench, and even the sarcastic and angry banter that is inevitable in a trial as highly charged as this one was.

■ Maryland, Attorney General's Office. Report of Attorney General Brent, to his excellency, Gov. Lowe, in relation to the Christiana treason trials, in the Circuit Court of the United States, held at Philadelphia. Annapolis, Thomas E. Martin, 1852. 19 p.

KF223.H35B7 LLRBR

The appointment of Maryland Attorney General Robert J. Brent to the Christiana prosecution team was extraordinary. He represented the state of Maryland in a federal prosecution in which Maryland was not a party. The U.S. district attorney, John W. Ashmead, was unhappy with this additional attorney who impinged on his authority and was not directly responsible to him.

Jealousies between Ashmead and Brent led to a refusal to share their information and evidence at the beginning of the trial. Thus when Brent and Ashmead finally shared ''important additional evidence, shewing the ramified and extensive character of the combination, forcibly to resist the laws of the United States,'' it ''was ruled out by the court, as inadmissible in so late a stage in the cause'' (p. 3). This error was largely caused by Brent, but he asserts that ''as I understand the opinion of the Court in their charge to the jury, no additional evidence on our part could have changed the result'' (p. 4). Brent reports to the governor that ultimately relations with Ashmead were amicable and mutually useful.

In his report, the Maryland attorney general complains that a number of aspects of the trial ''were greatly calculated to obstruct a fair and impartial trial'' (p. 4). Brent protests that the jury pool was stacked in favor of the prisoners, noting that the prosecution challenged fifty-one jurors the defense had accepted, and that when the final jury was selected, the defense had not used up all of its peremptory challenges. Brent accuses the U.S. marshal ''who summoned the jury'' of giving ''preferred seats in the court-room'' to male and female members of the antislavery society. Worse yet, Brent reports ''that free negroes were admitted through the Marshal's office into the court-room, when crowds of white citizens were kept outside the door.'' Brent attacks the marshal for other actions that Brent deems as sympathetic to the defendants. He blames the marshal's underlings for the escape of prosecution witnesses who were incarcerated to ensure their attendance at the trial (p. 4). Despite these complaints, Brent acknowledges that ''a large majority of the citizens of Philadelphia desired to see the laws faithfully and fairly executed'' (p. 6).

He bitterly assails Justice Grier for his opinion in the case and blames him for the outcome of the trial. He regards the decision ''as most disastrous at this time. It practically strikes dead the Fugitive Slave Act, whenever armed bands of negroes, encouraged by white men, may choose to resist the officer of the United States'' (pp. 16-17). (Throughout the report Brent fails to note that the accused were not tried for violating the Fugitive Slave Act of 1850, although convictions under that statute would have been easier to obtain than treason convictions.)

Brent concludes that Maryland should petition Congress for stronger legislation on this subject but should not attempt to seek further prosecutions over the Christiana incident. Brent's *Report* is bitter and often exaggerates the slights he suffered and the difficulties he encountered during the trial. It reflects Brent's anger that the strongest penalties were not meted out against the defendants.

■ A history of the trial of Castner Hanway and others, for treason, at Philadelphia in November, 1851. With an introduction upon the history of the slave question. By a member of the Philadelphia bar. Philadelphia, Uriah Hunt & Sons, 1852. 86 p.

Law Library

This pamphlet was published in response to Brent's *Report* and to the report of the hearings before Alderman Reigart, and because the "phonographic report of all the proceedings" had not yet been printed. The author, W. Arthur Jackson, was one of the defense counsel. He wished to provide a complete history of the case for the public and to correct and refute "the most glaring absurdities and incongruities contained in Mr. Brent's pamphlet" (p. 3).

Jackson begins with a twenty-seven-page essay describing how slavery became a national issue from the Constitutional Convention to the Missouri Compromise, from Texas Annexation and the Mexican War to the Compromise of 1850. It is generally partisan and antislavery. He follows with a fifty-four-page discussion of the Christiana case from the time Gorsuch arrived in Philadelphia to the attempts by the district attorney of Lancaster County to have Hanway and others indicted under state statutes after the federal prosecution failed. He exposes the inconsistent and self-serving testimony of U.S. Deputy Marshal Henry Kline and the questionable character of other prosecution witnesses.

At one point in the case a prosecution witness changed his testimony and undermined the government's case. Maryland Attorney General Brent believed this was the result of tampering with the witness. Jackson, on the other hand, asserts the government was at fault for trying to create false testimony and for using poor witnesses. In this particular instance the witness was notoriously feeble-minded, and his testimony should never have been solicited in the first place.

Jackson rebuts Brent's claims that blacks and antislavery society members were given unusual access to the courtroom by pointing out that many people were unable to get seats but that no one else complained of others getting special privileges. Indeed, he quotes a reporter as saying that no blacks or white women were seen in the courtroom at the very time Brent alleged special privileges for them.

Jackson's pamphlet is a very useful summary of the case and the strategy of the defense. Although partisan in the testimony Jackson chose to reproduce, the pamphlet nevertheless shows the weakness of the prosecution's case. It is also an important source for information about events involving fugitive slaves in Lancaster County before the Christiana incident and for events after Hanway's acquittal.

People v. *Allen*

(N.Y. Sup. Ct. 1852) (Unreported)*

Associated cases: *Charge to the Grand Jury: The Fugitive Slave Law*
2 Blatchf. 559, 30 F. Cas. 1013 (C.C.N.D.N.Y.
1851) (No. 18,262)
United States v. *Reed,* 2 Blatchf. 435, 27 F. Cas. 727
(C.C.N.D.N.Y. 1852) (No. 16,134)
United States v. *Cobb,* 25 F. Cas. 481 (C.C.N.D.N.Y.
1857) (No. 14,820)

On October 1, 1851, a fugitive slave in Syracuse, New York, named Jerry (or William Henry) was arrested on a false charge of robbery. He was then brought before U.S. Commissioner Joseph F. Sabine, who ordered him held as a fugitive slave and placed him in the custody of U.S. Deputy Marshal Henry W. Allen.

At the time of the arrest, Syracuse was filled with visitors attending both the State Liberty Party Convention and the New York State Fair. A crowd quickly gathered at the courthouse where Jerry was taken, and a number of lawyers offered their services to defend him. The most prominent of these attorneys was Gerrit Smith, a nationally known abolitionist soon to be a congressman from the Syracuse District.

During this hearing the crowd in the courtroom attempted to rescue Jerry. He escaped to the streets but was quickly recaptured and placed in the city jail. That night some five thousand people attacked the jail where Jerry was held. This rescue was carefully planned by Gerrit Smith, one white minister—Rev. Samuel J. May—and two black ministers—Rev. Jermain Loguen and Rev. Samuel Ringgold Ward. Jerry was successfully rescued and ultimately taken to Canada.

Thirteen rescuers were indicted by two different federal grand juries. One man, Enoch Reed, was convicted and died while appealing his case. All other prosecutions failed or were dropped. In retaliation for these indictments and as a symbolic attack on the federal government and the Fugitive Slave Act, a grand jury in Onondaga County indicted Deputy Marshal Allen for kidnapping.

■ Allen, Henry W., *defendant.* Trial of Henry W. Allen, U.S. deputy
marshal, for kidnapping, with arguments of counsel & charge of
Justice Marvin, on the constitutionality of the Fugitive Slave

---

* The Jerry Rescue Case

Samuel Joseph May (1797-1871). A Boston minister who settled in Syracuse, New York, May was active in the Jerry Rescue. Because of his earnest advocacy of temperance, peace, and most of all antislavery, May was dubbed "the Lord's chore boy" by the intellectual critic Bronson Alcott.
Lithograph by Seth Cole, Jr., 1871.

Law, in the Supreme Court of New York. Syracuse, Daily Journal Office, 1852. 122 p.

E450.A42

Jerry's arrest had been planned by the Fillmore administration to prove that the Fugitive Slave Act of Sept. 18, 1850, ch. 60, 9 Stat. 462, could be enforced in a Northern city noted for its powerful abolitionist movement. Coming after the Shadrach rescue and the

Christiana riot, the Jerry rescue proved to be a major embarrassment to the national government. The indictment of a federal marshal by the county grand jury simply added to this humiliation.

This report of the trial contains a list of the jurors, a copy of the indictment, and a brief transcript of the testimony in the case. This is followed by a "Note by the Reporter" declaring that the jury was irrelevant to the trial because the only issue before the court was the constitutionality of the Fugitive Slave Act. Next are an "Abstract of Gerrit Smith's Argument" (pp. 9-40) for the prosecution; the "Argument of S. D. Dillaye" (pp. 41-54) for the defense; the "Argument of George F. Comstock" (pp. 55-74) in closing for the defense; the "Argument of C. B. Sedgwick" (pp. 75-86) in closing for the prosecution; and "Judge Marvin's Charge" (pp. 87-98) directing the jury to acquit the defendant. This section is followed by the texts of the Fugitive Slave Acts of 1850 and 1793, the Constitution of the United States, and a speech by William Lusk Crandal, entitled "Can Slavery Be Law? A Word with the Members of the Pittsburg Convention."

According to the reporter of this case, W. L. Crandal, this trial "is the first one of the kind that has been brought since the Constitution of the United States was adopted" (p. 5). This was clearly not the first case involving the Fugitive Slave Clause or the act of 1850. However, it was the first time a federal marshal was indicted for kidnapping after arresting an alleged fugitive slave.

In arguing the case for the prosecution, Gerrit Smith acknowledges that Allen had acted under the act of 1850. Smith accepts the assertion that "If that is a Constitutional, valid law, under which the prisoner acted, and if he rightly interpreted its scope and claims, then he should be acquitted" (p. 9). But if the law is not constitutional, then Smith demands his conviction. Smith does not accept the notion that the marshal is "merely [a] ministerial officer" and should not be required to know the law (p. 9). On the contrary, he argues that an officer who "is required to swear to support not an Act of Congress, but the Constitution" should not enforce unconstitutional acts.

This preface out of the way, Smith offers seventeen reasons for declaring the 1850 act unconstitutional. For example, he asserts that there is no provision for a jury trial; the commissioner acts as a judge in violation of the rules set down in Article III; the difference in fees constitutes a bribe; the standard rules of evidence are ignored; the penalties do not allow discretion by the judge or jury; the compensation for all lost slaves is the same, despite the difference in the value of some slaves; the law recognizes slavery in the territories and the District of Columbia; the law suspends the writ of habeas corpus; and Congress does not have power to pass this type of legislation.

Smith ends his case with two arguments that underscore the

antislavery nature of this prosecution. He argues that ''the fugitive servant act of 1850 is Unconstitutional, because the Constitution is anti-slavery, and not pro-slavery.'' The reporter notes that ''Mr. Smith spent a couple of hours in arguing the Unconstitutionality of slavery'' and he ''frequently quoted from his own published writings, and from those of Lysander Spooner'' (p. 35). Finally, Smith asserts that the Fugitive Slave Clause of the Constitution ''does not refer to slaves'' and, therefore, the clause could not be used to remand fugitive slaves (p. 36).

In much shorter arguments, S. D. Dillaye and George F. Comstock refute Smith's presentation with a rather pedestrian summary of the Supreme Court and lower court cases affirming the Fugitive Slave Acts of 1793 and 1850. This is followed by the closing for the prosecution by Charles B. Sedgwick.

In directions to the jury, Judge R. P. Marvin agrees with Smith and Sedgwick that ''laws and Constitutions should be construed humanely, and in favor of liberty, when they will bear that construction, and it is not clear that another meaning was intended'' (p. 93). However, in this case it is clear to Marvin that the constitutional clause in question was clearly meant to provide for the return of fugitive slaves. He points out that most of the states at the time allowed slavery and that there was little or no debate over the clause at the Constitutional Convention. Marvin repeats the common notion that the Fugitive Slave Clause was inserted into the Constitution as part of the compromise necessary for union. He objects to the implications in Smith's argument that if the act of 1850 is constitutional, then the Constitution must be proslavery. Marvin simply declares that slavery ''is a *State matter*,'' and the Constitution ''is not an instrument defending, sustaining, or supporting slavery. It does not profess to interfere with it. It regarded slavery as *existing in the States*, and provided for contingencies which might happen, and which might, if not provided against, lead to collisions between the States, and endanger the peace and harmony of the States'' (p. 94). Furthermore, he declared that New York State could not be blamed for slavery. ''Some are held to service and labor against their will. This is a regulation of the States, and such State is responsible for it. Our own State is not. Our people are not. We have no right to interfere'' (p. 98). This being the case, a U.S. marshal could not be arrested under New York law for enforcing a federal law. Judge Marvin recommended acquittal, and the jury complied.

The Jerry rescue was a famous incident in the Northern protest against the Fugitive Slave Act. The indictment and trial of Allen was an attempt by antislavery activists to further display their contempt for the act. Allen's acquittal was probably a foregone conclusion, but the trial gave Gerrit Smith and others a new forum from which to attack slavery and the act of 1850. The publication of this pamphlet presents the most complete record of the trial, which was not officially reported. The pamphlet provided yet another instrument for antislavery leaders to publicize their positions and ideas. Coming two years after the Jerry rescue, this pamphlet served to remind Northerners that there were alternatives to rendition when fugitive slaves were seized.

■ Smith, Gerrit. Abstract of the argument on the Fugitive Slave Law, made by Gerrit Smith, in Syracuse, June, 1852, on the trial of Henry W. Allen, U.S. deputy marshal, for kidnapping. Syracuse, Printed for the Daily Journal Office [1852].

E450.S64

With the exception of pagination, this pamphlet duplicates exactly the abstract of Smith's argument provided in the more complete version of the report of this case made by W. L. Crandal. This pamphlet was printed to provide the public with greater access to Smith's arguments, the strongest arguments against the Fugitive Slave Act presented in this trial. His elaborate attack on the law is published here without the rebuttal of the defense attorneys or of Judge Marvin. At thirty-two pages it was easier to read and cheaper to produce and distribute than the more complete discussion of the trial in the larger pamphlet.

In re Anthony Burns

(U.S. Fugitive Slave Comm. Mass. 1854)
(Unreported)*

Associated cases: *United States v. Stowell*, 2 Curt. 153, 27 F. Cas. 1350 (C.C.D. Mass. 1855) (No. 16,409)
Ela v. Smith, 71 Mass. (5 Gray) 121 (1855)

The trial and rendition of Anthony Burns was one of the most dramatic and famous incidents in the enforcement of the Fugitive Slave Act of Sept. 18, 1850, ch. 60, 9 Stat. 462. After 1851 the federal government did not attempt to enforce the 1850 act in areas where such an attempt would have led to violence and perhaps a repetition of the Shadrach and Jerry rescues or the Christiana tragedy. At the same time,

---

*The Anthony Burns case

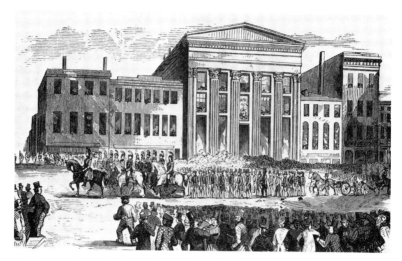

A Virginia slave, Anthony Burns (1834-1862) escaped to Boston in 1854, where he was seized by his master and, after a long hearing, was returned to servitude. Through the intervention of the Boston black community and the aid of some white philanthropists, Burns was subsequently purchased and brought North. He then attended Oberlin College and became a Baptist preacher, first in Indianapolis and later in St. Catherines, Ontario.

Frontispiece from Charles Emery Stevens, *Anthony Burns* (1856). LC-USZ62-39652

the Compromise of 1850 defused some of the national tension over slavery.

Both of these situations changed in 1854. In Congress, the Kansas-Nebraska debates spurred new interest in and massive Northern protest over the questions of slavery in the territories and the role of slavery in national politics. In Boston the arrest, trial and rendition of Anthony Burns once again made the Fugutive Slave Act the focus of national attention.

Burns was claimed by Charles F. Suttle of Alexandria, Virginia. According to Suttle, Burns had escaped by ship to Boston in March 1854. Burns then rather foolishly wrote a letter to his brother (also a slave owned by Suttle) which indicated his whereabouts. In May Suttle arrived in Boston and obtained an arrest warrant for Burns from U.S. Commissioner Edward G. Loring.

On the night of May 24, 1854, Burns was arrested by city officers on a specious charge of robbery and quickly taken to the courthouse, which was used by both state and federal authorities. Burns was then brought before U.S. Marshal Watson Freeman, who took him into custody under a warrant signed by Commissioner Loring. The next day (May 25), Burns was brought before Loring. Richard Henry Dana,

Theodore Parker (1810-1860). An antislavery minister in Boston, Parker was indicted but never tried for his role in the futile effort to rescue Anthony Burns. He later gave advice and helped raise funds for John Brown as one of Brown's ''secret six.''
From the *Illustrated London News*, September 27, 1856. LC-USZ62-52144

Jr., and Charles Mayo Ellis immediately volunteered to defend Burns. They obtained a postponement of the hearing until May 27 to prepare their case. On the night of May 26 there was a mass meeting in Faneuil Hall to protest Burns's arrest. This meeting was followed by a poorly planned and disastrously executed attack on the jail where Burns was held. Although one police deputy was killed, the attempt to rescue Burns failed.

The hearing before Loring began the next day (May 27) and lasted until May 31. During this time there were futile attempts to have Burns released under a state writ of habeas corpus or de homine re-plegiando, to have Suttle arrested for attempted kidnapping, and to purchase Burns from Suttle. On June 2 Commissioner Loring delivered his opinion. Despite conflicting testimony and imperfect evidence provided by Suttle, Loring declared Burns was indeed Suttle's slave. That day he was removed from the courtroom and placed aboard a U.S. revenue cutter for return to Virginia.

The trial and removal of Burns from Boston created one of the great spectacles of the late antebellum period. After the abortive rescue

John Hale (1806-1873). John Parker Hale was one of the first antislavery men to win election, and reelection, to the U.S. Senate. He was also a skilled attorney and used his forensic skills to help defend those accused of attempting to rescue Anthony Burns.
Carte de visite. LC-USZ62-42393

John Albion Andrew (1818-1867). A tireless antislavery lawyer, Andrew was particularly active in the Boston Vigilance Committee. As a state representative, he led the fight to have Edward G. Loring removed from his position as probate judge because Loring, as U.S. commissioner, had ordered the rendition of the fugitive slave Anthony Burns. In 1859 Andrew raised money for the defense of John Brown. He was governor of Massachusetts during the Civil War and used his position to pressure the Lincoln administration to allow blacks to enlist in the army. LC-USZ62-51916

attempt, the courthouse was heavily guarded and completely surrounded by a cordon of men. Because this building was owned and used by state authorities, this protection gave Bostonians the sense that their city was under martial law. The presence of artillery companies, U.S. Marines, and numerous other armed law enforcement personnel confirmed this.

After Loring decided in favor of the claimant, Burns was removed from the courthouse under heavy security. He was completely surrounded by police and military guards. The same military men had been guarding the courthouse for days. The streets between the courthouse and wharf were lined with troops, policemen, sheriff's deputies, and U.S. marshals. Among these guards were eight companies of artillery with various field pieces, a battalion of light dragoons, a regiment of light infantry, an additional battalion of light infantry, and various companies of militia and cadets. Much of the city was decorated in black crepe, and a coffin labeled ''Liberty'' was suspended over the street along Burns's route. Church bells tolled, most businesses were closed, and thousands gathered to cheer Burns and protest his removal. At a cost of as much as $100,000 the U.S. government proved it was possible to remove from Boston one slave, valued at around twelve hundred dollars, and place him on a federal revenue cutter for his return to bondage.

After Burns was returned, a number of Bostonians were indicted for the abortive rescue. However, none of these people were convicted, and the indictments themselves were quashed. In the meantime, the Massachusetts legislature passed (over a governor's veto) a series of ''personal liberty laws'' designed to prevent any future state complicity with the removal of a fugitive slave. In addition, Commissioner Loring was removed from his faculty position at Harvard Law School and, by a vote of the Massachusetts legislature, from his position as a Suffolk County probate judge.

■ The Boston slave riot, and trial of Anthony Burns. Containing the report
        of the Faneuil Hall meeting; the murder of Batchelder; Theodore
        Parker's lesson for the day; speeches of counsel on both sides,
        corrected by themselves; a verbatim report of Judge Loring's
        decision; and a detailed account of the embarkation. Boston,
        Fetridge and Co., 1854. 86 p.

                                E450.B92 Rare Book Room

    This pamphlet contains the legal documents, testimony, arguments of counsel, discussions between the bench and counsel, and other material connected with the case. It provides the full texts of the speeches of the counsel and the opinion of Commissioner Loring. In addition, it presents a chronological account of the events in Boston from the time of Burns's arrest until his removal. There is a report of the substance of the public meeting and the speeches given there, followed by an account of the rescue attempt. Various short articles, which appear to have been taken from Boston newspapers, are included, as is a fairly complete list of the various military companies and their officers used to guard Burns when he was taken to the wharf. There is a copy of Rev. Theodore Parker's sermon given on the Sunday after the arrest. A note at the end of the pamphlet by Suttle's attorney explains his version of why Burns was not purchased.

This pamphlet apparently went through a number of different printings. The various copies in the Library of Congress contain different colored wrappers. In addition, some have advertisements at the back of the pamphlet, while other copies do not. The pamphlet contains valuable primary source material about the trial and the events surrounding it. Indeed, the juxtaposition of all the material in this volume indicates the important connection between events in the courtroom and those in the streets.

■ Bowditch, William I. The rendition of Anthony Burns. Boston, Robert F. Wallcut, 1854. 40 p.

E450.B923

In a small pamphlet, William I. Bowditch, an antislavery lawyer, carefully analyzes the evidence and legal arguments presented before Commissioner Loring in the Burns case. From this information, he argues that the rendition was unjustified. Without offering any new information—most of his facts and quotations come from *The Boston Slave Riots and Trial of Anthony Burns*—Bowditch does present the facts concisely and clearly, pointing out the meaning of important testimony and the various ways this testimony could have been applied to the case. In addition, he rigorously compares the act of 1850 with the proceedings before Loring and concludes that Burns should not have been handed over to the claimant, Charles Suttle.

Bowditch begins by saying that he will not question the constitutionality of the 1850 act. He simply asserts that its ''constitutionality never has been, and cannot, as it seems to us, be successfully defended upon principle. Its only support is found in certain precedents, which have not as yet been overruled'' (p. 3). But, because Bowditch wishes to prove that Loring was not obligated to return Burns under the act, he is ''willing, for the purposes of the present discussion, to suppose that the Fugitive Slave Bill is constitutional, however groundless such supposition may be in point of principle'' (p. 4).

He then analyzes the provisions of the 1850 act that declare the type and standard of evidence and proof necessary for a rendition. He concludes that the sixth and tenth sections of the law detail ''two entirely distinct methods of proving the facts of owing service and escape'' (p. 8). One is through deposition or affidavit combined with ''satisfactory testimony'' before the commissioner. The second is by obtaining a certified court record from the state in which the escape was made. This record would then be presented to the commissioner and ''shall be held

and taken to be full and conclusive evidence of the fact of the escape''
and that service is due to the claimant (p. 7). Under this procedure the
claimant need not provide any other information, except to prove that
the person seized is in fact the person named in the certified court
record. Bowditch concludes that under the tenth section of the law ''the
Commissioner is *bound* to admit the truth'' of the facts stated in the
affidavit because it is part of a court record. But, under the sixth section,
the commissioner ''is left entirely free to make up his judgment as he
may think proper on all the testimony adduced'' (p. 8). After quoting
extensively from the evidence presented at the trial, Bowditch concludes
that Suttle was proceeding under the sixth section of the act and thus the
commissioner ought to have examined the evidence with great care
because it was not the evidence from a court record in Virginia.
Furthermore, Bowditch argues that the commissioner, as a court officer
operating in a free state, must lean toward freedom at all times.

Having established this technical interpretation of the act of
1850, Bowditch carefully applies the facts of Burns's case to this law.
He shows that there are great discrepancies between the evidence
produced by Suttle and that produced on behalf of Burns. Suttle's most
important witness is his friend William Brent, who traveled to Boston
with Suttle and testified that he had known Burns in Virginia. But Brent
does not accurately describe Burns and claims to have seen him in
Virginia at precisely the time impartial white witnesses claimed they
saw the alleged fugitive in Boston. Bowditch suggests that the person
arrested might not be Suttle's slave. He points out that the description of
Burns in Suttle's warrant might apply to at least fifty different men
''within ten minutes walk of Boston Court House'' (p. 22). He further
argues that Burns's most distinguishing feature—a broken bone in his
right hand which had caused a deformity—was left out of the description.
He states that from this omission ''we are bound to presume that it was
owing to the fact that no such mark existed on the hand of the genuine
Anthony Burns,'' and thus the wrong person was seized (p. 23).

Bowditch also argues that there is no evidence that Burns escaped
to Boston. Rather, Bowditch asserts that he was hired out to work on a
ship that took him there. Citing the *Lemmon* case (*People ex rel. Napoleon
v. Lemmon*, 5 Sand. 681 [N.Y. Super. Ct. 1852]), then making its way
through the New York courts, Bowditch suggests that Burns is not a
fugitive, because in fact he did not leave Virginia against his master's
will but rather his master put him in a position where he was inadvertently
taken to Massachusetts. Thus, under the precedent established by
Commonwealth v. *Aves*, 35 Mass. (18 Pick.) 193 (1836), Burns was
free.

Finally, Bowditch argues that because Burns was hired out at the
time of his alleged escape, he did not owe service or labor to his owner,

Suttle. Rather, under Virginia law (which Bowditch cites) Burns owed labor to the man who had hired him.

The main thrust of this pamphlet is that the Fugitive Slave Act of 1850 should be construed strictly. Bowditch is not on particularly strong ground in arguing that the wrong person was arrested or that Burns did not actually escape from Virginia. Despite the conflicting evidence, it seems likely that the man arrested as Anthony Burns was in fact the Anthony Burns owned by Suttle. Similarly, despite the fact that Suttle did not explicitly state that Burns had left Virginia against the will of his master, it seems likely that Burns did do this. Indeed, the letter to his brother in Virginia indicated this.

But if Bowditch is unconvincing in his suggestion that the man arrested was either the wrong person or not a fugitive, he is convincing in his assertions that the commissioner was not necessarily obligated to remand Burns to Suttle. He persuasively argues (1) that the commissioner has a great deal of flexibility in deciding the cases brought before him; and (2) that in a case in which a man's liberty is at stake, the law ought to be construed strictly and in favor of liberty.

In arguing for a strict adherence to the letter of the law, Bowditch suggests that any other method of interpreting the act is likely to bring about dangerous precedents or results. Only strict legal formalism can ensure that free men are not enslaved. After making these philosophical points, Bowditch shows in many ways that there were substantial technical reasons for *not* remanding Burns to Suttle.

■ Parker, Theodore. The trial of Theodore Parker, for the "misdemeanor" of a speech in Faneuil Hall against kidnapping, before the Circuit Court of the United States, at Boston, April 3, 1855. With the defence. Boston, Pub. for the author, 1855; Cambridge, Allen and Farnham, Printers, 1855. xx, 221 p.

E4550.P241

On June 7, 1854, U.S. Supreme Court Justice Benjamin R. Curtis charged a federal grand jury in Boston to seek indictments against those reponsible for the jail riot that failed to liberate Anthony Burns. This grand jury found no indictments and was ultimately dismissed. In October 1854 a second grand jury met and considered indictments against those who had spoken during the Faneuil Hall meeting just before the unsuccessful assault on the jail.

Among others, this grand jury included the brother-in-law of Justice Curtis. Before the second jury met, Rev. Theodore Parker had spoken out against the law and "the conduct of Judge Curtis, in a Sermon for the Fourth of July" (p.v). Parker was not surprised when the second grand jury indicted him: ''I knew the friends of the fugitive slave bill at Boston and Washington too well to think they would let the matter sleep; I knew that arts could be used to pack a jury and procure a bill'' (pp. v-vi).

Ten men, including Parker, Thomas Wentworth Higginson, and Wendell Phillips were indicted. On November 29, 1854, Parker was arraigned on various charges that he ''with force of arms, did knowingly and wilfully obstruct, resist, and oppose'' the rendition of Anthony Burns (p. xv). Parker gave bond for $1,500 and began to prepare for his trial, which was initially set for March 5, 1855, but was ultimately postponed until April 3 to allow Justice Curtis to attend.

The prosecution was made up of U.S. District Attorney Benjamin F. Hallett and Elias Merwin, a former law partner of Justice Curtis. Parker retained John P. Hale, the U.S. senator from New Hampshire, and Charles M. Ellis. Other defendants retained William L. Burt, Henry F. Durant, and John A. Andrew, who would later be the Civil War governor of Massachusetts.

The first man to be tried was Martin Stowell (thus the case *U.S. v. Stowell)*, but attorneys for all the defendants spoke before Justice Curtis. Senator Hale moved to quash the indictments because of irregularities in choosing the grand jury and inconsistencies within the indictments themselves. After argument by all the defense counsel and by Merwin and Hallett, Justice Curtis declared that he did not want to hear any rejoinder by Senator Hale. Instead, Curtis ruled that the indictments were bad because ''the allegation, on the indictment, that Edward G. Loring was a Commissioner of the Circuit Court of the United States for said District, was not a legal averment that he was such a Commissioner as is described in the bill of 1850'' (p. xix). Thus, on this rather flimsy technicality, the indictment against Stowell was dropped, and the prosecution entered a nolle prosequi in the other cases.

Parker claims not to have been surprised by these events because ''A great political revolution took place between'' his indictment and the commencement of the case, and Parker ''thought the Court would not allow the case to come to open argument'' (p. vi). It would have been difficult to convict any of the defendants on the charges against them because there was no direct evidence connecting them to the attempted rescue. Such a trial would only have provided a forum for antislavery ideas and would probably have embarrassed the Pierce administration. Theodore Parker had, however, put a great deal of work into his own defense. He did not want to see that work wasted, so he published his defense as a volume of over two hundred pages.

This volume contains an introduction to the case and the indictment of Parker, including copies of the indictments and other legal papers filed with the court (pp. i-xx). Parker's defense takes up the next

221 pages. Included in this printed defense are the texts of speeches made by Parker, Justice Curtis's charge to the grand jury, resolutions passed at various antislavery meetings, and other primary materials. Parker also gives histories of other attempted and successful renditions of fugitive slaves from Boston and a history of Curtis's involvement with slavery. Besides material directly related to slavery, Parker discussed good and bad judges and the history of the right to trial by jury, and generally sketches out the abuses of justice and the history of due process rights in England and America. The tone of this book is moralistic and connects antislavery with Christianity, justice, good, God's will, and American patriotism. He ends with "the religious lesson, that 'REBELLION TO TYRANTS IS OBEDIENCE TO GOD' " (p. 221).

Parker acknowledges that this defense would never have been allowed in a court of law. He presents it not as a legal document, but as a moral and political statement that uses his indictment to provide a forum for his antislavery beliefs.

■ Phillips, Wendell. Argument of Wendell Phillips, esq. before the Committee on Federal Relations (of the Massachusetts Legislature,) in support of the petition for the removal of Edward Greely Loring from the office of Judge of Probate, February 20, 1855. Boston, J.B. Yerrinton & Sons, 1855. 43 p.

E450.P552

Besides serving as U.S. commissioner, Edward G. Loring was also a judge of the probate court of Suffolk County. After the rendition of Anthony Burns, a number of petitions were presented to the Massachusetts legislature to have Loring removed from his office. The most articulate supporter of these petitions was Wendell Phillips, a leading abolitionist.

Phillips was a graduate of Harvard Law School and was said to be one of the finest students Justice Joseph Story had during the many years he taught there. However, a few years after he began to practice law, Phillips became an avowed anticonstitutionalist because he thought that document sinfully supported slavery. He renounced his oath as an attorney, although he occasionally took part in cases involving slaves or abolitionists. He also used his extensive skills to argue the cause of abolition before various committees of the Massachusetts legislature.

In supporting the petition for removal, Phillips asserts (1) that Loring's action in the Burns case was "in defiance of the solemn convictions and settled purposes of Massachusetts—convictions and purpose officially made known to him" (p. 20); (2) that the "very method" of the Burns trial "shows Mr. Loring unfit to be continued longer on the Bench,'' and Loring's arbitrary manner, his denial of certain motions, his treatment of the prisoner, and his managing of the hearing ''shows him unfit for the office of a Judge'' (p. 24); (3) that Loring decided the case before any arguments were made; and (4) that Loring's decisions and actions during the case directly violated settled law.

From the onset of his remarks, Phillips clearly argues that Loring should be impeached not because ''he has been guilty of some *official misconduct*'' (p. 6). Rather, Loring should be removed because he is morally unfit to hold an office of trust under the state's constitution. Phillips gives voluminous citations to support this position. In the end he concludes that the ''hunting of slaves is, then, a sufficient cause for the removal from a Massachusetts Bench. Indeed, I should blush for the State if it were not so'' (p. 39). In the end, Phillips did not need to blush, for by overwhelming majorities both houses of the legislature voted to remove Loring from his position. The Massachusetts governor refused to act on the legislature's recommendation, however, and it was not until 1858, with a new governor in office, that Loring was removed from the probate court.

■ Dana, Richard Henry. Remarks of Richard Henry Dana, Jr., Esq. before the Committee on Federal Relations, on the proposed removal of Edward G. Loring, esq. from the office of Judge of Probate. March 5, 1855. Boston, Printed by Alfred Mudge & Sons, 1855. 28 p.

E450.D23

Richard Henry Dana was one of the attorneys who argued on behalf of Anthony Burns. Dana opposed slavery but could not be considered a radical abolitionist. As a lawyer and a citizen, he believed the removal of Loring from his judgeship would be a dangerous precedent and would threaten the independence of the judiciary.

In this testimony before a legislative committee, he did not deny the right of the legislature to remove Loring. On the contrary, he agreed with Wendell Phillips (who had spoken for the removal less than two weeks earlier) that the legislature could remove a judge for something less than official misconduct. Dana simply argues that the removal of Loring would create a dangerous precedent. He suggests that ''If you remove Judge Loring because he executed the Fugitive Slave Law, other judges here or elsewhere, may be removed, because they do not'' (p. 12). He also suggests that once Loring is removed, future legislatures may remove other judges on political grounds or test their ''piety,'' "temperance," "moderation," "frugality," or "fidelity to the fundamental principles of the Constitution" (p. 12).

Besides these arguments of principle, Dana disputes many of the attacks Phillips made on Loring. He asserts that Loring conducted the trial fairly and went out of his way to ensure that Burns had adequate counsel and understood his rights. Dana dismisses as rumor Phillips's assertion that Loring informed the U.S. marshal of his decision long before he publicly announced it. Finally, Dana argues, as a prominent member of the antislavery Free Soil party, that the removal of Loring is improper. It will simply make the Free Soilers as bad as the other parties. He fears "that this step will involve the anti-slavery men of Massachusetts in a needless and doubtful issue, which they may live to regret; while we believe the course we recommend will secure the respect of all, and an ultimate ascendency to a sound and wholesome sentiment of liberty in the Commonwealth" (p. 28). Despite the logic of his argument, Dana's position was overwhelmingly rejected in the legislature, and Loring was ultimately removed from office.

In re Booth

3 Wis. 1 (1854)

Ex parte Booth

3 Wis. 145 (1854)

In re Booth and Rycraft

3 Wis. 157 (1855)

Associated cases: *United States ex rel. Garland* v. *Morris,* 26 F. Cas. 1318 (D. Wis. 1854) (No. 15,811)
United States v. *Rycraft,* 27 F. Cas. 918 (D. Wis. 1854) (No. 16, 211)
Ableman v. *Booth,* 62 U.S. (21 How.) 506 (1859)
Ableman v. *Booth,* 11 Wis. 517 (1861)
Arnold v. *Booth,* 14 Wis. 195 (1861)

The controversy surrounding the arrest and trial of Sherman M. Booth led to more litigation than any other fugitive slave case. In 1854 Garland, a slave owner from Missouri, obtained a warrant for the arrest of his slave, Joshua Glover. Glover was then seized and placed in the

Milwaukee County jail. Later that day the mayor of Racine, Wisconsin, where Glover had been seized, issued a warrant for the arrest of Garland for kidnapping Glover. Writs of habeas corpus were also issued, commanding the sheriff and marshal of the county to bring Glover before a county judge.

While these writs were being obtained, a mob, allegedly led by Booth and Rycraft, stormed the jail and rescued Glover. He safely escaped from the area and was never again arrested or seized. Garland was arrested by state officials but was subsequently released by a federal court on a writ of habeas corpus *(United States ex rel. Garland* v. *Morris)*. Rycraft and Booth were then arrested by the federal marshal, Ableman, for their role in rescuing Glover.

These arrests led to a protracted conflict between the Wisconsin state courts and the federal courts. Booth was first arrested by Marshal Ableman under the Fugitive Slave Act of Sept. 18, 1850, ch. 60, 9 Stat. 462. This arrest was not made under any warrant signed by a judge, and in the case *In re Booth* the Wisconsin Supreme Court released Booth on a writ of habeas corpus. Booth was then rearrested under a warrant from U.S. District Judge Andrew G. Miller. When Booth applied for a second writ of habeas corpus, the Wisconsin Supreme Court refused to release him, on the grounds that he should stand trial if properly indicted by a federal court. Thus, in *Ex parte Booth*, the plaintiff remained in prison. Booth was convicted in an unreported case, and Rycraft was convicted in *United States* v. *Rycraft*.

Both men appealed to the Wisconsin Supreme Court for still another writ of habeas corpus. In this case, *In re Booth and Rycraft*, the Wisconsin Supreme Court declared the Fugitive Slave Act of 1850 unconstitutional and freed Booth and Rycraft. The case was ultimately taken to the U.S. Supreme Court, where Chief Justice Taney, speaking for a unanimous Court, ruled that the federal laws were the supreme laws of the land and that the federal courts could not be overruled by state courts *(Ableman* v. *Booth)*. This decision was ignored by the state court, but Booth was nevertheless arrested by federal officials. He was subsequently rescued from prison and remained at large for over two months, all the while giving speeches at public meetings. Booth was later arrested again and remained in prison for almost six more months until President James Buchanan pardoned him in March 1861. During this period Booth's attorney, Byron Paine, was elected to the Wisconsin Supreme Court. After his release from prison, Booth remained active in antislavery politics as a Republican editor and politician.

■   Wisconsin, Supreme Court. Unconstitutionality of the Fugitive Slave Act. Decisions of the Supreme Court of Wisconsin in the cases of Booth and Rycraft. Milwaukee, R. King & Co., Printers, 1855. 218 p.

Law Library; E450.W81

This pamphlet contains the complete reports of *In re Booth*, *Ex parte Booth*, and *In re Booth and Rycraft*, as they appeared in volume 3 of the *Wisconsin Reports*. When that volume was printed, extra copies of the Booth cases were "struck off, so as to enable every one to obtain a copy" (p. iii). With the exception of a two-page preface, there is no difference between the material in this pamphlet and that found in the official report.

According to the preface, the publishers believe these cases are "of very great importance, not only to the profession, but to the people at large." All opinions, both for and against the Fugitive Slave Act are presented "so that both sides may be examined" (p. iii). The publishers believe these cases are about issues that affect citizens throughout the nation. The issues concern tyranny, despotism, the "right, duty and power of the States to protect their own citizens against the exercise of unconstitutional power, the inviolability of the Habeas Corpus, the independence of the States in the exercise of their reserved powers," and state sovereignty. Every "citizen is confidently commended to the careful study of the important decisions" published in this pamphlet because "Every citizen must take part in their final termination" (p. iv).

■ Booth, Sherman M., defendant. Unconstitutionality of the fugitive act. Argument of Byron Paine, esq. and opinion of Hon. A. D. Smith, associate justice of the Supreme Court of the state of Wisconsin. Habeas corpus trial. Before Justice Smith. In the matter of the petition of Sherman M. Booth for a writ of habeas corpus and to be discharged from imprisonment. [Milwaukee? 1854?] 35 p.

E450.B72

When Booth was arrested, he immediately petitioned for a writ of habeas corpus, which was granted by Justice A. D. Smith while the Wisconsin Supreme Court was on vacation. At that time Smith gave a long and elaborate opinion on why Booth should be released, which appears in volume 3 of the *Wisconsin Reports* on pages 7-49.

Smith's initial opinion is reprinted verbatim on pages 23-31 of this pamphlet. After Smith released Booth, the petition for habeas corpus was reviewed in *In re Booth* by the full court. The majority opinion, upholding Smith's action, was written by Chief Justice Edward V.

Whiton. That opinion, printed here on pages 31-35, corresponds to 3 Wisconsin 49-70.

The most important part of this pamphlet is not the opinions of the jurists but the arguments of counsel. According to the official reports, "The arguments of counsel in this case were long and able, but it is difficult to abreviate [sic] them, without materially impairing their force, and the plan of this volume will not permit their insertion at length" (3 Wisconsin 49). This pamphlet provides the complete argument of Booth's attorney, Byron Paine, and a short summary of the argument of U.S. District Attorney J. R. Sharpstein.

Paine's argument is a long and sophisticated attack on the constitutionality of the act of 1850, combined with an articulate rationale for the right of the state to interfere with the federal courts in this case. He asserts that "the power of the [state] court does not stop" at the door of the federal courthouse, but "if [the state court is] satisfied that the reason is insufficient, it may discharge from custody the citizen whose liberty has been unjustly invaded, and thus afford a peaceful and bloodless remedy for the dangers that impend over us. But if we fail here, we can go no further." And "If the people are driven unprotected from their State courts, the cloud that will settle down upon them can be lifted only by the dread ordeal of revolution, when falling back upon their reserved rights, amid scenes of violence and blood, they alter or abolish those governments that have failed to answer the great ends for which all governments are established" (pp. 3-4). Paine maintains that the only alternative to arbitrary federal power is the interference of the state courts in favor of justice and due process.

Unlike other lawyers in fugitive slave cases, Paine does not attempt to overwhelm the court with a laundry list of reasons why the act of 1850 should be declared unconstitutional. Instead he bases his argument on the three most obvious points of attack: (1) "that congress has no power to legislate upon the subject at all"; (2) that no "person claimed as a fugitive, may be reduced to a State of Slavery without a Trial by Jury"; and (3) "that it is unconstitutional because it vests the judicial power of the United States in a Court Commissioner contrary to the provisions of the constitution" (p. 4).

He specifically disavows any moral objections to the law, although in such a manner as to make clear to the court that there are moral objections that border on constitutional objections. Thus, he asserts "I do not stand here to oppose that law because it is a monstrous moral deformity—detestable in its purpose and detestable in its details, sinking to the depths of depravity to punish mercy as a crime, and sinking below the depths of contempt to offer a paltry bribe against freedom, to the petty tribunals it creates. I do not stand here to oppose it because it is a violation of the 'higher law' " (p. 4).

Paine then goes on to give detailed, convincing evidence that the Fugitive Slave Clause of the Constitution was directed at the *states* and not at the federal government. Among others, he quotes Daniel Webster, a vital supporter of the 1850 act, to prove his point. On the issue of commissioners he is equally strong. Paine cites Massachusetts Chief Justice Lemuel Shaw, suggesting that the use of commissioners is constitutional because the rendition is *not* a judicial procedure. Then he cites *Prigg* v. *Pennsylvania*, 41 U.S. (16 Pet.) 539 (1842), to show the U.S. Supreme Court believes it *is* a judicial procedure. His conclusion is that if the procedure is judicial, then the Wisconsin court ought to follow the implications of Shaw's arguments and declare the commissioner cannot constitutionally act. Both of these positions, on the judicial nature of the procedure and the lack of congressional power, are reinforced by voluminous references to court opinions, Madison's *Notes on the Constitutional Convention,* and many other legal and political sources. Paine devoted all of May 29 and part of the thirtieth to these arguments.

His arguments on the jury trial are less complete and less persuasive. He relies primarily on various treatises and the implications of numerous cases. He attempts to distinguish between a fugitive from justice and one from labor, arguing that the latter must be protected by a jury trial when seized, because unlike the former he will not get one after rendition.

Much of Paine's argument was influenced by, or directly borrowed from, the arguments made by Robert Rantoul, Jr., in the *Sims* case in 1851 in Boston. Paine had access to the Rantoul arguments because they had previously been published in pamphlet form. Thus, one of the main purposes of the publication and distribution of arguments in fugitive slave cases had been fulfilled: attorneys in one section of the country were able to share ideas, plans, and strategies with men of similar political views who lived far away and who might be personally unknown to each other. What failed for Rantoul in the *Sims* case worked quite successfully for Paine in the *Booth* case.

Ex parte Bushnell

9 Ohio St. 77 (1859)

Ex parte Langston

9 Ohio St. 77 (1859)

United States v. *Bushnell*

(N.D. Ohio 1859) (Unreported)

United States v. *Langston*

(N.D. Ohio 1859) (Unreported)

The Oberlin-Wellington rescue was the last major incident involving the Fugitive Slave Act to occur before the Civil War. In September 1858 Anderson D. Jennings of Macon County, Kentucky, came to Oberlin, Ohio, in search of some runaway slaves. Jennings did not find his own slaves, but he did see a black named John, who had escaped from John Bacon, a neighbor of Jennings. Jennings wrote to Bacon about John, and Bacon sent Jennings a power of attorney authorizing Jennings to arrest the fugitive.

A "gentleman-farmer" named Lewis Boynton sent his thirteen-year-old son to decoy John from the town of Oberlin. Outside the town John was seized by a federal marshal and taken to the county seat at Wellington. There he was being held in the Wadsworth Hotel when a rescue party arrived and surrounded the building. One witness estimated "as much as a thousand people [were] around and in" the hotel. He noted that a "great many of them had arms;—rifles, shotguns, etc. Should think there were five hundred guns in the crowd" (Shipherd, *History of the Oberlin-Wellington Rescue*, p. 18). This crowd soon surged into the building and seized John, who was spirited away and presumably taken to Canada.

A federal grand jury believed only about two hundred people were connected with the rescue. This grand jury, which included Lewis Boynton, among others, indicted thirty-seven men for "rescuing" or "aiding and abetting" the rescue of a fugitive slave (ibid., pp. 4-5). The indictments were handed down in December 1858, but the first trial did not begin until May 1859 and lasted ten days. In it Simeon Bushnell was convicted and sentenced to sixty days in jail and fined $600 plus court costs.

The U.S. district attorney then tried to bring the next man, Charles Langston, before the same jury that had convicted Bushnell. But Langston's attorneys successfully resisted this plan, and a new jury was called. By the time Langston was convicted, almost a month and a half had elapsed since the beginning of the first trial. At this rate the trials would have taken more than a year to complete, would have required more than three hundred jurors, and would have cost more than twenty thousand dollars.

From the beginning of the trials, the defendants had refused to post bail. Thus, they remained in jail as martyrs and at great expense and inconvenience to the government. In addition, Jennings and three men who had assisted in arresting John had been indicted under Ohio law for kidnapping, and Langston and Bushnell had brought their case before the Ohio Supreme Court on a writ of habeas corpus. In a three-to-two decision the Ohio court refused to interfere with the action of the federal courts. However, the prospect of two Kentucky citizens and two federal officials being convicted for kidnapping led to a compromise. The U.S. attorney agreed to drop all charges against the rescuers if the state officials dropped charges against Jennings and his comrades. This was accomplished, and all of the rescuers, including Langston and Bushnell, were released from federal custody.

■ Shipherd, Jacob R. History of the Oberlin-Wellington Rescue . . . Comp. by Jacob R. Shipherd. With an introduction by Prof. Henry E. Peck and Hon. Ralph Plumb. Boston, John F. Jewett and Co.; Cleveland, Henry P. B. Jewett; New York, Sheldon and Co., 1859. 280 p.

E450.S55

——[Reprint] New York, Negro Universities Press, 1969.

E450.S55 1969

This volume contains a vast amount of information about the cases connected to the Oberlin-Wellington rescue. It is divided into five large chapters. Chapter one gives a very brief history of the rescue and discusses the makeup of the federal grand jury, the arrests of those indicted, and the preliminary court actions through the striking of the first petit jury. Chapter two is a record of the trial of Simeon Bushnell. It includes most of the testimony, examinations and cross-examinations, the arguments of counsel for both sides, various legal motions, and the charge to the jury. Chapter three contains information about Bushnell's motion for a new trial and a record of the trial of Charles Langston. Chapter four details the sentencing of Bushnell and Langston and their appeals to the Ohio Supreme Court. The last chapter describes the indictments against Jennings and others and the compromise that was ultimately reached.

This book is particularly useful for its record of the federal court trials of Bushnell and Langston. Their cases were not officially reported by the trial judge. Thus, with the exception of scattered papers in the federal court archives, there is no official record of them. This book, however, reports much more than would have been officially reported.

It contains records of indictments, arguments, and testimony, which make it possible to know exactly what went on at these trials. Trained ''phonographic reporters'' took down most of the testimony and arguments of counsel at the trials. This material was supplemented with notes provided by the defense attorneys. The prosecution declined to participate in compiling this volume. Henry Peck and Ralph Plumb wrote the introduction while they were still in the Cuyahoga County Jail. The nonlegal material in this book, such as accounts of meetings and the celebrations after the release of the indicted abolitionists, appears to be taken from newspapers or accounts written down by witnesses to the events. The volume is sympathetic to the abolitionists and is ''affectionately inscribed'' to the ''Thirty-Seven Indicted and to all Who With Them Believe in the Doctrines of the Declaration of Independence'' (p. iii).

Despite the convictions, it appears from the record that U.S. District Judge Hiram V. Willson went out of his way to ensure a fair trial. Willson sustained a number of important defense objections on procedure and allowable testimony (pp. 18, 96, for example). At the trial of Charles Langston, the prosecution tried to use the same jury that had just convicted Bushnell, but when the defense attorneys objected, Willson ordered that a new jury be chosen. Finally, in his charge to the jury in Langston's case, Willson, realizing that Langston's being a Negro could in itself lead to his conviction, told the jurors that ''the first duty of a juror [is] . . . to divest himself of any and all prejudices he may have against the law itself, or of any partiality or ill-will he may have towards the accused'' (p. 166). Willson also told the jury that the government needed to prove every aspect of its charges before Langston could be convicted.

Willson had been a partner of the Free Soil radical Edward Wade before he was appointed to the bench, and this association suggests that he may have been somewhat sympathetic to those opposed to slavery. Willson's attempt to provide as fair and unpolitical a trial as possible may have been marred, however, by the clerk and U.S. marshal involved in choosing the jury. According to Shipherd, the clerk in Bushnell's case ''summoning without restriction whom he chose, was able to find only ten men out of the forty [in the jury pool] who sympathized politically with the defendants, while he found thirty who sympathized'' with the prosecution. The ten ''were immediately 'stricken' off by the District-Attorney, and the defense allowed their 'choice' of the remaining thirty'' (p. 14). Similarly, in Langston's case Shipherd claims the ''politics of this Jury were too marked to escape notice. They stood: nine Administration men, two Fillmore Whigs, and one Republican, who had no objections to the Fugitive Slave Law'' (p. 97).

The Oberlin-Wellington rescue was one of the important events of the late 1850s that captured the imagination of the nation and focused attention on the problem of slavery. The accommodation that freed those charged with the rescue was forced by the threat of state action against a Kentucky master and various federal officials. Yet, for all this, what is perhaps most important about this case is what did *not* happen. The Supreme Court of Ohio, in *Ex parte Bushnell* and *Ex parte Langston*, was given an opportunity to nullify federal law. Unlike the Supreme Court of Wisconsin, the Ohio court refused to take that step.

Commonwealth v. Myers

(Cumberland Cty. |Pa.| Ct. Quarter Sessions 1859) (Unreported)

In 1855 a Maryland slave owner named Elizabeth Warfield died. In her will, she directed that her slaves be set free. The probate court nevertheless ordered the sale of two slaves to settle Warfield's debts. This was done despite the fact that other property, particularly land, could have been sold to settle the debts. Later the court rescinded this order and directed that some of the slaves, including Emeline and her daughter Elizabeth, be sold for a term of years. In 1857 or 1858 Emeline, her daughter, and a slave named John Butler (Elizabeth's father) escaped to Pennsylvania. In 1859 they were seized by Emanuel Myers and taken back to Maryland. Myers was later arrested at the instigation of black and white neighbors of the Butler family. In this trial Myers was convicted of kidnapping under a Pennsylvania statute of 1847.

■ Myers, Emanuel, *defendant*. The trial of Emanuel Myers, of Maryland, for kidnapping certain fugitive slaves, had at Carlisle, Pennsylvania. November, 1859. |Carlisle? 1859| 10 p.

This pamphlet is the only printed report of Myers's case and appears to have been written directly from the original transcripts of the trial. It contains only the testimony, arguments of counsel, and speeches relevant to the conviction of Myers. It also presents the charge to the jury given by Judge Graham. Myers's case was heard in the Court of Quarter Sessions of Cumberland County. Three other men tried with him were acquitted. During the trial an attorney representing the state of Maryland was allowed to speak. He asserted that under the *Prigg* v. *Pennsylvania*, 41 U.S. (16 Pet.) 539 (1842), doctrine the Pennsylvania court did not have a legal right to question the status of a slave in Maryland. This lawyer declared the Pennsylvania court could ''only try whether the negroes alleged to have been kidnapped were in *fact* 'held to service' in Maryland . . . [and] the Court could not try the question of the *legality* of such *holding to service*—that any attempt to try the title of the negroes to their freedom would be an invasion of the rights of Maryland, under the Federal Constitution" (p. 7). Judge Graham rejected this argument and told the jury that they had a right to examine the issue of the blacks' legal status. This led to Myers's conviction.

United States v. Hossack

26 F. Cas. 378 (N.D. Ill. 1860) (No. 15,395)

United States v. Stout

(N.D. Ill. 1860) (Unreported)

In 1860 John Hossack was convicted of rescuing a fugitive slave. The trial was held before Judge Thomas Drummond, in the U.S. District Court for the Northern District of Illinois. The facts leading up to this conviction were disputed by prosecution and defense attorneys. Hossack's lawyers argued that the alleged slave was actually a free black, while the prosecution successfully argued he was actually the slave of a Missouri master named Richard Phillipps.

In October 1859 Phillipps journeyed to Jonesboro, Illinois, to claim a young black man named Jim Gray, who had allegedly escaped from him a month earlier. (Defense attorneys argued Gray had been kidnapped in Perry County, where he was peacefully employed by a farmer, but that the kidnappers took him only as far as Jonesboro because they were being followed by friends of Gray.) When Phillipps arrived in Jonesboro, Gray was in the local jail on the suspicion that he was a fugitive slave. However, the local sheriff would not release Gray to Phillipps because the sheriff had already been served with a writ of habeas corpus commanding him to bring Gray before Chief Justice John D. Caton of the Illinois Supreme Court.

The next day the sheriff, Mr. Albright, took Gray to Ottawa, Illinois, in response to Chief Justice Caton's writ. Phillipps then took a train to Springfield, Illinois, where the nearest U.S. commissioner could be found. The commissioner gave Phillipps a writ under the Fugitive Slave Act of Sept. 18, 1850, ch. 60, 9 Stat. 462, and ordered the local U.S. marshal to accompany Phillipps to recover the slave. The marshal and Phillipps caught up with Sheriff Albright before he arrived at Ottawa. Albright still refused to let Gray out of his custody, but he did agree to be deputized as a U.S. deputy marshal. Albright and Phillipps continued on to Ottawa.

At a hearing in Ottawa, Chief Justice Caton vacated his writ of habeas corpus and remanded Gray to Albright, who now acted not as a county sheriff but as a U.S. deputy marshal charged by the U.S. commissioner to bring Gray back to Springfield. Because there was some doubt as to whether Albright had been properly sworn in to his new position, Judge Caton administered an oath that made Albright's authority more official. This was done despite the fact that Caton and Albright were both *state* officials, and there was no federal authority to make Albright a federal deputy, except for a one-sentence appointment written by the U.S. marshal declaring, ''I hereby appoint A. N. Albright my special deputy to execute this writ'' (*Report of the Trial of John Hossack*, p. 250).

Caton's declaration that Gray was remanded to Deputy Marshal Albright caused confusion and commotion in the courtroom. Gray was urged to run, and with the help of the crowd he did so. The crowd in the courtroom and in the street below opened for Gray and closed around Albright and Phillipps. By the time they were able to get out of the courtroom, Gray was on his way to a waiting wagon, which sped him away. He was never seen again by any of the principals in this case.

Hossack and a second defendant, Joseph Stout, were subsequently indicted and tried before Judge Drummond. Hossack was convicted, but the jury recommended mercy. Drummond took this advice, fining Hossack only $100 and sentencing him to ten days in jail. A week later Stout was tried on essentially the same evidence as Hossack and received the same light sentence.

■ Hossack, John *defendant*. Report of the trial of John Hossack indicted for rescuing a fugitive slave from the U.S. marshal, at Ottawa, October 20th, 1859. Phonographically reported, including evidence, arguments of counsel & charge of the court. United States District Court for the Northern District of Illinois. Honorable Thomas Drummond, judge. February term, 1860. R. R. Hitt, reporter. Chicago, Press & Tribune Steam Book and Job Printing Office, 1860. 265 p.

Law Library

The prosecution of Hossack is reported in *Federal Cases* only by case number, 15,395, and case title, *United States* v. *Hossack*. This is followed by the short statement: ''Nowhere reported: opinion not now accessible.'' There is no report or case number for the prosecution of Joseph Stout. This pamphlet remedies that situation.

The *Report of the Trial of John Hossack* contains 130 pages of testimony, followed by the closing statements of two of the prosecution attorneys, the charge of Judge Drummond, and the argument for a new trial and arrest of judgment by Hossack's attorney. It presents neither opening statements by the lawyers nor the closing arguments of Hossack's lawyers. However, it includes the argument of the defense attorney in the prosecution of Joseph Stout. The reason for this is that for Hossack's case the "arguments for the Defense, by Messrs. [Joseph] Knox and [Isaac N.] Arnold who followed [U.S. District Attorney] Mr. [Henry S.] Fitch, were almost exclusively confined to a close and rigid examination of the testimony, and the discussion of certain technical objections." The pamphlet presents instead the arguments of E. C. Larned "in defense of Joseph Stout, the next of this series of cases," because it is "more general in its scope, and, from the comprehensive character of the topics discussed, of more permanent interest." The evidence in the two cases was basically the same. Additional testimony in the Stout case "is stated in the argument" of Larned (p. 160).

The testimony in this case focuses primarily on whether Hossack was involved in the rescue and whether Jim Gray was the slave of Phillipps. Phillipps and his sons testified as did Chief Justice John D. Caton of the Illinois Supreme Court. From this testimony, Hossack appears to be law-abiding, honest, hard-working, and successful. It shows that at one point in his life he refused to lease land he owned because the proposed tenant wanted to sell liquor on the premises. It is also clear that Hossack was actively involved in protesting the incarceration of Gray.

The argument by the U.S. district attorney is remarkable for its sarcastic nature and the ad hominem attacks he makes on Hossack, Hossack's attorneys, and all people opposed to slavery. The prosecution also spends a great deal of effort to link this case and the Fugitive Slave Act to such American heroes as Daniel Webster, Henry Clay, and George Washington. The arguments of Hossack's counsel (arguments made during the trial, the summation of Larned in *United States* v. *Stout,* and the argument for a new trial) are significant for their lack of emotion and political content. Hossack's lawyers base most of the defense on the technical requirements of the Fugitive Slave Act of 1850, other federal statutes, and the technicalities connected to any criminal indictment.

Unlike nearly all other fugitive slave cases, this case incudes no reference by the attorneys for the defense to the constitutionality of the act. This may be an indication that by this date antislavery attorneys realized that such arguments would get them nowhere and might alienate the bench. Instead of trying to embarrass the judge or attack the law, the attorneys in this case appear to have tried to build a case of sufficient strength to win an acquittal while granting the validity of the law.

This pamphlet is an important example of how ephemeral materials can supplement reported cases. To a bare case number and title with no date and no report, it adds a "phonographic" record of nearly everything that happened at Hossack's trial.

■ Hossack, John. Speech of John Hossack, convicted of a violation of the Fugitive Slave Law, before Judge Drummond, of the United States District Court, Chicago, Ill. New York, American Anti-Slavery Society, 1860. 12 p. (Anti-Slavery Tracts, no. 11, new series)

E449.A632, no. 11; E450.H82

After his conviction Hossack gave a short speech to Judge Drummond, explaining "why sentence should not be pronounced against" him (p. 1). Hossack describes his life, from his birth and boyhood in Scotland, to his migration to Quebec, to his ultimate settlement in Illinois. It is a patriotic statement, eloquently, if simply, arguing that abolition is a proper belief for all Americans. He declares:

> I first saw the light among the rugged but free hills of Scotland; a land, Sir, that never was conquered, and where a slave never breathed. Let a slave set foot on that shore, and his chains fall off for ever, and he becomes what God made him—a man. In this far off land, I heard of your free institutions, your prairie lands, your projected canals, and your growing towns. . . . I am, Sir, one of the pioneers of Illinois, who have gone through the many hardships of the settlement of the new country. I have spent upon it my best days, the strength of my manhood. . . . No living man, Sir, has greater interest in its welfare; and it is because I am opposed to carrying out wicked and ungodly laws, and love the freedom of my country, that I stand before you to-day. [pp. 4-5]

Unlike his attorneys, Hossack attacks the constitutionality of the Fugitive Slave Act. But he does so as a layman committed to freedom and abolition. He asks if the one provision of the Fugitive Slave Clause "transforms the Government into a monster of iniquity." He argues that it "violates both the letter and the spirit of the Constitution" because the Constitution is for a free people (p. 7). He refers to the preamble of the Constitution—"yes, Sir, *establish justice*"—the Declaration of Independence, the Founding Fathers, and the Bible (p. 6). He does not ask for mercy, as the jury has recommended, but argues that he should have no sentence pronounced against him because the Constitution supports freedom, justice, and liberty, and all he did in helping an alleged slave was to enforce the true meaning of the Constitution.

This pamphlet was printed by the American Anti-Slavery Society as part of the propaganda war against slavery. It adds a number of important details to the *Report of the Trial of John Hossack*, including the sentences that Hossack and Joseph Stout actually received.

■ Fitch, H. S. Argument of H. S. Fitch, Esq., United States District Attorney, on the Trial of John Hossack, Indicted for rescuing a fugitive slave from the United States deputy marshal, at Ottawa, Ill., Oct. 20, 1859; delivered in the United States District Court, in the Northern District of Illinois, Saturday, March 4, 1860. R. R. Hitt, Reporter. Chicago, Press & Tribune Book and Job Printing Office, 1860. 29 p.

Law Library

This pamphlet contains the final arguments to the jury of the prosecuting attorney in *United States* v. *Hossack*. The text is taken directly from the larger volume *Report of the Trial of John Hossack*, and, with the exception of the pagination, repeats exactly the text of pages 233−59 of the *Report*. It is apparent that the Chicago Press and Tribune Company printed the original *Report* with the expectation that the participating attorneys would want to purchase extra pamphlet editions of their own arguments.

Fitch's speech is a rather typical example of mid-nineteenth-century rhetoric. He begins by declaring, "I shall be brief. It is not my habit to make long speeches . . . " (p. 3). The rest of his "brief" talk takes up twenty-six printed pages. His actual speech was probably longer, because in a few places (pp. 9, 17, and 26) the text notes that Fitch read from various law books and reports of other cases. The argument is sprinkled with Latin phrases and references to or quotations from the Bible, the Founding Fathers, Henry Clay, Daniel Webster, Shakespeare, Molière, and Ben Johnson. The jury could not have doubted that Fitch was a learned man as well as a skilled prosecutor.

Fitch first offers the jury a summation of the evidence to prove the indictment. The evidence clearly shows that a slave named Jim escaped from his owner, Mr. Richard Phillipps of New Madrid, Missouri, and that Jim was later rescued from a jail at Ottawa, Illinois. There seems to be no doubt that Hossack was one of those responsible for the rescue.

But, proving that Hossack helped rescue a fugitive slave is only part of Fitch's task. More difficult no doubt was to convince a jury that such an act deserved punishment. To accomplish this Fitch had to dispute the morality and humanity of Hossack's act.

Throughout his argument Fitch is sarcastic and condescending toward Hossack. He equates rescuing a slave with stealing from the slave's owner. This is apparently an attempt to counter the traditional abolitionist contention that slaveholding was "manstealing." Fitch points out that Mr. Phillipps offered to sell the slave Jim for a thousand dollars. Fitch calculates that this would have merely required a fifty dollar donation from twenty abolitionists. "Think of it, gentlemen, a slave unfettered and no law broken—a brother ransomed and no authority insulted—a human being redeemed and no community disgraced, and all for fifty dollars." But, Fitch declares "such a course would have been inconsistent with the true spirit of fanaticism—a violation of all the well established rules of bigotry; besides, it would have been expensive, and Abolitionism seldom indulges in that kind of exercise." Fitch declares that Hossack and the other rescuers preferred "to season emancipation with a spice of larceny" and suggests that the "brute violence" of the rescue and the "principles of robbery" appealed to the rescuers. Hossack and his confederates are, in Fitch's view, "moral hypocrites and political prostitutes, [who] choose to proclaim their own shame and violate the Constitution" through "the dignity of a riot, by the valor of a mob" (p. 13).

Fitch also appeals to the prejudices of the jury. He refers to the fugitive slave as "the darkey" (p. 18). He asserts that only a craving for fame, "a morbid itch for notoriety," would lead men to rescue a fugitive slave. Fitch believes that Hossack acted only because of the support abolitionists received in other places. "Deprive these men [Hossack and his friends] of their half-witted admirers, their newspaper eulogies, their parade of counsel, and they would no sooner touch a negro than a lizzard" (p. 25).

Fitch ties Hossack's ideas and actions to his foreign birth, noting "Mr. Hossack belongs to this old guard of Abolitionists—a class of men not indigenous to the American soil" (p. 23). Somewhat inconsistently, he ties Hossack to William Lloyd Garrison and Wendell Phillips, the most extreme abolitionists in the nation (p. 25). The implications of these arguments are clear enough. Hossack is a foreigner with dangerous ideas who has teamed up with a group of notorious fanatics from the east coast.

Fitch argues that even Hossack's well known piety and Christian principles are suspect. "It has been conceded, I believe, that in all the relations of life he is an honest and honorable man; and he would not violate any injunction of the Decalogue—except the eighth commandment, and that only in reference to the southern people" (p. 25). Fitch argues that a good Christian must obey the laws of the land he lives in.

The outcome of this case shows that Fitch was partially successful. The jury convicted Hossack and in so doing asserted the importance of obeying the law. But, by recommending a lenient sentence (which the judge imposed) the jury showed that Hossack's motivations and goals were not inconsistent with those of his neighbors. By 1860 it seems that even in Illinois slavery and slave catchers could count on only the most minimal support from the general population.

United States v. *Gordon*

(C.C.N.D. Ohio 1861) (Unreported)

Gordon v. *United States*

U.S. Sup. Ct. 1862 (Cert. denied)

Rev. George Gordon was the antislavery president of Iberia College in Ohio. In May 1860 a slave owner from Kentucky attempted to seize Grandison Martin, an alleged fugitive slave then living in Iberia. A large crowd prevented the rendition of Martin, and the Reverend Gordon was indicted for leading this mob. In November 1861 Gordon was convicted of this crime and sentenced to serve six months in jail and to pay the costs of the prosecution plus a three-hundred-dollar fine. Gordon attempted to appeal this conviction to the U.S. Supreme Court, but that Court refused to hear the case on jurisdictional grounds "because the laws of the United States do not provide for such process in criminal cases" (Joliffe, *In the Matter of George Gordon's Petition*, p. 4). He therefore asked for a direct pardon from President Abraham Lincoln. On April 4, 1862, Lincoln granted this request. John Joliffe, a Cincinnati attorney and antislavery politician, argued Gordon's case in the petition to Lincoln.

■ Joliffe, John. In the matter of George Gordon's petition for pardon. John Joliffe, counsel for petitioner. Cincinnati, Gazette Company Steam Printing House, 1862. 56 p.

E450.G66

None of the cases surrounding Gordon's conviction was reported. Thus, this pamphlet provides most of the available information about Gordon's case. Joliffe's petition for pardon begins with a copy of the grand jury indictment and includes the original warrant for the arrest of the alleged slave Martin, the official notice of this indictment by the U.S. district attorney, and a copy of Lincoln's pardon.

Gordon did not apply for a pardon as a penitent. Rather, Joliffe asserted that Gordon ''CLAIMS a pardon exclusively upon the ground that the acts of Congress under which he is convicted are utterly null and void; because they are contrary to the Constitution of the United States'' (p. 4). Indeed, Joliffe argues that Gordon is so adamant about his right to a pardon on these grounds that the lawyer claims Gordon ''is NOT willing to receive a pardon upon any other ground. He makes no plea of penitence, no promise of amendment; he is not an applicant for mercy, —still less for favor. He does not wish the President, from any motive of pity or compassion, to pardon him at the expense of public justice, or of the Constitution of the United States; but, on the contrary thereof, he now claims pardon as a matter of RIGHT, and not as a favor'' (p. 4). Despite this principled stance, Gordon did in fact accept Lincoln's pardon, which asserted that the original ''sentence, though legal, was severe, and by his imprisonment and suffering he has atoned'' (p. iv).

The petition presented by Joliffe contains one of the most exhaustive examinations of the constitutionality of the Fugitive Slave Acts published at the time. Joliffe's first task is to show that under the Fugitive Slave Act of Sept. 18, 1850, ch. 60, 9 Stat. 462, the commissioners functioned in a judicial capacity. From this point he argues, as other antislavery lawyers did, that this was an unconstitutional delegation of power, because the commissioners were not appointed for life, given regular salaries, approved by the Senate, or in any other way chosen according to the procedures specified in Article III of the Constitution. Attorneys in other fugitive slave cases had made this point but usually based their entire argument on the statement in *Prigg* v. *Pennsylvania*, 41 U.S. (16 Pet.) 539 (1842), that the rendition process was judicial. Joliffe bases his argument on much more diverse sources. He cites more than twenty cases and a number of statutes and treatises to define a judicial procedure and then to show how that definition fits the rendition process.

While making his legal arguments, Joliffe is also aware of the political situation and of the circumstances created by the ongoing Civil War. He argues that if the act of 1850 is unconstitutional, then Gordon was acting patriotically when he opposed the law, ''at a time when the Constitution was trampled upon by thousands and tens of thousands of people; some by open warfare and others, less honorable and far more dangerous, by professing to support it while they were doing all that they could to secretly subvert it'' (p. 22).

Joliffe's second major point is that in the free states all people are presumed free. He supports this argument with a long series of citations from both the slave states and the free states. From this he argues that under the constitutional clause "*the claimant must prove his claim*" (p. 24). Thus, because the act of 1850 does not require the claimant to prove that the person arrested is in fact a slave owing service or labor in another state, and that he *escaped* from that state, Joliffe believes the law is unconstitutional. He supports this position by pointing out that the act requires no jury trial on these issues.

Finally, Joliffe states that the acts of 1793 and 1850 violate various sections of the U.S. Constitution. In an unusual constitutional argument, he asserts that the preamble to the Constitution is part of the nation's fundamental law, and a document designed "to secure the blessings of liberty" cannot support slavery (p. 52).

The last section of the petition for pardon rests primarily on arguments of natural and moral law, references to Magna Carta, the Constitution, and various other documents of first principles, and on political arguments. Joliffe asserts that in pardoning Gordon, Lincoln will "win for himself, as the Preserver of Magna Carta and Religious Liberty, imperishable renown." He urges Lincoln to "Seize, then, the glorious prize, while it is within your grasp, and secure to yourself the highest of all early honors—the honor of preserving the great charter of liberty, which, at Runnymeade . . . was wrung by the barons and people of England from King John" (p. 55).

$200 Reward.

RANAWAY from the subscriber, on the night of Thursday, the 30th of Sepember,

FIVE NEGRO SLAVES,

To-wit : one Negro man, his wife, and three children.

The man is a black negro, full height, very erect, his face a little thin. He is about forty years of age, and calls himself *Washington Reed*, and is known by the name of Washington. He is probably well dressed, possibly takes with him an ivory headed cane, and is of good address. Several of his teeth are gone.

Mary, his wife, is about thirty years of age, a bright mulatto woman, and quite stout and strong.

The oldest of the children is a boy, of the name of FIELDING, twelve years of age, a dark mulatto, with heavy eyelids. He probably wore a new cloth cap.

MATILDA, the second child, is a girl, six years of age, rather a dark mulatto, but a bright and smart looking child.

MALCOLM, the youngest, is a boy, four years old, a lighter mulatto than the last, and about equally as bright. He probably also wore a cloth cap. If examined, he will be found to have a swelling at the navel.

Washington and Mary have lived at or near St. Louis, with the subscriber, for about 15 years.

It is supposed that they are making their way to Chicago, and that a white man accompanies them, that they will travel chiefly at night, and most probably in a covered wagon.

A reward of $150 will be paid for their apprehension, so that I can get them, if taken within one hundred miles of St. Louis, and $200 if taken beyond that, and secured so that I can get them, and other reasonable additional charges, if delivered to the subscriber, or to THOMAS ALLEN, Esq., at St. Louis, Mo. The above negroes, for the last few years, have been in possession of Thomas Allen, Esq., of St. Louis.

WM. RUSSELL.

ST. LOUIS, Oct. 1, 1847.

Slave owners living in the border states always faced the possibility that their slaves would seek freedom. For Washington Reed and his family, liberty was just across the river, in Illinois. Southern Illinois, however, was never very friendly to blacks, and many slaves sought the safety of northern Illinois. Although still a relatively small town, Chicago in the late 1840s offered something of a safe haven for slaves who could reach it. Thus, the owner of the Reeds may have been correct in believing that Chicago was their destination. His assumption that a white man had helped them was probably the result of his racist notions, paranoia, and some factual possibilities. Most slave owners assumed that blacks were inferior to whites and thus could not escape on their own. They could only escape with help. Most Southerners also believed that there were far more abolitionists in the North than there actually were. Southerners were similarly, and mistakenly, prone to believe that all escapes were a result of abolitionist influence. Some slaves were aided by whites, particularly when they reached the free states, but this was by no means always the case.

Broadside Collection, Rare Book and Special Collections Division.

The just man shall be in eternal remembrance

Went to Prison for Teaching Colored Children.

Prudence Crandall (1803-1889). A Quaker schoolmistress from Connecticut, Crandall created an abolitionist cause célèbre when she opened her school to blacks in the face of violent local opposition. Connecticut passed a special law to prevent her school (and others like it, should any ever be built) from opening its doors to blacks from out of the state. Crandall defied this statute, but she was acquitted on technicalities. LC-USZ62-38166

Abolition and Abolitionists in the North

The pamphlets annotated in this section cover a variety of topics, all involving the activities of antislavery men and women in the Northern states. Some deal with opposition to slavery, whereas others concern actions against abolitionists by their neighbors.

Abolitionists were considered social radicals and outcasts. Most Northerners did not consider themselves to be abolitionists, and many Northerners despised those who did. Mob attacks on them were not uncommon, particularly in the 1830s. In addition to the Alton, Illinois, riots and the attacks on Prudence Crandall discussed in this section, there were riots in Cincinnati, Utica, New York City, Philadelphia, and Boston during that decade.

Crandall v. State

10 Conn. 339 (1834)

In 1832 Prudence Crandall, a young Quaker woman, opened a school for young ladies in the town of Canterbury, Connecticut. Crandall's school was designed to provide education beyond grammer school for girls whose families could afford the modest tuition. Encouraged by leaders of the community, she invested all of her own resources, and borrowed additional money as well to purchase a large house to serve as the school.

A few months after the school opened, Crandall admitted a black girl who was a graduate of the Canterbury schools and a member of the local church. However, a number of the patrons of the school objected to admitting black students, and the parents threatened to withdraw their children if Crandall continued this policy. Crandall responded by advertising that at the next term she would admit black students—and whites if they wished—into her school.

Town meetings were called to protest Crandall's position. In addition, when between fifteen and twenty black pupils arrived at the school, there were attempts to close the school through intimidation, violence, and threats of vagrancy prosecutions. Despite the refusal of village stores to sell products to Crandall, various minor attacks on the house, and excrement thrown in the school's well, Crandall's school remained open.

At this point the town officials turned to the legislature. In 1833 the Connecticut legislature passed a statute innocuously called "An Act for the Admission and Settlement of Inhabitants in Towns," May 24, 1833, ch. 9, 1833 Conn. Pub. Acts 420. This law prohibited the establishment of any schools "for the instruction or education of colored persons, who are not inhabitants of this State" without the permission of the civil authorities in the town where the school was to be set up.

In August 1833 Crandall was tried under this act. Because the jury could not agree on the verdict, the case was continued until the December session of the county court. During the October session of the superior court, however, the county prosecutor filed an information against Crandall, and she was tried in this court. David Daggett, who was chief justice of the Supreme Court of Connecticut, presided over this superior court case. Daggett instructed the jury that blacks were not citizens of the United States and therefore could not claim the protections of the U.S. Constitution. On the strength of this charge, Crandall was convicted. She immediately appealed to the Supreme Court of Connecticut.

In their arguments before the supreme court, Crandall's attorneys carefully avoided raising any technical objections to the information under which Crandall was tried or to any court procedure. The penalty for violating the statute was only a one-hundred-dollar fine. Crandall and her supporters were willing to risk paying this fine for a chance to get the law declared unconstitutional.

Despite the constitutional nature of the appeal, the court reversed Crandall's conviction on technical grounds. The court found the information to be insufficient because it did not set down all of the pertinent facts. Chief Justice Daggett dissented from this decision (and supported the earlier conviction he had presided over) on the grounds that the court could not decide an appeal on the basis of some error not alleged by the party appealing the case. However, for the majority of the court, this reversal on technical grounds allowed the court to dispose of an embrarrassing and potentially politically damaging case without reaching the constitutional (and political) issues.

In 1838 the legislature repealed the law under which Crandall was prosecuted, Act of May 31, 1838, ch. 34, 1838 Conn. Pub. Acts 30.

■ Crandall, Prudence, *plaintiff*. Report of the arguments of counsel, in the case of Prudence Crandall, plff. in error, vs. State of Connecticut, before the Supreme Court of Errors, at their session, at Brooklyn, July term, 1834, by a member of the bar. Boston, Garrison & Knapp, 1834. 34 p.

This pamphlet contains the arguments of counsel for both sides in Prudence Crandall's case. It was published by William Lloyd Garrison and Isaac Knapp, the abolitionist publishers (Garrison was also the editor) of the nation's foremost antislavery newspaper, the *Liberator*. About 75 percent of this pamphlet is devoted to arguments of the attorneys representing Crandall. Although most of the prosecution's arguments are the same as those published with the official report of the case, the arguments of Crandall's lawyers are greatly expanded here. It appears that Garrison and Knapp published these arguments to ensure their wider circulation and perhaps to allow them to be used by attorneys in other jurisdictions.

On behalf of Crandall, William W. Ellsworth argued that as citizens of other states, black school children had a right under the U. S. Constitution to attend school in Connecticut. He asserted if the children "were white, it is conceded they would be" allowed into the state (p.6). The whole question thus turned on color or race. But, Ellsworth argued, "A distinction founded in *color*, in fundamental rights, is *novel, inconvenient* and *impracticable*. Hitherto we have seen no such distinction: none in the ancient common law of England . . . none in that immortal instrument which our republican fathers put forth as the groundwork of all just government—the Declaration of our Independence," which declared, as he points out, that "all men are created *equal*" (p. 6).

Ellsworth went on to note that blacks had fought in the revolutionary armies and served their country in other ways. He observed that a survey of the constitutions of New York, Pennsylvania, Massachusetts, and other states, as well as the U. S. Constitution, revealed no clear distinctions based on color. He argued that the U. S. Congress supported the citizenship of free blacks when it required the territorial legislature of Missouri to remove from the proposed state constitution a clause that would have prohibited the migration or immigration of free blacks.

According to Ellsworth, if voting were a test of citizenship, then it was clear many free blacks could vote and therefore were citizens. However, he also suggests that voting might not be a test of citizenship, because many people, such as white women and children or those who lacked property qualifications, were citizens but could not vote. Thus, blacks from Connecticut and other states who could not vote might nevertheless be citizens. Ellsworth urges that a clear distinction exists between slaves and free blacks and that the black children who come to Connecticut for schooling are all free.

Finally, he concludes with a discussion of the Privileges and Immunities Clause of the U.S. Constitution. He declares that the statute *"is a repeal of the constitution"* because it attempts to deny rights to citizens of other states and because it unconstitutionally attempts to limit citizenship (p. 14).

Although the statute under which Crandall was convicted did not deal directly with slavery, it was still impossible to separate this case from the peculiar institution. Crandall's counsel tells the court, "we owe a debt to the colored population of this country, which we can never pay,—no, *never, never,* unless we can call back oceans of tears, and all the groans and agonies of the middle passage, and the thousands and millions of human beings, whom we have sent, and are sending, ignorant, debased and undone, to eternity" (p. 12). Later he notes that the law under consideration has a "connection with the subject of slavery, —that greatest curse and blight upon our country, and the greatest wrong ever done in our world." The law is "a most wanton and uncalled for attack upon our colored population," which compares unfavorably with "the moral example of England in her late act of emancipation" (p. 15).

Despite these references to slavery and morality, Ellsworth avoids the arguments based on natural law, the higher law, and moral justice that were used by most abolitionist attorneys. He does not try to shame the court into reaching a decision in favor of his client. But neither does he want to win on a legal technicality, although that is in fact how the court ultimately decided the case. Ellsworth takes the position that the "law is not denied for its impolicy," or immorality, "but for its *unconstitutionality*" (p. 15).

In his argument on behalf of the state, Andrew T. Judson raises the specter that "people may be driven away from their homes" if this law is not held constitutional (p. 15). He attempts to answer Ellsworth's constitutional arguments by asserting that the law is within the police powers of the state. He argues that schools are an issue of local concern, and thus the national government cannot interfere in them. He does not directly face Ellsworth's contention that if free blacks are citizens of some states then they must be granted the privileges and immunities of citizenship in other states. Rather he argues that the law deals solely with an educational issue. He also argues that blacks are not citizens of any state.

Judson supports his positions by essentially racist arguments, declaring that the state and boards of education may "exclude them [black schoolchildren] as a dangerous and destructive population'' (p. 16). People who believe blacks are citizens under the U.S. Constitution are "madmen," he says (p. 17), maintaining that it would have been odd for the Founding Fathers to "hold one portion of a *race of men* in bondage, while the other portion were made *citizens!*" This would have been a "strange inconsistency" (p. 18). The only way to make sense out of a constitution written by slaveholders is, according to Judson, to assume that no blacks were meant to be citizens. Judson concludes by arguing that "patriotism and love of country" do not dictate extending privileges and immunities to the black citizens of other states. He asks if Americans "shall surrender the country purchased by the blood of our fathers, up to another race of men." Judson thinks they should not, because "America is ours—it belongs to a race of white men, the descendants of those who first redeemed the wilderness" (p. 22).

The closing arguments, by Calvin Goddard for Crandall and Chauncey F. Cleveland for the state, reflect the two opening arguments. Neither was published with the original case in the *Connecticut Reports*, but this pamphlet provides them in addition to the more complete arguments of Ellsworth and Judson. The pamphlet ends with a note on the court's decision and a copy of the information originally filed by the prosecutor in the superior court.

State v. *Storrs*

(Northfield [N.H.] J. P. Ct. 1835) (Unreported)

George Storrs was a Methodist minister from Concord, New Hampshire, who was active in the antislavery movement. In 1835 the Anti-Slavery Society of Sandbornton and Northfield invited Storrs to preach and lecture in those two New Hampshire towns. On Sunday, December 13, 1835, Storrs was the guest minister at the Methodist Meeting House in Sandbornton Bridge. The next day he was to lecture in Northfield, but two town selectmen visited Storrs beforehand and asked him not to speak because they predicted his speech would incite a riot. They warned that if this occurred they would hold Storrs responsible. Storrs answered that it was "very strange that I should be held responsible for the doings of a mob, while I was only in the exercise of a constitutional right: I remarked that if I did or said anything unconstitutional the law was open, let me suffer for it." Storrs further asserted that he had been invited by the Anti-Slavery Society, "and for the time, I was their servant, if *they* chose *not* to have the lecture, I should acquiesce" (Storrs, *Mob, Under Pretence of Law*, p. 5).

Later that day Storrs began his lecture with "select portions of scripture" which denounced slavery (p. 6). Storrs then began a public prayer, which asked God to intervene on behalf of the president of the United States, the Congress, and various classes of men, including slaves. In the middle of his prayer for slaves, Storrs was arrested by a deputy sheriff on a warrant charging him "as a *vagrant* and an *idler* " (p. 6). This warrant was signed by Justice of the Peace Nathan Wells. Earlier that day Wells, in his capacity as town selectman, had attempted to dissuade Storrs from speaking. When Storrs was taken from the meeting hall he was greeted by an angry mob, which dispersed only on orders of the sheriff. An arresting officer told Storrs that "this is very unpleasant, but there was no other way to prevent a mob," except by arresting the speaker (p. 8). During the arrest one of the abolitionists in the audience, who was also a lawyer, attempted "to read the law relating to the disturbance of religious meetings," while pointing out that Storrs was praying at the time of the arrest. The sheriff "cried out, 'I care nothing about your law,' " and the arrest was made (p. 7).

Before Justice of the Peace Wells, Storrs was charged with being "an idle person and disorderly person, and wanton and lascivious in speech and behaviour, a common railer and brawler," who "neglects any lawful employment, and mispends his time going about . . . disturbing the public peace" (p. 9). This rather elaborate charge flew in the face of Storr's profession as a minister and was belied by his ability to post a $20 bond at this hearing. Storrs was thus free on bond and able to prepare for his trial later in the week.

At the trial the prosecution attempted to show that Storrs had no useful employment. Witnesses affirmed that he had been assigned to the Henniker, New Hampshire, circuit by his bishop, but that in fact he had never preached in that circuit. Rather, Storrs spent all of his time speaking at antislavery meetings and organizing abolitionist societies in New Hampshire. The prosecution failed, however, to show that Storrs was a troublemaker. Witnesses would not confirm that he had plotted to distribute incendiary literature or that he was a professional agitator. The prosecution could only show that Storrs was invited into New Hampshire communities by residents of these places and that often the residents were respectable citizens. Witnesses denied that Storrs lectured for fees or that he solicited public collections.

Storrs acted as his own attorney with great success. His cross-examinations undermined the prosecution by showing that many of the allegations against him were false. One prosecution witness, for example, declared that Storrs "expressed something about blacks, bought and sold like cattle in the market—and that they were very degraded—denied the Bible, and religious privileges." This testimony implied that Storrs was railing against slavery and perhaps asking for a violent end to the institution. On cross-examination, however, the witness agreed that Storrs did "pray that the slaves might be quiet, patient, and not *avenge themselves*" (p. 18). With such cross-examination, Storrs was able to prove his innocence.

When the prosecution closed its case, Storrs rose and declared: "I shall make no defence at *this time*. I am ready to hear the sentence of the Court." The judge immediately declared "that the Prisoner ought to be discharged," and at this point the case ended (p. 18). Two days later Storrs was in Bradford, New Hampshire, where the threat of mob action and lynch law was once again made. Storrs fearlessly spoke despite attempts to break into the meeting hall. No riot took place, and after the meeting Storrs "passed out through the mob" with a local minister, "without any other molestation than a little of the serpentine hissing." A second meeting took place without interruption because it was held on top of a steep hill "and the mobites had gotten their legs weakened by rum so as to make it difficult to climb" (p. 24).

■ Storrs, George. Mob, under pretence of law, or, the arrest and trial of Rev. George Storrs at Northfield, N. H., with circumstances connected with that affair and remarks thereon. Concord, Elbridge G. Chase, printer, 1835. 24 p.

E449.S885

Storrs was just one of many abolitionists who were threatened by mobs made up of "Gentlemen of Property and Standing." In the small towns of Ohio, New York, and New England, as well as in such cities as Cincinnati, Boston, Philadelphia, and New York, abolitionists were often harrassed, threatened, and sometimes physically harmed. The arrest and trial of George Storrs indicates that local authorities were willing to use the legal system to suppress abolitionists. This is not particularly surprising, since prosecutions of dissidents have often been initiated as a way of intimidating people with unpopular ideas.

Why Northerners feared abolitionists is a difficult question. Simple (and simplistic) explanations are (1) that abolitionists threatened the status quo, and thus undermined harmony in communities; (2) that abolitionists were viewed as troublemakers; (3) that the pervasive Negrophobia in the North led to attacks on abolitionists there; or (4) that Northerners feared the abolitionists would destroy the harmony of the Union and offend Southerners over issues (slavery and the rights of blacks) most Northerners preferred not to think about. More detailed analyses of this question can be seen in Gilbert Hobbs Barnes, *The Antislavery Impulse* (Washington: American Historical Association, 1933); Leonard L. Richards, *"Gentlemen of Property and Standing"*:

Anti-Abolition Mobs in Jacksonian America (New York: Oxford University Press, 1970); and Michael Feldberg, *The Turbulent Era: Riot and Disorder in Jacksonian America* (New York: Oxford University Press, 1980).

Storrs used his trial to publicize his cause. In doing this he was able to tie antislavery to the cherished American values of freedom of speech and freedom of religion. In his preface Storrs asserted that his arrest "reminds one of the scenes of by-gone days in Massachusetts, —about the middle and near the close of the seventeenth century, ere the fires of persecution had quite gone out, or at least while the spirit that enkindled them was yet in existence and in power." He tied this reference to the Salem Witch Trials directly to the American Revolution and the values of the new nation. "It is a melancholy proof that unhallowed opposition to moral good, to constitutional rights, may exist amidst the light of the nineteenth century, and in this boasted land of freedom. Yes, the rights so dearly purchased and so nobly maintained by our fathers, are now wrested from their sons by the hand of violence under the pretended sanctions of law! . . . Has it come to this?" he asked, even "while so many veterans of the revolution yet remain among us,—even while the last sun of these venerable men yet lingers above the horizon, the rich inheritance they have bequeathed to their country and their descendants, is trampled upon as a thing of little value?" (p. 3).

Besides the theme of constitutional rights, Storrs stressed two others in presenting his record of the trial. First, he directly tied his cause of antislavery to the cause of temperance. He notes in the pamphlet that one of the members of the mob drank himself to death and that many members of the mobs he faced were drunk (p. 9). He also sarcastically asked "the High Sheriff, whether, if it is probable that many abolitionists are to be arrested, as they are temperance men, he [the sheriff] cannot accommodate us with some Deputies whose *breath* is not so exceedingly offensive with RUM—especially if they are to be sent into the holy sanctuary to take us from our knees, while in the pulpit engaged in prayer" (p. 8).

The theme of temperance ties directly into his most important point: that abolitionists are fundamentally religious men, engaged in Christian activities. Throughout the pamphlet he stresses the religious nature of his activities and how the sheriff interrupted them. He provides a transcript of the proceedings of his trial. Much of his cross-examination of witnesses concerns the content of his sermons and prayers and his relationship to the church. At the end of this section of the pamphlet Storrs directs a few questions to "the public" on the propriety of New Hampshire's spending tax dollars on prosecutions such as his. Then Storrs directs "a few words to my *Christian* friends in particular" (p.

19). He asks these readers to "pray for them, pity them," who "have outraged our rights," because "they know not what they do." At the same time he declares there is a "perfect agreement of the *principles* of *abolition* with the Bible" (p. 20).

This pamphlet is the only existing printed record of this trial. Storr's arrest and trial were doubtless more of a help than a hindrance to the cause of antislavery for they allowed Storrs to publicize the outrages committed against him and at the same time to directly tie antislavery to constitutional freedoms, temperance, and religion.

State v. Gilman

(Alton |Ill.| Mun. Ct. 1838) (Unreported)*

Rev. Elijah P. Lovejoy was a Presbyterian minister and the editor of the *Observer*, a religious paper in St. Louis, Missouri. In 1835 and 1836 he began to attack slavery and Catholicism in his paper. By 1836 his increasingly harsh attacks on slavery aroused such strong public sentiment against him that he was forced to leave St. Louis. He moved his paper to the free state of Illinois and began publishing the *Alton Observer*.

By this time Lovejoy had become a committed antislavery activist. He helped organize an antislavery society in Illinois and turned his newspaper into an antislavery organ. Twice mobs destroyed his press in Alton. These mobs included ruffians from St. Louis. The St. Louis newspapers attacked Lovejoy and hinted that commerce between the South and Illinois (or at least Alton) would be seriously hurt if Lovejoy's press continued to function. The Illinois legislature and public officials urged Lovejoy to tone down his attacks on slavery or cease them altogether, but Lovejoy refused to be intimidated and ordered another press. This time Lovejoy let it be known that he and his friends would defend the press, with weapons if necessary.

On November 7, 1837, a mob attacked the warehouse containing Lovejoy's new press. Although Lovejoy and his allies asked for police protection, it was not supplied. The mayor of Alton did indicate, however, that Lovejoy could legally defend his own property. When the mob first attacked the warehouse, about fourteen men were inside. They fired on the mob and killed one member of it. The mob then retreated and sent the mayor of the town, John Krum, to talk with Lovejoy. The mob offered to disperse if Lovejoy and Gilman (the owner of the

---

*The Alton Trials

warehouse) would surrender the press. If not, the mob threatened to burn down or blow up the warehouse. Lovejoy refused to surrender his press, and a final assault was made on the stone warehouse. A ladder was placed against it, and men with torches climbed up to ignite the roof. Lovejoy went on to the roof with a weapon, and he was hit by five bullets. He died a few minutes later. The fire was then put out, and the press was thrown from a third-floor window and methodically destroyed.

In January 1838, a grand jury met to investigate the events of the previous November. From the beginning, officials in Alton had been extremely unsympathetic to Lovejoy. Nevertheless, it came as a shock to many when the city prosecutor asked the grand jury to indict Lovejoy's compatriots on a charge of riot for their defense of the press. Despite the irony of this situation, Winthrop S. Gilman, the owner of the warehouse, and eleven other men who had helped Lovejoy were indicted. The same grand jury also indicted eleven men for attacking the warehouse. The indictment of Gilman and the other eleven men from inside the warehouse encompassed everyone who had stayed to defend Lovejoy. The eleven indictments of the rioters, on the other hand, constituted only a small fraction of those who attacked the warehouse. More important, although the men who shot and killed Lovejoy were known, no one was indicted for murder.

Gilman and his codefendants were tried on January 16 and 17, 1838, before Judge William Martin. The trial was short, and it took the jury just fifteen minutes to acquit the defendants. On the nineteenth the trial of the attackers began, again before Judge Martin. This time the trial took less than a day to complete, but the jury deliberated overnight before acquitting those indicted for attacking the warehouse and destroying the press.

■ Alton trials: of Winthrop S. Gilman, who was indicted . . . for the crime of riot . . . written out from notes of the trial taken at the time by a member of the bar of Alton Municipal Court; also the trial of John Solomon . . . indicted . . . for a riot committed in Alton . . . written out from notes taken at the time of trial by William S. Lincoln. New York, John F. Trow, 1838. 158 p.
KF223.G5A7 1838 LLRBR

——[Reprint] Miami, Mnemosyne Pub. Co. [1969]
KF223.G5A7 1969

——[Reprint] [New York] Arno [1970]
KF223.G5A7 1970

The riot at Alton created the first martyr for the American anti-slavery movement. The antislavery society in New York commissioned Lovejoy's brothers to write a sympathetic memoir of him, and his brother Owen Lovejoy was propelled into a long and successful career in antislavery and Republican party politics. Throughout the 1830s, stationery, banners, papers, handouts, and other abolitionist propaganda used the slogan of Lovejoy—"the first MARTYR to American LIBERTY." In Boston, Wendell Phillips, a Brahmin lawyer, made his first abolitionist speech to decry the murder of Lovejoy. Lovejoy's death brought many others into the antislavery movement. More importantly, it made many Northerners sympathetic to the antislavery cause because it allowed abolitionists to link their crusade with civil liberties and constitutional rights for all men in the North. ·

The *Alton Trials* text states that this account was published because of the "deep and intense interest, throughout our whole country" in "the disgraceful and murderous affair at Alton, Illinois." The author of *Alton Trials* believed that two events had "increased the feeling, and created a great desire in the public to know the facts of the case." These events were the indictment of those who had helped Lovejoy defend his press and the acquittal of those members of the mob indicted for attacking the press. According to the publisher, the "publication of these trials has been loudly called for through several public journals" (p. 3).

The first eighty pages of the volume deal with the trial of Gilman and his associates. The remaining pages contain the record of the trial of the mob. Both records contain copies of the indictments, lists of jurors, arguments of counsel, and testimony of witnesses. Both trials appear to have been rather unsophisticated.

In Gilman's trial, jurors question witnesses, and in the second trial, one attorney for the defense offers an elaborate argument on a technical point of law, and another defense attorney declares, "I don't myself see any great force in the demurrer" (p. 87). Perhaps the most curious aspect of these cases concerns U. F. Linder, who is first identified as the attorney general (which he was not) (p. 5). In Gilman's trial Linder is part of the prosecution. He attempts in that case to convict Gilman for his defense of the press and the warehouse. In the trial of the mob, however, Linder appears as a private attorney, defending the mob. The city attorney, B. F. Murdock, on the other hand, prosecutes both cases.

In summation for the prosecution in Gilman's case, Linder attempts to tie Gilman to abolition and to play on the jury's fears and racial prejudice. He declares Gilman "violated the laws of man and God . . . for . . . a printing press! A press brought here to teach rebellion and insurrection to the slave; to excite servile war; to preach murder in the name of religion; to strike dismay to the hearts of the people, and spread desolation over the face of the land" (pp. 76–77).

In his defense of the rioters in the second trial, however, Linder avoids appeals to passion. Instead, he argues the evidence does not prove every specific item in the indictment. The prosecutor in the second case declares: "I am no abolitionist." But, he argues, "lawless acts of an unprincipled, an infuriated, a licentious mob" must be stopped (p. 156). Otherwise, the acts against Lovejoy and Gilman will soon be perpetrated on nonabolitionist citizens. He states that the destruction of the press is an attack on the constitution itself, which protects a free press. Despite the prosecution's passionate pleas, the jurors in both cases acquitted the defendants.

The death of Lovejoy and the destruction of his press made Alton a symbol of lawless violence. For many Northerners it also symbolized the threat of slavery and what first abolitionists and then Republicans would call the "Slave Power Conspiracy." The trials recorded in this volume were an anticlimax to the affair. It is likely that the jurors, all citizens of Alton, simply wanted to end the matter as quickly as possible. Their town had been disgraced and its reputation ruined. The acquittals may reflect a desire on the part of the citizens to remove any reason for further actions or appeals. Unfortunately, if this was the motivation of the jurors, it failed, for this volume was published because the acquittal of those who attacked Lovejoy was so clearly inconsistent with justice.

State v. *Post; State* v. *Van Beuren*

20 N.J. Law (1 Spencer) 368 (1845)

State v. *Post; State* v. *Van Beuren*

21 N.J. Law (1 Zab.) 699 (1848)

In 1844 the state of New Jersey ratified a new constitution. Article I, section 1, of that document asserted that: "All men are by nature free and independent, and have certain natural and unalienable rights, among which are those of enjoying and defending life and liberty, acquiring, possessing, and protecting property, and of pursuing and obtaining safety and happiness" (Stewart, *A Legal Argument*, p. 6).

At the time this constitution went into effect seven hundred to one thousand slaves were living in New Jersey. These slaves were all born before the passage of the New Jersey gradual emancipation statute of 1804. In addition, perhaps as many as three thousand children of

Alvan Stewart (1790-1849). A New York lawyer, Stewart advocated the radical theory that the Constitution was fundamentally antislavery. He believed that the Fifth Amendment gave the federal government the power to end slavery anywhere in the nation. Ironically, Chief Justice Taney would assert, in *Dred Scott* v. *Sandford,* that the same amendment protected slave property in the territories. In 1845 Stewart tried to apply his theories to the New Jersey Constitution, but the supreme court of that state, in *State* v. *Van Beuren* and *State* v. *Post,* rejected his arguments.
    Engraving by A. H. Ritchie. LC-USZ62-73263

slaves were living in New Jersey and held in indentured servitude under the 1804 act. Under that act, which was reaffirmed in 1820, the sons of slaves born after 1804 would remain servants until age twenty-five, and the daughters would be servants until age twenty-one (1820 N.J. Laws 679).

    In 1844 two slaves owned by John A. Post and the daughter of a slave indentured to Edward Van Beuren applied for writs of habeas corpus to test the status of slavery under the new constitution. Because this was a habeas corpus proceeding, the blacks were nominally represented by the State of New Jersey—thus the case is styled *State* v. *Post and State* v. *Van Beuren*. In fact, all three blacks were represented by the New York abolitionist attorney Alvan Stewart.

Before the New Jersey Supreme Court Stewart argued that the statement that "all men are by nature free and independent" implied that all people in the state of New Jersey must be free. In a three-to-one decision (with Chief Justice Joseph C. Hornblower dissenting), the court held that the constitution did not end slavery. The court asserted that all rights of man "must be understood in a modified sense according to the nature, the condition and laws of the society to which they belong" and that "Authority and subordination are essential under every form of civil society." With this analysis the court concluded that slavery was possible under the New Jersey Constitution, just as it was under the Declaration of Independence or the constitution of Virginia, which contained a similar clause, 20 N.J. Law (1 Spencer) 374, 375-76.

Slavery continued to exist in New Jersey until 1846, when all remaining slaves became indentured servants for life, 1846 N.J. Rev. Stat. 382. As indentured servants they had more rights than they had as slaves, but they were still not entirely free.

■ Stewart, Alvan. Legal argument before the Supreme Court of the State of New Jersey, at the May term, 1845, at Trenton, for the deliverance of four thousand persons from bondage. New York, Finch & Weed, 1845. 52 p.

Law Library; E449.S85

The proceedings in these two cases were initiated by the abolitionist Alvan Stewart, a highly successful lawyer from Utica, New York, whose professional fame came from his great ability to sway a jury. In 1835 Stewart helped organize the New York State Anti-Slavery Society. Two years later, in a speech before the society, he argued that slavery was unconstitutional because it violated the due process clause of the U.S. Constitution.

This position was considered a heresy by most abolitionists, who had been arguing that slavery was supported by the Constitution, which William Lloyd Garrison referred to as a "Covenant with Death." Stewart nevertheless continued to argue that slavery should be opposed through legal and constitutional means. He also argued that abolitionists should participate in electoral politics. In 1840 Stewart helped organize the Liberty party and was its candidate for the New York governorship.

Stewart's arguments before the New Jersey Supreme Court in

State v. *Post* and *State* v. *Van Beuren* reflect his constitutional and political philosophy. Through these cases, which concerned two slaves and one indentured servant, he hoped to rid New Jersey of the last vestiges of slavery in one court action. His argument is an amazing combination of history, morality, law, politics, philosophy, and constitutional analysis. He begins by asking ''the kind consideration of this Court, while he endeavored to break into a new, and almost uncultivated region, to explore and investigate the long neglected rights of man to his own body and soul'' (p. 6). Stewart asked the judges to imagine

> that glorious day, when the lion and the lamb shall lie down together? that day when the law, with its mercy, shall be extended to all, when none shall be so powerful as to override its injunctions, none so *low* as to fall beneath its merciful protection, defending all in their possessions: the rich man in his castle, the poor man in his liberty, and the value of his labor, whether in the wilderness, or the city, on the highway or in the closet; let this law of liberty brace the strong man on his journey, and its precious breathings fill the lungs of the infant in the cradle. [pp. 7-8]

This idealistic beginning was followed by a history of the development of Christianity, the founding of America, and the history of slavery in the Americas. Stewart verbally paints a picture for the justices of two ships headed for America. The first contains ''great and good men. Justice, mercy, humanity, respect for the rights of all; each man honored, as he was useful to himself and others . . . the good genius of America.'' This was the *Mayflower*, headed for Plymouth. The second ship is sinister, as ''if freighted with the elements of unmixed evil, hark! hear those rattling chains, hear that cry of despair . . . Listen to those shocking oaths, the crack of that flesh-cutting whip. Ah! it is the first cargo of slaves on their way to Jamestown, Virginia.'' One ship is ''a Parent, one of the prosperous labor-honoring, law-sustaining institutions of the North; the other the Mother of slavery, idleness, lynch-law, ignorance, unpaid labor, poverty, and duelling, despotism, the ceaseless swing of the whip, and the peculiar institutions of the South'' (p. 9).

Stewart asks the judges of the New Jersey court which side, in the conflict between good and evil, they wish to be on. But he does not expect them to choose solely on the basis of appeals to morality, religion, or history. He cites *Somerset* v. *Stewart*, 98 Eng. Rep. 499 (K.B. 1772), and the history of villenage in English law to show that slavery lacks solid legal support. He anticipates the argument that slavery is protected by the law of nations and asks, ''What was this law of Nations? That Christendom had a common right to plunder, burn, murder, enslave irredeemably, and make property of the inhabitants of that ill-fated continent [Africa], in and through all coming generations of their posterity. A *law of Nations!* that all law, justice, mercy, humanity, should be suspended, as to one quarter of the globe; a *law of Nations*, that piracy, murder, fraud, arson, kidnapping, ravishment and stealing, should be considered lawful'' (p. 15). Besides *Somerset* he points to acts of Congress and committee reports dealing with the African slave trade to show that in fact U.S. law opposes slavery. Citing Chief Justice Lemuel Shaw of the Massachusetts Supreme Judicial Court in the *Aves* case, Stewart argues that slavery is illegal in New Jersey just as it is in Massachusetts. He notes that the ''free and equal'' clauses of both states' constitutions are similar.

This legal argument is backed up with references to the Ten Commandments and the Exodus story. That in turn is supported by his old argument that the due process clause of the Fifth Amendment makes slavery illegal in the United States. Stewart concludes his opening argument, which took an entire day, by urging ''this Honorable Court to share in the unfading glory of opening this castle of slavery, New Jersey, with the key of the new Constitution and the other keys he had the honor to submit to this Court, by which to let the oppressed men go free'' (p. 45).

The next day, after arguments for Post and Van Beuren were heard, Stewart gave a four-and-one-half-hour summation. He again urges that the clause in the new constitution ends slavery in New Jersey. He notes that attorneys for the other side argued the clause was ''a mere braggadocio, a mere telling England that all men are free and independent by nature, and it is *so* said, to let England know that our people *know* that we are as good as her Lords and Commons, Kings and Queens.'' But, Stewart logically argues, why say this in 1844, ''when all danger is forever passed,'' especially since New Jersey had not written such language into the state constitution of 1776, when it would have meant something (p. 47). Stewart believes it is because the 1844 constitution was meant to accomplish the abolition of slavery in the state.

Stewart ends his summation with a plea for liberty and freedom. The pamphlet contains reporters' notes as well as Stewart's. One of the reporters states that at the end of his closing statement the ''scene was quite impressive. The auditory was numerous and highly respectable, and such was the impressiveness with which the closing appeal of the advocate for freedom was delivered, that no one seemed to like to be the first to speak to break the spell his eloquence had cast upon the assembly. At length, the Bench arose, the Chief Justice adjourned the Court'' (p. 52).

Stewart published this pamphlet ''to meet [the] desire'' of some men to read it in full and to ''contribute a single mite to the deliverance of my countrymen from Slavery'' (p. 4). For, despite the power of his forensics, he was unable to convince the judges of the New Jersey court to end slavery.

John Brown (1800-1859). On October 16, 1859, John Brown led twenty-two
armed men into Harpers Ferry on a raid intended to free the slaves of Virginia.
Portrait from *The Life, Trials, and Execution of Capt. John Brown* (New York,
1859), the first published account of his life and trial.

Abolitionists in the South

Next to slave revolts, slave owners feared abolitionists most. They believed abolitionists had organized to subvert their system from within, as well as to overthrow it from without, and had come to the South to encourage slaves to run away or revolt. There was no organized conspiracy to do this, and most antislavery leaders and organizations tried to allay fears by openly disavowing any agitations directed at slaves. The Garrisonians were also pacifists and consequently opposed any violent actions, including slave revolts. Other groups and leaders realized that activities in the South would be dangerous and for the most part futile.

Nevertheless, some abolitionists did go into the South to help slaves escape and, in the unique case of John Brown's raid at Harper's Ferry, Virginia, to lead a slave revolt. Some whites and blacks (most notably Harriet Tubman) organized forays into the South and helped slaves escape from bondage. As the materials annotated in this section indicate, a number of whites aided slaves in a less organized fashion, and they were caught in the act.

The punishments of these whites—particularly the branding of Jonathan Walker—were exploited by abolitionists in the North to expose the cruelties and danger of slavery even for whites. They also underscored the persistent claim by abolitionists that slavery and liberty were incompatible in the Union—that slavery would ultimately destroy all freedoms and rights. The proceedings described in these trials were used to support this position. Finally, the prosecutions and incarcerations of whites served as a propaganda vehicle for the antislavery movement.

It was possible to sell pamphlets, raise funds, and bring people into the antislavery movement through discussing cases such as those annotated in this section. It is therefore not surprising that many of these pamphlets were printed by individual abolitionists or abolitionist organizations. Selling a pamphlet on the case of Thomas Brown, Jonathan Walker, or Daniel Drayton accomplished a great many things for the antislavery movement. Such a pamphlet might raise money for the white victim of slavery or his family, educate the North about the evils and dangers of slavery, and attract new people to the movement.

Maryland v. *Gruber*

(Frederick Cty. [Md.] Ct. 1819) (Unreported)

In 1818 Jacob Gruber, an elder in the Methodist Church from Pennsylvania, attended a revival in Washington County, Maryland. When a scheduled speaker became ill, Gruber was obliged to give a sermon to a crowd of about three thousand whites and five hundred slaves and free blacks. Gruber spoke on the text from Proverbs: "Righteousness exalteth a nation, but sin is a reproach to any people."

In the sermon he "dwelt considerably on the sin of infidelity" and other ungodly activities and discussed slavery as a national sin. Gruber "contended that involuntary negro slavery was a violation of the moral and natural law, and a gross abuse of christianity; that it was in violation of the sentiments expressed by the American sages, in the declaration of independence; that it was reproachful to this nation to hold that sacred instrument in one hand, and a rod stained with blood in the other. He spoke of the cruelty of advertising and selling human beings, mixed with cattle" (*Trial of the Rev. Jacob Gruber,* p. 48). That Gruber spoke so strongly should have come as no surprise to his audience, since the Methodist Church had been opposed to slavery since the church was founded by John Wesley.

Gruber attacked cruel masters and warned that they would spend eternity in Hell for their sins. He praised kind masters, but warned that they could not control the actions of their children and their heirs. He urged kind masters to free their slaves, because otherwise there would be "mutual strife . . . between the negroes and the children of the present masters, there might be mutual death, and all be sent to destruction together" (p. 49). While condemning slavery, he urged slaves to be patient, obedient, and to avoid sin. Otherwise, they too would be condemned in the hereafter. Consistent with his role as a minister, Gruber prayed for all in his audience, and most especially for slaveowners and their slaves. He advocated peace and prayer and preached against violence on the part of the masters and the slaves.

This sermon was given in August 1818. In October Gruber was indicted by a grand jury on three counts of sedition and inciting slaves to rebel. He was tried the following March.

Gruber was represented by three attorneys—Mr. Pigman, Rev. David Martin (the editor of this pamphlet), and Roger Brooke Taney—who would later become chief justice of the U.S. Supreme Court. Taney was clearly the most important of the lawyers on Gruber's defense team. At Taney's urging a change of venue was granted, and the trial was held in the neighboring county of Frederick. Taney told the jury that this was done because a number of powerful men in Washington County had been members of the grand jury that indicted Gruber, so this might influence the petit jury. He pointed out that Gruber was not a man who ''shunned the decision of the men who knew him,'' because he was a stranger in both Washington and Frederick Counties. Rather, he shunned a jury made of ''frail men!'' who were ''liable to be influenced by the impulse of passion or prejudice without being aware of it'' (pp. 44, 45).

Taney's defense of Gruber rested on four points. First, Gruber's speech had violated no statute or law. Second, his speech and religious beliefs were both protected by the constitution of Maryland. Third, the masters who brought their slaves to the sermon should have been prepared for an antislavery sermon because it ''is well known, that the gradual and peaceable abolition of slavery in these states, is one of the objects, which the Methodist society have steadily in view. No slave-holder is allowed to be a minister of the church. Their preachers are accustomed, in their sermons, to speak of the injustice and oppressions of slavery'' (p. 36). Thus, if a master did not want his slaves to hear such ideas, ''it was in his power to prevent them from attending the assemblies, where such doctrines were likely to be preached. Mr. Gruber did not go to the slaves: they came to him. They could not have come, if their masters had chosen to prevent them'' (pp. 36-37). Finally, Taney and the other counsel for Gruber argued that the minister intended no harm to come from his sermons. He did not incite the slaves, but on the contrary, urged them to be peaceful. As Taney pointed out to the jury, ''if he did mean to stir up the slaves to insurrection, it must, at least, be admitted, that he at the same time, put the masters on their guard'' (p. 38). Since there was no insurrection after the sermon and no attempt on the part of Gruber to incite such an insurrection, Taney argued that Gruber had no criminal intent when he spoke.

The arguments of Taney, Pigman, and Martin were ultimately persuasive. Despite the fact that slave owners sat on the jury, Gruber was acquitted. The jury took only a few minutes to reach this verdict.

■ Gruber, Jacob, *defendant*. Trial of the Rev. Jacob Gruber, minister in the Methodist Episcopal Church, at the March term, 1819, in the Frederick County Court, for a misdemeanor. By David Martin . . . Fredericktown, Md. David Martin, 1819. 111 p.
        E445.M3G8 Toner Collection Rare Book Room

The indictment and trial of Gruber coincided with a dramatic change in the attitude toward slavery in the South and the North. During the trial Taney pointed out to the jury that this case was unique in Maryland's history. Before this trial criticism of slavery had generally been allowed in the state. Methodist ministers had often attacked the morality of owning slaves, as had Quakers in the state. Native Marylanders might have been more circumspect in their criticism of the institution than the minister from Pennsylvania was, but there was no doubt that slavery had been condemned from the pulpits of Maryland long before Gruber's sermon. As one defense witness, who was also a Methodist clergyman, put it:

> From prudent considerations I would not have preached in the same way, because, from his very frank manner persons might misrepresent him . . . but nothing escaped him that could induce me to believe for a moment, that he had a criminal intent. When Mr. Gruber spoke of the danger of mutual destruction between the children and slaves in the next generation, he offered up a prayer for them all: "the Lord have mercy on them," and it was then the general response of AMEN took place. [p. 47]

In part Gruber's indictment may have been the result of "his very frank manner" and in part it may have stemmed from the fact that Marylanders did not appreciate such criticism from an outsider. But, some of the motivation for the indictment appears to stem from a change in attitude about slavery.

By 1819 the limited questioning of slavery stimulated by the American Revolution was rapidly dying out. In addition, many slave owners felt under attack from the North because of the ongoing debates in Congress over the admission of Missouri into the Union as a slave state. In his speech in defense of Gruber, Rev. David Martin quoted Congressman James Tallmadge who had attacked slavery on the floor of the House of Representatives. He also quoted Jefferson's *Notes on the State of Virginia* to show that notable men who "have been exalted, not disgraced," spoke out against slavery and in favor of freedom of speech (p. 69). While Martin's references to Jefferson may have influenced the jury in favor of Gruber, it is not at all clear the same could be said for his use of Congressman Tallmadge. Indeed, many people in the South viewed Tallmadge as an evil man, who had unnecessarily attacked the institution that was the "cornerstone" of their society. Gruber, another Northerner, had come to Maryland and done the same thing. For this he was indicted. It was the forensic skills of Roger Taney, a famous local attorney, and the weakness of the prosecution's case, that led to this acquittal.

Taney, of course, would later become famous—or infamous—for his decision in *Dred Scott* v. *Sandford*, 60 U.S. (19 How.) 393 (1857). In that decision he denied the right of Congress to pass the Missouri Compromise and denied that blacks had any rights under the U.S.

Constitution. At the time of that case, Taney's supporters publicized his earlier defense of Gruber to prove that Taney was not malicious or evil.

This record of Gruber's case contains most of the pertinent material connected with the trial, including the presentment to the grand jury, the indictment, opening statements by the attorneys, most of the testimony, and most of the closing statements. Unfortunately, Taney's one-hour closing speech is not printed because "his continued ill health . . . rendered him unable to arrange the notes of his argument so as to enable the editor to report it" (p. 111). The editor simply notes that "Mr. Taney, in a speech of about an hour's continuance, with his usual eloquence and zeal made a most effectual and conclusive argument to the jury, on the part of Mr. Gruber. . . . After Mr. Taney concluded, the jury wishing to have some conversation on the subject in private, retired from the box, but immediately returned again, and answering to the usual call of the clerk, pronounced, through the foreman, a verdict of NOT GUILTY" (p. 111).

Besides this record of the trial, this report contains a small preface by Reverend Martin, a letter to Martin from Gruber, and a detailed "Sketch of the Sermon." This case was not appealed, and this is the only printed record of the trial.

Todd v. *Garrison*

(Baltimore [Md.] City Ct. 1829)(Unreported)

In 1829 William Lloyd Garrison moved to Baltimore, Maryland, to become coeditor, with Benjamin Lundy, of the newspaper *Genius of Universal Emancipation.* At the time, the *Genius* was the only major antislavery newspaper in the United States.

In 1830 Garrison wrote two articles denouncing Francis Todd, a shipowner from Garrison's hometown of Newburyport, Massachusetts. Todd had allowed his ship, the *Francis,* to be used to transport slaves from Maryland to New Orleans. Garrison considered this to be an "instance of domestic piracy" and believed that it was "no worse to fit out piratical cruisers, or to engage in the foreign slave trade, than to pursue a similar trade along our own coasts." Garrison printed this information "to illustrate New-England humanity and morality." He sent a copy of the article to Mr. Todd, as well as to the *Newburyport Herald.* He requested the editor of the *Herald* "to copy this article, or publish a statement of the facts contained herein . . . in order to enlighten the public mind in that quarter" (Garrison, *A Brief Sketch,* p. 7).

Following the publication of these two articles, Todd took legal action against Garrison. He sued Garrison for five thousand dollars

William Lloyd Garrison (1805-1879). An almost timid-looking man. Garrison was the firey editor of the *Liberator* and the single most important abolitionist in America. He, more than any other individual, was responsible for the building of antislavery organizations in the 1830s.

Engraving by L. Grozelier from a daguerreotype by Chase, copyright 1854. LC-USZ62-46114

"for injuring 'his good name, fame and reputation,' by publishing 'wicked, scandalous and malicious matter' in relation to himself" (ibid., p. 8). In addition, a Baltimore grand jury presented an indictment against Garrison, because he, "contriving and unlawfully, wickedly, and maliciously intending to hurt, injure and vilify one Francis Todd, and to deprive him of his good name, fame and reputation, and to bring him into great contempt, scandal, infamy, and disgrace . . . with force and arms . . . unlawfully, wickedly, and maliciously, did print and publish, and cause and procure to be printed and published" a newspaper article about Todd (ibid., p. 8). Garrison was convicted on this criminal charge and fined fifty dollars plus the cost of the prosecution.

Motions for a new trial were overruled, and Garrison entered a

Baltimore prison because he could not and would not pay his fine. While in jail, Garrison published an eight-page sketch of his trial and imprisonment. After forty-nine days he was released when Arthur Tappan, a New York philanthropist, paid Garrison's fine. Garrison left Baltimore immediately after his release and returned only once for a short visit.

Although Todd's suit was postponed, he ultimately won a $1,000 judgment against Garrison. Garrison did not contest this suit because he believed it would be impossible to get a fair trial. However, since he was no longer in Maryland and had no plans to return there, Garrison had no intention of paying Todd the money. Instead, Garrison remained in Boston as the publisher of the nation's most important and influential antislavery newspaper, the *Liberator*.

■ Garrison, William Lloyd. A brief sketch of the trial of William Lloyd
      Garrison for an alleged libel on Francis Todd, of Newburyport,
      Mass. Boston, Printed by Garrison and Knapp, 1834. 24 p.
            AC901.B3 vol. 39 Bailey Pamphlets Rare Book Room

Garrison first published an account of his trial in an eight-page pamphlet. In 1834 he republished it in a much larger format "at the request of many of my friends, and in order to rebut the defamation of my enemies" (p. iii). By 1834 Garrison was the most famous—and infamous— abolitionist in the country. He regularly berated the American Colonization Society for being a false friend of the slave and an enemy of free blacks. These stinging attacks led to counterattacks by the society, which charged Garrison with being a convicted felon. This pamphlet was published to refute that charge.

The pamphlet contains the full text of the allegedly libelous articles about Francis Todd. In addition it reprints the presentment to the grand jury, the indictment by the grand jury, and the motion for a new trial. Much of the testimony and some of the arguments of counsel are presented, but this material was written down only after the trial because Garrison "could procure no competent stenographer to report this trial" (p. 6). He regrets that the information in the pamphlet "is a mere skeleton of one grand, gigantic *whole*." He "did not take a single note at the trial . . . . The language is mine; but, I believe, the synopsis is substantially correct" (p. 13).

The main burden of Garrison's defense was inadvertently lightened by the prosecution. The prosecution witnesses did not deny that Todd's ship had carried slaves from Maryland to New Orleans. Indeed, they testified that the ship had carried more slaves than Garrison had claimed in his articles. With a sarcasm for which he would become famous, Garrison notes that one of the prosecution witnesses testified that the slaves on the ship "enjoyed the extatics of bliss, and were delighted at the prospect of realizing the pleasures of interminable slavery" (p. 11). Garrison argued that it was not a crime to transport slaves from one state to another. Therefore, it could not be a crime to write in a newspaper that someone had done this for a profit. There could be no libel if the newspaper article about a perfectly legal act also happened to be substantially correct in its facts. Furthermore, Garrison's attorney argued that there was no proof that Garrison had either written or authorized this article's publication. While technically a legitimate argument, this claim seems to undermine Garrison's moral position. Despite the fact that the alleged libel was substantially true, and hardly a libel because it alleged no legal wrongdoing, Garrison was convicted.

Besides a statement of the case, this pamphlet contains three sonnets Garrison wrote while in prison, an appendix that details Todd's civil suit for five thousand dollars, and reprints of editorial comment favorable to Garrison. A number of the editorialists (as well as Garrison) point out that America was "rejoicing over the triumph obtained on the other side of the water [France and England], in favor of the liberty of the press," while "at this very moment, attempts are making in Baltimore to punish, by a heavy fine, a citizen of the United States, for some remarks made by him whilst editor of a paper devoted to humanity and freedom" (p. 24).

United States v. *Crandall*

25 F. Cas. 684 (C.C.D.C. 1836)(No. 14,885)

Reuben Crandall was a botanist, physician, and surgeon. He was born in Conneticut and was the brother of the abolitionist school teacher Prudence Crandall (see *Crandall* v. *State,* 10 Conn. 339 [1834] in section on Abolitionists in the North). After studying medicine in Philadelphia and elsewhere he settled in Peekskill, New York. There he practiced medicine and gave no indication of being an abolitionist. In 1835 he moved to Washington, D.C., as the private physician of an invalid family. He had planned to move to the West after his family was settled in Washington. However, a position at a local college and the possibility of lecturing, botanical collecting, and research led him to stay in Washington.

Crandall rented a room in a commercial building to store his equipment, books, specimens, and various personal effects. While he was unpacking these belongings, a man named Henry King came to his office. King noticed some abolitionist pamphlets among Crandall's possessions and asked if he might borrow some of them. Written across the cover of some of the pamphlets, in Crandall's handwriting, were the words *"please read and circulate."* King examined the pamphlets and told Crandall "the latitude is too far south for these things; they won't do here," but "by your leave, I will take this and read it over." *(The Trial,* [Printed for the Proprietors], p. 9). King later left the pamphlet in another store and forgot about it. Some time after this Crandall was arrested on five counts "under the common law of libels, of publishing malicious and wicked libels, with the intent to excite sedition and insurrection among the slaves and free colored people of this District" *(The Trial,* p. 5). Crandall was held in jail for eight months, until his trial was held in April 1836.

Crandall was tried before the U.S. Circuit Court for Washington, D.C. Chief Justice William Cranch and Judges Buckner Thurston and James S. Morsell presided over this jury trial. Francis Scott Key (the author of *The Star Spangled Banner*) was the prosecuting attorney, along with J.M. Carlisle. At the time Key was the district attorney for the District of Columbia. Crandall was defended by R.S. Coxe and J.H. Bradley.

At the trial it was shown that Crandall did not distribute or circulate any pamphlets, except the one he lent to King. Crandall claimed that the written message "please read and circulate" had been placed on the pamphlets more than a year before he moved to Washington. Furthermore, he claimed that he was not an abolitionist and he had never been one. Finally, he claimed the pamphlets arrived in Washington either by accident or without his knowledge. Some of them, he claimed "were packed up, not by him, but by the lady of the house, as waste paper," when he moved to Washington with the invalid family *(The Trial,* p. 26). The rest he said were sent to him without his knowledge, request, or approval. He claimed he subscribed only to temperance papers. Letters from abolitionists in New York who had sent the material supported this position. But the court would allow neither this information nor depositions to be introduced as evidence without the consent of the prosecuting attorney. Despite the fact that it was impossible to actually bring these and other witnesses to Washington from New York and Connecticut, District Attorney Key refused to consent to the introduction of any depositions and letters.

Throughout the trial the prosecution atttempted to tie Crandall to the larger antislavery movement. References were made to his Northern background and citizenship. This particularly irritated his counsel, who noted:

> He was charged with being a northern man; a native of Connecticut, and a resident of New York. Have we, then, . . . lived to see the day when in a court of justice, in the federal city, under the very

eyes of Congress, and of the National Government, it can be urged against an individual arraigned at the criminal bar, as a circumstance of aggravation, or as a just ground for suspicion, that the individual comes from the North, or the South, from the East or the West? But we were told, that the Northern men were interlopers and intruders amongst us. [*The Trial*, pp. 43-44]

In addition to this appeal to regional bias, the prosecution noted that many Washingtonians had recently received pamphlets and newspapers mailed out, in bulk, from the New York offices of the American Anti-Slavery Society. Crandall, the prosecutors charged, was an agent of this society, whose purpose was to overthrow Southern institutions and create a revolt of the slaves.

During the trial the court consistently ruled against Crandall's attorneys on procedural matters and questions of the admissibility of certain evidence. Nevertheless, the jury acquitted Crandall after a short deliberation.

■ Crandall, Reuben, *defendant*. The trial of Reuben Crandall, M.D., charged with publishing and circulating seditious and incendiary papers, etc., in the District of Columbia, with the intent of exciting servile insurrection. Carefully reported, and compiled from the written statements of the court and counsel. By a member of the bar. Washington City, Printed for the Proprietors, 1836. 48 p.
Law Library; AC901.M2 vol. 31 Rare Book Room

This pamphlet contains most of the evidence, testimony, statements by the judges, and arguments of counsel in this trial. It does not contain the full speeches of the attorneys or judges or a total record of testimony. Most important, it lacks the judges' final charge to the jury.

The case involves four areas of law and social conflict. The first two areas are freedom of speech and slavery and race relations. Crandall was indicted for "publishing inflammatory and seditious libels" (p. 8). The pamphlets he possessed (and allegedly distributed) described slavery and some of its more barbaric aspects. The Washington officials feared they would stimulate a slave revolt.

The case must also be seen as a reaction to the development of Northern antislavery societies. Much of the testimony centers on the fact that similar pamphlets had been sent south from the New York offices of the American Anti-Slavery Society. In the 1830s, this society began to flood the South with literature designed to convince Southerners that slavery was wrong. It was sent to all prominent people, including newspaper editors, politicians, government officials, teachers, and most of all clergymen. This pamphlet campaign led to riots in Charleston and other Southern cities. Some postmasters attempted to prohibit the mailing or delivery of abolitionist literature. The mailing of these pamphlets convinced few, if any, Southerners that slavery was wrong. It did, however, lead to a backlash against abolition and a fear among many Southerners that the abolitionist movement was much larger than it actually was. Changes in printing technology and postal rates allowed the American Anti-Slavery Society to flood the South with pamphlets for a comparatively small amount of money. Thus, in Southern eyes the society appeared to be more powerful than it actually was.

Finally, this case must be viewed as part of the conflict between the American Colonization Society and the abolitionists. The prosecutor, Francis Scott Key, was a member of the Colonization Society. The pamphlets' attacks on that society, as well as their antislavery thrust, seem to have motivated the prosecution. Key defends the society from abolitionist attacks throughout his prosecution of Crandall.

The main thrust of Crandall's defense was a traditional defense against a libel, or seditions libel, prosecution. Crandall's attorney, R.S. Coxe, argued that the libels charged "were not upon individuals, nor the Government, but were said to be designed to excite the whole community." Thus, mere possession was not a crime. Only if it was proved that there was "publication or circulation with the intent charged" would it be possible to convict Crandall (p. 9). This position was maintained throughout the trial. Crandall's attorneys essentially denied the "facts of publication" in old fashioned libel law terms—that is, they denied that Crandall had "published" or distributed the pamphlets. Thus, he could not have committed the libel. In this case "publication" actually meant "distribution," since no one argued that Crandall actually published the pamphlets himself. Crandall's attorneys argued that the loaning of one pamphlet to "an intelligent and discreet citizen, without any sympathies with the abolitionists" could hardly be considered as an attempt to distribute the pamphlets with an intent to cause riot or insurrection (p. 43).

One of the curious aspects of this case is that a mulatto was allowed to testify against Crandall, despite opposition from his attorneys. This information was placed in the report of the case in Cranch's Circuit Court Reports (25 F. Cas. 689) but not put into this pamphlet. The willingness of the prosecutor to call a mulatto to the stand suggests the eagerness of Key to convict Crandall.

The police who arrested Crandall were also eager to convict him and exaggerated the evidence in their testimony. Constable H.B. Robertson had to be warned to avoid giving "your inferences . . . give us the facts, if you please" (p. 19). Constable M. Jeffers testified that Crandall, after he was arrested, admitted that he favored immediate emancipation. Jeffers testified that he responded to this by declaring emancipation "would be attended with dreadful consequences. We should all have our throats cut, and the next thing would be amalgamation." At this point, Judge Thruston asked: "Would the amalgamation occur after our throats are cut, Mr. Jeffers?" (p. 20).

Although the judges were generally hostile to Crandall, the jury ultimately acquitted him. However, the case still attracted a great deal of attention and sympathy for Crandall. He was, after all, kept in jail eight months before his trial. Vice President Henry Wilson, himself an abolitionist before the Civil War, later summed up the incident this way:

> The gross infringements by the Slave Power of the rights of whites, as well as blacks, the degrading and intolerable surveillance to which the nation submitted, and the torpidity with which the people regarded these flagrant outrages, find many examples in the history of these days. Of them is the case of Dr. Reuben Crandall . . . The enormity of this outrage [in Crandall's case] appears greater from the indictment under which he was tried . . .Such were the charges under color of which a Christian gentleman of culture and refinement was arrested, confined, and tried in the capital of this Christian nation. [Henry Wilson, *The Rise and Fall of the Slave Power in America* (Boston, 1872), 1:305-6]

■ Crandall, Reuben, *defendant*. The trial of Reuben Crandall, M.D. charged with publishing seditious libels, by circulating the publications of the American Anti-Slavery Society. Before the Circuit Court for the District of Columbia, held at Washington, in April, 1836, occupying the court the period of ten days. New York, J.R. Piercy, 1836. 62 p.

    AC901.B3 vol. 39 Bailey Pamphlets Rare Book Room

This pamphlet contains the most elaborate and complete record of Crandall's trial that exists. The copyright for this work was taken out by Crandall himself, and the differences between this version of the trial and the one published in Washington by "A Member of the Bar" reflect Crandall's interests. For example, the summations of Crandell's attorneys are printed here as they were given in court. The arguments are made in full. Also, the interaction between counsel and the bench is more fully reported and more personalized. The neutral and impersonal expressions, *the bench, the court,* or *the judge* are sometimes replaced by the name of the judge. This was not done consistently, however, because in other places *the court* appears before statements and questions. There are virtually no important factual differences in the material contained in these pamphlets. This one is simply longer, set in smaller type, and thus more complete.

■ Key, Francis Scott. A part of a speech pronounced by Francis S. Key, esq., on the trial of Reuben Crandall, M.D., before the Circuit Court of the District of Columbia, at the March term thereof, 1836, on an indictment for publishing libels with the intent to excite sedition and insurrection among the slaves and free coloured people of said District. Washington, 1836. 15 p.

LLRBR

This pamphlet was initially published in the November 1836 *African Repository*, the journal of the American Colonization Society. Key, a member of the Colonization Society, was the district attorney who prosecuted Crandall. The pamphlet and the article in the *Repository* contain what is purported to be part of Key's speech to the jury in this case. It is impossible to know how much of the speech is reproduced here because there is no complete copy of the speech printed anywhere else. This pamphlet does not directly cover any of the case's legal issues that Key undoubtedly discussed at the trial. Rather, it focuses on the nature of the Colonization Society and its relationship to the abolition movement.

The Colonization Society became an issue in the trial because many of the pamphlets and newspapers in Crandall's possession attacked it. The first count in Crandall's indictment charged that he possessed and either distributed or planned to distribute Arthur Tappan's "Reply to Mr. Gurley's letter, addressed to the Rev. R. R. Gurley, Secretary of the American Colonization Society." In his speech to the jury, Key also noted that Crandall possessed a copy of William Jay's *An Inquiry Into the Character and Tendency of the American Colonization and American Anti-Slavery Societies* (p. 8). Key quoted from Jay's pamphlet to show the dangers of Crandall's alleged libels. In addition, he went to great lengths to defend the Colonization Society and to attack the American Anti-Slavery Society.

Key argued that the "great moral and political evil" in the United States "is supposed to be slavery—but is it not plainly the whole coloured race?" He asked that if slavery was an evil, "do I not also in the same breath speak of emancipation as a far greater evil?" (p. 9). He went on to point out that the Colonization Society had helped numerous blacks escape both bondage and prejudice by removing them to Africa. But, Key asked, would the abolitionists recognize that the Colonization Society had accomplished more "than by all their [the abolitionists'] own labours?'' (p. 10). This, in fact, the abolitionists would not acknowledge, because their goal was emancipation of all the slaves. Such an emancipation, Key argued, would lead to disaster.

This pamphlet suggests that Key may have prosecuted Crandall in an attempt to vindicate the Colonization Society and destroy the Anti-Slavery Society. Certainly Key used the trial for this purpose. Indeed, during the trial it is at times difficult to determine whether Key is working for the government or the Colonization Society. What clearly emerges from this speech is that for Key the Colonization Society represented a legitimate answer to the problem of free blacks and slavery, and that the Society should be protected by the government. Thus, an attack on the Colonization Society was easily translated into a seditious attack on the government and the civil society.

In re Jonathan Walker

(Escambia Cty. [Fla.] Super. Ct. 1845)(Unreported)

Jonathan Walker was a ship owner and captain from Harwich, Massachusetts. In the 1830s and 1840s he spent time in Pensacola in the Florida Territory. While there he was generally accepted by the community. However, his outspoken opposition to slavery, and his willingness to be "on good terms with the colored people" led to problems. Twice during his first residence in Pensacola he was "called upon by different persons—the chief executive officers or mayors for the time being" and "it was intimated that there was danger in regard" to his safety because of Walker's "discountenance of some of their rules and customs respecting the association of white with colored men" (Walker, *Trial and Imprisonment* [1845], p. 9).

After living in Pensacola five or six years Captain Walker returned to Massachusetts. However, in June 1844 he once again returned to Pensacola. While there he agreed to help a number of slaves escape to the Bahama Islands, where they would be free under British law. During the voyage Walker became quite ill, and the ship ran out of water and began to drift. On July 8 the ship was aided by two salvage sloops near Cape Florida. Despite Walker's being in international waters, his ship was seized by these sloops and towed to Key West. There Walker was committed to jail in lieu of $1,000 bail to stand trial for stealing slaves.

He was subsequently taken to Pensacola by a steamboat "in the United States' employ" (ibid., p. 15). Because Florida was then a U.S. territory, this intervention by the national government was not illegal or improper. In Pensacola Walker was jailed in lieu of $10,000 bail. He

The author confined in the pillory.

Illustration from *Trial and Imprisonment of Jonathan Walker at Pensacola, Florida, for Aiding Slaves to Escape from Bondage* (Boston, 1845), written and published as antislavery propaganda.

Illustrations and text were designed to expose the evils of slavery. From *Trial and Imprisonment of Jonathan Walker* (Boston, 1845).

Jonathan Walker was branded with the initials SS for slave stealer and became known as the "man with the branded hand." Illustration from *Trial and Imprisonment of Jonathan Walker* (Boston, 1845).

was persuaded to sign over the deed to his ship to one of the owners of slaves he helped and was thus without any money. Throughout this period Walker was weak from his illness and still not fully recovered. He was held in double irons (hands and feet) and for some of this period was chained to another prisoner—a slave under sentence of death.

Walker was held in jail until November 1844, when he was finally brought to trial. The court appointed an attorney since he had no money to hire one. He had by this time been formally charged by the county grand jury that "with force and arms . . .[Walker] feloniously and unlawfully did entice to run away" four slaves. He was tried under four separate indictments, despite a protest from his court-appointed attorney that the indictments should be "arrayed against me for one act of offence, if it was an act at all" (ibid., pp. 35-36).

There was very little testimony and only a short charge to the jury. The jury deliberated on the first indictment about half an hour before returning a verdict of guilty. It "awarded him [Walker] to be branded on the right hand with the letters SS." After deliberating on the other three indictments, the jury sentenced Walker to the following additional punishments: he was to stand in the pillory for one hour, be imprisoned for fifteen days, and be fined $150 plus the court costs. (ibid., p. 39).

Walker subsequently received all these punishments. While Walker was in the pillory, the owner of some of the slaves he had helped took the covering off Walker's head so he would not be protected from the sun. He then threw two rotten eggs at Walker's face and head. For this act the man was ultimately tried and fined six and a quarter cents.

Immediately after his recommittal to jail, Walker was served with three more writs, for trespass and other offenses. He was held in jail until May 1845, when he was tried on these charges. The jury in that case was instructed to find him guilty and complied with the judge's instructions. However, the jurors also apparently believed that Walker had suffered sufficiently for his crime. He was thus fined $5 for each of the three indictments and released soon after that. He returned to Massachusetts where the narrative of his experiences was written.

■ Walker, Jonathan. Trial and imprisonment of Jonathan Walker, at Pensacola, Florida, for aiding slaves to escape from bondage. With an appendix, containing a sketch of his life . . . Boston, Published at the Anti-Slavery Office, 1845. 119 p.
> E450.W19 Toner Collection Rare Book Room

——The branded hand; trial and imprisonment of Johnathan Walker. [Reprint] New York, Arno Press, 1969. 119 p. (The Anti-Slavery Crusade in America)
> E450.W15 1969

——Trial and imprisonment of Johathan Walker, at Pensacola, Florida, for aiding slaves to escape bondage. A facsim, reproduction of the 1845 ed., with an introd. and index by Joe M. Richardson. Gainesville, University Presses of Florida, 1974. 119 p. (Bicentennial Floridiana Facsimile Series)
> E450.W15 1845a

——Trial and imprisonment of Jonathan Walker, at Pensacola, Florida, for aiding slaves to escape from bondage. With an appendix, containing a sketch of his life. . . . Boston, Published at the Anti-Slavery Office, 1846. 126 p.
> Law Library; E450.W192 Rare Book Room

Like many others of its type, these accounts of Walker's activities, imprisonment, and trials were written as antislavery propaganda. They were designed to both tell Walker's story and to expose the evils of slavery.

Walker makes it clear throughout his narrative that the South is not the only section to blame for slavery. Florida, at the time of his incarceration there, was a federal territory and presumably the responsibility of all Americans. He argues, for example, that the punishment of branding is inhumane and thus a "cruel and unusual punishment" prohibited by the Eighth Amendment to the U.S. Constitution. The Congress "having declared that no law of the territorial government, inconsistent with the United States laws, shall ever be *valid*," Walker thought he was punished illegally (p. 44). Walker prints a series of letters he received while in prison as well as letters and reports from the U.S. attorney for the territory, the Massachusetts government, and the Florida territorial government. He shows how the U.S. attorney lied to Massachusetts authorities about his health and prison conditions. This underscores the national complicity with his imprisonment and with slavery in general.

Walker's descriptions of his trials are very vague. His discussion of the first trial, for example, takes less than four pages, and most of that is devoted to reproducing the four indictments. However, Walker devotes a great amount of space to descriptions of prison conditions, the punishments of slaves taken to the prison, and the punishment of slaves owned by the jailers. He provides a prison diary with discussions of when and how often slaves were whipped. He analyzes the food he was given and his general treatment. Walker did not receive treatment as bad as that received by Thomas Brown in Kentucky when incarcerated for a similar crime (see *Brown's Three Years in the Kentucky Prisons*). However, prison conditions and his treatment were quite brutal.

The most important aspect of this case was Walker's punishment—being branded on the hand with the initials SS for slave stealer. Here the court in Florida gave the antislavery movement a marvelous propaganda device. Walker became known as the "man with the branded hand." His punishment proved to the world (or those who would listen to abolitionists) how barbaric and cruel slavery was, not just to blacks, but also to whites. These books are illustrated with woodcuts of Walker in the pillory (with eggs being thrown at him) and Walker being branded. They also contain a poem by John Greenleaf Whittier, "The Branded Hand." The Quaker poet was able to turn the branded hand and the brand itself to the advantage of the antislavery cause. He wrote:

> Welcome home again, brave seaman! with thy thoughtful brow
>   and gray,
> And the old heroic spirit of our earlier, better day—
> With that front of calm endurance, on whose steady nerve, in vain
> Pressed the Iron of the Prison, smote the fiery shafts of pain!
>
>   . . .
>
> Then lift that manly right hand, bold ploughman of the wave!
> Its branded palm shall prophesy, "SALVATION TO THE
>   SLAVE!"

Hold up its fire-wrought language, that whoso reads may feel
His heart swell strong within him, his sinews change to steel.

Commonwealth v. Webster

(Lexington Cty |Ky.| Ct. 1844) (Unreported)

Although raised in Vermont, Delia A. Webster visited Kentucky
in 1843 for health reasons. In Lexington she opened a school at the
urging of various ministers and other "persons of influence" (Webster,
A History of the Trial, p. 5). In September 1844 a Methodist minister
from New York named Calvin Fairbank began boarding at the same
house as Miss Webster. A few weeks later Fairbank and Webster went
on a trip to Millersburg. Webster spent a Sunday resting at a private
home in that town while Fairbank claimed to visit fellow clergymen in
the area. In fact, Fairbank used this time to take three slaves—Lewis
Hayden, Harriet Hayden, and their ten-year-old son—to Ohio. On returning to Lexington, both Fairbank and Webster were arrested for
slave stealing.

After her arrest Webster was placed in a room in a downtown
hotel and denied the right to counsel or the opportunity to communicate
with her friends. The basement of that hotel served as a jail, where
Fairbank was incarcerated and later shackled. Because Webster was
well connected in Kentucky, the sheriff intervened on her behalf. Cassius
M. Clay and an attorney named General McCalla were soon aiding her.
Webster was ultimately represented by three prominent and skilled
lawyers—Samuel Shy, Gen. Leslie Combs, and Madison C. Johnson.

Despite the skill of her attorneys and the lack of any evidence
directly connecting her to the crime, Webster was convicted and
sentenced to two years in the state penitentiary. The jury that convicted
her also sent a letter to the Kentucky governor, William Owsley, asking
that he immediately pardon her "before the sentence should be
pronounced" (ibid., p. 56). Owsley also received letters from such
notables as Henry Clay, and Sen. Samuel S. Phelps and Gov. William
Slade, both of Vermont. However, he refused to consider the case right
away because an appeal was pending.

Webster quickly asked for a new trial on the grounds that new
evidence had been found (since certain subpoenaed witnesses had not
appeared for the first trial), that the "Verdict is contrary to Law and
Evidence," that a letter found on Fairbank at the time of his arrest was
allowed to go to the jury, and this was "improper Evidence," and that
the "Court misinstructed the Jury" (ibid., p. 60). A large mob outside

the courtroom threatened to lynch the judge if he granted a new trial. Under these circumstances the petition for a new trial was denied.

Webster was then sent to the state penitentiary. There her prison experience turned out to be unexpectedly mild. While all the other prisoners "were lodged in dark cells," she "was permitted to be sole tenant of a small frame house with plain boarding . . . [which] was well furnished, and sufficiently large and commodious to answer the purposes of workshop, study, lodging, dining-room and parlor." The house was not locked, so she could enter and leave at will. She was well fed and not required to do any work, "but some light sewing was brought in for my own amusement" (ibid., p. 78). She had many visitors, including clergymen and legislators.

From the moment Webster entered prison there was a strong movement to pardon her. However, many people in the state opposed a pardon because she was viewed as an abolitionist who deserved to be in prison whether she actually committed the alleged criminal acts or not. The governor at first offered a pardon if she would agree never to return to Kentucky. This she would not accept.

Shortly after her imprisonment Calvin Fairbank was placed on trial. He denied Webster had anything to do with the escape, but he himself pleaded guilty to helping the slaves escape and was sentenced to fifteen years in the penitentiary. Wester was then pardoned after serving six weeks in the penitentiary. She had also spent five months confined in a hotel room while awaiting trial. Fairbank served four years and eleven months of his sentence before Gov. John J. Crittenden granted a pardon. Later Fairbank would serve another twelve years in the Kentucky penitentiary for aiding other slaves in their escape from bondage.

■ Webster, Delia A. Kentucky jurisprudence. A history of the trial of
        Miss Delia A. Webster. At Lexington, Kentucky, Dec'r 17-21,
        1844, before the Hon. Richard Buckner. On a charge of aiding
        slaves to escape from that commonwealth—with miscellaneous
        remarks, including her views on American slavery. Vergennes,
        Vt., E. W. Blaisdell, 1845. 84 p.
            AC901.M5 vol. 354, no. 1 Misc. Pamph. Rare Book Room

Webster wrote this pamphlet after her return to Vermont. In it she denies any knowledge of the plan to help the Hayden family escape bondage. Webster was not an abolitionist when she went to Kentucky, and when writing this pamphlet she claimed: "I have never yet read any publication issued by the Abolitionists" (p. 83). She did, however, "have . . . an utter abhorence of it [slavery], as a system of uncompounded wickedness, alike opposed to Christianity, and the principles of a Republican government." She thought it "almost as bad as the Devil and wicked men can make it'' (p. 83). But she also believed it wrong and misguided to encourage slaves to leave their masters. She was a supporter of Henry Clay in national politics, and did not ''approve of any thing which has a tendency to sow discord or to create feelings of animosity between the North and South'' (p. 84).

Given these statements, and Fairbank's insistence that she had nothing to do with his plot, it is likely that her claims of innocence were true. Throughout her ordeal she denied her guilt and naively expected the jury to acquit her. She also would not accept anything but a full pardon, because otherwise she might be admitting guilt. Her position is markedly different from that of the Reverend Fairbank, who never denied his actions, acknowledged them in open court, wrote about them in his memoirs, and did similar things after his release from prison (see Calvin Fairbank, *Rev. Calvin Fairbank During Slavery Times* [Chicago, 1890]).

Webster's account of her ordeal contains much of the testimony from her trial, as well as letters to her attorneys, petitions to the governor of Kentucky, and descriptions of her imprisonment. The pamphlet also contains a copy of an unsigned letter, allegedly written by Fairbank, in which the plot to aid the slaves is discussed in great detail. In this letter the author refers to a ''Miss W.'' who boarded at the same place as the writer. This was the main piece of evidence used to convict Webster. The letter, while mentioning a ''Miss W.'' does not indicate that she was a willing partner in the plan.

Webster's conviction appears to have been a result of community hostility toward Northerners in general and toward Webster and Fairbank in particular. Her case had many procedural peculiarities. She was not arrested under any legal process, but rather, she was requested to come to a hotel for her own protection. She was then locked in this place until she was indicted. Her boardinghouse room was searched while she was out of town, and there is an indication that some attempts were made to plant incriminating evidence among her possessions. During the trial all of the jurors and the witnesses stayed at the same hotel in which Webster was imprisoned. Finally, a large mob threatened the judge while he was considering her petition for a new trial. *Kentucky Jurisprudence* convincingly makes the case that where abolitionists, or alleged abolitionists, were involved, there was very little justice or jurisprudence in that state.

Commonwealth v. Garner

44 Va. (3 Gratt.) 624 (1846)

In 1845 six slaves escaped from Wood County, Virginia, into Ohio by crossing the Ohio River. A group of Virginians knew of this planned escape and were hiding on the Ohio side of the river when the slaves landed. They immediately seized the fugitives. In addition, they seized three citizens of Ohio who had met the slaves at the water's edge and helped them land in Ohio. These three Ohioans were forcibly carried across the river to Virginia where they were jailed, indicted, tried, and convicted of three felonies for enticing, carrying away, and assisting in the escape of the six slaves.

Garner and the two other convicted men appealed this decision on the ground that they had not been in the state of Virginia when they committed the alleged crime, and thus the Virginia courts had no jurisdiction in the case. Samuel F. Vinton of Marietta, Ohio, appeared as the defendants' attorney and as the representative of the governor of Ohio. Vinton concentrated most of his arguments on the jurisdictional issues and tried to avoid the issue of slavery. In a seven-to-five decision, the General Court of Virginia held that the jurisdiction of Virginia did not extend to the low-water mark of the Ohio River. Thus, Garner and the other defendants had never been in Virginia and could not be tried by a Virginia court. Their conviction was overturned, and they were released from jail.

■   Vinton, Samuel. Substance of an argument of Samuel F. Vinton, for the defendants, in the case of the Commonwealth of Virginia vs. Peter M. Garner and others, for an alleged abduction of certain slaves. Delivered before the General Court of Virginia at its December term, 1846. Marietta, O., Printed at the Intelligencer Office, 1846. 32 p.

Law Library; E450.V73

In his argument before the Virginia high court Samuel Vinton tries to avoid slavery and other controversial issues. He begins by noting that he will not talk about slavery or "the correspondence now going on, and not yet brought to a close, between the Executives of the two States, making mutual demands of certain persons as fugitives from justice." These two issues had been raised by opposing counsel, but were irrelevant to the issue before the court. Vinton asserts "I did not come here . . . to engage in those questions that are at issue between the slaveholders and the abolitionists." Nor does he wish to discuss, as the lawyers for the state of Virginia apparently had, "the comparative power and prowess of the people of Virginia and Ohio" (p. 1). Vinton does not believe the question of slavery, or even fugitive slaves, is at issue in this case. Furthermore, he suggests that if this is a case involving fugitive slaves, then the "principles laid down and settled" in the *Prigg* v. *Pennsylvania*, 41 U.S. (16 Pet.) 539 (1842), decision "raise, to say the least of it, a serious doubt whether the sole power to prescribe the punishment for such a case, is not vested in the Congress of the United States'' (p. 3). Thus neither Virginia nor Ohio had jurisdiction.

But for Vinton this is not a problem, because he asserts this case ''presents a simple question of boundary between the two States.'' He only ''regret[s] exceedingly that this question, so important to the State of Ohio, should have arisen out of a transaction having any connexion with slaves or slavery, since this adventitious circumstance creates a prejudice against the case, and gives it an outward appearance of being something different from what it in reality is, and which the mind has a natural tendency to associate with the question that does in fact arise.'' Vinton is sure the Virginia court will not be ''in the least degree, influenced by the outward and accidental form in which this question is presented'' (p. 3).

Having separated the boundary and jurisdictional question from the issues of slavery and abolition, Vinton then develops a long and detailed argument on the nature of boundaries, riparian law, conflicts of law, and international law. He discusses the early charters of Virginia and the other colonies, the cession of the Northwest Territory, the admittance of Ohio into the Union, various U.S. Supreme Court decisions, and the statutes of the federal government and some of the states. At no time does the issue of slavery again intrude on his argument.

Vinton's success led to the freedom of Garner and avoided a major conflict between Virginia and Ohio. By directing the Virginia court to the boundary issue, and away from the slavery issue, Vinton succeeded in defusing what could have been a serious interstate conflict. Vinton was correct that the simple boundary question was complicated by the issue of slavery. But, it seems unlikely that any other issue could have led to the seizure of people in Ohio by Virginians who claimed that acts committed in Ohio were indictable in Virginia.

Drayton v. *United States*

7 F. Cas. 1063 (C.C.D.C. 1849)(No. 4,074)

Daniel Drayton was a sea captain from Philadelphia. In April 1848 he arrived in Washington with a shipload of wood. His main purpose however was to transport a family of nine slaves to Philadelphia. Other slaves were informed of the possibility of escape, and on the night of the proposed rendezvous seventy-six slaves boarded Drayton's rented schooner, the *Pearl*. A day later the *Pearl* was captured by a steamer manned by some of the owners of the missing slaves. Drayton was jailed and subsequently indicted under a 1737 Maryland statute that provided jail terms of up to twenty years for stealing slaves. He was also indicted for helping slaves escape, which carried a $200 penalty for each slave he aided.

At the time there was great public clamor to be as harsh as possible against Drayton. Thus he was indicted on forty-one separate counts of stealing slaves, because the slaves found on the *Pearl* belonged to forty-one different District of Columbia owners. He was also indicted on seventy-four separate counts of helping slaves to escape. Two of the slaves were owned by Virginia masters and did not come under the District of Columbia jurisdiction. Drayton was indicted and tried under Maryland statutes because at this time the District of Columbia was governed by Maryland laws as modified by Congress. However, because his crime took place in the federal district, he was tried in federal courts and could ultimately be pardoned by the President of the United States.

The many separate indictments were designed to ensure conviction and maximum punishment for Drayton, even if some of the juries failed to reach a verdict or acquitted him. Drayton argued that the larceny indictments were untenable because he had helped the slaves escape to gain their freedom and had not stolen them for his own personal gain. He further noted "of both these acts charged against me"—stealing slaves "and the helping them to escape from their master—I could not be guilty" (Drayton, *Personal Memoir*, pp. 72-73).

In his first trial Drayton was convicted of larceny. Before the jury in that trial had finished its deliberations, however, the district attorney began a second larceny trial. Drayton was convicted in both of these and sentenced to twenty years in prison.

The district attorney also prosecuted Mr. Sayres, who was the owner of the *Pearl* and who had been on board at the time of its capture. Sayres was acquitted of larceny in two separate trials. An agreement was then reached. Sayres pled guilty to the seventy-four indictments for transporting the slaves and was fined $150 per slave. He was to remain in prison until the fines were paid. He was allowed, however, to appeal his case on the legal issues. Sayres remained in jail while appealing his case because the fine remained unpaid.

Drayton then appealed to the U.S. Circuit Court, which overturned his conviction. The court ruled that the trial judge did not properly instruct the jury on the meaning of larceny and on the requirement that the prosecution needed to prove Drayton intended to steal the slaves for his own enjoyment or for pecuniary gain. Despite this reversal, the district attorney again brought Drayton to trial on the larceny charge, but this time he was acquitted in two successive trials. At this point the district attorney "agreed to abandon the remaining larceny cases" in return for Drayton's "consent to verdicts in the transportation cases on the same terms with those in the case of Sayres" (ibid., p. 101). Drayton agreed to this and was fined a total of $10,060 and ordered to remain in prison until he paid his fine.

Drayton and Sayres remained in prison, unable to pay their fines, until August 1852, when President Fillmore pardoned them. This pardon was accomplished through the political intervention and a legal brief of Charles Sumner. Other politicians, including Reps. Joshua R. Giddings and Horace Mann and Sens. John P. Hale, Salmon P. Chase, and William H. Seward, also intervened on behalf of Drayton and Sayres.

■ Drayton, Daniel. Personal memoir of Daniel Drayton, for four years and four months a prisoner (for charity's sake) in Washington jail. Including a narrative of the voyage and capture of the schooner Pearl. Boston, Bela Marsh; New York, American and Foreign Anti-Slavery Society, 1855. 122 p.

E450.D76

The case of Drayton and Sayres became something of an antislavery cause célèbre until their pardon. Numerous antislavery politicians took part in their defense and brought the issue of their imprisonment to the floors of the House and Senate. In Boston there were mass meetings to protest their incarceration.

Drayton's memoir recounts his life from childhood until his pardon and release from prison. It is an excellent example of how the antislavery movement used the trial of one man to attack the entire system of slavery and its influence on the nation. Drayton tells of his experiences as a ship captain before he began to help slaves, and how slaves often asked him to take them to freedom. He discusses his conversion to religion and to antislavery.

In great detail he explains how he was treated with unnecessary harshness after his arrest because of the nature of his crime. Similarly, he describes how a mob tried to silence Gamaliel Bailey's antislavery newspaper, the *National Era,* after Drayton's arrest. He quotes speeches by Southern senators and congressmen ''in honor of the new French revolution, the expulsion of Louis-Philippe, and the establishment of a republic in France'' to show the hypocrisy of slaveholding in a ''free'' country (p. 26). These speeches were later introduced as evidence to prove that the slaves who ran away by boarding Drayton's schooner could have gained their ideas of liberty from the words of slaveholders.

Drayton's *Memoir* also contains much of the testimony and legal arguments from his trials. It includes the speeches of the attorneys, the charge of the judge, and the kind of testimony presented. This material was not published in any other form and is useful background and supplementary information to his reported appeal, *Drayton* v. *United States.*

In re William Chaplin

(D.C. 1851)(Unreported)

William Lawrence Chaplin was born in Groton, Massachusetts, in 1798. The son of a Presbyterian minister, he was educated at Andover Academy and Harvard College. He later practiced law, edited newspapers, and became a temperance reformer. In the 1840s he moved to Washington, D.C., where he argued a number of cases on behalf of slaves who claimed to be free. Because of his reputation as a man opposed to slavery, Chaplin was ultimately asked to aid two slaves who had recently left their masters.

The slaves were owned by Rep. Robert Toombs and Rep. Alexander H. Stephens, both of Georgia. Chaplin was planning a trip to Pennsylvania, and friends of the two runaways asked him to take the slaves along. He agreed to do this. However, Chaplin's carriage was already under surveillance by a professional slave catcher named John Goddard. Goddard and his men easily intercepted them on the road leading out of Washington. They beat Chaplin and wounded one of the slaves when they shot into the carriage.

Goddard took Chaplin to the civil authorities, who placed him in the District of Columbia jail. The district attorney attempted to tie Chaplin's activities to the city's antislavery newspaper, the *National Era*. However, Chaplin denied any connection between his action and the newspaper, or its editor, Dr. Gamaliel Bailey. Goddard and the district attorney also hoped to severely punish Chaplin. But they quickly discovered that the only crime Chaplin could be convicted of was the rather minor change of "assisting the two slaves to escape: the penalty for which, by the laws in force in the District, is, at the utmost, but two hundred dollars for each slave" (*The Case of William L. Chaplin*, p. 27).

Goddard then decided that he had not captured Chaplin in the District of Columbia but, rather, in Maryland. A complaint was soon lodged with authorities in Maryland, and Chaplin was charged both with assault and battery on Goddard and with slave stealing in Maryland. Meanwhile, the district attorney in Washington proceeded to obtain an indictment for slave stealing against Chaplin. This was done despite the precedent set in the case of Daniel Drayton, where the "Circuit Court of the District had solemnly decided . . . that a state of facts precisely like that in Mr. Chaplin's case *would not sustain a charge of larceny,* and that it amounted, at most, only to the misdemeanor of assisting slaves to escape" (p. 29). At the urging of the Washington district attorney, bail was set at $6,000. As soon as this bail was paid, Chaplin was seized and

Robert Toombs (1810-1885). A Whig congressman and senator from Georgia, Toombs worked hard for the passage of the Compromise of 1850. Although initially a Unionist, he became secretary of state of the Confederacy in 1861. One of his slaves was among those who tried to escape with William Chaplin in 1851. LC-USZ62-13683

turned over to Maryland officials. There Chaplin's bail was set at the extraordinary amount of $25,000.

It took some time for Chaplin to raise this bail. But even after it was raised it was almost impossible for Chaplin's friends to find any citizens of Maryland willing to act as sureties and bail bondsmen. However, after six weeks of negotiations and searches, two men, both

Alexander Hamilton Stephens (1812-1883). A Georgia congressman, Stephens opposed secession, although he was a vigorous advocate of states' rights. In 1861 he became vice president of the Confederate States of America. By this time he had had firsthand experience with a union that was half slave and half free. One of his slaves had tried to escape from Washington with the aid of William Chaplin.

Brady-Handy Collection. LC-BH82-4439

slaveholders, agreed to sign for his bond. They received $19,000 from Chaplin's lawyers. Chaplin was then taken to Annapolis, where a sympathetic judge received the bail in a secret proceeding. They thought secrecy was necessary because they feared a mob would attack and perhaps lynch Chaplin if he were publicly released from jail.

Chaplin believed he would get a fair trial in neither Maryland nor the District of Columbia. The high bails set in both places were an indication of the hostility toward him. In addition, the charges in both cases were apparently without any legal foundation. He had never been to Maryland, so the indictments in that state represented a total misuse of the judicial process. In the District Columbia he was charged with larceny, when his only crime was helping slaves to escape. In both cases it was clear that Goddard and his associates were prepared to perjure themselves. Under these circumstances, Chaplin left Maryland and did not return for his trial. "Thus, after an imprisonment of six weeks at Washington, and of thirteen more at Rockville [Maryland], was Mr. Chaplin delivered out of the hands of the Philistines; not, however, till his friends had paid for him the enormous ransom of $25,000" (p. 49).

■ The case of William L. Chaplin; being an appeal to all respectors of law and justice, against the cruel and oppressive treatment to which, under color of legal proceedings, he has been subjected, in the District of Columbia and the state of Maryland. Boston, Published by the Chaplin Committee, 1851. 54 p.

E450.C45

This book "is addressed to the whole people of the United States" insofar as it "relates to the treatment of Mr. Chaplin, in the District of Columbia" (p. 3). The advertisement at the beginning notes: "The District is theirs" (p. 3). The aspects of Chaplin's case that relate to Maryland are directed "to the good citizens of that State; who are bound, if they are able, to preserve the integrity of their own laws, and the impartiality of the administration of justice by their own State tribunals" (p. 3). The book is designed to let the nation know about Chaplin's suffering and, no doubt, to raise money to pay for the tremendous cost of freeing him.

Most of the book describes the arrest and treatment of Chaplin. Detailed descriptions of the jails he stayed in, the conditions of inmates, and statements about slavery in the District of Columbia are all designed to gain sympathy for the antislavery cause and Chaplin. In addition, in an eleven-page discussion, the authors attempt to show that slavery is illegal in the District of Columbia. They base this position on four connected arguments. First, the laws of the district were based on the laws of Maryland, as of 1800. Second, all laws of Maryland were initially based on the charter of Lord Baltimore, which prohibited any laws "repugnant or contrary . . . to the laws, statutes, and rights of this our kingdom of England" (p. 6). Third, the *Somerset* decision of 1772 declared slavery illegal in England. This was supported by many other English cases. Therefore, any laws creating slavery in Maryland before 1772 were not binding. Fourth, no Maryland statutes creating slavery in the state were passed after the Revolution and before 1800. Thus, slavery in the District of Columbia must be illegal.

In re Thomas Brown

(Union Cty. [Ky.] Ct. 1854)(Unreported)

Thomas Brown was a peddler who in 1850 moved from Cincinnati to Henderson, Kentucky. He was a devout Methodist and, as such, opposed to slavery. This, plus his free-state origins, made him suspect in Kentucky. Brown's mode of travel was "a small spring wagon, drawn by two horses. It had black oil-cloth curtains that could be fastened down tightly, as was necessary to protect the goods [he carried for sale] from the weather" (*Brown's Three Years,* p. 6).

In May 1854 he traveled to Evansville, Indiana, to sell some clothing his wife had made. On his return to Henderson he was stopped by two men from Evansville, who accused him of "assisting a woman and her children to escape from Union County [Kentucky]" into Indiana (ibid., p. 8). Brown refused to yield to these professional slave catchers, since they lacked any writ or other legal authority. However, he was later arrested under a writ issued by a sheriff in Henderson. He was quickly taken to the Union county seat of Morganfield and held under $5,000 bail. Because he was unable to pay this amount, he remained in the county jail awaiting trial at the next circuit court.

Although arrested in May 1854, Brown was not tried until April 1855. During this period he was kept in the Union County jail in an underground cell that could only be reached through a trap door. The cell, sixteen by eighteen feet, had no toilet facilities. Thus "maggots were crawling over the floor" (ibid., p. 11). After his trial Brown remained in this cell until his transfer, a few weeks later, to the Kentucky state prison.

Before Brown's trial, allegations were printed in an Evansville, Indiana, newspaper that those who helped arrest him had been bribed by U.S. Senator Archibald Dixon. The testimony against Brown initially came from three sources: an Indian (who was ineligible to testify under

Kentucky law), a young Irish boy, and a man named Ward. Just before Brown's arrest, the Indian and the Irish boy had been tried for helping slaves escape in Indiana but had been acquitted. Ward had allegedly been paid to secure Brown's arrest. At his trial a fourth man, James Steele, also testified against Brown. A group of citizens from Steele's home county presented an affidavit asserting "we believe him to be inordinately avaricious. So much so, that the prospect of gain would materially influence his testimony in a court of Justice" (ibid., p. 13).

Nevertheless, on the strength of the testimony of these four witnesses, Brown was convicted and sentenced to two years, this time in the penitentiary. This sentence did not begin until he arrived at the penitentiary. However, he was not sent there until two weeks after his conviction. At first Brown was whipped and beaten and put to hard labor. Later, however, he became a prison messenger, until he was finally released in May 1857.

■ Brown, Thomas. Brown's three years in the Kentucky prisons, from May 30, 1854, to May 18, 1857. Indianapolis, Courier Company Print., 1857. 21 p.

E450.B88

This pamphlet was published after Brown's release from prison. One reason for its publication was to raise money for the Brown family. It sold for twenty-five cents a copy and could be purchased from Mrs. Brown in Indianapolis. A note on the back of the pamphlet stated the terms of sale and declared: "It is hoped that those who sympathize with the family, that has suffered so much, will encourage the sale of this entire edition, and thereby relieve, in a slight degree, their present needs."

The pamphlet contains the only available printed account of Brown's trial. However, most of the text is devoted not to the trial, but to prison conditions and Brown's encounters with runaway slaves while in prison. Throughout the case Brown denied any wrongdoing. In the pamphlet itself he is evasive. In the end, the pamphlet declares that Brown "suffered for no crime, and had no remorse to aggravate the cruelties inflicted upon him and his fellow convicts. The only charge brought against him, was that of being neighbor to those who fell among thieves, and even that, bribed testimony failed to substantiate" (p. 21). Brown was clearly opposed to slavery and believed that slaves were neighbors who had fallen "among thieves." Brown certainly did not condemn those who helped slaves escape. It is unclear, however, if he actually helped any slaves escape before his arrest.

Commonwealth v. Brown

(Jefferson City |Va.| Cir. Ct. 1859)(Unreported)

John Brown's raid at Harpers Ferry, Virginia, was the most
spectacular event of the 1850s. At the time of his raid John Brown was
famous—or infamous—for his activities in the Kansas Territory. There
he had been involved in the armed conflicts between free-state settlers
and slave-state settlers. In May 1856 two free-state settlers were murdered
by a band of proslavery men. A day or two later the free-state city of
Lawrence was invaded by proslavery men, and two newspaper offices
and a number of other buildings were destroyed. In retaliation for these
and other acts, Brown led an attack on the proslavery Pottawatomie
settlement, in which five proslavery men were killed. Later Brown
engaged in various guerrilla activities from his settlement near Osawatomie. Brown, or "Osawatomie Brown" as he was known, became a
symbol of free-state resistance in Kansas. When a cease-fire was finally
achieved in Kansas, Brown and his sons left the territory. During this
period two of Brown's sons were imprisoned on false charges, and a
third, Frederick, was killed by proslavery forces.

In 1857 Brown went to Boston where he sought and gained
support for an invasion of the South to free the slaves. Among those
who contributed to his plans were Gerrit Smith, Dr. Samuel G. Howe,
Rev. Thomas Wentworth Higginson, George L. Stearns, Rev. Theodore

After seizing the armory at Harpers Ferry, John Brown waited there for slaves to
join him and was trapped in the engine room. From *The Life, Trials, and
Execution of Capt. John Brown* (New York, 1859).

"Attack on the Insurgents at the Bridge by the Railroad Men," Harpers Ferry.
From *The Life, Trials, and Execution of Capt. John Brown* (New York, 1859).

Parker, and Franklin B. Sanborn. Before Brown launched his invasion of Virginia, he returned once more to Kansas under the nom de guerre Shebel Morgan. While in Kansas he crossed the border into Missouri, where he liberated eleven slaves and successfully brought them to Canada while authorities chased him the entire eleven hundred miles in an eighty-two day odyssey. After this Brown returned to the East and made final preparations for his foray into Virginia.

As a military operation Brown's raid was disastrous. It was a mixture of careful preparation and military planning, wild hopes, and foolish expectations. Brown rented a farmhouse in nearby Maryland in July 1859. From there he made his plans to seize the U.S. armory.

On the night of October 16, 1859, Brown led an armed group of twenty-two men into Harpers Ferry, where they seized the armory and announced they had come to free the slaves of Virginia. Brown hoped the slaves in the area would join him, and he would then arm them from weapons in the arsenal and with pikes stored at a nearby farm. He then planned to lead an uprising of slaves and end slavery in the South. Brown brought with him a "Provisional Constitution and Ordinances for the People of the United States."

Brown ignored the advice of the famous black abolitionist Frederick Douglass, who warned him that slaves would not know of the raid, and even if they did most would be reluctant, fearful, or unable to join him. He failed to leave Harpers Ferry after successfully seizing the armory because he was waiting for the slaves to join him and, he was ultimately trapped in the building's engine house. He allowed some

Samuel Gridley Howe (1807-1876). Dr. Samuel G. Howe was one of the leading physicians in antebellum America, and he was an expert on the care and education of the deaf and other handicapped people. He was also a member of the Boston Vigilance Committee, which aided fugitive slaves. He aided John Brown and was one of the "secret six." His fame was somewhat overshadowed by that of his wife Julia Ward Howe, the author of the "Battle Hymn of the Republic."

Engraving by H. W. Smith. LC-USZ62-26637.

people to escape after they discovered his activities, and thus word of the raid reached nearby towns and eventually the nation's capital.

There was some fighting between Brown and local citizens on the morning of October 17. By the afternoon Brown was surrounded by local militia, and that evening U.S. Marines arrived under the command of Col. Robert E. Lee and Lt. J. E. B. Stuart. On October 18 the marines battered down the doors of the engine house and captured Brown and his remaining force. Of the twenty-two men in Brown's force, five escaped, ten were killed (including two of Brown's sons) and seven, including Brown himself, were captured. His son Watson and others were killed under flags of truce or while attempting to surrender. Once fighting broke out in Harpers Ferry, the residents respected neither white flags nor raised hands.

Brown was wounded during the attack on the armory but survived to stand trial. He was indicted on October 25, a week after the invasion was put down, and was placed on trial the same day. On October 31 he was found guilty of conspiring with slaves to rebel and of committing murder and treason. He was sentenced to death and hung on December 2, 1859.

In the period between his conviction and execution, Brown wrote eloquent letters to friends and supporters. These were widely printed in the Northern press. In them he explained his humanitarian motives and defended his failed mission. These letters made Brown a hero, particularly among the intelligencia of the North. They brought tears to the eyes of millions of readers as he expressed, with power and emotion, his love of freedom and his hatred of slavery. In one letter he declared: "They cannot imprison or chain or hang the soul. I go joyfully in behalf of millions that have no rights that the great and glorious Christian Republic is bound to respect. Strange change in morals, political as well as Christian, since 1776. I look forward to other changes in God's good time, believing that 'the fashion of this world passeth' away" (Brown to Thomas B. Musgrove, Nov. 17, 1859).

While in prison he persuasively portrayed himself as a Christian martyr, a messenger of God, whose sole purpose on earth was to die so that the innocent slaves might be set free. Even his failure was part of God's plan. To one minister he wrote: "Had Samson kept to his determination of not telling Delilah where his great strength lay, he would probably have never overturned the house" (Brown to Rev. Heman Humphrey, Nov. 25, 1859). In his "Plea for Captain John Brown" Henry David Thoreau wrote:

> He did not go to the college called Harvard, good old Alma Mater as she is. . . . But he went to the great university of the West, where he sedulously pursued the study of Liberty, for which he had early betrayed a fondness, and having taken many degrees, he finally commenced the public practice of Humanity in Kansas, as you all know. Such were *his humanities,* and not any study of grammar. He would have left a Greek accent slanting the wrong way, and righted up a falling man.

> Some eighteen hundred years ago Christ was crucified; this morning, perchance, Captain Brown was hung. These are the two ends of a chain which is not without its links. He is not

Old Brown any longer; he is an angel of light. ["A Plea for Captain John Brown," *Writings of Henry David Thoreau,* vol. 6, pp. 358-69, first printed in James Redpath, *Echoes of Harpers Ferry* (Boston, 1860)]

Sometime after this plea Brown was finally hung. The poet Whittier wrote:

John Brown of Osawatomie,
  They led him out to die.
When lo, a poor-slave-mother
  With her little child pressed nigh.
Then the bold, blue eyes grew tender,
  And the old, hard face grew mild,
And he stooped between the jeering ranks,
  And kissed the negro's child.

[*New York Independent,* December 22, 1859; quoted in Julius Ables, *Man on Fire: John Brown and the Cause of Liberty* (New York: Macmillan, 1971), p. 368]

Brown himself left a prophetic and simple summation of the whole affair: "I John Brown am now quite *certain* that the crimes of this *guilty land will* never be purged *away*; but with Blood. I had *as I now think; vainly* flattered myself that without *very much* bloodshed; it might be done" (quoted in Stephen B. Oates, *To Purge This Land with Blood: A Biography of John Brown* [New York: Harper & Row, 1970], p. 351).

■ Brown, John, *defendant.* The life, trial and conviction of Captain John Brown, known as "Old Brown of Osawatomie," with a full account of the attempted insurrection at Harper's Ferry. Compiled from official and authentic sources. New York, Robert M. De Witt [1859] 100 p.

E451.L72 Rare Book Room

——The life, trial and execution of Captain John Brown, known as "Old Brown of Osawatomie," with a full account of the attempted insurrection at Harper's Ferry. Compiled from official and authentic sources. Including Cooke's confession and all the incidents of the execution. New York, Robert M. De Witt [1859] 108 p.

E451.L73 1859 LLRBR

This book was the first published account of John Brown's life and trial. The first edition appeared a week before Brown's execution. That this book was published so quickly after Brown's arrest and trial indicates the instant appeal, both political and commercial, that Brown seemed to have in the North. *The Life, Trial and Conviction* was prepared in only a few weeks. It contained engravings of Brown and his associates and sold for twenty-five cents. An account of Brown's execution, a copy of his will, "John Brown's Last Letter to his Family," and the confession of his associate, John E. Cooke, were added to the second edition, which came out in the weeks following Brown's death.

According to the introduction this book was published because "the madness of the attempt, the boldness—amounting to heroism—of the handful of men who were concerned in the movement, and especially the romantic history and personal character of the chief actor, have awakened in the public mind an ardent desire to know more of the man and his intentions." The editor hoped to "gratify this desire" for information about Brown, and "to record, in convenient form, the facts concerning the outbreak and its suppression" (p. 7). The editor no doubt also expected to profit from growing Northern interest in the case.

The volume begins with a brief biographical sketch of Brown. This includes a short history of his exploits in Kansas, followed by very brief sketches of the other participants in the raid. The bulk of the book is devoted to the attack on Harpers Ferry and Brown's trial.

The biography is quite sympathetic to Brown but recognizes some of his faults—or at least his unusual characteristics. He is compared with "such fanatics as Peter the Hermit . . . Joanna Southcote . . . Ignatius Loyola . . . or Don Quixote. . . . It was Brown's idea that he was divinely appointed to bring American Slavery to a sudden and violent end" (pp. 7-8). He is described as a man of "firmness, conscientiousness, and self-esteem, indicating a stern will, unswerving integrity, and remarkable self-possession" (p. 8). His business failures in early life are blamed on evil and greedy men or other forces beyond his control. He is portrayed as a peaceful man "honorable and just" whose "insane fanaticism" was "impelled . . . by stimulations applied by others to his ardent and fearless temperament" (p. 10).

The descriptions of the attack on Harpers Ferry and the trial in this book comes from eye-witness accounts, letters, recorded public statements, and trial transcripts. What emerges is the clear desire of the Virginia authorities to ensure a speedy execution of Brown after a trial that appeared fair but that in fact would not delay proceedings or give Brown a chance to defend himself or escape. Most of the forms of a fair trial were present in Brown's trial, but little of the substance.

Brown was severely wounded at Harpers Ferry. At the time of his capture "he had a severe bayonet wound in his side, and his face and hair were clotted with blood'' (p. 35). Nevertheless, he was interrogated immediately after his arrest. A week later he was indicted and placed on trial that same day. Throughout the trial Brown lay down on a pallet, except when he was able to muster the strength to rise and address the court. Brown was arrested with a large sum of money on him, but this was confiscated, and he was not allowed to use it to support his defense.

The court appointed two local attorneys to defend Brown. When the case opened Brown immediately asked for a delay in the proceedings. He noted ''I have been promised a fair trial,'' but that at the moment he was unable to attend the trial because of his health. ''I have a severe wound in the back, or rather in one kidney, which enfeebles me very much. But I am doing well, and I only ask for a very short delay of my trial, and I think I may get able to listen to it; and I merely ask this, that, as the saying is, 'the devil may have his dues,' no more. I wish to say, further, that my hearing is impaired, and rendered indistinct, in consequence of wounds I have about my head. I cannot hear distinctly at all; I could not hear what the Court has said this morning'' (p. 62). Brown's court-appointed attorneys also argued for a delay on health grounds and because ''he has heard to-day that counsel of his own choice will be here, whom he will, of course, prefer'' (p. 62).

The prosecutor opposed any delay because ''the condition of things'' would ''render it dangerous to delay.'' Despite Brown's obvious wounds, the prosecutor thought Brown was fit to stand trial. He did not mind if Brown imported attorneys, as long as they would do nothing ''to weaken our present position, and give strength to our enemies abroad . . .'' (p. 62). It was clear that Brown would be given a fair trial only if fairness did not delay the proceedings or alter the expected outcome. The court refused all of Brown's requests and immediately began to choose a jury.

On the second day of the trial the court received a telegram from the neighborhood in Ohio where Brown once lived, asserting that Brown was insane. Brown rejected this defense, but again requested a delay of the trial until counsel from the North could arrive. He also expected witnesses to arrive. The prosecutor declared Brown would get a fair trial ''according to the laws and policy of the State of Virginia'' (p. 65).

On the third day of the trial George H. Hoyt of Boston arrived to aid in Brown's defense. Hoyt, however, was not an experienced attorney, but was ''quite a youth'' (p. 71). The prosecutor tried to prevent Hoyt from joining the defense team because, although a member of the Boston bar, Hoyt had failed to bring proof of that membership with him. Judge Daniel Parker, in one of his few rulings in Brown's favor, allowed Hoyt to assist in the defense. The court, however, did not recess to allow Hoyt to prepare his case. Instead, testimony continued and on that day the prosecution rested its case.

Brown had asked that a number of witnesses be subpoenaed for him. When called, however, they were not in the courtroom, and it was clear the Virginia authorities had not attempted to ensure these witnesses' arrival. Brown then "arose from his mattress, evidently excited," and addressed the court. "I discover that, notwithstanding all the assurances I have received of a fair trial, nothing like a fair trial is to be given me" (p. 76). He recounted his physical condition, the fact that he was not allowed access to his money to hire someone to serve his subpoenas, and his lack of counsel. He again asked for a delay. Brown "then lay down again, drew his blanket over him, and closed his eyes and appeared to sink in tranquil slumber" (p. 77). Hoyt, who had arrived that day, reiterated the request for a continuance. The prosecutor ranted that the trial was fair and challenged the relevance of Brown's witnesses. Brown's court-appointed attorneys then resigned from the case. At this point the court did adjourn.

On the fourth day of the trial, Samuel Chilton of Washington, D.C., and Henry Griswold of Cleveland, Ohio, arrived to take over Brown's defense. They stressed that Brown had not attempted to kill anyone and that he might have destroyed the city but did not. On the other hand, Brown's son was killed under a flag of truce, and others in the party were murdered in cold blood after they surrendered or as they attempted to surrender. Some of the bodies of Brown's men were mutilated during the battle. Finally, they argued that Brown could not have committed treason against the state of Virginia because he was not a citizen of that state and therefore owed no allegiance to it.

The judge and jury rejected these legal arguments. Brown was found guilty after three-quarters of an hour of deliberations. In addressing the court before sentencing, Brown declared his only object was "to free slaves." He denied that any others were involved in his plans or that he had "any disposition to commit treason or excite slaves to rebel or make any general insurrection." He acknowledged that "Considering all the circumstances, it has been more generous than I expected" (pp. 94-95). Brown was sentenced to die on December 2 and that sentence was duly carried out.

This book details the execution. It also contains a short history of various slave revolts in the South, including that of Nat Turner, and transcripts of interviews with Brown, including those conducted by Rep. Clement Valladingham of Ohio and Sen. James Mason of Virginia. Its illustrations depict Brown and the events at Harpers Ferry. While not portraying Brown as an innocent martyr, the book is sympathetic to the man and his cause. More importantly, it allows Brown and the participants in the raid and trial to speak for themselves.

A

JOURNAL

OF THE

PROCEEDINGS

IN

The Detection of the Conspiracy

FORMED BY

Some *White* People, in Conjunction with *Negro* and other *Slaves*,

FOR

Burning the City of *NEW-YORK* in AMERICA,

And Murdering the Inhabitants.

Which Conspiracy was partly put in Execution, by Burning His Majesty's House in Fort GEORGE, within the said City, on Wednesday the Eighteenth of *March*, 1741. and setting Fire to several Dwelling and other Houses there, within a few Days succeeding. And by another Attempt made in Prosecution of the same infernal Scheme, by putting Fire between two other Dwelling-Houses within the said City, on the Fifteenth Day of *February*, 1742; which was accidentally and timely discovered and extinguished.

CONTAINING,

I. A NARRATIVE of the Trials, Condemnations, Executions, and Behaviour of the several Criminals, at the Gallows and Stake, with their *Speeches* and *Confessions*; with Notes, Observations and Reflections occasionally interspersed throughout the Whole.

II. AN APPENDIX, wherein is set forth some additional Evidence concerning the said Conspiracy and Conspirators, which has come to Light since their Trials and Executions.

III. LISTS of the several Persons (Whites and Blacks) committed on Account of the Conspiracy; and of the several Criminals executed; and of those transported, with the Places whereto.

By the Recorder of the City of NEW-YORK.

Quid facient Domini, audent cum talia Fures? Virg. Ecl.

NEW-YORK:

Printed by *James Parker*, at the New Printing-Office, 1744.

Fires in the city of New York in March and April 1741 provoked fear of slave revolts and suspicion of conspiracy. Title page from *A Journal of the Proceedings in the Detection of the Conspiracy* (New York, 1744), by Daniel Horsmanden.

Slave Revolts

Throughout the existence of slavery in America, masters often tried to convince themselves that blacks were somehow less than human, which justified their enslavement. The slave owners also invented, or perpetuated, other rationales for the peculiar institution. One of these was that slaves were basically content and even happy in their situation. Indeed, masters believed that such contentment was logical because they believed the slaves incapable of surviving without the help of whites. One of the classic defenses of slavery in America was based on the notion that the Africans were rescued from ignorance, heathenish ways, and inadequate food when they were taken to America.

Most masters no doubt honestly believed they treated their slaves well and that their slaves were happy and content. Some slaves may indeed have been happy. Many were no doubt resigned to, if not content with, their situation. They probably understood that a successful escape was difficult, if not impossible, and that a successful revolt against their white masters was ridiculous to even consider. In the slave South the whites had the power, organization, and knowledge to easily defeat any revolt. Even in those sections of the Deep South where slaves made up a majority of the population, whites were still firmly in control.

Despite these conditions there were some major, and many minor, slave revolts in what is now the United States. There were also slave revolts in some of the British colonies in the Caribbean (see Appendix). The two most famous slave revolts—the Stono Rebellion of 1739 in South Carolina and the Nat Turner Rebellion of 1831 in Virginia—led to trials, but neither was reported at the time. Thus, they are not part of this annotated bibliography. The original manuscript transcripts made during the trial of Nat Turner have been reproduced in modern, commercially printed anthologies and are available to scholars.

In re New York Slave Conspirators

(N. Y. Sup. Ct. 1741-42) (Unreported)*

Between March 17 and April 6, 1741, the city of New York suffered a series of devastating and mysterious fires. Ten fires in all—

*The New York Slave Conspiracy, 1741-42

197

eight of them in a single week, and four in a single day—destroyed much of the city. The first and most damaging of the fires destroyed a good portion of Fort George, the seat of the colony's government, the residence of the governor, and the symbol of authority, safety, and stability. There were also a number of robberies that were apparently connected to the fires. At the same time these fires were burning the city, Great Britain—and thus her colony of New York—was involved in a war with Spain known as the War of Jenkins' Ear. During the war a number of New Yorkers were engaged in combat, some Spaniards were captured and incarcerated in New York City, and the colony of Georgia was invaded by Spanish soldiers.

Coinciding with a fear of slaves and with the rash of fires, these wartime conditions produced a panic within the New York government. City officials believed the fires were part of a larger plot by slaves, Spanish agents, captured Spanish seamen, and a few greedy whites to overthrow the city in a general slave rebellion. While attempts were being made to put out the fires on April 6, a slave was seen running from a burning building. This led to an alarm that *"the negroes were rising"* (Horsmanden, *The New-York Conspiracy*, p. 29). This cry, combined with other events, led to mass arrests and trials of slaves. Although some slaves confessed to being part of a large conspiracy and thus were spared the rope or the faggot, it is unlikely such a huge conspiracy existed.

As early as March 1, a slave was arrested for theft. That same week a white woman known as Peggy was also arrested. She was notorious for prostitution and various liaisons with black men. She was charged with aiding in the theft of silver items and other goods. It was not until the fires of mid-March and April, however, that officials in New York connected these, and other isolated arrests for robbery with a larger conspiracy. On April 8, a white tavern owner and his wife, John and Sarah Hughson, were arrested and "charged as accessaries to divers felonies and misdemeanors." The prostitute Peggy had rented a room from the Hughsons, and it appeared that they were connected to numerous robberies and the fires. On April 11 the common council met and concluded that the recent fires "were occasioned and set on foot by some villainous confederacy of latent enemies" (ibid., p. 31). Two more slaves were arrested on April 13 and another on the seventeenth.

A grand jury met on April 21 to consider the fires, robberies, and illegal selling of liquor to slaves and began examining witnesses on April 23. Peggy had been in jail for almost two months. Although she was given a chance to turn state's evidence with the promise of a "recommendation to the governor for a pardon," she "positively denied knowing any thing" about the fires (ibid., p. 41). On April 24, the Hughsons, Peggy, and two slaves were indicted and their trials set for the next day. However, their trials were at first postponed three days, and then the attorney general moved that they be postponed until May 1. On that day the two slaves were tried and convicted. Trials resumed on May 6, and the Hughsons were convicted of receiving stolen property.

Up to this point in the trials there had been little proof of a conspiracy or any direct evidence to tie the Hughsons and Peggy to the fires. However, accumulating testimony and depositions indicated to the authorities that a great conspiracy existed. On May 11 the first two slaves convicted of robbery were hanged while wearing chains. The next day the Hughsons and Peggy were brought to trial on the new charge of "conspiring, confederating and combining with divers negroes and others, to burn the city of New York, and also to kill and destroy the inhabitants thereof" (ibid., p. 61).

From that day until August 31 the city saw a long series of arrests, trials, and executions. Ultimately 20 whites and 154 black slaves were arrested. Four of the whites—the Hughsons, Peggy, and a purported Catholic priest—were hanged. The Hughsons' daughter was convicted and sentenced to death, but later pardoned. Seven other whites were discharged or pardoned "on security of departure from the province" (ibid., tables following p. 385). The slaves faced even worse fates. Thirteen were burned to death at the stake and another eighteen were hanged. Seventy-one were transported out of the colony, most going to the sugar-producing islands in the Caribbean, where their life expectancy would be short.

More of the slaves might have been executed or perhaps imprisoned had the existing facilities allowed this. But, by July 4 the jail was "thronged with negroes committed as confederates in the conspiracy, many whereof had made confessions of their guilt in hopes of pardon . . . and others who were pardoned and turned [state's] evidence" (ibid., p. 235). The jailers feared that "considering the season of the year, that such numbers closely confined might be apt to breed an infection." Thus, forty-one were chosen for transportation out of the colony. That same day, however, another black was taken from the jail and "executed according to sentence . . . at the stake" (ibid., pp. 235-36). When this particular slave was taken to be burned to death, the "wretch set his back to the stake, and raising up one of his legs, laid it upon the fire, and lifting up his hands and eyes, cried aloud, and several times repeated the names" of the other slaves "who he had said first brought him into this plot" (ibid., p. 237). Later that evening these slaves were arrested. Despite the attempts to empty the jails in early July, arrests kept them full.

Trials, executions, and deportations continued throughout the summer. The last burning at the stake took place on July 18. Blacks were hanged as late as August 15 and both whites and blacks were being deported in September and October. The last major trial began on July 21 and did not conclude until August 29. This was the trial of John Ury, a white man indicted on charges that he with "malice afore-thought wickedly, maliciously, voluntarily, wilfully, and feloniously, did counsel, abet, procure and encourage" blacks and some whites to destroy the city (ibid., p. 288). The prosecution argued that Ury, "as a popish priest, baptized Hughson, his wife and daughter, and Kerry [alias Peggy], and also divers negroes, and told them then, and at several other times, that he could forgive sins, and that he forgave them their sins relating to the plot" (ibid., p. 289). Ury never admitted that he was in fact a Catholic or a priest, but others testified that he was. Some of the most damaging testimony came from Sarah Hughson, the daughter of John and Sarah Hughson. She testified in exchange for her life, since she had already been convicted and sentenced to death.

After the execution of Ury on August 29 the trials began to wind down. However, as late as February and March 1742 there were still fears of a slave uprising. On March 15, 1742, a slave was executed for arson. Although this did not lead to mass arrests, some other slaves were arrested, and the grand jury investigated the situation.

The final chapter of the New York conspiracy took place on September 2, 1742. A white woman named Mary Burton received a reward of eighty-one pounds from the common council of the city. Burton was herself an indentured servant under the control of John and Sarah Hughson. At great personal risk she had informed on her master. Ironically, Burton did not get the full one hundred pounds reward offered by the New York Common Council, because nineteen pounds had already been spent by the city to purchase Burton's indenture so that she could legally (and safely) testify against her master.

■ Horsmanden, Daniel. A journal of the proceedings in the detection of the conspiracy formed by some white people, in conjunction with Negro and other slaves, for burning the City of New-York in America, and murdering the inhabitants. Which conspiracy was partly put in execution, by burning His Majesty's house in Fort George . . . the eighteenth of March, 1741, and setting fire to several dwelling and other houses there, within a few days succeeding. And by another attempt . . . on the fifteenth day of February, 1742 . . . New-York. Printed by James Parker, at the New Printing-Office, 1744. 205 p.

F128.4.H81 Rare Book Room

——The New York conspiracy, or a history of the Negro plot, with the journal of the proceedings against the conspirators at New-York in the years 1741-2 . . . [2d ed.] New-York, Printed and published by Southwick & Pelsue, No. 3, New-Street, 1810. 385, [7] p.

——[Reprint] New York, Negro Universities Press [1969] 385 p.

——Edited with an introd. by Thomas J. Davis. Boston, Beacon Press [1971] 491 p.

The report of Daniel Horsmanden contains six sections: a preface, an introduction, the "Journal of the Proceedings Against the Conspirators at New-York in 1741," a conclusion, an appendix, and tables of those arrested and the disposition of their cases. Most of the book, pages 35-349, contains the "Journal of the Proceedings." The information there appears to be a reasonably complete record—although not a word-for-word transcript—of the trials.

It is difficult to trace all the evidence presented against each defendant in the journal of proceedings. Much of the evidence used in one trial would later be used (without any direct reference) in another trial. For example, on June 24 the court record noted "[i]ntimation having been given for some time past, that there had of late been Popish priests lurking about the town, diligent inquiry had been made for discovering them, but without effect; at length information was given, that one Ury, alias Jury, . . . was suspected to be one, and . . . he was taken into custody this day . . . [and] was committed to the city jail" (p. 182). Ury's trial, however, did not begin for almost another month. In the meantime numerous references to Ury and other defendants were made in various trials. The trials of the whites are much better documented here than those of the blacks. This probably reflects the racism of the period and the status of the defendants. Stronger evidence was needed to convict and execute a white than a black.

Throughout the trials there is a constant fear of Catholicism and a rather vague conspiracy. In his conclusion Horsmanden places most of the blame for the conspiracy and the burnings on the existence of a Catholic conspiracy. He declares that "if such priests had not been here (and some of capacities much superior to Ury's) there would have been no such plot; for upon this and no other footing can it be accounted for" (pp. 353-54). In a time of international tension and conflict between Catholic Spain and England, the colonial officials could easily blame any discontent on "popery."

In addition to fear of the Catholic church, these trials have an aspect of hysteria reminiscent of the Salem Witch Trials. Much of the evidence used would have been unacceptable in courts of the time, had not hysteria prevailed. Ury's conviction in particular seems to have been based on the unproven fear that he was a Catholic priest, rather than on any direct proof that he actually took part in the conspiracy. Indeed, despite the massive amount of material in this book, it is unclear whether or not there was any organized conspiracy. It is quite clear that if the Hughsons and some slaves had conspired together their plans did not involve most of those arrested, or even most of those executed. That most, but not all, of the executions took place in May, June, and the first eighteen days of July suggests that fear of the conspiracy may have died down after that. It is also possible that by that time more sober voices in the community suggested, as in Salem, that things had gone far enough. At the end of the conclusion the author declares that "a plot there was, and as to the parties and bloody purpose of it, we presume there can scarce be a doubt amongst us at this time" (p. 372). Such a statement suggests the New York authorities wished to convince their readers (and perhaps themselves, or at least their neighbors) of the propriety of their actions—actions which left eighteen smoldering corpses, and another twenty-two bodies hanging from the gallows.

The Denmark Vesey Conspirators

(Charleston [S.C.] Magis. Ct.)(Unreported)*

In 1817 Denmark Vesey, a free black in Charleston, South Carolina, began to plan a slave insurrection or revolution. His plans were disrupted in 1820 when white authorities forced an all-Negro church to disband. By 1821, however, a new Negro church was organized, and Vesey took up where he had left off. He used the church as a departure point for his rebellion. He was a lay preacher in the church as well as an organizer outside the church.

Vesey revealed his plans to five other blacks, who in turn organized recruits. Vesey initially planned to begin his rebellion on Sunday, July 14, 1822. However, in late May a house servant told his master that someone had attempted to recruit him for a rebellion. The recruiter, William Paul, confessed and named two conspirators who were above him in Vesey's hierarchy. These men, Mingo Harth and Peter Poyas, laughed at the accusations and convinced investigators that William Paul was crazy. Harth and Poyas were then released. On June 8 William Paul again confessed to authorities, and a trusted slave of

---

* The Denmark Vesey Conspiracy

Governor Thomas Bennett was named. This slave, Ned Bennett, also denied that any conspiracy existed.

In the meantime, Vesey moved the date of the rebellion up to June 16. On June 14, however, another slave confessed that a rebellion was about to take place. The militia was called out to police the streets of Charleston, and intense investigations began. In the next two months, 135 slaves were arrested. Of the ninety-seven who went to trial, thirty-five were hanged and forty-three were transported out of the United States and the rest were acquitted.

Vesey was a talented carpenter who was literate in English and spoke other languages as well. He had originally purchased his own freedom with winnings from a lottery. But he was unsatisfied with personal freedom as long as other blacks remained enslaved. Many of Vesey's ideas came from the Bible, the general notions of liberty prevalent in the United States, and reports of the congressional debates over admitting Missouri into the Union. Vesey incorrectly believed that many Northerners would support a slave uprising in the South. He was particularly influenced by Rufus King's speeches in Congress. South Carolinians blamed the Vesey plot on abolitionists and Northern agitators, although the record clearly shows this was not the case. Rather, Vesey organized the revolt himself. The plot led to fears in South Carolina and the rest of the South that there was a giant conspiracy to overthrow slavery. The discovery of Vesey's planned rebellion also led to a polarization of the North and the South. In the years after the Vesey plot, South Carolina would lead the South on the road from nullification to secession.

Blaming the North, abolitionists, and other outside forces for the Vesey conspiracy did not, however, eliminate the causes of slave discontent. Nor did it remove the fear of a rebellion. Despite the trials, hangings, and deportations, Charleston's white population could not rest easy after the plot was discovered. It was estimated that Vesey recruited up to nine thousand slaves and free blacks. But only 135 blacks were arrested. The report of the trials indicated how incomplete the investigative process was:

> That Peter [Poyas] was engaged in enlisting, was positively proved; but so scrupulously and resolutely to the last did he observe his pledge of secrecy to his associates, *that of the whole number arrested and tried, not one of them belonged to Peter's company.* Monday [another conspirator] acknowledged that he had kept a list, but had he not become state's evidence, but had died without disclosing as Peter did, as well might we have doubted that *he kept a list.* In the course of the trials it was also stated, that Vesey had a variety of papers and books relating to this transaction, *which he burnt when the discovery of the*

intended attempt was made. Monday also burnt his list, *and probably so did Peter at the same time.*

As these leaders only communicated to each other the numbers, and not the names of those whom they had engaged, and who constituted their company; and as with the exception of Monday, none of them betrayed their associates; the companies of Vesey, Peter, Ned, Rolla and Gullay Jack have escaped detection and punishment. [Kennedy and Parker. *An Official Report of the Trials of Sundry Negroes,* (p. 25-26)]

In the years following the discovery of the plot, no one in Charleston could know how many conspirators remained, to perhaps rise up at a later time. Throughout the 1820s Charleston was plagued with fires of mysterious origins. Rumors of rebellions and plots abounded. The Vesey conspiracy trials removed the immediate threat of a rebellion but did little to remove the anxieties of the whites in South Carolina.

It is estimated that Vesey and his coconspirators recruited as many as nine thousand slaves in Charleston and the surrounding area. Vesey had plans for six simultaneous attacks on Charleston. Two different groups of slaves were to attack the arsenal from opposite sides of the building. Vesey himself planned to enter the arsenal in disguise (wigs were made for this purpose) before the attacks began. Another slave wore around his neck the key to a store that sold rifles and powder. Still another slave had access to various stables in the city, and was preparing to have a slave cavalry on the streets within minutes after the rebellion was to begin. Vesey depended on the lax atmosphere in the city and the weakness of the slave patrols to make it possible for his forces to seize Charleston before any successful defense could be organized. The city's night watchman would provide the signal to Vesey's troops, when he announced that it was midnight, and all was well. It is unclear what Vesey planned to do after the city was taken. It is likely, however, that he could have seized the city if the plans had not been betrayed.

■ Vesey, Denmark, *defendant.* An official report of the trials of sundry Negroes, charged with an attempt to raise an insurrection in the State of South Carolina: preceded by an introduction and narrative; and in an appendix, a report of the trials of four white persons, on indictment for attempting to excite the slaves to insurrection. Prepared and published at the request of the Court, by Lionel H. Kennedy & Thomas Parker, members of the Charleston bar, and the presiding magistrates of the court. Charleston, Printed by James R. Schenck, 1822. 188, x, 4 p.   Law Library

——[Reprint] The trial of Denmark Vesey. Introduction by John Oliver Killen. Boston, Beacon Press [1970] 175 p.

KF223.V4K4 1970

The authors of this book, Lionel H. Kennedy and Thomas Parker, were South Carolina magistrates who presided over the trials of the alleged conspirators. The trials themselves were held in secret "in consequence of the peculiar nature of the investigations" (p. iii). This volume is not a complete record of the trials. Rather it "presents the prominent features of the late contemplated insurrection . . . and is ingenuously characterized, as furnishing 'a very brief abstract of the testimony offered in the cases brought before the Court'" (p. iii).

The book contains six parts. The first section is an introduction to the trials. It includes a discussion of the trial procedures and the statute under which the trials were held. The authors go to some length here to show that some aspects of elemental due process were observed throughout the trials. Among other things, they note that accused slaves were allowed to have lawyers if their owners wished to provide them. Free blacks, on the other hand, were allowed to provide their own attorneys or conduct their defenses for themselves, as they chose. No black could be convicted of a capital offense without direct evidence from two witnesses. The accused were allowed to question the witnesses against them and sometimes to confront their accusers. Because many of the slaves testified under immunity *and* with a promise of anonymity, not all of the accused faced their accusers or were allowed to cross-examine them. The court itself was made up of two magistrates and five freeholders.

The authors admit, however, that despite these attempts to ensure due process, the court departed "in many essential features, from the principles of the common law, and some of the settled rules of evidence" because the court could not adopt rules that were "repugnant to, nor expressly excepted by . . . statute, nor inconsistent with the local situation and policy of the state" (p. vi).

The second section of this volume contains a "Narrative of the Conspiracy and Intended Insurrection. Amongst a Portion of the Negroes in the State of South-Carolina. In the Year 1822" (p. 11). This forty-three-page history of the events is based primarily on the evidence presented in the trials. It describes Vesey and his activities in Charleston before the conspiracy was under way. It details how Vesey organized a hierarchy based on cells. No one knew anyone outside of his own group, except for some of the principal organizers. It also details the extent of the preparations, including the sources of weapons and horses. Some weapons had been made in advance, others had been stolen and hidden. Most of the weapons, however, would have been seized in the first few hours of the insurrection. The authors concluded, "Had the plot not been discovered, and the Insurrection commenced at the appointed time, they would not have been found unarmed" (p. 34). Furthermore, the authors thought that only by "the timely discovery of this plot, Carolina has been rescued from the most horrible catastrophe with which it had been threatened, since it has been an independent state.'' Kennedy and Parker believed ''success could not possibly have attended the conspirators, yet before their suppression, Charleston would probably have been wrapped in flames—many valuable lives have been sacrificed—and an immense loss of property sustained by the citizens . . . whilst the plantations in the lower country would have been disorganized, and the agricultural interests have sustained an enormous loss'' (pp. 60-61).

The third section, the records of the trials, includes testimony, depositions, cross-examinations, confessions, and sentences of the court. It contains the trial records of all the principal leaders of the conspiracy. Where slaves were acquitted there is usually little record of the trials, other than to note ''there was little or no testimony'' against them (p. 84, for example). The court decided that there were two classes of offenses: those that warranted a death penalty, and those which did not. The former category was for those who had actively participated in planning the rebellion, tried to recruit new conspirators, donated money or material to the rebellion, or took a leadership role. The latter category was for slaves who were recruited and who agreed to join the rebels, but otherwise took no part in organizing or planning. These slaves or free blacks were not executed. Instead, they were sentenced to be transported out of the United States. Some slaves who were guilty of crimes that merited a death sentence had their sentences commuted to transportation out of the country because they cooperated with the investigation. In other cases the court sentenced men to death but recommended that the governor of the state pardon them as long as they agreed to be transported out of the nation. Although these trials were conducted in an atmosphere of hysteria and without due process protections for the accused, there were nevertheless a large number of acquittals. Some of these verdicts resulted from a lack of evidence combined with the desire not to execute valuable slaves. But even with an acquittal, the court was not always certain that the proper verdict had been achieved. In one case, for example, ''The COURT *unanimously* found PRINCE NOT GUILTY— but suggested to his owner to send him away'' (p. 154).

The fourth part of this volume is ''A CALENDAR, *Comprising those Arrested, their owner's names, the time of their commitment, and the manner in which they were disposed of* '' (p. 183). This ''calendar'' contains eight separate lists of names and a ''RECAPITULATION'' giving a numerical count for each category. The eight categories are: (1) executed; (2) sentenced to death, but recommended by the court to the governor for transportation out of the country; (3) sentenced to death, but ''since respited by the Executive . . . with a view to the commutation of their punishment'' by deportation (p. 184); (4) convicted and initially sentenced to deportation to be carried out ''by their masters, under the direction of the City Council'' (p. 185); (5) sentenced to transportation to be carried out by the state (applied to free blacks); (6) acquitted, but the court nevertheless suggested their masters transport them out of the country; (7) acquitted and discharged; (8) arrested, but never brought to trial because of insufficient evidence.

The fifth part is an appendix that details the cases of four men accused and convicted of *"a Misdemeanor in inciting Slaves to Insurrection"* (p. 189). These men contacted blacks during the insurrection scare and offered to join them. It is unclear where the sympathies of these men actually lay. During the investigation of one man, it became clear ''he looked for a *handsome pecuniary reward* for the services he was to render [to the blacks], and hinted that *the freedom of the blacks was an object of no importance to him''* (p. v, appendix). His greed earned him a one-year prison sentence and a $1,000 fine. ''This sentence, unless modified by a pardon, will doubtless amount to imprisonment for life, since the circumstances and character of the prisoner, will effectually prevent him from paying the fine, or giving the security'' for his good behavior that the sentence also required (p. v, appendix). Two other whites convicted were fined $100 and sentenced to three months in jail, while the fourth man received a six-month sentence and a $500 fine. These men were all indicted and convicted under common law because they had taken no *actions* that would have allowed their indictment under the criminal statutes. They did not actually attempt to start a slave insurrection or take part in one. Of the four, three were foreigners, with obvious accents. The fourth, a native South Carolinian, had a criminal record and had been recently convicted of counterfeiting.

The last section of this book contains ''extracts'' from a local newspaper describing other slave insurrections and scares. It ends by urging that the federal government supply a military force to put down slave revolts, if necessary.

This is the best and most complete primary record of the trials connected to the Vesey Conspiracy. But the trial records in this volume are incomplete and much of the testimony is summarized. The book contains numerous and sometimes confusing cross-references connecting evidence at one trial to that of another. This confusion is perhaps indicative of the manner in which the trials themselves took place.

Many of the leaders of the conspiracy were executed immediately after their trials. Thus, there are often references to trials that took place after the trial—and even execution—of one individual. These supplementary references are used to assure the reader that the court was justified in its verdicts and sentences. Given the presence of attorneys for the conspirators and the number of acquittals, it is clear that the court sought to give reasonably fair trials to the slaves and free blacks arrested.

On the other hand, it is clear from the evidence here that many of those convicted would not have been convicted on similar evidence if they were whites charged with plotting a rebellion. Surely whites would not have been hung on the basis of these charges or the evidence presented. But South Carolina had already suffered one major slave revolt (the Stono Rebellion in 1739), and the people of Charleston were not willing to risk another. Although no act of rebellion actually took place in Charleston, the court treated Vesey and many of his cohorts as if they had committed great acts of violence and mayhem.

■ Hamilton, James, Jr. An account of the late intended insurrection among a portion of the blacks of this city. Published by the authority of the Corporation of Charleston. Charleston, Printed by A.E. Miller, 1822. 48 p.

AC901.W7 vol. 88, no. 3
Wolcott Pamphlets Rare Book Room

————— Negro plot. An account of the late intended insurrection among a portion of the blacks of the City of Charleston, South Carolina. Published by the authority of the Corporation of Charleston. 2d ed. Boston, Printed and published by Joseph W. Ingraham, 1822. 50 p.

AC901.M7 vol. 36, no. 2, and vol. 52, no. 13
Moore Pamphlets Rare Book Room

On August 13, 1822, the city council of Charleston passed a resolution that "the intendant be requested to prepare for publication, an account of the late intended insurrection in this city, with a statement of the trials and such other facts in connexion with the same as may be deemed of publick interest" (p. 2). In complying with this resolution the intendant, James Hamilton, concluded that "a full publication of the prominent circumstances of the late commotion" was the "most judicious course, as suppression might assume the appearance of timidity or injustice." Among other things, he thought there could "be no harm in the salutary inculcation of one lesson, among a *certain* portion of our population, that there is nothing they are bad enough to do, that we are not powerful enough to punish" (p. 2).

Hamilton's account is much smaller and less complete than the Kennedy and Parker volume. It repeats much of the information contained in the larger book. Many of the trial "records" in this book are simply one paragraph summaries of the evidence used to convict or acquit someone. Nevertheless, the volume contains important and useful supplementary information not reported by Kennedy and Parker. For example, we learn that Rolla, one of the ring leaders, was able to call five witnesses as part of his defense.

There is also an appendix that gives the full text of the important confessions of various conspirators and contains the text of ''An Act for the Better Ordering and Governing Negroes and other Slaves in this Province,'' May 10, 1740, No. 670, 7 Stat. S.C. 397 (1840). Vesey and his comrades were tried under this act, which was passed in the wake of the Stono Rebellion of 1739. Finally, the book contains eight tables and a ''Recapitulation'' of those arrested, tried, convicted, executed, acquitted, and transported out of the country.

Perhaps the most interesting insights in this volume are found in the many footnotes offered by the editor giving supplementary facts, describing important individuals, and explaining events. More importantly, they reveal the ambivalences and fears of Hamilton, and presumably the Charleston establishment that he represented.

The most useful of these notes concerns Peter Poyas, one of Vesey's original conspirators. One of the first tried and executed, he died without giving any confession. Indeed, he allegedly laughed when asked if he would murder his own master. Only after his execution did the full extent of his activities become known. Hamilton devoted less than one page of this report to the trial of Poyas. He footnotes this account with the following statement:

> After the execution of Peter, his guilt, in the most flagrant degree, became most abundantly established; affording, in every particular, the strongest corroboration of the testimony by which he had been convicted. It was apparent that he was the most efficient of all the ringleaders, and one who possessed the largest share of the confidence of Denmark Vesey, who was, in every sense of the term, the father of the plot. Peter was a slave of great value, for his colour, a first rate ship-carpenter. He had the confidence of his master in a remarkable degree, and had been treated with indulgence, liberality and kindness. [p. 14]

For the slaveowners of Charleston the activities of a man like Peter were particularly disturbing. Valuable, skilled and appearing to be a model slave, Poyas was well treated and apparently pampered and indulged within the confines of the peculiar institution. Yet he was a ringleader in a planned revolt that would have led to the death of his kind and indulgent master. If one could not trust Peter, then who indeed could trust any slaves?

ARGUMENT

OF

JOHN QUINCY ADAMS,

BEFORE THE

SUPREME COURT OF THE UNITED STATES,

IN THE CASE OF THE

UNITED STATES, APPELLANTS,

vs.

CINQUE, AND OTHERS, AFRICANS,

CAPTURED IN THE SCHOONER AMISTAD, BY LIEUT. GEDNEY,

DELIVERED ON THE 24th OF FEBRUARY AND 1st OF MARCH, 1841.

WITH A REVIEW OF THE CASE OF THE ANTELOPE,

REPORTED IN THE 10TH, 11TH AND 12TH VOLUMES OF WHEATON'S REPORTS.

NEW YORK:

S. W. BENEDICT, 128 FULTON STREET.

1841.

Title page from *Argument of John Quincy Adams before the Supreme Court of the United States* (New York, 1841), an argument not printed in court reporter Richard Peters's record of the trial in the case of the *United States* v. *The Amistad*.

The African Slave Trade

Perhaps no aspect of slavery was viewed with more distaste than the African slave trade. Its abolition was the first object of numerous antislavery organizations in America and Great Britain. Many slaveowners admitted that the slave trade was barbaric and immoral, even while they defended slavery itself.

The slave trade was viewed with such disgust because of the brutalities associated with it. It is estimated that only one out of every three potential slaves actually survived to reach America. The rest died in Africa or on board ship in what was known as the "middle passage." During the middle passage slaves were crowded into the hulls of ships under conditions that led to disease and often death. Many Africans, believing that in death they returned to their homeland, chose to commit suicide rather than remain chained inside a ship. Profits from the slave trade were so great that even with a high mortality rate those who financed the trade could expect a good return on their investment.

At the Constitutional Convention in 1787, there were numerous debates over the slave trade. Not surprisingly, the trade was opposed by delegates from the Northern colonies that were already taking steps to end slavery. But the trade was also opposed by delegates from Maryland, Delaware, and Virginia. Delegate John Dickinson of Pennsylvania considered "it as inadmissible on every principle of honor & safety that the importation of slaves should be authorized" in the new Constitution (Max Farrand, *The Records of the Federal Convention of 1787*, 4 vols. [New Haven: Yale University Press, 1937] 2:372). The delegates from South Carolina, Georgia and, to a lesser extent North Carolina, threatened to walk out of the Convention if any attempt was made to prohibit the African slave trade. A compromise was ultimately reached, allowing the trade to continue for another twenty years, after which Congress would have the right—although not the obligation—to end the importation of slaves from Africa. James Madison predicted this additional twenty years would produce "all the mischief that can be apprehended from the liberty to import slaves" (Farrand, *Records*, 2:415).

In 1808 legislation enacted at the urging of President Thomas Jefferson ended the slave trade (Slave Trade Prohibition Act of March 2, 1807, ch. 22, 2 Stat. 205). By that time over eighty thousand slaves had been imported into the United States since the Constitution was ratified. After the slave trade was prohibited, illegal importations continued. Perhaps as many as fifty thousand additional slaves were imported into the United States between 1808 and 1865.

While many Southerners thought the slave trade wrong, or even immoral, few were willing to prosecute a slave trader. Southern congressmen and senators, as well as judges and presidents, were also unwilling to actively enforce the laws prohibiting the trade. The United States Navy made a valiant attempt to catch ships involved in the trade, but it was understaffed and underfinanced for this job. Many slavers were never intercepted.

Most of the enforcement of the laws prohibiting the slave trade was carried on by the British navy (see Appendix). At the same time the United States prohibited the trade, the British Parliament also took steps to end it. The British navy actively patrolled the coast of Africa and stopped ships flying any flags except the American flag. In addition, the British government successfully pressured other European nations to end the trade.

Although few slave ships were captured, those that were apprehended were usually brought to the United States and condemned. While the captains and crews (not to mention the financial backers) were not ordinarily punished severely, the ships were confiscated. As the discussion of the *Wanderer*, 29 F. Cas. 150 (D. Mass. 1860) (No. 17, 139), shows, however, a condemned slaver could easily be purchased by other slave traders and put back into service.

By the late 1850s some Southern nationalists argued that the African trade should be reopened. Although a minority, they were influential in preventing the enforcement of the laws prohibiting the trade. Not until the Civil War began would a slave trader be sentenced to the maximum allowed for this type of piracy—death by hanging.

Charge to the Grand Jury

(C.C.D. R. I. 1819)(Unreported)

This charge was given to the federal grand juries in Boston and Providence by U.S. Supreme Court Justice Joseph Story while attending to his circuit court duties during the 1819 term. It is not entirely clear to what cases, if any, this charge is directly related. Story does urge a vigorous prosecution of those who violate the statutes prohibiting the slave trade. The charge undoubtedly reflects Story's concern with the enforcement of the recently enacted Slave Trade Prohibition Acts.

Joseph Story (1799-1845). Story was an associate justice of the U.S. Supreme Court, a professor at Harvard Law School, and one of the preeminent legal scholars of the nineteenth century. Story initially opposed slavery and spoke out against it from the bench in his charges to federal grand juries to investigate the illegal slave trade. By 1842, however, Story's position on slavery was less clear. His opinion in *Prigg* v. *Pennsylvania* supported the Fugitive Slave Act of 1793 even though that statute violated some due process protections.

From a painting by Chappel; copyright 1862 by the publishers Johnson, Fry & Co. LC-USZ62-5762

The Act of April 10, 1818, ch. 91, 3 Stat. 450, provided that any person accused of illegally participating in the slave trade must prove that the blacks in his possession were imported legally. The Act of

March 3, 1819, ch. 51, 3 Stat. 532, gave the president new power to enforce the ban on the African slave trade. It also provided for forfeitures of ships engaged in the trade and new punishments for people convicted of violating the prohibitions against the trade.

The first four pages of this charge cover the general question of piracy on the high seas. Story warns that "there are hordes of needy adventurers prowling upon the ocean, who under the specious pretext of being in the service of the Patriot Governments of South America, commit the fowlest outrages." He declares that piracy "threatens the most serious mischiefs to our peaceful commerce" (Story, *A Charge*, p. 1). Story defines piracy "according to the common law" as "those acts of depredation and robbery at sea, which if committed upon land would amount to felony there." Piracy is robbery, theft, violence, or murder on the high seas, and under recent statutes of the United States to help curb it, the pirate, "on conviction, [will] suffer death" (ibid., p. 2). He details five types of piracy, including murder, robbery, assault, mutiny, or attack by an American citizen of an American ship "under colour of any commission or authority from any foreign prince or state, or on pretence of authority from any person" (ibid., p. 3).

After discussing these usual forms of piracy, Story turns "to that most detestable traffic, the *Slave Trade*." He finds this trade "so repugnant to the natural rights of man and the dictates of justice, that it seems difficult to find for it any adequate justification" (ibid., p. 4). Story urged the grand jury not to tolerate the trade in any form. It was an evil that needed to be done away with.

■ Story, Joseph. A charge, delivered to the grand juries of the circuit court, at October term, 1819, in Boston, and at November term, 1819, in Providence, and published at their unanimous request. [Boston, 1819?] 8 p.

Law Library

This charge did not mention any specific violation of the laws prohibiting the slave trade. Nor do there appear to have been prosecutions in 1819 in Story's circuit. However, in 1820 Story heard the cases of *United States* v. *La Coste*, 26 F. Cas. 826 (C.C.D. Mass. 1820)(No. 15,548) and *United States* v. *Smith*, 27 F. Cas. 1167 (C.C.D. Mass. 1820) (No. 16,338), which may have begun with indictments during the 1819 term.

Story's charge is remarkable for its vehement attack on the slave trade, slave traders, and slavery in general. It is also unusual because of the incorporation of economics, statistics, and public policy into the charge. Story acknowledges that "It is to be lamented indeed, that slavery exists in any part'' of the United States, but this was ''not an evil introduced in the present age.'' Rather it was ''entailed upon a part of our country by their ancestors.'' The slave owner, Story sanguinely declared, looked for ''a safe and just remedy for its gradual abolition'' which he thought was possible because ''christianity . . . prepared the way for a gradual abolition of slavery'' (p. 4). Story clearly did not want to engage in any sectional attacks. Thus he ascribed to slave owners a desire (which they probably did not have) to eventually end slavery. Similarly, he blamed slavery on the acts of previous generations, rather than living slave owners.

He also noted that New Englanders had participated in the slave trade and were still doing so. ''I wish I could say . . . that New England and New Englandmen were free from this deep pollution. But there is some reason to believe that they who drive a loathsome traffic, 'and buy the muscles and bones of men,' are found here also.'' They might be few in number, ''but our cheeks may well burn with shame while a solitary case is permitted to go unpunished'' (p. 5). Indeed, it was to a grand jury of New Englanders that Story urged vigorous prosecution of slave traders.

Men who participated in the slave trade were, to Story, the worst sort of men. There were ''men calling themselves Christians who degrade the negro by ignorance to a level with brutes, and deprive him of all the consolations of religions.'' He hoped that ''virtuous men would by their abhorrence stay its polluted march, and wicked men would be overawed by its potent punishment.'' But this was not the case. ''We have but too many melancholy proofs from unquestionable sources, that it is still carried on with all the implacable ferocity and insatiable rapacity of former times. Avarice has grown more subtle in its evasions. . . . American citizens are steeped up to their very mouths (I scarcely use too bold a figure) in this stream of iniquity'' (p. 5). The participation in this ''*inhuman* traffic'' needed to be stopped (p. 6).

Story supported his assertion that the traffic was inhuman with a detailed discussion of the trade. Working from data presented to the English Parliament by Wilberforce and ''a man immortalized by his virtues, the intrepid Thomas Clarkson,'' Story asked the grand jury to allow him to pass ''from these cold generalities to some of those details which are the ordinary attendants upon this trade.'' (p. 5-6).

Story told the jurors that from 1768 until the abolition of the trade, about one hundred thousand slaves were taken from Africa each year. Half of these were ''*kidnapped people.*—This mode of procuring them includes every species of treachery and knavery. Husbands are stolen from their wives, children from their parents, and bosom friends from each other.'' Others are captured by ''predatory expeditions [that] go out at night, set fire to the villages, whcih they find, and carry off the wretched inhabitants. . . . The practice is indeed so common, that the remains of deserted and burnt villages are every where to be seen on the coast.'' Other slaves were people convicted of crimes at ''mock trials for the purpose of bringing them within the reach of the royal [slave] traders'' (p. 6).

Story then described the trip to the coast ''in droves or caufles, as they are called,'' with the slaves chained or harnessed together. Their conditions on board ship, the chains they were required to wear, that ''custom to make them jump for exercise as high as their fetters will allow them; and if they refuse they are whipped until they comply. This the slave merchants call dancing, and it would seem literally to be the dance of death.'' In the middle passage they were confined

> so that it is impossible to stand erect in most of the vessels, and in some scarcely to sit down in the same posture. If the vessel be full, their situation is truly deplorable . . . and here their situation becomes wretched beyond description. . . . Some go down apparently well at night and are found dead in the morning. Some faint below and die from suffocation before they can be brought upon deck . . . the motion of the ship rubs the flesh from the prominent parts of their body and leaves their bones almost bare. . . . [Often] the whole place becomes covered with blood and mucus like a slaughter house. . . . During the time that elapses from the slaves being put on board on the African coast to their sale in the colonies about one fourth part, or twenty-five thousand per annum are destroyed—a mortality which may be easily credited after the preceding statement. [pp. 6-7]

''Nothing,'' Story asserted, ''can exceed the terror which the wretched Africans exhibit'' when they arrive in the New World and are examined for sale and then sold. And that terror is justified, for ''about one half perish within two years from their first captivity.'' The slave trade thus presents ''a picture of human wretchedness and human depravity, which the boldest imagination would hardly have dared to portray, and from which (one should think) the most abandoned profligate would shrink with horror'' (pp. 7-8).

Story asked the grand jury to investigate the trade when possible so that ''at least one human being may have been saved from sacrifice by our vigilance in enforcing the laws'' (p. 8). In asking the grand jury to do this, he was proud that to the United States ''belongs the honor as a nation, of having set the first example of prohibiting the further progress of this inhuman traffic'' (p. 4). But, Great Britain, he lamented, had been more vigorous in stopping the trade. ''May America not be behind her in this glorious work,'' Story declared. He hoped ''by a generous competition in virtuous deeds'' America could ''restore the degraded African to his natural rights, and strike his manacles from the bloody hands of his oppressors'' (p. 5).

Story's charge to the grand jury was in part stimulated by his recent examination of the records of the slave trade as presented to the British Parliament. Before that time he ''had no conception . . . of the vast extent of misery and cruelty occasioned by its ravages'' (p. 6). But, the facts of the trade had converted Story into something of an abolitionist (at least for the moment—see also the discussion in this volume of *Prigg* v. *Pennsylvania*, 41 U.S. |16 Pet.| 539 |1842|). He reminded the grand jurors that the public documents of the United States declared ''that all men are born free and equal, and have certain unalienable rights.'' Americans ''boast of our noble struggle against the encroachments of tyranny . . . and yet that there are men among us who think it no wrong to condemn the shivering negro to perpetual bondage'' (pp. 5-6). Story did not mind taking up the time of the grand jurors, because they needed to have their minds awakened ''to the absolute necessity of constant vigilance in the enforcement of the laws on this subject'' (p. 6). He believed Americans ''in vain . . . expend our wealth in missions abroad for the promotion of christianity; in vain shall we rear at home magnificent temples to the service of his most High; if we tolerate this traffic, our charity is but a name, and our religion little more than a faint and delusive shadow'' (p. 8). In the ringing slogan of the British abolitionists, and in one of the most extreme antislavery statements by a U.S. Supreme Court justice, Story asked his fellow New Englanders, ''May not the miserable African ask 'Am I not a man and a brother?' '' (p. 6).

United States v. *The La Jeune Eugénie*

26 F. Cas. 832 (C.C.D. Mass. 1822)(No. 15, 551)

The Slave Trade Prohibition Act of March 2, 1807, ch. 22, 2 Stat. 205, prohibited the importation of slaves into the United States after June 1, 1808. This act authorized the president ''to employ armed vessels to cruise on any part of the coast, where he might judge attempts would be made to violate the act, and to instruct the commanders of armed vessels to seize, and to bring in, vessels found on the high seas contravening the provisions of the law.''

Earlier statutes prohibited ''the citizens of the *United States,* from being engaged in the transportation of *slaves* from *Africa*, or elsewhere, to any foreign port'' (*A Report of the Case*, p. 1). The Acts of Apr. 20, 1818, ch. 91, 3 Stat. 450, Mar. 3, 1819, ch. 101, 3 Stat. 532, and May 15, 1820, ch. 113, 3 Stat. 600, further regulated the African slave trade. These laws prohibited any participation in the trade by Americans or American-owned ships. They provided that such ships could be lawfully seized as prizes, and anyone arrested for participating in the trade "shall be adjudged a pirate, and on conviction shall suffer death" (ibid., p. 3).

In 1821 the armed schooner *Alligator,* under the command of Robert F. Stockton, seized the schooner *Jeune Eugénie* off the coast of Africa "and captured her on the suspicion of her being engaged in the *slave trade*" (ibid., p. 3). At the time of this action the *Jeune Eugénie* was flying the French flag and carried French papers indicating that she belonged to French citizens resident in Guadaloupe. The vessel's papers and the crew claimed that the ship sailed to Africa to procure a cargo of palm oil. The ship's papers also indicated that the schooner was built in the United States and not transferred to her French owners until after the passage of the U.S. act of 1818 that facilitated the prosecution of slave traders.

Despite the alleged purpose of this ship's voyage, the *Jeune Eugénie* appeared to be fitted out as a slaver: "The vessel was equipped in the manner that is usual for the slave trade; she had two guns, a false or moveable deck, and a large quantity of water and provisions, and water casks, quite unusual in ordinary voyages, and indispensable in this particular class of voyage" (ibid., p. 50). On board were also handcuffs and fetters. There was also testimony from observers on the African coast who said the ship was procuring a cargo of Africans.

The prosecution argued that the *Jeune Eugénie* was a slaver fraudulently sailing under the French flag. This was an attempt to avoid the rigors of the American statutes. He asserted that even if the ship were truly owned by Frenchmen, the U.S. court should "take notice of the *French ordinances* against that traffic, and the ship being rightfully in the possession of the court," the ship could not be returned to the owners (ibid., p. 7). Such a decision was warranted because the "slave trade was contrary to the law of nations, because it was a violation of the *law of nature* . . . it was merely a barbarous, unauthorized, private, piratical warfare, carried on against *Africans* to make them *slaves*" (ibid., p. 7). Thus, attorneys for the United States argued that the *Jeune Eugénie* was the lawful prize of the United States and the crew of the *Alligator*.

William Sullivan, the attorney for the owners, argued that the ship was not engaged in the African slave trade. Nor was there any reason to believe the French registry of the ship was not genuine. He noted: "This vessel was not found with slaves on board. She is brought in on *suspicion* of intending to take them on board. And although we entirely, and absolutely deny, any intention of the supposed character, yet it may be admitted that the American law might subject an American vessel, under like circumstances, *to trial*. But by what law can an

American court, *in time of peace,* condemn, or withhold restitution of, a vessel of a foreign nation, which is found engaged in the African slave trade?'' (ibid., p. 12).

This case was argued in the U.S. Circuit Court in Boston, Massachusetts, before U.S. Supreme Court Justice Joseph Story. In an elaborate and detailed opinion, Justice Story ruled that the *Jeune Eugénie* was indeed participating in the slave trade. He could not ''entertain doubts as to the real destination and employment of this vessel . . . [for] [u]pon the evidence in the case it is irresistibly established to my mind, that the sole purpose of the voyage was a traffic in slaves'' (ibid., p. 50). Nor was he convinced that the ship was legitimately French. The ship ''was sailing under the customary documents of France, as a French vessel,'' and in ''ordinary cases'' this documentation would have been *prima facie* a sufficient proof, that the vessel was really owned by the persons whose names appear upon the papers. In ordinary times, and under ordinary circumstances, ''when disguises are not necessary or important to cloak an illegal enterprize, or conceal a real ownership, the ship's papers'' would be accepted as proof of ownership (ibid., pp. 50-51).

But, this was not an ordinary case. Indeed, ''if the trade is such, that disguises and frauds are common; if it can be carried on only under certain flags, with safety or success,'' then ship's papers could not be accepted as proof of ownership or even proper registry. Story's court was ''accustomed to know, how easily they are procured by fraud and imposition upon public officers, and how eagerly they are sought by those, whose cupidity for wealth is stimulated and schooled by temptations of profit, to all manner of shifts and contrivances'' (ibid., pp. 50-51). Thus, Story thought it ''no hardship'' for him to require the claimants ''to shew the bill of sale, by which they acquired their title; to give the names of the American owners; and to establish to a reasonable extent, that the transfer was for a valuable consideration'' (ibid., p. 53). Story was ''not satisfied that the property is owned as claimed'' by the French claimants, and thus he would not order the ship returned to them (ibid., p. 54).

However, this conclusion did not necessarily mean that the ship was owned by Americans. All Story held was that the French claimants had no right to the ship. But Story did not believe that Stockton and his crew had a legitimate claim to the ship either, because it was not proved to be an American vessel.

Story asserted that the African slave trade was piracy and condemned by international law. ''It begins in corruption, and plunder, and kidnapping'' (ibid., p. 69). It leads to ''lawless wars, and rapine, and kidnapping, and ending in disease, and death, and slavery,—it is of this traffic, in the aggregate of its accumulated wrongs, that I would ask, if it be consistent with the law of nations? . . . We are not to be told, that war is lawful, and slavery lawful, and plunder lawful, and the taking away of life is lawful, and the selling of human beings is lawful'' (ibid., p. 71). Slavery, Story conceded, might exist under local laws, but such local statutes could not justify the slave trade. He noted that ''scarcely a single maritime nation of Europe'' had failed ''in the most significant terms, in the most deliberate and solemn conferences, acts, or treaties'' to acknowledge ''the injustice and inhumanity of this trade; and pledged itself to promote its abolition'' (ibid., p. 74). France, England, and the United States had all agreed to stop the slave trade.

These conclusions left Story in somewhat of a dilemma. The claimants of the *Jeune Eugénie* had not proved their ownership, and, indeed, there were good reasons to believe the ship was actually owned by U.S. citizens. But this could not be proved. Thus, the ship could not be libeled and claimed as a prize by Captain Stockton. Nor could it be turned over to the French claimants. The ship had been involved in the slave trade, so the secret American owners did not come forward to claim the ship and perhaps contest the case. What then could Story do with the ship? He had two alternatives. He could turn the ship over to the U.S. government ''as unclaimed property, or forfeited property,'' or it could be turned over to the ''Sovereign of France, if he should choose to interpose a claim, or assert a right to proceed against it in his own courts for the supposed forfeiture'' (ibid., p. 89). Story chose the latter course because it made the United States ''not a principal, but an auxiliary, in enforcing the interdict of France, and subserves the great interests of universal justice'' (ibid., p. 90). Story was sure ''the American courts of judicature are not hungry after jurisdiction in foreign causes, or desirous to plunge into the endless perplexities of foreign jurisprudence'' (ibid., p. 92). The slaver flying the French flag was thus to be turned over to the French government. This act would ''enforce the policy, common to both nations, of repressing an odious traffic, which is denounced by both'' (ibid., p. 90).

■ Jeune Eugénie (Schooner). A report of the case of the Jeune Eugénie, determined in the Circuit Court of the United States, for the First Circuit, at Boston, December, 1821. With an appendix. By William P. Mason. Boston, Wells and Lilly, 1822. 108 p.

LLRBR

This pamphlet was published by the official court reporter because ''the interesting nature of the case of the Jeune Eugénie required that it should not be withheld from the Public until the volume of Reports, in which it would regularly appear, should be put to press'' (advertisement, before p. 1, unpaginated). It contains the entire opinion as it would later appear in the official reports. It also contains a more elaborate and complete text of the arguments of counsel for the claimants than appeared in the official reports. The abbreviated outline of the argument for the libelants is the same in this pamphlet as it later appeared in the official report.

In addition to the arguments of counsel, the statutes under consideration, and Story's opinion, this pamphlet includes an appendix that gives a short summary of important cases and statutes cited during the arguments or by Story. The most interesting of these is the opinion of Judge William Peter Van Ness in the case of the schooner *Plattsburgh* (S.D. N.Y. 1821) (Unreported). This case was later argued before the U.S. Supreme Court as *The Plattsburgh*, 23 U.S. (10 Wheat.) 133 (1825). Although a report of the case, upholding the lower court decision, is available, there is no printed report of the opinion of Judge Van Ness in any of the official reports of the lower federal courts. This brief, two-page summary of the case may be the only printed text of the lower court decision in the case. Van Ness declared that the slave trade was prohibited by the law of nations, and this was used to support the argument of the libelants, as well as Story's opinion.

Story's opinion is one of the strongest condemnations of the slave trade in American law. It is a thorough examination of the trade and its position in international law. He examines the trade in all its complexities. In condemning the *Jeune Eugénie*, Story builds a strong case for the immorality of the slave trade on the premise that if "the African slave trade be prohibited by the law of nations . . . it will not, I presume, be denied, that confiscation of the property ought to follow" (pp. 67-68). He cites a number of English cases, the state papers of the U.S. Congress, and even British statesmen to support his position. He quotes William Pitt's speech of 1792: "There is something of horror in it, that surpasses all the bounds of imagination" (pp. 70-71).

His decision is based on the facts of the trade, including the destruction of African civilization and the horrors of the middle passage. He concludes the trade is "founded in a violation of some of the first principles, which ought to govern nations. It is repugnant to the great principles of christian duty, the dictates of natural religion, the obligations of good faith and morality, and the eternal maxims of social justice." It is thus "sufficient to stamp any trade as interdicted by public law, when it can be justly affirmed, that it is repugnant to the general principles of justice and humanity" (pp. 73-74). On these high grounds, as well as the statutes of the United States and the rest of the western world, Story condemns the slave trade and ships participating in it.

United States v. The Amistad

40 U.S. (15 Pet.) 518 (1841)

Gedney v. L'Amistad

10 F. Cas. 141 (D. Conn. 1840) (No. 5,294a)

In August 1839 the schooner *Amistad* was boarded by Lieutenant Gedney, commander of the United States Coast Guard brig the *Washington,* in Long Island Sound, near New Haven, Connecticut. On board, Lieutenant Gedney found two Cuban slave owners, a Cuban slave who was serving as the cabin boy, and thirty-nine Africans. On June 28 the *Amistad* had left Havana with five white men, a slave cook and the slave cabin boy, and fifty-three Africans who had been recently imported into Cuba. On the fourth night at sea the Africans broke their chains and revolted. The captain, the cook, and two sailors were killed. The slave owners—Pedro Montez and José Ruiz—were spared because they convinced the Africans they could steer the ship back to Africa.

Throughout July and most of August Montez and Ruiz sailed the ship in an easterly direction during the day and at night reversed course and sailed west and north, hoping to reach one of the slave states of the United States. Instead, on August 26 they reached Long Island. By this time a number of the Africans had died from exposure and lack of food and water. The ship was seized by Lieutenant Gedney and taken to New London, Connecticut.

In New London the Africans were jailed for murder, mutiny, and piracy. Montez and Ruiz were treated as the lawful owners of the *Amistad* and the slaves on board. Montez and Ruiz claimed the ship and wanted to take possession of it as soon as possible. This might have occurred, had not others also made claims to the *Amistad*. When Lieutenant Gedney boarded the *Amistad* two sea captains, Henry Green and Peletiah Fordham, were negotiating with some of the Africans who had come on shore to buy food and water. They were planning to board the ship and claim it for salvage, but they were preempted by Lieutenant Gedney.

Green and Fordham, as the first men to deal with the *Amistad* Africans, entered a claim to the ship in the form of a libel for salvage. Their libel was the third to be brought before the U.S. District Court. When he reached New London, Lieutenant Gedney immediately sued out a libel for himself and the crew of the *Washington.* Ruiz and Montez also sued out a libel. Finally, the U.S. district attorney sued out a fourth libel on behalf of the U.S. government.

John Quincy Adams (1767-1848). A former president, Adams was a leading antislavery congressman throughout the 1830s and 1840s. His stature, fame, and experience brought prestige to the antislavery movement. His argument in the *Amistad* case presented a powerful indictment of American policy toward the African slave trade.

Engraving by H. Wright Smith from a painting by A. B. Durand. LC-USZ61-173

This last action, by the U.S. attorney, was particularly confusing in that it asked the court to take a number of different actions, some of which were mutually exclusive. At the insistence of the Spanish minister to the United States, the U.S. attorney asked that the court turn the Africans over to Montez and Ruiz. But he also asked that the Africans be turned over to the president of the United States, so that he might return them to Africa. Later, on November 19, the U.S. attorney entered still another claim, demanding that the schooner, cargo, and Africans be

Lewis Tappan (1788-1873). Lewis Tappan was a successful New York merchant who devoted much of his time, energies, business experience, and wealth to opposing slavery. The cause of the *Amistad* was only one of many that he supported.

Engraving by G. R. Hall, copyright 1875 by Virtue & Yorsten. LC-USZ62-47919

returned to their lawful owners "in pursuance of the treaty between the United States and Spain" *(Gedney* v. *L'Amistad,* 10 F. Cas. 141, 142). Finally, to complicate matters further, the adult Africans "were committed for trial, for murder on the high seas, at the Circuit Court" *(The African Captives,* p. iii).

Immediately after the *Amistad* was seized, abolitionists began to organize a committee to defend the Africans. Roger S. Baldwin, a lawyer in New Haven, took charge of their defense, with the aid of New

Roger S. Baldwin (1793-1863). A Connecticut lawyer, Baldwin successfully argued the case of the *Amistad* before the U.S. Supreme Court. Whereas John Quincy Adams presented a bitter political denunciation of the federal government's treatment of the *Amistad* captives, Baldwin presented a convincing legal argument. His participation in this case as an advocate of antislavery did not hurt his career in relatively conservative Connecticut. In 1844 he was elected governor of the state and the following year he was reelected. In 1847 he was elected to the U.S. Senate, where he opposed slave expansion.

Engraved for the *American Review* by A. H. Ritchie, from a daguerreotype by Brady.

York attorneys Seth P. Staples and Theodore Sedgwick and Ellis Gray Loring of Boston. Lewis Tappan, a New York philanthropist, organized a committee to oversee fund raising, legal defense, education and religious instruction, and other aspects of the struggle to free the Amistads (as the Africans were called) and return them to Africa not as heathens, but as missionaries. Tappan was aided by Simeon St. Jocelyn and Joshua Leavitt.

In New Haven a number of Yale faculty members and students began to teach the Amistads English and Christianity. The greatest obstacle to the defense of the Amistads, as well as to their education, was a language barrier. None of the Africans spoke any English or Spanish. Thus, it was impossible to communicate with them beyond basic sign language and pointing. This fact alone was obvious proof that the Amistads were not Cuban slaves, but in fact had been illegally imported into Cuba *very* recently. But it also made it impossible to hear their version of the events on board the *Amistad* and prepare a legal defense against the murder charge or the attempt by the government to send them back to Cuba.

On September 18 the first legal action surrounding the Amistads began. Although most of the Africans on the ship were men, there were also three young girls. All of them were jailed when Lieutenant Gedney seized the ship. Thus, the first action by the abolitionist attorneys was to ask the U.S. Circuit Court for a writ of habeas corpus on behalf of the young girls, on the ground that they were not charged with any crime and thus should not be in jail. On September 18 U.S. Supreme Court Justice Smith Thompson, who was attending to circuit duties at the time, issued the writ, returnable the next day. An attorney for the U.S. marshal argued that the girls should be held as witnesses for the murder prosecution of the male adults, because Lieutenant Gedney had libeled the ship for salvage and they were part of the ship's cargo, because Pedro Montez had libeled the ship as well, and because the U.S. government had claimed the ship and its contents on behalf of the Spanish government.

While this case was in progress, the judge was interrupted by the foreman of the federal grand jury that was sitting at that time. The grand jury wanted instructions on whether to charge the Amistads with murder on the high seas. In a critical ruling, Justice Thompson decided that whatever happened aboard the *Amistad* took place in international waters on a Spanish ship and was thus beyond the jurisdiction of the United States. Thus, no murder charges could be brought against the Amistads. However, Justice Thompson refused to release the Amistads from custody because their status had yet to be determined. Instead, he sent the entire matter to the district court, where it would be decided after a full hearing into all the evidence and full arguments by the counsel for all the parties.

Immediately after Justice Thompson adjourned the circuit court, Judge Andrew T. Judson convened the U.S. District Court. Judson was a Connecticut Democrat who, before being appointed to the bench, had prosecuted Prudence Crandall for opening a school to teach black girls. (See Prudence Crandall's case, pp. 138-43.) Thus, abolitionists feared he would be unlikely to rule in their favor. However, his first rulings must have confused the lawyers for all of the parties. He declared that slavery did not exist in Connecticut, and thus there would be no salvage allowable for the value of the Africans. They were not property in Connecticut. He also ordered the U.S. marshal to find some place other than the jail to house them because they were no longer held under criminal charges. He directed the marshal to ensure that the Africans were adequately fed and especially that they were adequately clothed and given proper medical attention, for the next hearing in their case would not be until November. Judson did offer to allow the Africans to be released on bail, but he decided that bail must be based on their "appraised value" as slaves in Cuba. This was unacceptable to the abolitionists defending them, and the Amistads were instead returned to the custody of the marshal.

Between these hearings in the circuit and district courts in September and before the resumption of the proceedings in November, someone was found who could communicate with the Africans in their native tongue of Mende. He was James Covey, a twenty-year-old native of Africa serving on a British warship. Covey had been rescued from a slave trader by the British navy and was thus fluent in Mende and English. He was able to translate for the Amistads and allow their side of the story to be told. He was able to confirm what was apparent to all who cared to investigate the issue: the Amistads had all been born in Africa and were recently kidnapped and taken to Cuba, in violation of Spanish law prohibiting the African slave trade.

Although scheduled for the November term of the court, the case of the *Amistad,* reported as *Gedney* v. *L'Amistad,* did not reach the U.S. District Court until January 1840. By this time the case had become a national and international issue. The Spanish government was vigorously demanding the return of the Africans so they could be tried for murder in Cuba. Northerners, including many who were usually opposed to the antislavery movement, supported the right of the Africans to return home. President Martin Van Buren wanted to get rid of the ship, its passengers, and the problems it brought for his administration as soon as possible. Van Buren expected that Judge Judson would rule in favor of returning the Amistads to Cuba. Thus, he ordered the *Grampus,* a United States Navy schooner, to dock in New Haven harbor and immediately after the verdict to take the Africans out of the country before an appeal could be initiated. John Quincy Adams would later castigate the administration for this action in his argument before the Supreme Court in this case.

Van Buren's actions ultimately proved to be futile, because

District Judge Judson, much to the surprise and pleasure of the abolitionists and other supporters of the Africans, ruled that the Amistads should be returned to their native land. Referring to the two apparent leaders of the Amistads, Judson declared: "Cinquez and Grabeau shall not sigh for Africa in vain. Bloody as may be their hands, they shall yet embrace their kindred." In his final decree Judson ordered that all the Africans "be delivered to the president of the United States to be transported to Africa, there to be delivered to the agent, appointed to receive and conduct them home" (10 F. Cas. 141, 151). Judson also awarded Lieutenant Gedney one-third of the value of the ship itself as salvage. Captains Green and Fordham had never set foot on the ship and were thus awarded nothing. The slave cabin boy was to be returned to his owner, as provided for by treaties between Spain and the United States. The ship and its goods (except of course the Africans) were to be turned over to the Spanish government after payment to Gedney and his crew of one-third the appraised value of the ship plus their costs in salvaging it and towing it to port.

The U.S. government, on behalf of the Spanish government, appealed this case to the Supreme Court. Heard in February 1841, the oral arguments lasted eight days. Writing for the Court, Justice Joseph Story upheld most of the district court's decision. However, he reversed the part of Judson's decree that commanded that the Africans be turned over to the president of the United States to be returned to Africa. Instead he ordered "that the said negroes be, and are hereby, declared to be free, and that they be dismissed from the custody of the Court, and be discharged from the suit and go thereof quit without day" 40 U.S. (15 Pet.) 518, 598.

This may have been a greater legal victory for the Africans than the order that they be turned over to the president. It allowed them to choose where they wished to live and made them, in effect, totally free people. However, it proved to be a mixed blessing. The Amistads and their friends lacked the resources necessary to send them back to Africa immediately. The Amistads did not reach their homeland until January 1842.

The case of the *Amistad* was a major cause célèbre for its two-year duration. It brought to the United States living proof of the horrors of the African slave trade. It also provided a forum for abolitionists and others opposed to slavery. As a legal case it involved three levels of the federal courts, the president of the United States, the secretary of state, the attorney general, a former president, the governments of Spain and Great Britain (which tried to intervene on behalf of the Africans), and a host of lawyers in a complicated adjudication of treaties, state law, federal law, Spanish law, and international law. Almost buried underneath the weight of this mountain of legal paper, treaties, and arguments, were the lives and futures of thirty-nine innocent victims of kidnapping. Perhaps what is most remarkable about this case is that in the end these people received some measure of justice.

There are three pamphlets annotated here that discuss this case. The first details the original seizure of the ship and the initial hearings before Justice Thompson. There is no printed reported of that case, and thus this pamphlet is a particularly useful supplement to the reports dealing with this case. The second and third contain Roger S. Baldwin's and John Quincy Adams's arguments before the U.S. Supreme Court. Adams's argument is also an important supplement to the printed case, since the court reporter, Richard Peters, did not print any of Adams's arguments with the case. The pamphlet containing Baldwin's argument simply supplements the extensive reporting of his argument by Peters.

■ U.S. Circuit Court (2d Circuit). The African captives. Trial of the prisoners of the Amistad on the writ of habeas corpus, before the Circuit Court of the United States, for the District of Connecticut, at Hartford: Judges Thompson and Judson. September term, 1839. New York, 1839. 47 p.

LLRBR

The *Amistad* case was essentially three different cases. First, there was an attempt to prosecute the *Amistad* captives for murder and piracy on the high seas under American law. Second, there was an attempt by abolitionists to have the Amistads released under a writ of habeas corpus. Third, there was a very complicated case involving the salvage rights for the ship (and for the slaves) and an attempt to have the Amistads returned to Spanish authorities.

This last case was argued in the United States District Court for Connecticut as *Gedney* v. *L'Amistad*, 10 F. Cas. 141 (D. Conn. 1840) (No. 5,294a). It was then appealed to the U.S. Supreme Court as *United States* v. *The Amistad*, 40 U.S. (15 Pet.) 518 (1841). The attempted prosecution failed to materialize because of the charge to the federal grand jury by U.S. Supreme Court Justice Smith Thompson. This charge to the grand jury was not officially reported; nor was the habeas corpus hearing before Justice Thompson. This pamphlet, however, presents both.

Although no author appears on this pamphlet's title page, it was probably written by Lewis Tappan, a leading New York abolitionist and philanthropist who organized and directed the Amistads' defense. The pamphlet begins with an introductory account of the discovery and seizure of the *Amistad* and a discussion of its defense committee. This is followed by the "Case of the Africans," which appears to be a transcript of the habeas corpus hearing before Justice Smith Thompson and District Judge Andrew T. Judson (p. 7).

New York attorneys Seth P. Staples and Theodore Sedgwick, Jr., represented the Africans at the habeas corpus hearing. They sought the release of the three African girls who had been found aboard the *Amistad*, but because of their sex and their youth were not charged with any crimes. An attorney for Ruiz and Montez argued that the girls were slaves and should not be released. In addition, the U.S. district attorney argued that they were (1) needed as witnesses in the criminal prosecution, (2) claimed "for salvage" by Lieutenant Gedney, (3) claimed by Montez and Ruiz, and (4) claimed by the Spanish government. For these reasons the U.S. attorney believed they should be held along with the rest of the Amistads.

On the third day of the hearing Roger S. Baldwin joined Staples and Sedgwick to defend the rights of the Africans. Both Baldwin and Sedgwick attempted to enter into a substantive discussion of the status of the three girls. They were interrupted, however, by the foreman of the federal grand jury. That grand jury was sitting in the same building and investigating the possible criminal actions that could be taken against the Africans. The foreman asked Justice Thompson for a charge, which Thompson refused to give until the jury presented him with facts. The foreman returned with a statement of the facts about what happened aboard the *Amistad*. At this point the habeas corpus hearing was suspended while Thompson examined the facts and told the grand jury he would give it a charge later in the day.

The hearing then resumed with Baldwin discussing a number of substantive issues in the case. Among other things, Baldwin tried to get the case moved from Connecticut to New York on the assumption that the district judge there would be more friendly than the antiabolitionist Judson. Baldwin argued that the ship was closer to New York State than to Connecticut when it was found. While this effort failed, Baldwin did get a major concession from Judge Judson. In commenting on the question of salvage rights, Judson declared "that the District Court had no power to sell these persons," although it might have the power to return them to their Cuban owners (p. 14). Baldwin further argued that the Africans had committed no acts that violated U.S. law, but on the contrary, if anyone had violated the law it was either Lieutenant Gedney for boarding the ship and bringing the Africans into the United States, or Montez and Ruiz for slave trading. Baldwin also investigated the treaties between the United States and Spain to show that the United States had no obligation to return the Africans to Montez and Ruiz or to turn them over to the government of Spain. While supposedly arguing for the freedom of the three African girls, Baldwin was laying the groundwork for a defense of all of the Africans.

Baldwin's argument clearly surprised the U.S. attorney and the attorney for the Cubans. The hearing lasted for another two days, and it was only on the last day that the U.S. attorney was able to organize his thoughts, and the precedents, to refute Baldwin and Staples, who also came prepared for full arguments in the case. Baldwin's argument may also have influenced Justice Thompson's charge to the grand jury. The charge is also printed in this pamphlet.

In his charge Thompson concludes:

> the Courts of the United States have no jurisdiction in the case. Admitting that this offence—if it was an offence—and on that question I express no opinion—that offence was committed on board a Spanish . . . vessel, with a Spanish crew and commander, and Spanish papers, as a mere coasting vessel, on the Island of Cuba. The question arises, whether this Court had jurisdiction of an offence committed on board a Spanish vessel of that character. It must be either an offence against the laws of the United States or the laws of nations. [p. 22]

It was clearly not an offense against U.S. laws, nor did it appear to be an offense against the law of nations. Therefore, Thompson told the grand jury not to bring any indictments against the Africans. Thus, the timely attempt to have the three girls released may have set the stage for the defeat of the proposed indictments.

However, Staples and Baldwin were unable to have the girls released from custody. Justice Thompson asked Mr. Staples: "What is to be done with them?" if they were released. Staples answered: "I suppose, if they have committed no offence against the laws of the United States, nothing can be done with them." This did not satisfy Thompson who retorted: "My object is really to get information. If they are dismissed what provision will be made for them?" Staples suggested they "would be provided for as foreign paupers" (p. 28). This matter was left standing without any conclusion. Staples and Baldwin also introduced the translated affidavit of one of the Africans to show the Africans were not slaves. This too is printed here. However, despite the overwhelming evidence that these girls had committed no crime and were illegally held as slaves, Thompson would not release them. Instead, he ultimately deferred to the arguments of the U.S. attorney, who wanted all the Africans held because the government wished to return them to the Spanish government.

After four days of hearings and deliberations, Justice Thompson ultimately declared that he was "not prepared, as yet, to dispose of the case under consideration *finally*." He declared that this was no longer a question of what to do with the three girls but, indeed, what to do with all the Africans. Because they were no longer held under criminal charges "the embarrassment felt by the Court extends to all the persons held in custody" (p. 37). He therefore decided to hear yet another afternoon of arguments.

Here the whole question of the African slave trade was raised as well as the propriety of the U.S. government becoming involved with the case. These arguments did not clear up the matter. They were essentially a rehash of the arguments of the past few days. Justice Thompson had finally realized that this case was simply too complicated to be decided at a habeas corpus hearing. Thus, the court issued a number of decrees.

First of all, the Africans were no longer held as potential criminals. Thus, they were to be released from jail. Nor could they be sold as salvage because slavery was not recognized in Connecticut. However, they might be owned by Ruiz and Montez, and therefore they should be retained in some type of custody in the eventuality that they would have to be returned to Cuba. Finally, the whole issue had to be remanded to the district court, where all the facts could be brought out and the issues cleared up. In the meantime, the Africans were remanded to the custody of the U.S. marshal, who was ordered to find suitable lodgings for them.

Immediately after this ruling, Judge Judson opened the district court and ordered the marshal to take care "to see that the prisoners were comfortably situated, provided with clothes suited to the season, that they had proper and sufficient food, medical attendance, &c." (p. 47). Judson offered to allow the prisoners to be released from custody, but only if the bail put up amounted to their value in Cuba. For, although they might not be property in Connecticut, it was as yet unclear if they were property in Cuba. This offer of bail was rejected by the abolitionist attorneys. However, the author of the pamphlet did note that this offer exposed slavery and the government's involvement with it in "its hideous bearing" that could be "calculated to open the eyes of the people in the free States to the extent of their entanglements in the guilt and dangers of slavery" (p. 47).

This pamphlet is the best existing record of the habeas corpus hearing and the grand jury investigation connected to this case. It illustrates how quickly the abolitionists were able to mobilize legal talent to defend the Amistads as well as publish an account of their plight for Northern readers. This quick reaction may have saved the lives of the Africans. It certainly set the stage for their ultimate return to Africa.

■ Adams, John Quincy. Argument of John Quincy Adams, before the Supreme Court of the United States, in the case of the United

States, appellants, vs. Cinque, and others, Africans, captured in
the schooner Amistad, by Lieut. Gedney, delivered on the 24th
of February and 1st of March, 1841, with a review of the case
of the Antelope, reported in the 10th, 11th and 12th volumes of
Wheaton's Reports. New York, S. W. Benedict, 1841. 135 p.
LLRBR; E447.A21 Toner Collection Rare Book Room

——[Reprint] New York, Negro Universities Press [1969]
E447.A2 1969

——[Reprint] Argument in the case of the United States vs. Cinque.
New York, Arno Press, 1969.
E447.A2 1969b

    In the official report of this case, the reporter planned "to insert
the able and interesting argument of Mr. Adams, for the African appellees;
and the publication of the 'reports' " was "postponed in the hope of
obtaining it, prepared by himself." But Adams did not send Richard
Peters his arguments, and they were not printed with the report of the
case. Ultimately Peters concluded that "the necessary omission of the
argument is submited with less regret" because "many of the points
presented by Mr. Adams, in the discussion of the cause, were not
considered by the court essential to its decision: and were not taken
notice of in the opinion of the court, delivered by Mr. Justice Story" 40
U.S. (15 Pet.) 518 at 566. While Adams was unable to put the finishing
touches on his argument before the volume of *United States Reports*
went to press, he did make sure the arguments were available in the
form of this 135-page pamphlet.
    Adams did not take any part in this case in the district or circuit
courts. Nor did he want to argue it before the U.S. Supreme Court. At
the time of this argument he was seventy-four years old. In his illustrious
career he had been a diplomat, a U.S. senator, a secretary of state, and
president of the United States (1825−29). After his defeat for reelection
in 1828 Adams did not retire to a life of well-deserved rest. Instead, at
the age of sixty-three he was elected to the U.S. House of Representatives, where he served until his death in 1848.
    At the beginning of his career Adams had been an attorney of
some skill. His name had been entered as an attorney of the Supreme
Court in 1804, but the last case he argued before that court was in 1809.
Thus, when first approached to argue this case Adams declined. He
claimed that his age, the business of the House of Representatives, his
long absence from the legal profession, and his notoriously bad temper
made him a poor choice as co-counsel for Roger Baldwin. Only the
personal pleas of the abolitionist-philanthropist Lewis Tappan and the

abolitionist attorney Ellis Gray Loring convinced Adams that he was vital to the cause of the Amistads.

After Adams agreed to argue the case he wrote in his diary, "I implore the mercy of God so to control my temper, to enlighten my soul, and to give me utterance, that I may prove myself in every respect equal to the task." In his opening remarks Adams expressed his feelings of inadequacy to the Court. He thought an apology "might well be expected where I shall perhaps be more likely to exhibit at once the infirmities of age and the inexperience of youth" (p. 3). In some ways Adams exhibited his "infirmities," his "inexperience," and also his temper.

His argument was delivered over a three-day period and contains over 100,000 words. Just beneath the surface of his legal points was his rage at slavery, the slave trade, and the U.S. government's complicity in this case in particular. Justice Joseph Story, who delivered the "opinion of the court," wrote to his wife that Adams's argument was "extra-ordinary." "Extraordinary, I say, for its power and its bitter sarcasm, and its dealing with topics far beyond the record and points of discussion." In spite of this, Adams and his arguments were important to the case. Adams's stature as a former president and a former secretary of state was particularly important in convincing the Supreme Court to uphold Judge Judson's decision.

Adams's argument is more political, historical, philosophical, and moral than legal. He quotes many unusual sources, including Jonathan Swift, Shakespeare, and Justinian. He declares that his greatest consolation in this case comes "from the thought that this Court is a Court of JUSTICE" (p. 3). He begins his argument by demanding that the Court apply justice to this case, because he would show that "another Department of the Government of the United States has taken, with reference to this case, the ground of utter injustice . . . " (p. 4).

The main thrust of Adams's argument was to show that : (1) the Amistad captives were not legally slaves under Spanish law because they had been illegally brought to Cuba in violation of statutes prohibiting the African slave trade; (2) no treaties between the United States and Spain required that the United States return slaves to Spain; (3) the U.S. government had no legitimate interest in the outcome of the case, and, therefore, although Adams did not explicitly state it, the United States had no standing as a party to the suit; and (4) the U.S. government had illegally, unconstitutionally, and immorally interfered on behalf of the Spanish claimants and against the Africans.

To support these positions, Adams relies primarily on the correspondence between Secretary of State John Forsyth and authorities in Spain and Great Britain, the actions of President Martin Van Buren, various statutes of Spain and the United States, and the text and circumstances of treaties between the United States and Spain. He shows that the United States attempted to return the Africans to Cuba, despite the fact that there was overwhelming proof that they were not legally slaves, even under Spanish law. Adams shows that the Spanish government had been arrogant, insulting, and threatening toward the American government in these negotiations, while the U.S. government violated principles of American and international law in a corrupt attempt to please the Spanish government.

The Spanish government demanded three things of the United States: (1) that "the vessel be immediately delivered up to her owner"; (2) that "it be declared that no tribunal in the United States has the right to institute proceedings against, or to impose penalties upon, the subjects of Spain" in this case; (3) that "the negroes be conveyed to Havana, or be placed at the disposal of the proper authorities in that part of Her Majesty's dominions, in order to their being tried by the Spanish laws which they have violated" (pp. 15–16).

Adams notes that to comply with these demands the U.S. president "should first turn himself into a jailer, to keep these people safely, and then into a tipstaff to take them away for trial among the slave-traders of the baracoons. Was ever such a demand made upon any government?" Where, Adams asks, "in the law of nations is there a warrant for such a demand?" (p. 16). Adams believes the secretary of state should have responded to these demands by informing the Spanish government "that such a demand was treating the President of the United States, not as the head of a nation, but as a constable, a catchpole—a characater that it is not possible to express in gentlemanly language" (pp. 29-30). Throughout his argument Adams is indignant that the Spanish would dare treat the American president and the American institutions with such disrespect. As the man who negotiated the Adams-Onís treaty which led to the acquisition of Florida, Adams could present a strong case that this was not how Spain should conduct business with the United States. Indeed, in discussing the demand for the return of the Africans, Adams, the former secretary of state, declares: "I will speak of my own knowledge, for it happened that on the renewal of the treaty in 1819, the whole of the negotiations with the then minister of Spain passed through my hands, and I am certain that neither of us ever entertained an idea that this word *merchandise* was to apply to human beings" (p. 21).

The most insulting aspect of the Spanish-American negotiations over the Amistads was a threat by the Spanish minister that there would be some sort of retaliation if the Africans were not returned. But Adams does not dwell on this matter. Instead, he submitted the text of the letter of the Spanish minister to the secretary of state and tells the Court: "There are a few portions of this letter, which I had rather your Honors would read when you are together in consultation, than to read them myself in this place. I will not trust myself to comment upon them as they deserve. I trust your Honors, in the pursuit of JUSTICE, will read them, as the document will be in your hands, and you will see why I abstain from doing it'' (p. 24). However, Adams nevertheless implies that it was because of this threat that ''the President of the United States was to issue his *lettre de cachet,* and send these unfortunate individuals to Cuba'' (pp. 24-25).

However indignant Adams is over the conduct of the Spanish government, he reserves his greatest contempt for the actions of Secretary of State John Forsyth and President Martin Van Buren. He cannot understand why the government has tolerated these insults. Worse yet, the government actually tried to accede to Spain's demands. When the case was in the district court, President Van Buren sent the vessel *Grampus* to wait in New Haven harbor. Van Buren expected the decision to go against the Africans, and at that point they were to be summarily placed on the *Grampus* and sent to Cuba. Quoting from correspondence between Secretary of State Forsyth and the U.S. district attorney, Adams reads the instructions: '' 'If the decision of the Court shall be such *as is anticipated,* the order of the President is to be carried into execution, unless an appeal is actually interposed.' '' But, he was '' 'NOT TO TAKE IT FOR GRANTED THAT IT WILL BE INTERPOSED.' '' Adams notes: ''The Government then confidently 'anticipated' that the negroes would be delivered up; and the Attorney was directed not to allow them a moment of time to enter an appeal. They were to be put on board of the Grampus instantly, and deprived, if possible of the privilege of appealing to the higher Courts. Was this JUSTICE?'' (p. 79). Thus, Adams concludes, it was ''deliberately intended by a President of the United States'' to dispose ''of the lives and liberty of thirty-six human beings!'' Almost unable to contain his temper Adams continues, ''Will this Court please to consider for one moment, the essential principle'' of this action? ''Will this Court inquire, what,'' if this had happened

> would have been the tenure by which *every* human being in this Union, man, woman, or child, would have held the blessing of personal freedom? Would it not have been by the tenure of Executive discretion, caprice or tyranny? Had the precedent once been set and submitted to, of a nameless mass of judicial prisoners and witnesses, snatched by Executive grasp from the protective guardianship of the Supreme Judges of the land *(gubernativa-mente,)* at the dictate of a foreign minister, would it not have disabled forever the effective power of the Habeas Corpus?''
> [pp. 79-80]

Throughout his long and, indeed, tedious argument, Adams returns to the same theme: that the U.S. government had conspired with the Spanish government to return the Amistads to Cuba, even though under both Spanish and American law they were not legally slaves. Rather, they were free men of the nation of Mende who had been kidnapped and illegally brought to Cuba. When Lieutenant Gedney boarded the *Amistad* he showed great sympathy for the slave owners on board and no sympathy for the Africans. The secretary of state told the Spanish authorities that this sympathy had become national. But, Adams wonders, "if the sympathies . . . had been felt for all the parties, in due proportion to their sufferings and their deserts, who were the pirates and robbers? Were they the Africans?" (p. 20). Adams thinks not.

While most of Adams's argument centers on diplomatic communications and the actions of the Van Buren administration, he does deal with one major legal precedent, the case of the *Antelope*. In that case Africans intercepted at sea had been returned to Spain. This was an extremely complicated case, heard by the Supreme Court on three separate occasions, as well as argued in circuit and district courts. It involved the laws of Spain, the United States, Portugal, Great Britain, and other nations, as well as international law. Between the time it was argued and the seizure of the *Amistad,* new laws had been passed, both in Spain and the United States. Thus, after almost forty pages of argument, Adams was able to distinguish the *Antelope* from the *Amistad.* In part he rests this argument on the statement of Chief Justice John Marshall, that in the case of the *Antelope,* "no principle was settled" because the court was so divided and the issues so unusual. With the *Antelope* precedent out of the way, Adams ends his argument. He had tried to convince the court that no precedents stood in the way of upholding the lower court decision, and that justice and the law were on the side of the Africans.

■ Baldwin, Roger S. Argument of Roger S. Baldwin, of New Haven, before the Supreme Court of the United States, in the case of the United States, appellants, vs. Cinque, and others, Africans of the Amistad. New York, S. W. Benedict, 1841. 32 p.
LLRBR

Roger S. Baldwin was the first attorney to speak before the U.S. Supreme Court on behalf of the *Amistad* Africans. His argument and presentation were overshadowed by that of John Quincy Adams both because of the fame of Adams and because of the length at which Adams spoke. Baldwin's oral arguments are printed in this pamphlet. The material in this pamphlet is more extensive than that published with the case in Peters's reports, although in substance they vary only slightly. The only major portion of Baldwin's argument that was deleted by Peters concerns the history of the case and some general arguments on the right of either the U.S. government or the Spanish government to claim the Amistads.

For the most part Baldwin avoids the emotion, sarcasm, and political analysis presented by John Quincy Adams. Instead he concentrates on an analysis of Spanish law and the treaties between the United States and Spain. He also analyzes the law of New York State, where the *Amistad* initially landed, to show that slaves entering that state are free, unless they are fugitives under the U.S. Constitution. This was also true for Connecticut, where the Amistads were later taken. Baldwin admits that a state may choose to return a fugitive slave or a fugitive from justice to another country, but he asserts that "the question of the surrender of fugitive slaves to a foreign claimant . . . is left to the *comity of the States* which tolerate slavery" (p. 15). He argues: "The government of the United States has nothing to do with it" (p. 15). He supports this contention with documentation from Adams's official correspondence with various American ambassadors when he had been secretary of state in 1818. Baldwin no doubt had access to this information because Adams was his co-counsel.

In analyzing Spanish law Baldwin concentrates on the fact that the Amistads could speak no Spanish and therefore must not be Cuban slaves. Rather, they must be illegally imported Africans. As such they could not be claimed as slaves by anyone.

In confronting the alleged piracy of the Africans, Baldwin uses treaties with Spain as well as those with Tunis and Algeria to show that slaves who revolt against their masters on the high seas have never been considered pirates. He asks the Court: "Was it ever supposed that if an Algerine corsair should be seized by the captive slaves on board of her, it would be the duty of our naval officers or our Courts of Admiralty to re-capture and restore them?" (p. 22). The object of Cinque and his fellow captives, was not, however, piracy, "but the deliverance of himself and his companions in suffering, from unlawful bondage." Under Spanish and Cuban law "they owed no allegiance to Spain," and therefore "they were guilty of no crime, for which they could be held responsible as pirates." Baldwin asks the Court: "Suppose they had been impressed American seamen, who had regained their liberty in a similar manner, would they in that case have been deemed guilty of piracy and murder?" (p. 23).

Finally, in answering the question of piracy and the return of fugitive slaves, Baldwin asserts: "The United States, *as a nation,* is to be regarded as a free State. And all men being presumptively free" meant that the interpretation of "property" in treaties between Spain and the United States could not refer to slaves (p. 23). This argument was acceptable to the Court in 1841, although after the *Dred Scott* v. *Sandford* decision, 60 U.S. (19 How.) 393 (1857), it may have been less tenable.

Throughout his argument Baldwin is restrained and avoids the attacks of Adams. However, there is some passion in his speech. He ends by asking the Court to "VINDICATE THE HONOR OF OUR COUNTRY AND THE CLAIMS OF HUMANITY AND JUSTICE" (p. 32).

In re Bates

2 F. Cas. 1015 (D.C.S.C. 1858)(No. 1,099a)*

In August 1858 the U.S. brig *Dolphin* intercepted the brig *Echo* in the waters near the Florida Keys. On finding 320 Africans on board the *Echo*, the *Dolphin* seized the ship as a slaver and took it to Charleston, South Carolina. Some of the crew members were Americans, and some were Spaniards. The ship appeared to be owned by its captain, E. C. Townsend, of Providence, Rhode Island. For reasons that are unclear, the *Dolphin* dropped Townsend off at Key West on its way to Charleston. Townsend was later arrested in Boston but does not appear to have been tried for his actions in this case.

Sixteen crewmen, however, were taken to Charleston and jailed. In September they sued for a writ of habeas corpus before District Judge Andrew Gordon Magrath after a grand jury had refused to find a bill against them. In this case, Judge Magrath refused to free the accused slave traders. In a politically shrewd move, the U.S. government hired Isaac W. Hayne, the attorney general of South Carolina, to argue against issuing the writ.

By April 1859 the sixteen crew members had been indicted and were tried in the federal circuit court before Judge Magrath and U.S. Supreme Court Justice James M. Wayne. The prosecution presented overwhelming evidence that the *Echo* was American owned, was a slaver, and had violated the statutes making slave trading an act of piracy. The defense relied entirely on the argument of the defense attorneys and presented no evidence. In his charge to the jury, Justice Wayne urged that the facts be applied to the laws without any political considerations. However, the jury appears not to have followed this advice. It took the jury an hour and a half to find all of the defendants innocent on all the indictments. The prisoners were immediately discharged after this verdict was received.

*The *Echo* Cases

James Moore Wayne (1790-1867). James M. Wayne was a Georgia Democrat whose loyalty to President Jackson earned him an appointment to the Supreme Court in 1834. As a nationalist, Wayne upheld federal prohibitions on the slave trade during the trial of the *Echo*. As a slaveholder, he quite naturally supported Taney's position in *Dred Scott*. Although his son was a Confederate officer, Wayne opposed secession and remained on the Court until his death.
Brady-Handy Collection. LC-BH82-5007

■ Hayne, Isaac William. Argument before the United States Circuit Court, by Isaac William Hayne, esq., on the motion to discharge the crew of the Echo. Delivered in Columbia, S. C., December, 1858. Reported by Douglass A. Levein. Albany, N.Y., Weed, Parsons & Co., 1859. 24 p.

LLRBR

When the *Echo* was first captured, the crew members were arrested and incarcerated in Charleston. Information about the *Echo* was sent to the federal grand jury then in session, "but the Grand Jury had

Isaac W. Hayne (b. 1809). An extreme states' rights advocate, Isaac Hayne had served as clerk of the 1832 South Carolina Nullification Convention. In 1858 the federal government hired him to help prosecute the case of the brig *Echo*, hoping that his presence would deflect any states' rights prejudices the jurors might have had against a federal prosecution.

Engraving by F. Girsch. From John Livingston, *Portraits of Eminent Americans Now Living* (New York, 1853-54).

ignored it'' and refused to indict the prisoners (p. 4). At the conclusion of that term the prisoners sought a writ of habeas corpus to have them released from custody. This case was brought as *In re Bates* before Federal District Judge Andrew Gordon Magrath.

The federal government hired Isaac William Hayne to help argue this case. At the time Hayne was the attorney general for the state of South Carolina and a leading politician. Hayne was hired for at least two reasons. First, he was a prominent state politician, states' rights advocate, and Southern nationalist in a state that felt itself increasingly alienated from the national government. The federal prosecutors no doubt reasoned that Hayne might be more persuasive before Judge Magrath, and to the public at large, than would be the federal prosecutor. This was especially important because District Judge Magrath, although an appointee of President Franklin Pierce, was a fire-eating Southern nationalist in his own right. Magrath's political position is symbolized by his role in the secession crisis and during the Civil War. The day after Abraham Lincoln's presidential victory, Judge Magrath resigned his position. He later became a district judge under the Confederate Constitution and then governor of South Carolina in 1864. The second reason for hiring Hayne had to do with the nature of the legal arguments. Although an action in the federal court, the rules for granting or not granting the writ of habeas corpus were based in part at least on state law. Hayne, more than U.S. District Attorney James Connor, understood the state law at issue.

Hayne began by noting that there was no law or procedure that required the judge to free the prisoners. And, since the U.S. district attorney wished to prosecute the crew of the *Echo*, the prisoners ought to be detained for another term. That the first grand jury to hear evidence in the case did not indict the crew members did not stop "the District Attorney from acting according to his sense of duty, on his best judgment . . . " (p. 7). Thus, Hayne argued that the prisoners should remain in custody until the evidence was brought to a grand jury in the upcoming term.

This led directly to the second, and more politically sensitive, issue: whether the act prohibiting the African slave trade was constitutional. Here Hayne argued that the Slave Trade Prohibition Act of May 15, 1820, ch. 113, 3 Stat. 600, providing severe penalties for those convicted of slave trading, had been passed "without opposition or division" (p. 8). Since then "the powers of the General Government have been brought much into question, and have been very thoroughly discussed, in the South in particular, and in South Carolina, most especially. But no one, not even "Mr. Calhoun—*clarum et venerabile nomen*!" had ever "brought about any discoveries as to the law in question" (p. 8).

Hayne asserted that he favored a strict construction of the U.S. constitution. He argued that the national government was one of strictly limited, enumerated powers. But he asserted that within those powers Congress clearly had the power to enforce its laws and punish law-breakers. Furthermore, Hayne argued that Congress had the power to regulate commerce, to make treaties, and to punish piracy. Finally, he noted that Congress was given the right to interfere with the African slave trade after the year 1808. The slave trade clause was adopted "as a compromise, and although it was afterwards attacked, it was defended by Gen. [Charles] Pinckney, who had previously fought against it," in the Constitutional Convention, "on the ground that it *was* a compromise." Indeed, during the ratification debates in South Carolina Pinckney asserted "that he gave up the right to Congress with very great reluctance, and was prepared to go home and give up the Union altogether, rather than consent to yield the power at once" (p. 22). Given this historical evolution of the slave trade clause in the constitution, it was clear to Hayne that the act prohibiting the slave trade was indeed constitutional.

Finally, Hayne asked whether this case could "be regarded as a question of States Rights, or of Southern Rights" (p. 24). There was no conflict between state and national rights. The states did "not pretend to claim power in this behalf; nor has any interposition of the shield of State Sovereignty for the protection of the citizen been suggested" (p. 24). The prisoners, after all, were flying the national flag, in international waters when they were arrested. Indeed, it appeared that the *Echo* may have been headed to Cuba, rather than any U.S. port. Since it could not be doubted that the federal government had the right to prevent the African slave trade with the United States, then "certainly the South, as a section, is not affected by the trade elsewhere. If *we* are not to have slaves imported, is it to affect us to interfere with the importation into Cuba?" (p. 24). Clearly not by Hayne's interpretation. Moreover, in this case citizens of the South were not even involved. The ship was owned by a man from Rhode Island, and "not one solitary Southern man can be found . . . among the prisoners before the Court. . . . Every American among the crew. . . . hailed from North of the Potomac." Hayne asserted: "The act was not sectional in its inception, and had not been sectional in its operation" (p. 24).

On the strength of Hayne's argument Judge Magrath ruled against the defendants, who were then held for trial. The case was reported as *In re Bates,* but it contained none of the arguments of counsel. This pamphlet is the only printed record available of Hayne's contribution to this case.

This pamphlet was printed by the printing company owned by Thurlow Weed, a leading New York Republican and a close ally of William Henry Seward. The connections between Magrath and Hayne in South Carolina and Seward and Weed in New York in this case are particularly interesting. These New York Republicans were, by 1859, the sworn political enemies of the South Carolina fire-eaters led by such men as Hayne and Magrath. Indeed, the election of a Republican president in 1860 would lead to Magrath's resignation from the federal bench and the subsequent secession of South Carolina. Moreover, at first glance it appears odd that Magrath and Hayne would have sided with the federal government in a case that apparently attacked the morality and justice of slavery, as well as perhaps hurting the institution. The issues, and the alignments are not, however, as odd as they first appear.

A number of Southern nationalists opposed a reopening of the African slave trade for many reasons. First, some considered the trade unnecessarily brutal and violent. It was morally repugnant even to men who considered slavery in the United States to be a positive good for both masters and slaves. Second, some Southerners thought the slave trade was dangerous because it would bring fresh Africans to the South who might lead revolts. There were also economic considerations. The importation of new slaves would perhaps diminish the value of slaves already in the United States. Finally, in this case it was Northerners, and not Southerners, who would go to jail. Hayne no doubt saw this case as proof of the hypocrisy of Northerners who condemned slavery while participating in the slave trade. In the propaganda war between the North and the South, this was wonderful evidence for Southern nationalists.

For Northern Republicans this was also a useful case. Hayne's argument did suggest that the slave trade was immoral and wrong. If that was the case, then slavery itself was perhaps wrong. In addition, Hayne's support of the federal government in the late antebellum period was a welcome change from the states' rights cry in the South. Thus, Weed and Parsons printed Hayne's arguments. The crew of the *Echo* remained in prison to await their trials.

■ Bates, R. T., *defendant*. Report of the trials in the Echo cases, in federal court, Charleston, S. C., April, 1859; together with arguments of counsel and charge of the court. By J. Woodruff, phonograph reporter. Columbia, S. C., Steam-Power Press of R. W. Gibbes, 1859. 115 p.

LLRBR

This book records the trials of the crew of the *Echo*. The only existing record of the case, this volume contains a statement of the cases, names of counsel engaged, the testimony, arguments on the evidence, arguments on challenging the jurors, lists of the jurors, oral arguments or speeches of the five attorneys in the case, the charge of Justice Wayne, and the verdict.

According to this report two trials were conducted before Wayne: one for the American defendants and one for the crew members who were not American citizens. Some of the jurors in the first trial also served in the second, despite a protest from the U. S. district attorney, James Conner. In both trials, all the defendants were acquitted.

Very little testimony was presented in this case. The prosecution called eight witnesses, some of whom only testified about the ownership of the *Echo*. The defense called no witnesses at all but would be ready to argue its case the next day. Before arguments began, the court allowed the prosecution to call one more witness, despite protests from the defense counsel.

The defendants were represented by Col. Maxey Gregg, Leonidas Spratt, Edmund Bellinger, and a Mr. DeTreville. The arguments of the four are similar in almost all respects. Indeed, Bellinger began his argument (he was the second defense attorney to speak) by declaring that "his colleague (Col. Gregg) had left him little to do, save to repeat what had already been said" (p. 21). These arguments centered on the constitutionality of the act prohibiting the African slave trade. They argued that Congress was not explicitly authorized to pass laws punishing those engaged in the trade. Thus, the statutes under which the prisoners stood indicted were both an unauthorized action by the Congress and an unconstitutional infringement on states' rights and state sovereignty. Underlying all of these arguments was the need to protect slavery from federal interference. In summation DeTreville (the last defense attorney to speak) declared:

> [L]et me recur again to the subject upon which, in the beginning of my remarks, I declined to dwell for fear of exciting your anger and indignation, I mean the character of this law which you are summoned by Federal authority to enforce. I speak of it to denounce it, not only as oppressive and tyrannical, but as most insulting to us who are slaveholders, and whose fathers were slaveholders and saw no crime in the slave trade. I speak of it as it is, a gross indignity to the freemen of this State who have never known any condition of society which was not identified with the institution of slavery . . . . this Act of 1820, it is written as a part of our history, that our fathers were sea-robbers and pirates; for if the slave trade is now piracy and theft, so it was always. Is it not a thing to complain of, that our own Congress should deliberately record this infamous falsehood of our ancestors? Was not the enactments of this law a much more sensible cause for disunion than ever were the tariff laws? and yet we resisted the one, but have tamely submitted to the other . . . . Great is the wrong which the mere passage of this law has inflicted, but infinitely greater is the insult that we, the descendants of those who were once engaged in the slave trade, should be required to enforce it. If this law is true, then are we the descendants of pirates, and our slaves are entitled to their freedom, for *their* parents *were* stolen and there is no shadow of title by which we can hold them. [p. 95]

The act of 1820 was an act of "our enemies" to undermine slavery in South Carolina (p. 95). DeTreville urged the jurors to disregard the law and free the prisoners.

U. S. District Attorney Conner urged the jury to ignore the passionate arguments of the defense attorneys. He noted: "You are told that this question involves great political events." But he urged that these arguments "have no place, no weight, in the decision of a question before a legal tribunal. Public opinion and political expediency have nothing to do with the administration of justice" (p.104). The defense counsel had noted that the fugitive slave law was not enforced in the North. But, Connor argued, this was irrelevant. To reject the law was "to follow the example of fanatics" (pp.104-105). Justice Wayne also reminded the jury to support the law and avoid political considerations. He went on to warn the South Carolinians on the jury: "Your constitutional rights will be taken from you to a much greater extent than you can possibly protect them in South Carolina, if you take from the Courts the power to determine the constitutionality of the law" (p. 108). But these efforts to secure the enforcement of the law were to no avail. It took the jury less than an hour to acquit the American defendants and a half hour to acquit the others.

The Wanderer

29 F. Cas. 150 (D. Mass. 1860)(No. 17,139)

United States v. Corrie

25 F. Cas. 658 (C.C.D. S.C. 1860)(No. 14,869)

The schooner *Wanderer* was initially built for a member of the New York Yacht Club, who wanted the fastest boat on the seas. It was later sold to Captain W. C. Corrie, who acted for a syndicate of Savannah, Georgia, investors led by Charles A. L. Lamar. The *Wanderer* made a successful slave-trade voyage to Africa in 1858, but publicity after the slaves were sold in Georgia and South Carolina led federal authorities to investigate the ship. The *Wanderer* was subsequently condemned and repurchased by Lamar at auction in Savannah.

Lamar sent the ship back to Africa on another successful slave-trading mission. In 1859 he sold part interest in the ship to a captain named Martin. Martin and Lamar planned yet another slaving expedition. Martin, however, apparently never paid, nor intended to pay, Lamar for the *Wanderer*. Instead, he gathered a crew and on sudden notice left Savannah before the ship was fully loaded. There were some shortages of food and provisions, as well as a lack of charts and navigational instruments. Many of the sailors did not have their clothes or personal possessions on board when they were ordered to depart. The ship left the port "without having obtained from the Customs House any clearance or proper papers for that purpose" (*The Schooner Wanderer*, p. 28). There was no pilot aboard, and the ship ran aground a few times before successfully reaching open water. Sailors on board were ordered to remain and were forced at gunpoint to sign the ship's articles. They were not informed of the nature of the voyage until the ship was out of the harbor, and then they were told they would be killed if they tried to leave the ship.

This hasty departure was probably due to Lamar's impatience for the money owed him. On the day before the ship left, Lamar asked the collector of the Port of Savannah "to order Captain Day, of the Revenue Cutter, to take position in the river to prevent the Wanderer from leaving the port without her proper clearance." Lamar told the collector that "he had sold an interest in the Wanderer to the captain, and that he had so frequently disappointed him by not coming up to pay . . . that he (Lamar) began to think that he (the captain) was a damned rascal, and would attempt to steal the Wanderer from him" (ibid., p. 28-29).

The *Wanderer* sailed to the Azores where provisions were purchased but never paid for. Two young women were also taken aboard there on the premise that the captain and the first mate would marry them and take them to America. However, the captain said "he was going to take them with him, and trade them off for a certain number of negroes [slaves]" (p.166). In his haste to leave these islands with his as yet unpaid-for provisions, the captain ordered the ship to sea before the ship's carpenter came back on board. He was thus left in the Azores. By this time the ship's name had been changed to the *William*, and the captain produced false papers indicating he was sailing to Greece and Turkey.

The captain next headed to the Canary Islands. On the way he hailed a French ship to obtain more provisions and directions, since the ship was still without proper charts and equipment. The captain left the *Wanderer* and boarded the French boat. In his absence, the crew, under the direction of the first mate, resolved to abandon their captain. They quickly raised the sail and headed for Boston. Upon reaching that city they turned the ship over to federal authorities and claimed the ship in lieu of their wages and for its salvage value. The U. S. government at the same time proceeded against the ship as a slaver.

In a trial before District Judge Peleg Sprague, Charles A. L. Lamar claimed the *Wanderer*, which he argued Captain Martin had stolen from him. He also argued that the ship had not participated in the slave trade, and that there was no conclusive evidence that it was a slaver. For these reasons Lamar claimed the ship should not be condemned but should be returned to him. During the trial Lamar sold, or transferred, any claim he might have in the ship to his father, Gazaway Bugg Lamar, one of the leading financiers in Georgia and, like his son, a sometime participant in the slave trade. G. B. Lamar posted a bond of $5,940 for the ship's appraised value and took possession of the *Wanderer* before the trial began. Lamar also posted a $1,000 bond for court costs.

In his opinion condemning the *Wanderer*, Judge Sprague concluded that there could be no doubt that the ship was a slaver. That no slaves were found on board or that there was not a great deal of slaving equipment, such as chains and fetters, did not matter. There was an abundance of testimony from the crew that the captain was headed for the coast of Africa to buy, steal, or kidnap slaves. Given the wording of the law, it did not matter who actually owned the ship. Sprague declared that the slave trade was "a traffic so denounced and so criminal" that it would "assume every disguise, false pretense and deception, which fraud and ingenuity can devise, and calls for the most stringent measures for its prevention; one of which is to enlist the owner of the vessel to prevent her being so employed in violation of law, by holding him responsible for such use to the extent of his ownership" (29 F. Cas. 150, 152). Sprague did not investigate the culpability of Lamar in this enterprise, although there was much evidence to suggest he knew of the ship's destination and plans.

■ Wanderer (Schooner). The United States of America, by information, versus the Schooner Wanderer and cargo. For the United States, C. L. Woodbury, District Attorney; for the claimant, Circuit Court of the United States. In Admiralty. John A. Andrew, A. G. Browne, Jr. Boston, Prentiss & Deland, Printers, 1860. 188 p.
Law Library

This book contains most of the records of the case. Among other items, it contains copies of the information, the warrant to the marshal, the marshal's return, an inventory of the perishable cargo and what it was sold for, numerous motions, the appraisal of the ship, numerous stipulations by the parties, and 170 pages of testimony and affidavits. The book ends with the court's decree condemning the ship. The only relevant pieces of information not contained in this volume are the arguments of the attorneys and the opinion of Judge Sprague.

Most of the testimony consists of depositions from crew members and the two women taken from the Azores. Most of the crew members asserted that they knew nothing of the real purpose of the ship's voyage until they were at sea and forced, at gunpoint, to agree to the captain's demands. Descriptions of the captain indicate that he drank heavily throughout the trip and was a notorious bully. He openly displayed his weapons and kept the ship's cannon loaded throughout the voyage. One irony of the voyage concerns the *Echo*, which Captain Martin tried to hail to get directions and food. This ship was also engaged in the illegal slave trade. In April 1859 the *Echo* had been acquitted by a jury in Charleston, South Carolina, of violating the federal laws prohibiting the slave trade. It, of course, avoided the *Wanderer* and would not stop to answer its hail.

NEGROES
FOR SALE.

☞ Will be sold at public auction, at Spring Hill, in the County of Hempstead, on a credit of twelve months, on Friday the 28th day of this present month, 15 young and valuable Slaves, consisting of 9 superior Men & Boys, between 12 and 27 years of age, one woman about 43 years who is a good washer and cook, one woman about twenty-seven, and one very likely young woman with three children.

Also at the same time, and on the same terms, three Mules, about forty head of Cattle, plantation tools, one waggon, and a first rate Gin stand, manufactured by Pratt &Co.

Bond with two or more approved securities will be required. Sale to commence at 10 o'clock.

E. E. Hundley,
W. Robinson,
H. M. Robinson.

Spring Hill, Jan. 6th, 1842.

A broadside from January 1842 advertises the sale of slaves in Hempstead County, Arkansas. Broadside Collection, Rare Book and Special Collections Division.

Miscellaneous Trials and Cases

Not all of the trials involving slaves fit into neat categories. In this section of the bibliography are the annotations of those pamphlets that are more or less left over. Some involve murder trials. One deals with the legislative attempt to reverse a Mississippi Supreme Court decision allowing a master to free his slaves. Another, *Elkison* v. *Deliesseline*, 8 F. Cas. 493 (C.C.D. S.C. 1823) (No. 4,366), involves a major issue of constitutional law and international affairs.

King v. *Mark and Phillis, Slaves*

(Charlestown [Mass.] Super. Ct. 1755)(Unreported)

Mark and Phillis were the slaves of Capt. John Codman of Charlestown, Massachusetts. In 1755 they carefully planned their master's murder. Mark obtained some "potter's lead" as well as some arsenic. These poisons were administered by Phillis when serving food to her master. The arsenic was mixed with water and put in his chocolate, his watergruel, and other foods. The poison was given about seven times, before Codman died in July 1755.

Mark, Phillis, and some other slaves were quickly arrested and questioned. Phillis and Mark refused to confess to the crime, although they did not deny knowledge of it. Rather, they blamed each other and other slaves. In September 1755 they were tried and convicted for petit treason. Mark was hanged until dead, and then his body was removed and hung in chains. From this record it appears that Mark's body was left for a number of years. Phillis, in conformity with English statutes, was burned to death.

■ Goodell, Abner Cheney, Jr. The trial and execution for petit treason, of Mark and Phillis, slaves of Capt. John Codman, who murdered their master at Charlestown, Mass., in 1755; for which the man was hanged and gibbeted, and the woman was burned to death. Including, also, some accounts of other punishments by burning

251

in Massachusetts. Cambridge, John Wilson and Son, University
Press, 1883. 39 p.

This pamphlet was published about 130 years after the events
described took place. It is a reprint of an article that initially appeared in
the *Proceedings of the Massachusetts Historical Society*. The paper was
reprinted because this was "the only known instance of the infliction of
the common-law penalty for petit treason, in New England" and was
nowhere else reported (p.3).

Codman was apparently a strict master who made life intolerable
for his slaves. Three of them, Mark, Phillis, and Phebe, planned his
murder by obtaining poison from other slaves in the Boston area. Mark,
the leader of this group, was literate and "signed his examination . . . in
a bold, legible hand. He professed to have read the Bible through, in
order to find if, in any way, his master could be killed without inducing
guilt" (p.4). Mark concluded this could be done without violating God's
commandments. The slaves believed they could successfully accomplish
this murder because they believed other slaves in the area had poisoned
their masters and not been prosecuted.

This pamphlet is part narrative and part legal documents. It
includes the coroner's inquest; the examinations of the slave Quaco, of
Phillis, and of Mark; a mittimus against the slave Robin; the indictment;
various subpoenas; a record of the conviction; and the death warrants.
Quaco, Robin, and Phebe were involved in the crime but were apparently
not indicted. It is likely they testified at the trial (the trial records are not
included in this pamphlet and probably no longer exist) and were
transported out of the colony instead of being executed.

Besides this case, the pamphlet contains the records of a number
of other harsh executions in Massachusetts and England. Some of these
involved slaves. In 1681 the slave Marja was burned at the stake after
being convicted of arson. The body of a male arsonist was burned along
with Marja, but after this criminal had been hanged. This slave had been
convicted for arson but was not an accomplice of Marja. However,
Marja did have a male accomplice who was jailed and then transported
out of the country.

The different penalties for men and women in these cases are
striking. They are the result of English law, which provided death by
burning for women convicted of petit treason, and hanging and gibbeting
for men. Initially the men probably suffered more than women under
these laws, since the men were hanged until they passed out, but not
until they died. They were then "eviscerated, then beheaded" (p. 28)
before the hanging horses dragged them through the streets. In
Massachusetts, however, it appears that the men were simply hanged

until dead, after being dragged to the place of their execution. These harsh penalties were imposed because both poisoning of a master and arson were considered crimes against the state—petit treason—and thus severely punished. English legislators and jurists saw killing one's master or burning down his house as an act of revolution or treason against the state.

People v. *Amos Broad*

(N.Y.C. Recorder's Ct. 1809) (Unreported)

Amos Broad and his wife Demis were indicted for beating and assaulting two of their slaves. Amos was indicted twice, once for beating his adult female slave, Betty, and once for beating Betty's three-year-old child, Sarah. Demis Broad was indicted only for beating the child.

These indictments were the result of the unusually harsh treatment of these slaves. One witness testified she "had seen much cruelty on the part of Mr. and Mrs. Broad toward their servants, had seen Mr. Broad strip the slave Betty naked in the coldest weather, when the snow was on the ground . . . whip her in the kitchen, and afterwards turn her out into the yard, and keep her there half an hour; the slave begged for her cloaths, which after much entreaty he permitted her to have, ordering her at the same time to beg his pardon" (*The Trial of Amos Broad*, p. 6). Another witness testified that on a different occasion, Mr. Broad had poured water on Betty and made her stand out in the cold until it froze on her. This witness had seen Mrs. Broad "kick the infant [Sarah] in the breast till it gasped for breath." At another time Mrs. Broad did "whip and kick the child, throw a case knife at her head, which cut so large a gash, and made her bleed so excessively, that Doctor Gamage was sent for to sew it up" (ibid., p. 6). Other witnesses testified that Mr. Broad made Betty "drink the glauber salts out of the bowl" when she was not ill (ibid., p. 11). The same person saw Mr. Broad "also when Betty brought a teapot, because he said she had put too much water in it, order her to hold out her hand, and pour boiling water upon it; using at the same time this expression—'Am not I a good doctor to doctor negroes?' " (ibid., p. 11).

When all the testimony had been given the defense attorney did not give a summation. Instead he "made a proposal; that the defendant should voluntarily manumit the mother and her child, and also, the third slave named Hannah, whose case was not involved in the present indictment" (ibid., p. 15). Mr. Broad was allowed to leave the courtroom and return home accompanied by an officer and some members of the New York Manumission Society (its full name was the New-York

Society, for Promoting the Manumission of Slaves and Protecting Such of Them as Have Been or May Be Liberated). Manumission papers were prepared and "the astonished victims were delivered" into the "benevolent charge" of the Manumission Society. The foreman of the jury then pronounced a guilty verdict upon both defendants and "expressed openly their [the jurors'] opinions, that the forefeiture of the slaves was by no means an adequate punishment" (ibid., p. 16). Mr. Broad returned to jail, while his wife was apparently freed on her own recognizance.

Three days after this conviction that court was convened for sentencing. The Broads' attorney argued that the court should show mercy, despite the heinous nature of the crime. He asserted, among other things, that Mrs. Broad was pregnant, and the jailing of her husband would be too much of a shock in her condition. He suggested a fine would be appropriate, for "if the defendant is a sordid man, punish him by his avarice, and that will make him feel. Let him suffer in his property, by the loss of the servants he has ill treated. Add to that such a fine as may make him feel still more," which would hurt him, but not his innocent children (ibid., p. 17).

The prosecution mocked these pleas to humanity, the pleas for the welfare of Broad's family. "He has a wife! the mother of five children! and he, their father! Gracious heaven! How does this thought recoil upon his head? Where were the tender feelings of a father, when he could kick and buffet a poor baby . . . " (ibid., p. 21). As to only fining Broad, the prosecution asked, "Might not every culprit say, I have money, I can buy impunity, and pay my debt to justice with my purse?" (ibid., pp. 23-24). The court ultimately accepted this demand for more than a fine. Mr. Broad was fined the rather large sum of $500, but he was also sentenced to sixty days in jail and required to post a peace bond of $1,000 before he could leave prison. Mrs. Broad, because of her pregnancy, was not jailed, but was fined $250 for her conviction.

■ Broad, Amos, *defendant*. The trial of Amos Broad and his wife, on three several indictments for assaulting and beating Betty, a slave, and her little female child Sarah, aged three years. Had at the Court of Special Sessions of the Peace, held in and for the City and County of New-York, at the City-Hall, of the said city, on Tuesday, the 28th of February, 1809. Present, the Hon. Pierre C. Van Wyck, *Recorder*. Peter Mesier and James Drake, *esquires, aldermen*. To which is added, the motion of counsel in Mr. Broad's behalf, to mitigate the imprisonment of his person, and impose a fine—and the reply of Mr. Sampson. Also, the prayer of invocation of Mr. Broad, to the Court, for mercy, and the address of his Honor, the Recorder, on passing Sentence on the Defendants. New York, Printed by Henry C. Southwick, 1809. 31 p.

Law Library

This case was brought by the New York Manumission Society, which apparently provided an attorney, Mr. Sampson, to be co-counsel for the district attorney. Despite the origin of the prosecution, the judge refused to accept the challenge to one of the jurors who was a member of the Manumission Society. Thus, at least one of the jurors was predisposed toward conviction when the trial began.

This report of the trial includes lists of the jurors, the panel of judges, and the attorneys. It also contains most of the testimony and speeches of the counsel for both sides, the speech by Mr. Broad before sentencing and a summary of the speeches at sentencing, as well as the sentence. It is a fairly complete record of this trial, which took place at one of the lowest levels of the New York court system and would have been unrecorded but for this pamphlet. The pamphlet was published because the information was "too interesting to humanity and good morals, to be sunk in silence or oblivion." The Manumission Society thought "there never was a case more deserving of universal notice; never one more characteristic of a nation's justice; none ever offered to humanity a more generous triumph . . . " (p. 3).

The outcome of this case was clearly a triumph for the Manumission Society. First, it led to the unexpected liberation of three slaves. It also punished a master for mistreating his slaves. Finally, it may have put other masters on notice that they could not inhumanely punish or beat their slaves. By the time this case was brought, slavery was being gradually abolished in New York. Indeed, it is unclear under the New York Gradual Emancipation statute how the child Sarah could have been a slave for life. Most likely she was bound to serve the Broads only until she reached age twenty-five. Yet, because of the gradual nature of its emancipation law, there were still slaves, and slave owners, in New York. Nevertheless, as this case shows, slavery in New York or anywhere in the North was not what it had once been and clearly was nothing like Southern slavery. In the South a master could treat his slaves in any manner he chose. Short of premeditated murder, the master could not be criminally or civilly indicted or charged for assaults or batteries on slaves. In New York, the law protected not only the life but also the physical safety of the slave.

Elkison v. Deliesseline

8 F. Cas. 493 (C.C.D. S.C. 1823)(No. 4,366)

In December 1822 South Carolina passed "an act for the better regulation of Free Negroes and Persons of Color, and for other purposes," Act of Dec. 21, 1822, No. 2277, 7 Stat. S.C. 461 (1822). The third section of this act regulated the ingress of free black seamen from "any other State, or *foreign port.*" The law required that such black sailors be "seized and confined in gaol until such vessel, shall clear out and depart from this state." The captain of the ship that brought these sailors was required to pay the costs of their incarceration before they could be removed from the state. If the captain failed to pay these expenses, he was "liable to be indicted; and on conviction thereof shall be fined in a sum not less than one thousand dollars, and imprisoned not less than two months." Free blacks left in the state were to "be deemed and taken as absolute slaves, and sold in conformity" with existing statutes (8 F. Cas. 493).

The purpose of this statute was not to enslave free Negroes, although some could be enslaved under its provisions. Rather, the South Carolina legislature hoped to discourage or completely stop free blacks from coming into the state as merchant seamen. The act was passed in the wake of the Denmark Vesey conspiracy (see section on slave revolts). Many South Carolinians believed that Vesey and his coconspirators had been influenced by free black seamen who brought antislavery literature and ideas with them. By jailing Negro seamen when they entered the state, the legislature hoped to stop the spread of antislavery ideas among South Carolina's slaves.

Immediately after the passage of the Negro Seamen's Act, there were complaints that it would create havoc in interstate commerce and probably lead to an international conflict with England or some other nation that employed free blacks. The federal government took an interest in the law and attempted to negotiate with South Carolinian authorities to prevent its enforcement. Secretary of State John Quincy Adams participated in these negotiations as well as in communications with British officials who were worried about the safety of their citizens. In June 1823 Adams informed a British official that measures had been taken "for effecting the removal of the cause of complaint . . . and will prevent the recurrence of it in the future" (8 F. Cas. 493). And indeed this appeared to be a correct assessment of the situation. From "that time the prosecutions under this act were discontinued," and state officials acknowledge "this law has been complained of on the ground of its unconstitutionality and injurious effects upon our [South Carolina's]

William Johnson (1771-1834). Supreme Court justice William Johnson was a nationalist from the bastion of state sovereignty, South Carolina. While attending to his circuit court duties, Johnson declared that South Carolina's laws regulating black seamen were unconstitutional. For this decision in *Elkison* v. *Deliesseline*, Johnson became a pariah in his home state.

From a photograph of a painting, artist and owner unknown, resembling a miniature by Charles Fraser. Prints and Photographs Division. LC-USZ6-915 commerce and foreign relations.'' Thus the officials ''have shown every dispostion to let it [the law] sleep'' (8 F. Cas. 493).

A number of citizens in South Carolina, however, would not let the issue die quietly. They formed the South Carolina Association and agitated for strict enforcement of the Negro Seamen's Act. Their activities led to the arrest of Henry Elkison in 1823. Elkison was a free black born in Jamaica and a seaman on the British ship *Homer*, which was based in Liverpool. After Elkison's arrest the British consul in Charleston made official protests and initially sought Elkison's release through diplomatic channels. This tactic failed, and Elkison then sued in U.S. Circuit Court for one of two remedies. He asked the court to grant him a writ of habeas corpus on the grounds that he was illegally held in jail under an act that was unconstitutional and void. If this relief was impossible, he asked for a writ de homine replegiando, which would bring his case before a jury.

This case was heard by Justice William Johnson, a justice of the U.S. Supreme Court who was hearing circuit court cases in his native South Carolina when the action was brought. Although brought as a suit against the sheriff of Charleston, no attorneys appeared on behalf of the state. Rather, the case was defended by two attorneys for the ''South Carolina Association,'' Isaac E. Holmes and Benjamin Faneuil Hunt.

In his decision Justice Johnson reached three conclusions. First, he declared that the Negro Seamen's Act was an unconstitutional interference with the commerce clause of the Constitution as well as an unconstitutional interference with the treaty-making powers of the federal government. His discussion of the statute was harsh and angry. He let his South Carolina neighbors know, in no uncertain terms, that he would vigorously oppose their disunionist tendencies. Second, Johnson found that although Elkison was held in custody under an unconstitutional statute, the federal court had no power to release him through a habeas corpus proceeding. His third conclusion, however, was that he had no reason not to issue a writ de homine replegiando. This writ might not in the end free Elkison, and indeed Johnson doubted it would. But as a matter of common law, Johnson could not refuse to grant it. In this case Johnson condemned the statute without actually effecting any change in its enforcement.

A year after this case, the South Carolina statute was modified to exempt free blacks serving on U.S. or foreign naval vessels by the Act of Dec. 20, 1823, No. 2319, 7 Stat. S.C. 463 (1823). But this law remained on the books until the Civil War. It and similar statutes in Louisiana led to a number of controversies between these two states and some Northern states.

■ Johnson, William. The opinion of the Hon. William Johnson, delivered
on the 7th August, 1823, in the case of the arrest of the British
seaman under the 3d section of the state act, entitled, "An act
for the better regulation of free Negroes and persons of colour,
and for other purposes," passed in December last. Ex parte
Henry Elkison, a subject of his Britannic Majesty, vs. Francis
G. Deliesseline, Sheriff of Charleston District. [Charleston,
S.C., 1823?] 15 p.

Law Library

This pamphlet was apparently published by Justice William
Johnson shortly after his decision in the case. It contains Johnson's
opinion and is virtually the same as the opinion that appears in the
Federal Cases. Its publication was probably designed to convince South
Carolinians of the necessity of accepting federal authority over commerce
and treaty making. Johnson may have also hoped to deflect criticism
from extremists in his state. If these were indeed his motives for publishing
his opinion, Johnson failed. Benjamin F. Hunt responded with a pamphlet
of his own (see following annotation), and Johnson was ostracized in his
home city and state. Finally, South Carolina continued, undeterred, on
its long road to secession.

In his opinion Johnson went out of his way to criticize the statute
and those who supported it. He notes that its enforcement could have
disastrous results. In one case, for example, the enforcement of the law
left not a "single man on board the vessel to guard her in the captain's
absence" (p. 3). Potentially there were even greater dangers. "Let it be
observed that the law is 'if any vessel,' (not even the vessels of the
United States excepted,)" comes into the state, the free blacks on board
would be seized and subject to enslavement (p. 5). Johnson asked: "But
what shall we say to the provisions of this act as they operate on our
vessels of war? Send your Sheriff on board one of them, and would the
spirited young men of the navy submit to have a man taken?" (p. 11).
The law of South Carolina threatened to force that state to go to war
with the national government, Great Britain, France, Morocco, Algiers,
Lascar, Sierra Leone, and a number of states of the Union. Enforcement
of the statute would lead to the "United States involved in war and
confusion" (pp. 6-7).

Besides international and domestic conflict, the law subverted
the Constitution. The law was "altogether irreconcilable with the powers
of the general government; that it necessarily compromits the public
peace, and tends to embroil us with, if not separate us from our sister
states; in short that it leads to a dissolution of the union, and implies a
direct attack upon the sovereignty of the United States" (p. 5). For a
patriotic South Carolinian and a devoted Unionist like Johnson, the law

was a double anathema. It would destroy the commerce and peace of his home state and it would destroy the Constitution and the Union itself. Fortunately for Johnson the law was so blatant a violation of the Constitution that he had no qualms about declaring it null and void. Besides violating the commerce clause, the law infringed on the national government's inherent power to conduct foreign affairs. "In order to sustain this law, the state [of South Carolina] must also possess a Power paramount to the Treaty-Making Power of the United States, expressly declared to be a part of the supreme legislative power of the land." And, even if the state had such a power, which it most emphatically did not, a statute such as this one still could not be passed, "without furnishing a just cause of war." The seizing and enslaving of foreign nationals was a violation of international law. Even the exclusion of certain classes of foreigners could be accomplished only "by treaty" (p. 9). Johnson had no doubts that the clause of the statute under which Elkison was jailed "is clearly unconstitutional and void" (p. 15).

After demolishing the constitutionality of the statute, Johnson turned to the remedy. He noted that it was "an obvious mockery" for a party to "have a right to his liberty and no remedy to obtain it" (p. 11). Nevertheless Johnson could not issue a writ of habeas corpus. Either by accident or because it was "studiously calculated," the law left those arrested under it "remediless" (p. 11). Because it was a state prosecution the federal courts were prohibited from interfering in the case. As to the writ de homine replegiando, Johnson asked: "what right I have to refuse it?" and found he had none (p. 13).

Johnson found this writ to be one "of common right" that "contains upon the face of it, its own death-warrant if it be not legally grantable in any particular case" (p. 13). Thus, he could grant the writ, but it was his "opinion extrajudically" that there was "the most serious doubt whether this writ could avail the party as against the sheriff, but as against his vendee, there is not a question that it will well lie at common law" (p. 14).

Thus, Johnson accomplished a legal finesse as deft and as useful as the one Chief Justice John Marshall executed in *Marbury* v. *Madison*, 5 U.S. (1 Cranch) 137 (1803). Johnson declared the statute under consideration unconstitutional, and in doing so supported the integrity of the Constitution, the Union, and the power of the federal government. At the same time he avoided issuing an order the South Carolina government might have flagrantly ignored.

The importance of Johnson's opinion is perhaps underscored by the origin of the copy of this pamphlet in the Library of Congress collection. The pamphlet in the Law Library was originally owned by the Department of State. In his opinion Johnson details the attempts by Secretary of State John Quincy Adams to negotiate a settlement in the case, even though he could not "officially take notice of Mr. Adams' letter" to British officials. Johnson put this information into his opinion "to show that our administration has acted in good faith with that of Great Britain" (pp. 4-5). While unable to persuade South Carolina to change its policies, Johnson at least hoped to defuse a potential crisis with Great Britain. It is no wonder the Department of State kept a copy of his opinion in its library.

■ Hunt, Benjamin Faneuil. The argument of Benj. Faneuil Hunt, in the case of the arrest of the person claiming to be a British seaman, under the 3rd section of the state act of Dec. 1822, in relation to Negroes, &c., before the Hon. Judge Johnson, Circuit Judge of the United States, for 6th Circuit. Ex parte Henry Elkison, claiming to be a subject of his Britannic majesty, vs. Francis G. Deliesseline, Sheriff of Charleston District. [Charleston, S.C.] Printed by A. E. Miller, 1823. 22 p.

Law Library

This pamphlet contains the argument of Benjamin F. Hunt before Justice Johnson in *Elkison* v. *Deliesseline*. It was published after Justice Johnson published his opinion in the case because Hunt thought "it equally my right and duty to appeal also to the public." In addition, he believed that "to understand the decission [*sic*] and do simple justice to the unsuccessful advocate, the *case* should be reported, or his arguments *stated* with at least as much plausibility as they were *originally* presented at the hearing; and, as in this instance, the honourable Judge has thought proper to link my humble reputation with his own high name, by frequently naming me, I will venture to withdraw myself as far as possible" from "so intimate a union" with Johnson and present the case directly to the people. Hunt was sure his argument would look better "*by itself* . . . than when its mangled parts are scattered through the opinion of the learned Judge." So, to satisfy "repeated requests to publish" his argument, Hunt prepared this pamphlet. "My *case*," he asserted, "was made for me. I am responsible only for my *argument*" (pp. 1-2).

An additional reason for this pamphlet was to dispute part of Johnson's opinion. Johnson had declared that South Carolinian officials had agreed with John Quincy Adams that the Negro Seamen's Act should not be enforced. Johnson went on to blame Hunt and the South Carolina Association for bringing on this crisis. Hunt argued this was not the case at all. He said that Maj. James Hamilton, the intendant of Charleston (and the author of a pamphlet on the Vesey Conspiracy) had flatly rejected the British officials' arguments. He said of one of the letters by the British diplomats, "Its language was objectionable and not sufficiently respectful when applied to the proceedings of *an Independent State*," and assured Hunt that no promise had been given, "that the arrests would not be repeated" (p. 2). The notion that South Carolina was "*an Independent State*" was one of the major themes in Hunt's argument.

The title of this pamphlet illustrates a second theme. Hunt titles this case *Ex parte Henry Elkison "Claiming" to Be a Subject of His Britannic Majesty* (quotation marks added). For Hunt and his racist colleagues, a black could not be a "subject" or "citizen" of any state or nation. Thus, the law that discriminated against free blacks could not offend any nation. By refusing to acknowledge that Negroes (slave or free) had any rights that South Carolina needed to respect, Hunt was able to present his case for the validity of the statute. The final aspect of this argument was that the laws were necessary for the safety and security of the state. Hunt planned to win his case by establishing:

> [1] That the provision of the law now in question, is one which a sovereign State may enact without violating the laws of nations, or affording any just grounds of offence.
>
> [2] That South Carolina was a sovereign State, prior to, and at the time she entered into the Federal Compact.
>
> [3] That the right which South Carolina possessed to pass such a law, was one, which from its nature, under the peculiar circumstances of her slave population, she could not and has not surrendered to the Federal Government.
>
> [4] That the convention [treaty] of 1818, between Great Britain and the United States, does not interfere with the perfect right of the State, to pass and enforce the provision of the law in question, and if it did, it would not be obligatory under the State, inasmuch as the treaty-making power, can make no stipulation which shall impair the rights, which by the constitution are reserved "to the States respectively, or to the people" [p. 4].

Citing Emmerich de Vattel's works on the laws of nations, Hunt argued that a sovereign state was free to exclude from its borders whomever it chose. He argued that this was a quarantine law similar to those used by other states for diseases. South Carolina "dread[ed] the moral pestilence which a free intercourse with foreign negroes will produce" (p. 7). This, Hunt argued, was a constitutionally sanctioned police protection and not an interference with commerce. He pointed out that

> New-York subjects our vessels to quarantine, and confines our citizens to her hospitals, although we have no faith in

> contagion. Yet, if we confine *her* negro cooks to a particular
> spot in Charleston, we are told it is a violation of the
> Constitution! We have much more reason to believe in the
> moral contagion they introduce, than in the importation of
> yellow-fever. However, as New-York judges for herself upon
> one point, South-Carolina has the same right to decide on the
> other, especially as she conceives her interests and safety,
> are at stake [p. 13].

Somewhat disingenuously, Hunt declared: ''All that South-Carolina has
done in the provission [sic] under discussion, is to require free persons
of colour, when they arrive, to take up their abode in a very airy and
healthy part of the city, until the vessel in which they came is ready to
depart'' (p. 6). This was surely a curious way to describe the city jail. It
also ignored the possibility of lifetime enslavement if a ship captain did
not, for whatever reason, pay for the black seamen's lodging in this
''airy and healthy part of the city'' (p. 6).

Hunt also argued quite strenuously that Elkison could not apply
for a writ of habeas corpus or a writ de homine replegiando because
South Carolina law allowed blacks (slave or free) no access to those
writs. He asserted that under the laws of his state ''persons of colour are
only entitled to the writ of *ravishment of ward*, sued out by guardian''
(p. 18). ''The right of a free negro to sue *without Guardian* in our State
Court has never been recognized'' (p. 20). Free blacks were ''liable to
be tried in the same way as *slaves*'' and in no other way (p. 20). Thus,
Hunt asserted that Elkison had no right, on his own, to bring an action.

Hunt's argument is an important example of the merging of
states' rights theory with proslavery legal theory. Hunt is blind to the
possibility that other jurisdictions might consider blacks citizens—and
even equals. Thus, he can see nothing to make South Carolina's law
unusual or unconstitutional. To him, it is simply a police regulation to
protect the state from the ''contagion'' of free blacks. Similarly, he
argues that South Carolina is a sovereign state with the same rights
under international law as any other nation. The two arguments and
positions are neatly tied together: ''South-Carolina, as a perfect State,
could not surrender [the right to pass this law] without being guilty of an
act, tending to self-destruction'' (p. 14).

People v. *Corse*

(N.Y.C. Recorder's Ct. 1839) (Unreported)

In August 1838 a slave owner named John P. Darg arrived in
New York City with his wife, about eight thousand dollars in cash, and a

slave named Thomas Hughes. Darg was a professional gambler from New Orleans. Hughes was a trusted slave who had a wife and children in New Orleans who were also owned by Darg. Darg's assumption that Hughes would not leave him proved ill-founded, however, for a few days after their arrival in New York Hughes disappeared, taking with him all of his master's money.

Hughes was aided by a black living in New York named Henry Clark. Clark took Hughes to a well-known Quaker abolitionist named Isaac T. Hopper. Hopper had "never taken any measures to make a slave dissatisfied with his condition, or to induce him to leave his master's service." But Hopper declared that "when fugitive slaves have called upon me and asked for my protection, I could not take any steps to return them into bondage; in me it would be a crime to do so" (p. 4). Thus, when Hopper discovered Hughes was indeed a fugitive he "gave directions that he [Hughes] should leave my house," and this was done that day (p. 4). The next day there was an advertisement in a New York paper offering a $1,000 reward "for the apprehension and return of a mulatto man, who it was said, had stolen seven or eight thousand dollars" from Darg (p. 4). The advertisement also indicated that the fugitive slave would be freed once the money was returned.

Hopper soon became involved in searching for the missing Hughes and the money. Hopper did not believe in slavery, but he was also opposed to larceny. He engaged Barney Corse, a white abolitionist and David Ruggles a black abolitionist and editor, in this project. It quickly became apparent that Henry Clark and perhaps some other free blacks were involved in attempting to obtain most of this money for themselves and that Clark was holding $5,800 of the money for Hughes. The rest of the money had been spent or given to other people, including $1,025, which was by this time in Albany, New York, in the hands of a friend of one of Clark's friends.

Before leaving for Albany to help secure this money, Corse entered into a contractual agreement with John P. Darg. Corse agreed to act as Darg's agent in obtaining the stolen money, but not in returning Hughes. Darg agreed to pay for Corse's expenses and to manumit Hughes after the money was returned. In the meantime, Hughes voluntarily returned to his master after he discovered that "those who were willing to afford him protection as a suspected fugitive slave, would not conscientiously harbor him after they discovered he was a felon" (p. 5).

After almost all of the money had been recovered, arrangements were made to return it to Darg. While Corse was counting out the money, two police officers, Merritt and Peck, burst into the room and "arrested Barney Corse for compounding a felony" (p. 18). Later David Ruggles was arrested. Both men were indicted, along with Hopper, Henry Clark, and Hopper's son-in-law, James S. Gibbons. Ruggles was held in jail for two days "notwithstanding there was no shadow of proof against him" (p. 5). During that period bail was offered for Ruggles, but the police did not allow a bail hearing for two days.

Corse was tried twice on these charges, and both times the judge gave the jury a charge quite favorable, indicating the jury ought to acquit him. In both cases, however, the juries could not reach a verdict. After almost a year and a half of legal actions, a nolle prosequi was entered in all the cases. In the meantime the fugitive slave Hughes was convicted of larceny and sentenced to two years in prison. He was also manumitted so that his testimony might be used against Corse and Hopper. He was promised freedom and a light sentence for his perjured testimony. Hopper fully understood Hughes's actions, for "What higher bribe could be offered to any man, than a manumission from slavery?" (p. 8).

After charges were dropped against Hopper, Corse, and the other defendants, Hopper sued John P. Darg for the $1,000 reward he had offered for the return of his money. Hopper did not initiate this action for financial gain, but rather because "it appeared to me reasonable and just that Darg should pay the expenses that his own pe[r]fidy would occasion," and because this was the only way Hopper could "insure a legal investigation of the charges" against him, since the prosecutors did not want to bring him to trial (p. 15). This civil suit was not completed before this pamphlet was published.

■ Hopper, Isaac Tatem. Exposition of the proceedings of John P. Darg, Henry W. Merritt, and others, in relation to the robbery of Darg, the elopement of his alleged slave, and the trial of Barney Corse, who was unjustly tried as an accessary. New York, I T. Hopper, 1840. 39 p.

E450.H79

This pamphlet consists of four parts: a narrative by Hopper; a narrative by James S. Gibbons giving other details of the events; a "synopsis" by Hopper; and a transcript and account of the first trial of Barney Corse, in the Court of Sessions, in March 1839. This pamphlet was published for two apparent reasons. First, Hopper wanted to clear his name and, more importantly, that of his young friend, Barney Corse, "a worthy member of the Society of Friends, and exceeded by few for benevolence and kindness of heart" (p. 15). Second, he wished to expose the actions of the police, certain judges, and of course the slaveholder, Darg.

Darg appears in this pamphlet as the epitome of venality. He apparently hatched a plot with the police that would have allowed him to regain his slave, not have to pay any reward, and extort money from Corse and Hopper. The police appear in even a worse light. They participated in the arrest and imprisonment of men who committed no crimes and in fact were good citizens trying to return stolen money. Through their actions "a respectable citizen is dragged from his home and confined in a loathsome jail, among criminals, without the least proof of his having committed any crime, and that too, after competent bail has been offered" (p. 5). The wife of Henry Clark was threatened, searched, and harassed, even though officer "Merritt did not pretend to have any warrant for arresting" her (p. 6).

The motives of the police and Darg are twofold: greed and a desire to harass—and perhaps jail—abolitionists. Officer Peck is quoted as declaring, "we mean to scorch old Hopper like H---, for it is such as him that we want" (p. 6). The treatment of Ruggles and Mrs. Clark is part of this antiabolitionist attack. Ruggles was illegally arrested, "but he was a colored man" (p. 5). His arrest and that of Mrs. Clark, "an unoffending, helpless female, arrested without a warrant, menaced and imprisoned without a crime even *alleged* against her" led Hopper to believe that all justice in New York was in danger (p. 7). "If such outrages are tolerated," he warned, "may we not soon expect to see an inquisition established, and thumb-screws applied, in the city of New-York" (p. 7)? And although such actions might be first taken against blacks, Hopper wished to emphasize the danger of the precedent. "If such oppression may be tolerated in the case of a colored man, why not in that of a white man? For the law knows no difference" (p. 5).

While not explicitly arguing the position, Hopper's pamphlet fits neatly into a long line of antislavery documents warning that unchecked slavery would ultimately destroy freedom and justice for whites, as well as blacks. Indeed, Hopper hoped this pamphlet might help protect against that eventuality. He thought the case (and no doubt this discussion of it)

> will have a beneficial influence upon the police, they have learned that oppression and injustice will not always go unrebuked, and it may serve to stimulate the Court of Sessions to keep a more strict, supervisory care over that department. Having had an opportunity, I have been gratified in observing a determination in the Recorder to correct some abuses found in it; his vigilance and independence entitle him to the gratitude of his fellow-citizens; and if duly supported, in a very little time, I have no doubt, we shall witness a thorough reformation. [p. 16]

Ross v. *Vertner*

6 Miss. (5 Howard) 305 (1840)

Ross v. *Duncan*

1 Freem. (Miss.) 587 (Ch. Ct. 1839 or 1840)

In 1834 Captain Isaac Ross prepared a will directing his executors to take Ross's slaves to Liberia and free them. The will was modified a few years later to give Ross's daughter, Mrs. Margaret A. Reed, the use of the Ross estate until her death. After that Ross directed that his slaves be taken to Liberia. In 1836 Ross died. Mrs. Reed then had a will written in her own name directing her executors, Rev. Zebulon Butler and Dr. Stephen Duncan, to carry out her father's wishes. Mrs. Reed died in 1838. At that point the legal heirs of Margaret Reed and Isaac Ross sued to have both wills overturned.

In 1839 the Mississippi Chancery Court upheld the Ross and Reed wills. The court accepted the argument that it would have been against Mississippi law and policy to free the slaves within the state. This was because it was against Mississippi law to free any slaves in the state without the consent of the legislature. "No one can by his mere act, unsanctified by the public authority, set his slave free in this country [Mississippi], either by will or deed. And hence what he cannot do himself, cannot be done by trustees. That which he cannot do by his own act whilst living, cannot be done by his executors when he is dead. No man can delegate to another a power which he does not himself possess." *(Ross* v. *Duncan,* 1 Freem. (Miss.) 587, 698). By this very argument, however, the judge ruled that the slaves could be sent to Liberia and freed, because that was a power Ross had in his own lifetime. Indeed, with a certain irony the court ruled that a master must have the right to take his slaves anywhere he chose. It would be impossible to suggest otherwise "without a manifest absurdity. The power to have done so, resulted to the testator as the owner of the slaves from his acknowledged right of absolute dominion" *(Ross* v. *Duncan,* 1 Freem. (Miss.) 587, 699). In *Ross* v. *Vertner* this decision was upheld by the Mississippi High Court of Errors and Appeals.

At this point the heirs of Ross and Reed tried a new tactic. They attempted to overturn this decision through direct legislative intervention. A resolution introduced in the Mississippi House of Representatives declared that the manumission of the Ross and Reed slaves was a "dangerous example" and therefore, the Mississippi legislature "will not consent to the manumission either directly or indirectly of the slaves

mentioned in the last wills and testaments of the said Isaac Ross and
M. A. Reed, nor will they [*sic*] consent to the transportation of said
slaves to Africa or elsewhere, for the purpose of being there manumitted''
(pp. 7-8). This resolution was passed without debate or dissent in the
Mississippi House of Representatives.

The following day, by a one-vote majority, it was tabled in the
state senate. The tabling motion declared that the bill should lay on the
table until ''Monday next,'' which happened to be a day after the
session of the legislature ended. The man who made this rather shrewd
motion was Sen. John Ker. Two days later, when Ker was not on the
floor of the senate, an attempt was made to take the resolution off the
table and debate it. Ker arrived back on the floor in time to object and
force a careful examination of the minutes of the senate. This proved
that the motion could not be resurrected without a vote to reconsider.
Thus, the legislative attempt to defeat the wills and to overturn the
decisions of the courts failed.

■ Ker, John. A brief history of an attempt during the last session of the
Legislature, in 1841, to interfere with the judgments of the
courts, in relation to the wills of the late Captain Ross and Mrs.
Reed. Natchez, Printed by Baldwin & Risk, 1842. 13 p.
E445.M6K3; AC901.BF vol. 22, no. 9 Rare Book Room

This pamphlet appears to have been published by a group of
Ker's neighbors, who wrote to the senator to discover the true version of
what took place. It may have been published by them at Ker's request,
to protect the senator's reputation in his hometown of Natchez. The first
part of the pamphlet is a letter to Ker asking for information. The
remaining pages consist of Ker's answer, which includes the wording of
the resolutions and a new statute that was passed to prohibit such
manumissions in the future.

Ker's position in this pamphlet is that a legislative interference
with the decisions of the courts was illegal and very dangerous. Ker tells
his constituents:

> The people have been called upon to rise up and put the laws at
> defiance—calls have been made upon the Legislature to usurp
> power not granted to them by the people in the Constitution, to
> annul the solemn decrees of the Courts—to wrest from the hands
> of citizens property which has been devised to them under the
> laws of the State. And shall it be said that you and I have no
> concern with these extraordinary movements? If we quietly fold
> our arms and acquiesce in such proceedings, what security, I

ask, have any of us for the protection of law to our property, our lives, or our liberty? . . . *We may be the next victim to the ruthless hand of lawless usurpation and violence.* [pp. 12-13]

This pamphlet shows that a law-abiding majority existed in the Mississippi Senate in 1841. It also shows how extreme some members of that state's legislature could become on the issue of slavery. In February 1842 the Mississippi legislature passed "An Act to amend the several acts of this State in relation to free negroes and mulattoes," Act of Feb. 26, 1842, ch. 4, s.2, *Miss. Laws* 65. This act made it an offense for free Negroes to enter the state. A first offender would receive a whipping. On a second conviction such a free black could be sold into slavery. In addition, the law prohibited any manumissions, even out of the state, by will or testament.

The Remarkable Case of Potter Jackson (London, 1807?) concerns a free black man who worked as a seaman and who was cruelly beaten by a ship's captain during a voyage in 1805.

Appendix
British Cases

Slavery was not simply an American problem. The British continued to participate in the peculiar institution long after the thirteen American colonies had won their independence. Indeed, there were far more slaves under British rule than under American rule. Slavery flourished in the British-owned sugar islands of the Caribbean as well as in Bermuda, British Honduras, and other colonies. Slaves could be found in parts of Canada as well, although the institution never developed there to any great degree. After the Revolution, however, a number of Loyalists took their slaves with them as they headed to Canada or to Britain itself. Despite the decision in *Somerset* v. *Stewart,* there were perhaps twenty thousand slaves living in England in 1830.

Besides owning slaves, Englishmen trafficked in them. For a long time the Royal Africa Company had a monopoly on the slave trade. When that monopoly ended, the company, along with many small entrepreneurs, continued to trade in human beings from Africa. Britain joined the United States in prohibiting the slave trade in 1808, but unlike the U.S. Navy, the Royal Navy was given the ships and the authority with which to enforce the ban.

The fight for abolition in England centered around two objects. First was the abolition of the slave trade itself, which was accomplished in 1808. This was followed by an attack on slavery in the Empire. This reached fruition in 1833 with the passage of an act that led to an end to slavery throughout the Empire (3-4 Wm. 4, ch. 73 [1833]). After the passage of this act, the British antislavery movement continued to attack American slavery vigorously.

Before 1775 all English legal precedents had some impact on American law. Thus, many northern states assumed that *Somerset* v. *Stewart* was part of their common law. After 1775 American courts continued to cite new British cases where they were deemed appropriate to an issue at law in the United States. Both nations, after all, had legal systems based on the same common law. Since a common law ruling in England might be appropriate to American conditions as well, Americans watched English courts. At the same time, American and British abolitionists worked together on the same causes. The cases in this appendix include some of the pamphlet material connected to transatlantic slavery and the movement to end it.

The King v. Rev. John Smith

(British Guiana, 1823) (Unreported)

In 1817 the London Missionary Society sent Rev. John Smith, a Methodist minister, to the British colony of Demerara, British Guiana, to instruct slaves in the Christian religion. Upon his arrival it became immediately clear that many of the planters in the colony did not want Smith there. Until 1814 the colony had been under Dutch control, and many of the leading planters were Dutch. The Dutch planters particularly disliked an English minister interfering with their slaves and educating them. Many of the English planters also disliked the practice of sending ministers to instruct slaves in religion. This mistrust was based on two very realistic appraisals and one apparent misunderstanding of the probable results of missionary work.

The planters were correct in believing that many of the missionaries were abolitionists and would use their position to report on conditions in the slave colonies in the hopes that these reports might lead to the end of slavery. As the prosecutor at Smith's trial noted, the minister "avows an aversion to slavery" (London Missionary Society Report, p. 147). They also realized that the ministers would try to interfere with the treatment of slaves and to pressure masters to eliminate their more barbaric customs and practices. This in fact happened, and the planters resented it. The planters also believed, and the facts indicate this was an erroneous belief, that instructing slaves in Christianity would make them more likely to revolt. In fact, most of the slaves executed after the Demerara revolt had neither been baptized nor received instruction in religion. Most of the slaves who had been baptized did not join in the revolt, and some actually protected their masters. The few church-going slaves who did participate in the revolt had particular personal grievances, the most notable being the threat that some of these slaves were about to be sold away from their families to settle debts or estates. Of the more than two thousand slaves executed after the revolt, fewer than ten had been baptized.

The Demerara slave revolt began on August 18, 1823, and was, for the most part, over within three or four days. By August 31 all of the rebels had been captured. The rebellion was almost bloodless, and there was little destruction of property. It appears that only three whites were killed by the rebels. In defending the conviction of Smith for encouraging the rebellion, a member of Parliament was reduced to the following discussion of the loss of property:

> As to the loss of property, I would ask, whether the effect of this
> temporary suspension of the course of common affairs was not

highly prejudicial to the interests of property; and though the effect of the insurrection might not have been the destruction of property by fire and plunder, yet I would inquire if the necessity of compelling individuals to abandon their civil, for exclusively military, occupations, is not to be considered as highly detrimental to their interests; and whether, in fact, they did not sustain a severe loss in their property by this removal from their customary avocations?

[*Substance of the Debate in the House of Commons,* p. 66]

When compared to the terrible loss of life in the Nat Turner Rebellion (1831) or the Stono Rebellion (1739), or the loss of property through arson in New York City in 1741, it is clear that the Demerara slave revolt was mild—almost nonviolent.

This lack of violence may be attributed to the causes of the revolt. The slaves in Demerara outnumbered the whites by more than twenty to one. In many cases they controlled plantations and tied up owners and overseers or put them in the stocks usually reserved for slaves who misbehaved. The whites were not murdered, however, because the slaves on Demerara believed they were already free by the law of England.

In July 1823 the British government had sent a set of instructions to the government of Demerara on how slaves were to be treated. These instructions had called for an elimination of some of the excesses of some slave owners and also would have required the slaves to be given a few rights. These regulations were met with "great alarm and feverish anxiety . . . amongst the White part of the population" (*Substance of the Debate in the House of Commons,* p. 5). These regulations were debated by the whites but not implemented.

The blacks in the colony were aware that something important concerning their welfare had arrived from Great Britain. "There existed the general impression, that some extension of grace and bounty had been made to them." But the whites would not let the slaves know what was in these instructions. "In the ignorance which was so studiously maintained as to the nature of it, their hopes were proportionately excited— they knew that something had been done, and they were inquisitive to know what it was. The general conversation amongst them was, 'Has not our freedom come out? Is not the King of Great Britain our Friend?'" (*Substance of the Debate,* p. 6). Under these circumstances, the slaves revolted in hopes that they could force the government to reveal the contents of the instructions from England and gain their freedom.

Rumors of a revolt had been circulating since July. Indeed, on August 15, three days *before* the revolt began, martial law was declared in the colony. Three days after the revolt began, "when it had been substantially quelled," Smith was arrested and "dragged too from his home and his family, at a time when his life was attacked by a disease which, in all probability, would, in any circumstances, have ended in his dissolution." He was "first imprisoned, in that sultry climate, in an unwholesome fetid room, exposed to the heat of the sun. This situation was afterwards changed, and he was conveyed to a place only suited to the purposes of torture, a kind of damp dungeon, where the floor was over stagnant water, visiable through the wide crevices of the boards" (*Substance of the Debate*, p. 8). Smith was kept in this jail until October 14 when he was tried on various charges and, after a month-long trial, convicted and sentenced to death. Smith appealed to the British Parliament to review his case, but died while the appeal was pending. The London Missionary Society nevertheless petitioned the House of Commons to review the case in an attempt to officially clear Smith's name and the society and to perhaps impress upon the colonial slave owners the need to respect missionaries sent to instruct their slaves.

Smith was initially arrested for refusing to join the militia in putting down the revolt. He told the officer who seized him that he could not serve in the militia because of his position as a minister and reminded the officer that this exemption was sanctioned by British law. However, under martial law the militia officers brazenly ignored imperial law. Although the revolt was completely over by the end of August, martial law was continued until January 15, 1824. It was under martial law that Smith was tried, and because of this he was court-martialed.

Smith was officially charged with "promot[ing], . . . discontent and dissatisfaction in the minds of the negro slaves towards their lawful masters, managers, and overseers" long before the revolt broke out, and "thereby intending to excite the said negroes to break out in such open revolt and rebellion against the authority" of the masters. The indictment also charged that on the day before the revolt began Smith "advised, consulted, and corresponded with a certain negro named Quamina, touching and concerning a certain intended revolt and rebellion of the negro slaves within" the colony. A third count charged that Smith knew about the planned revolt but did not tell anyone about it. A fourth count charged that after the revolt began "Smith, then well knowing the said Quamina to be an insurgent engaged therein . . . did not use his utmost endeavours to suppress the same, by securing or detaining the said insurgent Quamina, as a prisoner, or by giving information to the proper authorities, or otherwise, but, on the contrary, permitted the said insurgent Quamina to go at large and depart, without attempting to seize and detain him" or tell authorities where he was (*London Missionary Society Report*, p. 2).

Smith was found guilty on all four counts, although the court found him guilty of only parts of three of the counts. Nevertheless the court sentenced him ''to be hanged by the neck until dead.'' However, the judges added, ''But the Court, under all the circumstances of the case, begs humbly to recommend the Prisoner, John Smith, to mercy'' (*London Missionary Society Report*, p. 179). Smith remained in prison until February 6, 1824, when he died of diseases he had been suffering from since before the revolt.

On April 13, 1824, Sir James Mackintosh introduced a petition on behalf of the London Missionary Society to have the House of Commons investigate Smith's trial. After studying documents about the case for over a month, the issue was debated on June 1 and 11, 1824, on a motion of Henry Brougham. The Tory administration of Prime Minister Robert Jenkinson, earl of Liverpool, opposed the motion to condemn the court-martial and posthumously acquit Smith. By a vote of 146 to 193, the motion of Brougham was defeated.

■ Smith, John, *defendant*. The London Missionary Society's report of the proceedings against the late Rev. J. Smith, of Demerara, minister of the gospel, who was tried under martial law, and condemned to death on a charge of aiding and assisting in a rebellion of the Negro slaves; from a full and correct copy, transmitted to England by Mr. Smith's counsel, and including the documentary evidence omitted in the parliamentary copy; with an appendix; containing the letters and statements of Mr. and Mrs. Smith, Mrs. Elliot, Mr. Arrindell, etc.; and, also, the society's petition to the House of Commons. The whole published under the authority of the directors of the said society. London, Published by F. Westley, 1824. 204 p.

LLRBR

The London Missionary Society published this book to do justice to the society and to Rev. John Smith and to put pressure on the House of Commons to acquit Smith in its review of the case. The first 180 pages are devoted to the ''Proceedings of a General Court-Martial,'' which appears to be an exact transcript of the trial (p. 1). This section is followed by a selection of letters from Smith, his wife, and others involved in the case. It also includes a copy of the petition introduced into the House of Commons by Sir James Mackintosh.

Three aspects of the trial are particularly interesting. First, it appears that Smith was on trial as much for his actions before the revolt as he was for any part he may have had in the revolt. In the second sentence of his opening remarks, the prosecutor declares: ''I shall first adduce in evidence, that the prisoner, even from the beginning of his arrival in this colony, has begun to interfere with the complaints of the different negroes upon the estates in the district where he has been admitted as a regular missionary'' (p. 3). Throughout the trial there are references to what Smith taught blacks, that he admonished owners for mistreatment of slaves, and that he made blacks understand that they were oppressed.

Second, most of the testimony against Smith was presented by slaves. Although Smith protested this, his protest was rejected. Had Smith lived in the United States, this testimony (at least in the slave states) would have been inadmissible. In their desire to convict Smith, the planters in Demerara were even willing to sanction the rather dangerous precedent of using slave witnesses against a white man.

Third, the testimony for the most part appears to be unconvincing. Much of it was easily refuted by Smith. Some of it appears to have been blatantly false. For example, the slave Bristol claimed he was ''a deacon, and one of the duties of the deacons is, to instruct the candidates for baptism, and to teach them to read.'' The purpose of this testimony was to show that the slaves Smith educated were leaders of the revolt. However, the slave Bristol also admitted during his testimony that ''he cannot read'' (p. 139). In a number of cases slaves testified against Smith and their testimony was then refuted by other slaves. The court, in all of these cases, appears to have been more willing to believe the slaves who testified against Smith, than those who supported him. This was true, even when the overwhelming evidence was in Smith's favor. In other parts of the trial Smith was prevented from calling whites to the stand who could refute evidence against him (p. 144).

Finally, it is clear that any knowledge that Smith may have had of the coming revolt was held by others in the community as well. This is supported by the fact that martial law was declared three days *before* the revolt began. Clearly Smith was singled out, not because he knew of the revolt and did not warn the white community, but because of his past actions as a minister to the slaves.

■ Smith, John, *defendant*. The missionary Smith. Substance of the debate in the House of Commons on Tuesday the 1st and on Friday the 11th of June, 1824, on a motion of Henry Brougham, esq. respecting the trial and condemnation to death by a court martial of the Rev. John Smith, late missionary in the colony of Demerara. With a preface, containing some new facts illustrative of the subject. Published with the sanction of the London Missionary Society. London, Printed by Ellerton and Henderson, 1824. 255 p.

Law Library

This volume, also published by the London Missionary Society, contains the speeches delivered during the parliamentary debate over Smith's trial. In addition, the fifty-four-page preface provides facts the Society hoped would sway public opinion, since the House of Commons had already disposed of the case. It points out that the leader of the revolt was not executed after he agreed to testify against Smith (p. xvii). It also points out that many of those slaves who testified against Smith recanted their testimony before they were executed. The preface gives a short history of the revolt and trial as well as some lurid and gruesome descriptions of the treatment and condition of slaves in the colony.

Among the important facts the preface records is that fewer than ten of the two thousand slaves executed had been baptized by Smith. If baptism had any effect on the slaves it was to decrease the likelihood that they would revolt. Indeed, on those few plantations where Smith was allowed to freely preach and instruct, there was little or no trouble, and few slaves from those plantations joined the revolt. This may be because the type of masters who would allow Smith to preach were also likely to be more kind to their slaves. But it may also be that Smith's mission had the effect of lessening tensions and the possibility of rebellion.

The speeches in the House of Commons cover the trial in great detail. Not surprisingly those opposed to slavery, such as William Wilberforce, Henry Brougham, and Sir Joseph Yorke, spoke for the Missionary Society resolution. The supporters of the government in power spoke against the resolution. One of the major weaknesses of this pamphlet concerns the actual vote. It appears that the House did not vote on the Missionary Society resolution, but rather on some motion to substitute or table that resolution. Those in favor of the resolution are recorded as voting *against* the motion on the floor, while those opposed to Smith and the Missionary Society voted in favor of the motion on the floor. Unfortunately, it is unclear what motion was voted on. The pamphlet does include a list of which Members of Parliament voted for and which voted against the motion on the floor, and, of course, this includes the final tallies.

The King v. *Kimber*

(London Central Crim. Ct. 1792) (Unreported)

John Kimber was captain of the *Recovery*, a vessel engaged in the African slave trade and the West Indian trade. In 1791 the *Recovery* sailed from Bristol to Calabar, in Africa, and then to Grenada before returning to Bristol. Some time after his return to Britain, Kimber was tried in admiralty court for murdering a slave on the voyage between Africa and Grenada.

According to prosecution witnesses, Kimber had arbitrarily beaten one of the slaves, a young girl about fourteen years old, almost from the beginning of the voyage. This girl had gonorrhea, appeared lethargic, and would not eat or exercise. One witness also claimed that she had a stiff knee, which made it difficult for her to walk. To cure her of these ills, Kimber suspended the girl from a rope, first by one hand, then by the other, then by one foot, upside down, then by the other, and finally, by both hands. Each suspension lasted about five minutes. During some of the suspensions Kimber beat the girl with a whip. The five suspensions took place for about thirty minutes. The girl went into convulsions soon after this and died three days later.

The chief prosecution witness was the ship's surgeon. He did not report this incident when the ship landed in Grenada because he feared for his life. Instead, he waited until the ship returned to Bristol. At that point he spoke to William Wilberforce, a member of Parliament active in the movement to abolish the slave trade. Wilberforce mentioned this incident in a speech in the House of Commons, and afterwards Kimber was prosecuted on a complaint lodged by the Committee to Abolish the Slave Trade. The prosecuting attorney for the Crown was Sir William Scott, later Lord Stowall and judge of the High Court of Admiralty.

The main defense of Captain Kimber did not rest on denying the allegations. Indeed, no evidence was presented to show that Kimber had not beaten this girl or that she had not died three days later. Instead, he presented witnesses who undermined the credibility of the ship's surgeon, Dr. Thomas Dowling, and the third mate, Stephen Devereux. Both were accused of malicious intent and seeking revenge for disagreements with Kimber. Dr. Dowling had in fact been in a short fist fight with Kimber while under his command, and for that minor mutiny he was put in irons for one day, not allowed to eat with the officers for the rest of the voyage, and docked half of his pay. Witnesses for Kimber alleged that when Dowling returned to Britain he told them he would ruin Kimber. Other witnesses told of Kimber's good character and of Devereux's bad character. Many of Kimber's character witnesses were involved in the slave trade themselves.

The jury apparently believed the witnesses who attacked Devereux and Dowling. Without even waiting for summations, the jury declared Kimber innocent. An attempt was made to arrest Dowling and Devereux for perjury. The outcome of that attempt is unknown. Kimber had also been indicted for murdering a second slave, but since the evidence in that case also came from Dowling and Devereux, Kimber was summarily acquitted on that charge.

This case was reported in two different pamphlets. Both of them present the same general facts, although they supplement each other in different places. However, there is a decidedly different slant to the pamphlets.

The first, annotated here, was published by friends of Kimber (if not Kimber himself) "in vindication of innocence." The authors of this pamphlet "were pleased to see his Royal Highness the Duke of Clarence present" during the trial and "the beam of benevolence shown in his eye, when the NOT GUILTY was pronounced by that sacred deposit of the subjects liberty, a BRITISH JURY" (p. 5).

The second pamphlet annotated here, on the other hand, was published to help expose the "atrocity of that unnatural and abominable custom" of the slave trade. It was hoped that pamphlets such as this one would help lead to "an immediate and total abolition of a cruel and inhuman traffic" (pp. v-vi). The authors of this pamphlet "lamented that a personage of the first rank, who could have no other motive except that of love for uncontroulable [*sic*] tyranny, should become so strenuous an advocate for slavery" (p. vi). In case any reader did not know who this "person of the first rank" was, the pamphlet ended by noting: "His Royal Highness the Duke of Clarence was present the whole time, and appeared from his looks and gestures, to be particularly interested, in favor of the man who was accused of having murdered a slave" (p. 36).

■ Kimber, John, *defendant*. The Trial of Captain John Kimber, for the supposed murder of an African girl, at the Admiralty Sessions, before the Hon. Sir James Marriott, Knt. (Judge Advocate) and Sir William Ashurst, Knt. &c. on Thursday, June 7, 1792. For which he was most honorably acquitted, and the two evidences for the prosecution committed to Newgate to take their trials for wilful and corrupt perjury. London, Printed by William Lane [1792] 43 p.

LLRBR

This pamphlet contains most of the testimony of this case and the opening arguments by Sir William Scott. It also contains what appears to be the indictment, although it is not printed as such (pp. 7-9). A brief "Address" at the beginning of the pamphlet declares that it was printed in "vindication of innocence." The address advises the readers that by "exercising their own judgment they will see, on what principle CAPTAIN KIMBER (who was so honourably acquitted) was brought to his trial" (p. 5).

In his opening statement, Sir William notes "a circumstance

which will probably be brought before you [the jury], which is to affect the credit of the surgeon of the ship; namely that he had on some other occasion given a different representation of this matter" (pp. 11-12). Scott simply hoped his explanation of this would satisfy the jury. This admission by Scott does not appear in the second, antislavery, pamphlet annotated here.

Kimber's defense is clearly apparent in this pamphlet. He attempts to discredit and attack the prosecution witnesses. At one point his attorney asks Dr. Dowling, "This is your prosecution?" to which Dowling replies, "No, sir, it is not." The attorney then asks, "Your disclosure of the EXTRAORDINARY MURDER was casual?" Dowling replies, "It was I who communicated it to Mr. WILBERFORCE the day before his *speech* in the House of Commons" (p. 30). Kimber's attorney attempted, with apparent success, to make Kimber's prosecution into a personal vendetta by two disgruntled crewmen, who went so far as to complain to a member of Parliament.

At another point Kimber's attorney tried to show that Dowling must be lying because no other crewmen (except the third mate) complained about the incident. The attorney asked, "Pray sir, I take it for granted then, that this must have occasioned on board the ship, a great deal of attention, discussion, and observation upon it [the death of the girl]?" Dowling's answer may not have helped the prosecution, but it certainly a damning comment on the slave trade: "No, sir, such things are customary on board slave ships" (pp. 19-20).

The proslavery—or at least proslave trade—sentiment represented by this pamphlet and Kimber's defense is shown in the witnesses who spoke for his defense. One was a Capt. Thomas Phillips, who also dealt in slaves. He declared that he had known "Captain Kimber twenty-five years; he has borne the character of a *humane good tempered man*" (p. 42). This same Captain Phillips denounced Dr. Dowling for feeding the slaves fresh fruit, which he believed "produced laxes, and brought on death" (p. 42). Another witness, a Bristol merchant connected to the slave trade, denounced Dowling. That slave traders were acceptable witnesses for the defense suggests that the strong sentiment against the African slave trade that appeared in nineteenth-century England was not particularly widespread at this time. Thus, one slave trader could call another a *"humane good tempered man,"* and this would be accepted as a legitimate character reference by an English jury.

■ Kimber, John *defendant*. The trial of Captain John Kimber, for the murder of two female Negro slaves, on board the Recovery, African slave ship. Tried at the Admiralty Sessions, held at the Old Bailey on the 7th of June, 1792. Before Sir James Marriot,

&c. taken in short hand by a student of the Temple. To which is added, observations on the above trial. London, Printed by C. Stalker [1792] 36 p.

Law Library

This pamphlet was published by those opposed to slavery and the slave trade. The author hopes it will help end "that unnatural and abominable custom" and "lead to an immediate and total abolition of a cruel and inhuman traffic" (pp. v-vi). Despite Kimber's acquittal, the author believes the prosecution was "evidently a necessary and useful measure. It may afford a salutary lesson to those captains of slave ships, and masters of slaves, who should hereafter attempt to commit such horrid outrages as" Kimber was charged with. The author thinks "the circumstances here related, (for such barbarities have doubtless been often practiced) fill the minds of men universally with horror against the present system: until tyranny shall at length give way to public opinion, and liberty and happiness be restored to human beings" (pp. vi-vii).

Although most of the facts in this pamphlet are the same as those in the one previously annotated, there are a few differences. In all likelihood neither pamphlet is incorrect; rather, each emphasizes different events. The abolitionist author of this pamphlet explicitly points out that Kimber was charged with murdering two slave girls, not one. He also includes the testimony that shows that Kimber beat the slave who died many times before the fatal beating was administered. The description of the beatings is also more graphic here. Because this slave was sick, she

> could not eat, as the other slaves did, nor join in any of their amusements, at which the Captain was so irritated, that he used to flog her himself with a whip, the handle of which, was one foot long, and the lash two. About three weeks after they had sailed, he beat her in this manner with uncommon severity; and on the 22nd of December, perceiving her not to dance with the other negro women, he ordered a boy to bring a teakle, one end of which was fastened to the *mizen stay,* and the other to one of her hands, and by this she was lifted up from the deck, and remained suspended for about five minutes: and during that time she was bounsed up and down, or in other words, lifted up, and let fall again, by the way. . . . She was then taken down and suspended in the same manner by the other arm. She was next lifted up by one leg; and afterwards by the other; until at last she was taken up for the fifth time by both hands, and underwent a fifth excruciating suspension . . . While she continued hung up by both hands, the prisoner lashed her inhumanly with his whip: and when she was let down, he forced her to walk without any

> assistance down the hatchway: this she was unable to do, having
> got but two or three steps, when she slipt all the rest of the way.
> [pp. 4-6]

The next day "she was welted in several parts of her body, her hands
were swelled in consequence of the hanging and her legs disfigured in a
shocking manner; after this the witness saw her in convulsions" (p.
6). Three days later she died.

Besides this description of the slave's punishment and death,
this pamphlet offers more complete answers by the prosecution witnesses.
Thus, in both pamphlets defense attorneys ask Dr. Dowling if he
administered mercury to aid the sick girl. But in this one his answer is
not a simple no. Rather, the complete answer appears: "No: it was
improper for her complaint" (p. 13). Thus, the first pamphlet makes
Dowling appear to be incompetent and not a trustworthy witness. Here
he appears more competent, and thus the case against Kimber is
strengthened.

Furthermore, his disclosure of the murder does not appear to be
as conspiratorial in this pamphlet. He did not tell anyone of it, until
William Wilberforce questioned him about the slave trade in general.
"It was upon that occasion he told him the circumstance of the
murder . . . without having the remotest intention of prosecuting him
[Kimber]. And he moreover observed that outrages of that nature were
so common on board the slave ships, that they were looked upon with as
much indifference as any trifling occurrence, their frequence had rendered
them familiar" (p. 18). Thus, the prosecution does not appear in this
pamphlet to be the result of a vendetta by Dr. Dowling, while the first
pamphlet annotated here gives that impression.

This pamphlet concludes with four pages of observations about
the case. The author asks

> why was there not such a defense set up by Captain Kimber, as
> could, in the minds of the people, have acquitted him of the
> horrid act which was sworn against him? Did he bring forward
> a single witness to contradict the charges of his accusers? What
> became of all the seamen and servants on board his ship, who
> were in England at the time he was apprehended, and who might
> have been brought into Court to declare at once that the prisoner
> did not commit murder; without having recourse to the miserable
> shift of proving perjury against Mr. Dowling and Devereux, in
> points that had nothing to do with the prosecution? Were none
> of the RECOVERY'S crew to be found, or was Captain Kimber
> afraid that they would have all conspired against his life? [pp.
> 34-35].

While Kimber was not convicted, the Committee for the Abolition of the Slave Trade, which brought the case, no doubt benefited from the publicity created by this pamphlet, for it allowed them to expose the horrors of the trade. It would, however, take another sixteen years to pass legislation prohibiting the trade.

Jackson v. *Livesly*

(K. B. 1806) (Unreported)

Potter Jackson was a free black born in New York in 1774. In 1786 he signed on with a merchant ship. For the next twenty years he worked on various ships, including some connected to the British navy. He served as both a steward and a seaman. In 1805 he was in Jamaica when he joined the crew of the *Lord Stanley Guineaman*, which was returning to Liverpool after selling its cargo of slaves in Jamaica.

For most of the last month of this voyage the captain whipped Jackson regularly. Other members of the crew were also ordered to beat Jackson. The reasons for these beatings are unclear. Jackson was charged with a minor theft, although the captain does not appear to have actually believed Jackson had committed any crime. During the time that Jackson received these beatings he was given little food and sometimes compelled to drink sea water. At other times sea water was poured all over his back. On one occasion the chief mate put Jackson in a cask of water and attempted to drown him. But crew members intervened to prevent his cold-blooded murder. On another day "the captain seemed bent on exercising a fresh species of torture" and declared: "'I'll flog you no longer like an Englishman, but will give it you West Indian fashion.' I was then flogged from my posteriors down to my hams. The pain I endured from this fresh mode was excessive; and the punishment so severe as to lay open my privities in a most shocking manner" (*The Remarkable Case*, p. 17).

When not being flogged Jackson was required to do regular seaman's work, including being ordered "up to the fore top from morning till night; [the captain] thinking no doubt from my weak state I should not be able to keep my hold, and might thereby fall a sacrifice to the waves" (p. 20). When not working, Jackson was kept in irons. The beatings finally ceased when the chief mate refused to participate any longer because, as he declared, "the man is dying—*for the blood is now gushing from his eyes and breast*" (p. 19).

When the ship reached Liverpool, Jackson was secretly brought ashore where he was "so shocking a spectacle" that he had difficulty obtaining lodging, "no one caring to grant an asylum to an object whose death was daily expected.'' However, he was finally taken in by the ''regulating surgeon of Liverpool,'' who expected him to die soon (p. 22). While staying with this doctor ''large pieces of flesh of eighteen inches long, and near one inch thick'' came off of his back (p. 22). Jackson's recovery took more than nine months, and after that he was weak and unable to work or even walk easily. At this point he went to London to institute a suit against the captain of his ship.

This suit was ''an action for assaulting, putting in irons, and falsely imprisoning and flogging'' Jackson. Only two witnesses appeared for Jackson, the second mate and the doctor who had saved his life. The defendant produced no witnesses. The judge declared that this case was ''one of the most unparalleled cruelty. . . . The defendant appeared to have added insult to barbarity, in a way the very lowest degree of human depravity could scarcely account for. A disclosure of such savage and, as appeared, unprovoked cruelty . . . never before disgraced the annals of a British Court of Justice'' (pp. 30-31). It took the jury only a few moments to declare judgment for Jackson and award him five hundred pounds in damages.

■ Jackson, Potter, *plaintiff*. The remarkable case of Potter Jackson (formerly steward of the Echo sloop of war) giving an account of the most cruel treatment, he received from Captain Lively, (commander of the Lord Stanley slave-ship) and his chief mate; by assaulting, imprisoning, putting in irons, and cruelly flogging him: which caused blood to burst from his eyes and breast, and large pieces of flesh to come from his back, occasioned by the unmerciful flogging he received, of upwards of one thousand lashes, written by himself. With the trial before the Right Hon. Lord Ellenborough in the Court of King's Bench, Guildhall, London, on Thursday, July 10, 1806; when a jury returned a verdict, five hundred pounds damages!! London, Printed for and sold by the unfortunate sufferer, at R. Butters' [1807?] 31 p.
Law Library; HT857.S5 vol. 6 Rare Book Room

Despite the large judgment in his favor, Jackson was destitute when this pamphlet was published. The money had not yet been paid, and ''should the Defendant, with an intention still to further harass and distress him [Jackson], move for a new trial, it will then be a considerable time longer before this matter can be again settled'' (p. iii). It was indeed unclear if the defendant would ever return to Britain and pay the money at all. Thus, Jackson published this pamphlet to raise money from its sale and to stimulate charitable efforts on his behalf.

The pamphlet contains a number of striking illustrations of

Jackson's being beaten and of his back after the beatings. Furthermore, Jackson declares his availability for those who wish to interview him, or see his scars and wounds, before they donate to his cause.

This pamphlet is not directly about the slave trade or slavery. Yet, it is an insight into the actions of slave traders and of the treatment of slaves and free blacks in the early nineteenth century. That Jackson was flogged ''West Indian fashion'' suggests that there were clearly different standards of punishment for white and black seamen and for freemen and slaves (p. 17). Jackson was treated like a slave, even though he was not one. The record of the trial shows that Englishmen would not accept this treatment of a free man, and most likely indicates that people in England would not have allowed such treatment of slaves in the metropolis.

The King v. *Pedro de Zulueta*

18 Cent. Crim. C. 1038 (London 1843)

Pedro de Zulueta was a partner in a shipping and import-export firm that had maintained offices in London for at least twenty years and offices in Spain for seventy years. In 1839 Zulueta's company purchased a vessel recently seized, but not convicted, for involvement in the slave trade. The ship was renamed the *Augusta* and refitted under Zulueta's direction. In 1840 this ship was seized by Captain Hill of the *HMS Saracen*, one of the ships deployed off the African coast to suppress the African slave trade. The *Augusta* was taken to Sierra Leone, where the Vice-Admiralty Court condemned the ship. This condemnation was later upheld by the Privy Council, and the house of Zulueta and Company was implicated in the illegal slave trade.

Zulueta later testified before a committee of the House of Commons about the incident. His testimony was inaccurate in some places and inconsistent in others. At the insistence of members of the British and Foreign Anti-Slavery Society, the connections between the *Augusta* and Zulueta were examined by Sir George Stephen, an author, attorney, and antislavery activist and son of one of the early English opponents of slavery, Sir James Stephen. Sir George took the information about Zulueta to government solicitors and to the secretary of the treasury who agreed that Zulueta should be indicted. An indictment was not obtained until August 1843 because of the difficulty in collecting all the relevant documents, which were by this time scattered in England and Africa.

Zulueta was brought to trial on October 27, 1843. The trial lasted until October 30, when Zulueta was acquitted. To convict Zulueta the prosecution would have needed to prove that when captured the *Augusta* was on a slave-trading voyage, or a voyage related to the slave trade, and that Zulueta knew that the *Augusta* was to be used in this manner and thus was responsible for its activities.

Neither of these facts was easy to establish because if the *Augusta* was involved in the illegal trade, and if Zulueta knew of this activity, then Zulueta and the captain did an excellent job of hiding the true intent of the voyage. The most damning evidence against Zulueta consisted of a series of circumstances and facts that needed to be carefully connected. Since these connections would have led to felony convictions, it is no wonder that Zulueta and others covered their tracks well.

The route and actions of the *Augusta* indicate that the ship probably was involved in the slave trade. The *Augusta* left Liverpool and promptly ran into a fierce storm. Rather than return to port, it continued on to Cádiz, despite complaints from the crew that there were closer ports that could be safely reached. At Cádiz the captain discharged some of his English crew and took on Spaniards. He also took on cargo and letters on consignment which were owned by Martinez and Co., notorious for its involvement in the slave trade. The *Augusta* then proceeded to the part of the African coast known as the Gallinas. According to experts on the African slave trade and the prosecution:

> The sole trade carried on there [the Gallinas] is the slave trade. It consisted of a few, . . . five, of what are called barracoons. It is hardly necessary I should state that a barracoon is a place in which slaves are kept; that slave traders, by attacking a village, or other means, take possession of the people, who are taken down to warehouses erected for their use—barracoons they call them—places where they are kept until an opportunity arises, whereby they may be shipped off either to the Havannah or to Cuba: . . . [The Gallinas] is not a trading place in any other way. Slaves are purchased by the barter of cotton goods or other goods from England . . . There is no other trade but the mere slave trade. [*Trial of Pedro de Zulueta, Jun., on a Charge of Slave Trading*, p. 251].

However, despite the destination of the ship—and the cargo, which consisted of items used in the African slave trade—it was impossible to prove that the *Augusta* was involved in the trade. This is because the *Augusta* had none of the special equipment—such as extra water containers, chains, or false decks—usually associated with the trade. The prosecution argued that this was because the owners were being very careful. The prosecution suggested two reasons for the lack of slaving equipment. One was that such equipment would be provided by the slave sellers in Africa. The second, and perhaps more plausible reason, was that the trade no longer required one ship to bring goods *and* carry Africans. Thus, the *Augusta* was simply carrying the goods to pay for a load of slaves that another ship would then transport to Cuba.

The prosecution had planned to tie Zulueta to the voyage by also prosecuting two other men. One was a Spaniard named Bernardos who had once been captain of the *Augusta* and was involved in the slave trade. However, Bernados was in Cuba when the indictments were handed down and naturally did not return for his trial. The second was the captain of the *Augusta*, Thomas Jennings. However, Jennings managed to remain in hiding until just before the trial began. At that point he argued that he had already been tried for the crime of slave trading, and to now try him on conspiracy with Zulueta and Bernardos would be illegal. Thus, the trial of Jennings was postponed. Much of the evidence the prosecution planned to use was not allowed because it focused on Jennings. Had Jennings been tried with Zulueta, it is likely the case for a conspiracy would have appeared stronger. The main evidence against Zulueta was thus reduced to the testimony of British naval officers and an analysis of the circumstances of the voyage. This did not convince the jury, which acquitted Zulueta.

Zulueta, as a prosperous businessman, called numerous character witnesses. They testified to his good reputation. Zulueta also shrewdly began his trial by complimenting the jurors. As a foreigner he was entitled to a jury that was half English and half foreign. But he declined this, declaring, "I am as safe in the hands of Englishmen as of any body" (ibid., p. 239). This may have made the jury more sympathetic to him.

This prosecution was initiated by private individuals. At the end of the case, the lawyers for the prosecution asked the court to order that the expenses be paid by the Crown. This the court did, because it agreed "that it was a very proper case for inquiry" (ibid., p. 410).

■ Zulueta, Pedro de. Jr., *defendant*. Trial of Pedro de Zulueta, jun., on a charge of slave trading, under the 5 Geo. IV, cap. 113, on Friday the 27th, Saturday the 28th, and Monday the 30th of October, 1843, at the Central Criminal Court, Old Bailey, London. A full report from the short-hand notes of W. B. Gurney, Esq. With an address to the merchants, manufacturers, and traders of Great Britain, by Pedro de Zulueta, Jun., Esq., and documents illustrative of the case. London, C. Wood & Co., 1844. 410 p.
LLRBR Law Library

———[Reprint] New York, Negro Universities Press [1969]
Law Library

This account of Zulueta's trial was published by Zulueta to clear his name and reputation from any connection with the African slave trade. It begins with an address by Zulueta, which is followed by "opinions of legal authorities" and over two hundred pages of documents, letters, evidence, and reports connected to the case. This is followed by about twenty-five pages of trial documents, such as the indictments for felony and conspiracy, some affidavits, and the initial hearings. Pages 225 to 410 are devoted to the trial itself. This appears to be a complete record of the trial, taken by a competent stenographer.

Zulueta's opening address is dedicated to "The Merchants, Manufacturers, and Traders of Great Britain." It is a strenuous and indignant statement in which Zulueta tries to clear his name while he condemns "the absolute recklessness" of the charges against him (p. xii). Zulueta describes his case as "one of an unprecedented character" in which "a merchant, to all practical purposes a British merchant . . . finds himself suddenly arrested . . . whilst in the pursuit of his ordinary business" (p. ix). Zulueta also lectures the British and Foreign Anti-Slavery Society for their part in this prosecution. He declares: "Crime is, indeed, a just object of abhorrence; but a society, like the Anti-Slavery Society, is specially bout to guard themselves against the danger of encouraging one species of crime in their attempt to put down another" (p. xxv). Zulueta warns that prosecutions such as his will threaten the commerce and trade of England with Spain, Cuba, Brazil, and the United States, as well as Africa, because all of those places are connected to the illegal slave trade, as well as legal slavery. He ends with a plea to the House of Commons "whether the position of merchants in mercantile intercourse with countries in which slave trade and slavery exist" will be such that these merchants will "be undone before we are even heard in our defence," simply because they trade with such countries. He is willing that those who knowingly participate in the slave trade be prosecuted. Zulueta only wants the prosecution of innocent men (like himself) to be stopped.

■ Zulueta, Pedro de, Jr., *defendant*. Trial of Pedro de Zulueta, Jun., in the Central Criminal Court of the city of London, on the 27th, 28th, and 30th of October, 1843, on a charge of slave-trading. Reported by J. F. Johnson, short-hand writer, with introductory and concluding remarks, by the Committee of the British and Foreign Anti-Slavery Society. 2d ed. London, Ward & Co., Office of the British and Foreign Anti-Slavery Society, 1844. 95 p.

JX4447.Z8 1844

This pamphlet was published by the British and Foreign Anti-Slavery Society. It contains a short introduction by the society, followed by an account of the trial. Unlike the volume published by Zulueta, this is not a transcriptlike report of the trial. Rather, much of the proceedings are summarized, and the amount of material is much less than in the more complete record of the trial. Nevertheless, this appears to be a wholly accurate account of the trial, and its smaller size makes the account much more readable.

The account of the trial is followed by the text of a series of letters between the captain of the *Augusta*, the slave trader Martinez, and slave traders on the coast of Africa in the Gallinas. Because these letters were neither written nor received by Zulueta they were excluded as evidence at the trial. This section of the book also includes part of the *Augusta's* log and cargo manifest. These documents tie the ship to the slave trade in ways more direct than was possible at the trial, where this evidence was excluded.

This pamphlet was published to show that, despite his acquittal, Zulueta may have participated in the slave trade. It was also published to clear the society and Sir James Stephen of ''any interested or officious intermeddling in this case'' (p. v). At the end of the account of the trial the society added two pages of ''concluding remarks.'' This statement contains nine separate arguments: (1) ''that, in point of fact, British capital *is* employed in the African slave-trade''; (2) that evidence of British complicity in the trade ''is all but inaccessible'' because most of the illegal acts take place outside of the country and because of inadequacies in the law; (3) that the support of Zulueta by the mercantile community'' gives rise to a painful doubt, whether indirect slave-trading is regarded by commercial men with just abhorence, and whether the principle of it may not be considered even as legitimate''; (4) that the findings of the Grand Jury, and the awarding of the costs to the prosecutor by the Judges on the ground that the case was a fit one for inquiry'' leads to the conclusion that the parliamentary investigation was inadequate; (5) that the ''mysterious and unexplained inaction of the law officers of the Crown'' after Zulueta was indicted ''bears a painful appearance of an unwillingness on the part of the Government to incur the odium of prosecuting men of mercantile eminence''; (6) that it is ''inexpedient and unsafe to place the representatives of commercial interests on any [Parlimentary] committee, whose duty it is to inquire into slave trading offences''; (7) that authorities did not properly clear the *Augusta* when it sailed and this should lead to an investigation; (8) that Parliament should still examine Zulueta; and (9) ''that the only effectual means of abolishing the slave-trade is the abolition of slavery'' (pp. 74-75).

The King v. Hodge

(Tortola [Brit. V.I.] Oyer & Terminer 1811)(Unreported)

In 1811 Arthur Hodge, a planter on the island of Tortola in the British West Indies, was indicted for the murder of his slave, Prosper. After a three-day trial, Hodge was convicted by a jury and sentenced to death. He was subsequently hanged.

Prosper was initially beaten for causing a mango to fall off of a tree. On the first day he was beaten for more than an hour "with a certain instrument of punishment commonly called a cart-whip, made of wood and rope" (p. 43). Under Hodge's direction, during this beating Prosper was naked, held face down on the ground by other slaves, and received more than one hundred lashes. Part of this beating was administered by Hodge and part by the other slaves. On the following day Prosper was "tied to a tree . . . and the flogging was repeated; he was then licked so long that his head fell back, and could not bawl out any longer" (pp. 95-96). Prosper was then put in chains and taken to the plantation's "sick-house" where he remained for about ten days, until he died.

According to the prosecution's chief witness Prosper was not fed during this time nor did be receive medical aid. He died "by licking, confinement and starvation—he had no black skin upon him, he was all cut to rags . . . The back part of him [had no skin]—at the time of his death crawlers [insects] were in him" (p. 97). Another witness reported: "I saw Prosper some days before he died, in a cruel state, so bad, I could not go near him for the blue flies" (p. 112). Two weeks before the fatal beating Hodge had knocked Prosper down with a rock and then beaten him with the rock.

Prosper was apparently killed in July 1808, although the indictment declares he died in October 1807. His body was ultimately exhumed for this trial.

■ Hodge, Arthur, *defendant.* A report of the trial of Arthur Hodge, esquire, (Late one of the members of His Majesty's Council for the Virgin Islands) at the Island of Tortola, on the 25th April, 1811, and adjourned to the 29th of the same month; for murder of his Negro man slave named Prosper. Stenographically taken by A. M. Belisario, esquire, one of the grand jury who found the bill of indictment and certified to be impartial and correct by His Honor Richard Hetherington, esq. President of the Virgin-Islands, and

President of the Court on this trial. Middletown, Conn., Tertius Dunning, 1812. 136 p.

This pamphlet contains most, but not all, of the evidence and argument presented at this trial. The most important material lacking is the transcript of the defense counsel's closing arguments. Some witnesses testified, but their testimony is not recorded here. However, despite these omissions this record of the trial seems to be generally complete and very useful.

This case has a number of legal curiosities that distinguish it from similar cases in the United States. First, the indictment of Hodge was at common law. In 1811 in most of the slave states it would have been difficult, or impossible, to indict an owner at common law for murdering his slave. Second, the jurors asked some of the witnesses questions. Third, and perhaps most important, the chief prosecution witness was a free black woman. In the slave states (and some of the free states) it was illegal for a black to testify against a white.

Hodge was apparently indicted because he was notoriously cruel and barbaric in treating his slaves. The prosecution introduced testimony about such treatment to show the nature of Hodge's character. The prosecution also entered into evidence a number of depositions alleging that Hodge had murdered a number of other slaves and tortured many more. A slave named Tom "between three and four years ago, was by the order of the said Hodge, laid down and cart-whipped without intermission, for at least an hour." He was then "taken up and carried to the sick-house, from whence he never came out, but *died* in about a week after said cartwhipping" (pp. 8-9). Two women slaves had boiling water poured down their throats. The witness describing this said that she "did not see the boiling water poured down their throats, because she had not the heart to be present; but heard the screams of Margaret, and saw both Margaret and Else running afterwards with scalded mouths, &c. That they lived sometime after in a miserable condition, always complaining of their stomachs until their deaths, that they never got better, but died" (pp. 10-11). The day before the slave Margaret died she had been beaten on the head so that the witness "could have laid her three fingers" into "the hind part of her head" (p. 11). A ten-year-old slave boy was beaten until "the skin [was] all off" his back, and he soon died (p. 11). Although Hodge kept a "sick-house," he never sent a doctor to it, and he usually only put slaves in it who had been beaten so severely he expected them to die.

Hodge's conduct appears to have offended the slave-holding white population of the community. The prosecution noted that Hodge's lawyers claimed *"it was no greater offence in law for his owner to kill him* [the slave Prosper], *than it would be to kill his dog."* The solicitor general declared: "My God! Are we patiently to hear such a declaration?" (p. 77). Quoting this statement later on, the prosecutor told the jury:

> Not one of you who heard the declaration, but felt indignant at the assertion. Even the long exploded disgrace to British liberty, the ancient state of villeinage, to which West-India slavery seems more nearly allied than any other condition or bondage I can compare it to; even villeinage, which gave to the Lord the manors, a property in their villeins, so they could not leave their service without permission . . . which even permitted him to beat his villein with impunity, was nevertheless so regulated, so restrained by law, that the persons of villeins, were protected against any atrocious injuries of the Lord; for the Lord could neither maim nor kill his villeins, but was obliged to call in the assistance of the law, whenever it became necessary to inflict *capital* punishment [p. 82].

Clearly, the acts of Hodge were beyond the pale of legitimate actions, even for an owner of slaves in the West Indies. Hodge himself realized this at his trial. Before sentencing, he noted: "I am sensible the country thirsts for my blood . . ." (p. 184).

The solicitor general's argument suggests that slavery in the West Indies was akin to villeinage, which is historically doubtful. But, his assertion again distinguishes this case from those involving slaves in the United States. Most American courts would not apply the concept of villeinage to American slavery. Such an application would have implied that slaves had certain rights at common law, which might have ultimately undermined the system of slavery. In addition, it would have created a "class-based" society that Southern judges rejected in theory, although slavery obviously supported it in practice.

This pamphlet was published in Connecticut for what were apparently antislavery motives. The publisher leaves to the reader "the moral and political effects, this report is calculated and likely to produce." He hopes the readers will draw their own conclusions about such issues from "the very able speeches of the learned Counsel" (p. 5). Most likely, however, he expects the readers to learn how evil slavery could be.

Selected Bibliography of Secondary Sources

Alilunas, L. "Fugitive Slave Cases in Ohio prior to 1850." *Ohio State Archaeological and Historical Quarterly* 49 (1940): 160−84.

Alpert, J. L. "Law of Slavery: It Did Happen Here." *American Bar Association Journal* 55 (June 1969): 544−46.

"American Slavery and the Conflict of Laws." *Columbia Law Review* 71 (1971): 74−99.

Avins, A. "Involuntary Servitude in British Commonwealth Law." *International and Comparative Law Quarterly* 16 (1967): 29−55.

Barzel, Y. "Economic Analysis of Slavery." *Journal of Law and Economics* 20 (1977): 87−110.

Bell, D. G. "Slavery and the Judges of Loyalist New Brunswick." *University of New Brunswick Law Journal* 31 (1982): 9−42.

Belz, H. *Emancipation and Equal Rights: Politics and Constitutionalism in the Civil War Era*. New York, 1978.

Berns, W. "The Constitution and the Migration of Slaves." *Yale Law Journal* 78 (1968): 198−228.

Bestor, A. "The American Civil War as a Constitutional Crisis." *American Historical Review* 64 (1964): 327−52.

——— . "State Sovereignty and Slavery—A Reinterpretation of Proslavery Constitutional Doctrine, 1846−1860." *Journal of the Illinois State Historical Society* 54 (1961): 117−80.

Bollinger, L. C. "Homer of the Pacific: Melville's Art and the Ambiguities of Judging Evil." *Michigan Law Review* 75 (1977): 823−44.

Boskin, J. *Into Slavery: Racial Decisions in the Virginia Colony*. Philadelphia, 1976.

Brackett, J. R. "The Status of the Slave, 1775−1789." In *Essays in the Constitutional History of the United States* Ed. John Franklin Jameson. Boston and New York, 1889.

Brown, W. H. *An Historical Sketch of the Early Movement in Illinois for the Legalization of Slavery*. Chicago, 1865.

Calhoun, E. "Thirteenth and Fourteenth Amendments: Constitutional Authority for Federal Legislation against Private Sex Discrimination." *Minnesota Law Review* 61 (1977): 313−62.

Campbell, S. *The Slave Catchers: Enforcement of the Fugitive Slave Law,
    1850–1860*. Chapel Hill, 1970.
Catterall, H. T. *Judicial Cases Concerning American Slavery and the Negro*. 5
    vols. Washington, 1926.
———. "Some Antecedents of the Dred Scott Case." *American Historical Review*
    30 (1924): 56–71.
Cobb, T. R. R. *An Inquiry into the Law of Negro Slavery in the United States of
    America*. Philadelphia and Savannah, 1858.
Cochran, W. C. *The Western Reserve and the Fugitive Slave Law: A Prelude to
    Civil War*. Western Reserve Historical Society Publication no. 101.
    Cleveland, 1920.
Collins, D. G. "The United States Owes Reparations to the African States for
    the Slave Trade." *Howard Law Journal* 16 (1971): 314–33.
Commager, H. S. "Constitutional History and the Higher Law." *Pennsylvania
    Magazine of History and Biography* 62 (1938): 20–40.
Corwin, E. S. "The Dred Scott Decision in the Light of Contemporary Legal
    Doctrines." *American Historical Review* 17 (1911): 52–69.
Coulter, E. Merton. "Four Slave Trials in Elbert County Georgia." *The Georgia
    Historical Quarterly* 41 (1957): 237–46.
Cover, R. M. *Justice Accused: Antislavery and the Judicial Process*. New
    Haven, 1975.
Cushing, J. D. "The Cushing Court and the Abolition of Slavery in Massachusetts:
    More Notes on the 'Quock Walker Case.' " *American Journal of Legal
    History* 5 (1961): 118–44.
Davis, D. B. *The Problem of Slavery in the Age of Revolution*, Ithaca, 1975.
Dowd, M. D. "Justice Story and the Slavery Conflict." *Massachusetts Law
    Quarterly* 52 (1967): 239–53.
DuBois, W. E. B. *The Suppression of the African Slave Trade to the United
    States of America, 1638–1870*. Cambridge, Mass., 1896.
Dunn, J. P. *Indiana: A Redemption from Slavery*. Boston, 1900.
Eckert, R. L. "Antislavery Martyrdom: The Ordeal of Passmore Williamson."
    Pennsylvania Magazine of History and Biography 100 (1976): 521–38.
Edwards, John C. "Slave Justice in Four Middle Georgia Counties." *The
    Georgia Historical Quarterly*, 57 (1973): 265–73.
Ehrlich, W. *They Have No Rights: Dred Scott's Struggle for Freedom*. Westport,
    Conn., 1979.
———. "Was the Dred Scott Case Valid?" *Journal of American History* 55
    (1968): 256–65.
Elden, G. "'Forty Acres and a Mule,' with Interest: The Constitutionality of
    Black Capitalism, Benign School Quotas and Other Statutory Racial
    Classifications." *Journal of Urban Law* 47 (1969–70): 591–652.
Fehrenbacher, D. E. *The Dred Scott Case: Its Significance in American Law
    and Politics*. New York, 1978.
Fiddes, E. "Lord Mansfield and the Sommersett Case." *Law Quarterly Review*
    50 (1934): 499–511.
Finkelman, P. *An Imperfect Union: Slavery, Federalism and Comity*. Chapel
    Hill, N.C., 1981.

———. "The Law of Slavery and Freedom in California, 1848–1860." *California Western Law Review* 17 (1981): 437–64.

———. "*Prigg* v. *Pennsylvania* and Northern State Courts: Antislavery Use of a Proslavery Decision." *Civil War History* 25 (1979): 5–35.

———. "The Treason Trial of Castner Hanway." In *American Political Trials*. Ed. M. R. Belknap. Westport, Conn., 1981.

Fisher, R. A. "Granville Sharp and Lord Mansfield." *Journal of Negro History* 38 (1943): 381–89.

Fishback, M. M. "Illinois Legislation on Slavery and Free Negroes, 1818–1865." *Transactions of the Illinois State Society* 9 (1904): 414–32.

Flanigan, D. "Criminal Procedure in Slave Trials in the Antebellum South." *Journal of Southern History* 40 (1974): 537–64.

Fogarty, G. P. "Slaves, Quakers, and Catholic Marriage in Colonial Maryland." *Jurist* 35 (1975): 142–61.

Fogel, R. and S. Engerman. "Philanthropy at Bargain Prices: Notes on the Economics of Gradual Emancipation." *Journal of Legal Studies* 3 (1974): 377–401.

Fox-Genovese, E., and E. D. Genovese. *Fruits of Merchant Capital: Slavery and Bourgeois Property in the Rise and Expansion of Merchant Capitalism*. New York, 1983.

Franklin, J. H. *The Emancipation Proclamation*. Garden City, N.Y., 1963.

Geiser, K. F. "Redemptioners and Indentured Servants in the Colony and Commonwealth of Pennsylvania." *Yale Review Supplement* 10 (1901): 337.

Genovese, E. D. "Slavery in the Legal History of the South and the Nation." *Texas Law Review* 59 (1981): 969–98.

———. "When the Slaves Left Old Marster." *Civil Liberties Review* 2 (Winter 1975): 67–76.

Gerteis, L. S. *From Contraband to Freedman: Federal Policy toward Southern Blacks, 1861–1865*. Westport, Conn., 1973.

Goodell, W. *Views of American Constitutional Law in Its Bearings upon American Slavery*. Utica, N.Y., 1845.

Handlin, O. and M. Handlin. "The Origins of the Southern Labor System." *William and Mary Quarterly*, 3d ser., 7 (1950): 199–222.

Harris, N. D. *The History of Negro Servitude in Illinois*. Chicago, 1904.

Henderson, W. C. "The Slave Court System in Spartanburg County." *Proceedings of the South Carolina Historical Association*. 24 (1976).

Henry, H. M. *The Police Control of the Slave in South Carolina*. Emory, Va., 1914.

Hesburgh, T. M. "Justice in America: The Dream and the Reality." *Wisconsin Bar Bulletin* 50 (1977): 17–21.

Higginbotham, A. L. *In the Matter of Color: Race and the American Legal Process, the Colonial Period*. New York, 1978.

———. "Racism and the Early American Legal Process, 1619–1896." *Annals of the American Academy of Political Science* 407 (1973): 1–17.

———. "Relevance of Slavery: Race and the American Legal Process." *Notre Dame Law Review* 54 (1978): 171–80.

Hindus, M. S. "Black Justice under White Law: Criminal Prosecutions of Blacks in Antebellum South Carolina." *Journal of American History* 63 (1976): 575−99.

———. "The Contours of Crime and Justice in Massachusetts and South Carolina, 1767−1878." *American Journal of Legal History* 21 (1977): 212−37.

———. *Prison and Plantation: Crime, Justice, and Authority in Massachusetts and South Carolina, 1767−1878.* Chapel Hill, N.C., 1980.

Horowitz, H. W. "Choice-of-Law Decisions Involving Slavery: 'Interest Analysis' in the Early Nineteenth Century." *University of California at Los Angeles Law Review* 17 (1970): 587−601.

Howington, A. "Not in the Condition of a Horse or an Ox: *Ford v. Ford*, the Law of Testamentary Manumission, and the Tennessee Court's Recognition of Slavery Humanity." *Tennessee Historical Quarterly* 34 (1975): 249−63.

Hudson, R. O., and J. Durham. *The New York Daily Tribune and Passmore Williamson's Case: A Study in the Use of Northern States' Rights.* Wichita, 1974.

Hurd, J. C. *The Law of Freedom and Bondage in the United States.* 2 vols. Boston and New York, 1858 and 1862.

Hurd, R. C. *Treatise on the Right of Personal Liberty, and on the Writ of Habeas Corpus, and the Practice Connected with It, with a View of the Law of Extradition of Fugitives.* Albany, 1858.

Hyman, H. M., and W. M. Wiecek. *Equal Justice under Law: Constitutional Development, 1835−1875.* New York, 1982.

Jaffa, H. V. "Equality as a Conservative Principle." *Loyola University Law Review* 8 (1975): 471−505.

Johnson, A. "The Constitutionality of the Fugitive Slave Acts." *Yale Law Journal* 31 (1921): 161−82.

Johnson, W. B. "The Origin and Nature of African Slavery in Seventeenth-Century Maryland." *Maryland Historical Magazine* 73 (1978): 236−45.

Jordan, W. D. "Modern Tensions and the Origins of American Slavery." *Journal of Southern History* 28 (1962): 18−30.

———. *White Over Black: American Attitudes toward the Negro, 1550−1812.* Chapel Hill, N.C., 1968.

Katz, J. *Resistance at Christiana: The Fugitive Slave Rebellion, Christiana, Pennsylvania: September 11, 1851. A Documentary Account.* New York, 1974.

Kettner, J. *The Development of American Citizenship, 1608−1870.* Chapel Hill, N.C., 1978.

Kiely, T. F. "Hollow Words: An Experiment in Legal Historical Method as Applied to the Institution of Slavery." *DePaul Law Review* 25 (1976): 842−94.

Kuper, T. F. "Thomas Jefferson and Slavery." *New York State Bar Journal* 42 (1970): 125−32.

Kutler, S. *The Dred Scott Decision: Law or Politics?* Boston, 1967.

Lang, M. *Defender of the Faith: The High Court of Mississippi 1817−1875.* Jackson, 1977.

Lee, C. R. *The Confederate Constitutions.* Chapel Hill, N.C., 1963.

Leslie, W. R. "A Study in the Origins of Interstate Rendition: The Big Beaver Creek Murders." *American Historical Review* 57 (1951): 63−76.

Levy, L. W. "The 'Abolition Riot': Boston's First Slave Rescue." *New England Quarterly* 2 (1952): 85−92.

——. *The Law of the Commonwealth and Chief Justice Shaw.* Cambridge, Mass., 1957.

——. "Sims' Case: The Fugitive Slave Law in Boston in 1851." *Journal of Negro History* 35 (1950): 39−74.

Levy, L. W., and H. B. Phillips. "The *Roberts* Case: Source of the 'Separate but Equal' Doctrine." *American Historical Review* 56 (1951): 510−18.

Litwack, L. F. *North of Slavery: The Negro in the Free States, 1790−1860.* Chicago, 1961.

Lynd, S. *Class Conflict, Slavery, and the United States Constitution: Ten Essays.* Indianapolis, 1967.

MacNaul, W. C. *The Jefferson-Lemen Compact: The Relation of Thomas Jefferson and James Lemen in the Exclusion of Slavery from Illinois and the Northwest Territory with Related Documents.* Chicago, 1915.

McClendon, R. E. "The *Amistad* Claims: Inconsistencies of Policy." *Political Science Quarterly* 48 (1923): 386−412.

McDougall, M. G. *Fugitive Slaves: 1619−1865.* Boston, 1891.

McManus, E. J. "Antislavery Legislation in New York." *Journal of Negro History* 46 (1961): 208−16.

——. *Black Bondage in the North.* Syracuse, 1973.

——. *A History of Negro Slavery in New York.* Syracuse, 1966.

Miller, J. B. "Monster of the Spanish Main." *Juridicial Review,* 1970, pp. 97−114.

Misner, R. L., and J. H. Clough. "Arrestees as Informants: A Thirteenth Amendment Analysis." *Stanford Law Review* 29 (1977): 713−46.

Morris, T. D. "'As If the Injury Was Effected by the Natural Elements of Air, or Fire': Slave Wrong and the Liability of Masters." *Law & Society Review* 16 (1982): 569−99.

——. *Free Men All: The Personal Liberty Laws of the North, 1780−1861.* Baltimore, 1972.

Nadelhaft, J. "The Somerset Case and Slavery: Myth, Reality, and Repercussions." *Journal of Negro History* 51 (1966): 193−208.

Nanda, V. P., and M. C. Bassiouni. "Slavery and the Slave Trade: Steps toward Eradication." *Santa Clara Law Review* 12 (1972): 424−42.

Nash, A. E. K. "Fairness and Formalism in the Trials of Blacks in the State Supreme Courts of the Old South." *Virginia Law Review* 56 (1970): 64−100.

——. "A More Equitable Past? Southern Supreme Courts and the Protection of the Antebellum Negro." *North Carolina Law Review.* 48 (1970): 197−242.

——. "Negro Rights, Unionism, and Greatness on the South Carolina Court of Appeals: The Extraordinary Chief Justice John Belton O'Neall." *South Carolina Law Review* 21 (1969): 141−90.

——. "Reason of Slavery: Understanding the Judicial Role in the Peculiar Institution." *Vanderbilt Law Review* 32 (1979): 7−218.

——— . "Texas Justice in the Age of Slavery: Appeals Concerning Blacks and the Antebellum State Supreme Court." *Houston Law Review* 8 (1971): 438−56.

——— . "The Texas Supreme Court and Trial Rights of Blacks, 1845− 1860." *Journal of American History* 58 (1971): 622−42.

Nelson, W. E. "Impact of the Antislavery Movement upon Styles of Judicial Reasoning in Nineteenth Century America." *Harvard Law Review* 87 (1974): 513−66.

Nogee, Joseph L. "The Prigg Case and Fugitive Slavery, 1842-1850." *Journal of Negro History* 39 (1954): 185−205.

Nye, R. B. *Fettered Freedom: Civil Liberties and the Slavery Controversy.* East Lansing, Mich., 1949.

O'Brien. W. S. J. "Did the Jennison Case Outlaw Slavery in Massachusetts?" *William and Mary Quarterly*, 3d ser., 17 (1960): 219−41.

Olshausen, G. "American Slavery and Its Aftermath." *Guild Practitioner* 30 (1973): 69−73.

O'Neall, J. B. *The Negro Law of South Carolina.* Columbia, 1848.

Paludan, P. S. *A Covenant with Death: The Constitution, Law, and Equality in the Civil War Era.* Urbana, 1975.

Parker, J. *Personal Liberty Laws, (Statutes of Massachusetts) and Slavery in the Territories (Case of Dred Scott).* Boston, 1861.

Patton, James W. "The Progress of Emancipation in Tennessee, 1796-1860." *Journal of Negro History* 17 (1932): 67−102.

Pease, J. H. and W. H. Pease. *The Fugitive Slave Law and Anthony Burns: A Problem in Law Enforcement.* Philadelphia, 1975.

Phillips, W. *Review of Lysander Spooner's Essay on the Unconstitutionality of Slavery.* Boston, 1847.

Poole, W. F. *Anti-Slavery Opinions before the Year 1800.* Cincinnati, 1873.

Reid, J. P. "Lessons of Lumpkin: A Review of Recent Literature on Law, Comity, and the Impending Crisis." *William and Mary Law Review* 23 (1982): 571−624.

Riga, J. P. "American Crisis over Slavery: An Example of the Relationship between Legality and Morality." *American Journal of Jurisprudence* 26 (1981): 80−111.

Robinson, L. *Slavery in the Structure of American Politics, 1765−1820.* New York, 1970.

Ryan, H. R. S., "Ex parte John Anderson." *Queens Law Review* 6 (1981): 383−88.

Shaw, W. C. "The Fugitive Slave Issue in Massachusetts Politics, 1780−1837." Ph. D. diss., University of Illinois, 1938.

Siebert, W. H. *The Underground Railroad from Slavery to Freedom.* New York, 1898.

Sirmans. M. E. "The Legal Status of the Slave in South Carolina, 1670− 1740." *Journal of Southern History* 28 (1962): 462−73.

Spooner, L. *A Defence for Fugitive Slaves against the Acts of Congress of February 12, 1793, and September 18, 1850.* Boston, 1850.

——— . *The Unconstitutionality of Slavery,* Boston, 1845.

Stealey, J. E. "The Responsibilities and Liabilities of the Bailee of Slave Labor in Virginia." *American Journal of Legal History* 12 (1968): 336−53.

Stephenson, M. W., and D. G. Stephenson. "'To Protect and Defend': Joseph Henry Lumpkin, the Supreme Court of Georgia, and Slavery." *Emory Law Journal* 25 (1976): 579−608.

Stroud, G. M. *Sketch of Laws Relative to Slavery in the Several States of the United States of America*. Philadelphia, 1827.

Szasz, T. S. "Sane Slave: Social Control and Legal Psychiatry." *American Criminal Law Review* 10 (1972): 337−56.

Taylor, Rosser H. "Humanizing the Slave Code of North Carolina." *North Carolina Historical Review* 2 (July 1925): 323−31.

tenBroek, J. *The Antislavery Origins of the Fourteenth Amendment*. Berkeley, 1951.

Turner, J. "Use of the Courts in the Movement to Abolish American Slavery." *Ohio State Law Journal* 31 (1970): 304−20.

Tushnet, M. V. *The American Law of Slavery, 1810−1860: Considerations of Humanity and Interest*. Princeton, 1981.

——. "American Law of Slavery, 1810−1860: A Study in the Persistence of Legal Autonomy." *Law and Society Review* 10 (1975−76): 119−84.

——. "Approaches to the Study of the Law of Slavery." *Civil War History* 25 (1979): 329−38.

Umozurike, U. O. "African Slave Trade and the Attitudes of International Law towards It." *Howard Law Journal* 16 (1971): 334−49.

Walvin, J. "Black Slavery in England." *Journal of Caribbean History* 7 (1973): 68−86.

Watson, A. "Morality, Slavery, and the Jurists in the Later Roman Republic." *Tulane Law Review* 42 (1968): 289−303.

Wiecek, W. M. "Slavery and Abolition before the United States Supreme Court, 1820−1860." *Journal of American History* 65 (1978): 34−59.

——. "*Somerset:* Lord Mansfield and the Legitimacy of Slavery in the Anglo-American World." *University of Chicago Law Review* 42 (1974): 86−146.

——. *The Sources of Antislavery Constitutionalism in America, 1760−1848*. Ithaca, 1977.

——. "The Statutory Law of Slavery and Race in the Thirteen Mainland Colonies of British America." *William and Mary Quarterly*, 3d ser., 34 (1977): 258−80.

Wheeler, J. D. *A Practical Treatise on the Law of Slavery: Being a Compilation of All the Decisions Made on That Subject, in the Several Courts of the U.S. and the State Courts*. New York, 1837.

Wright, M. T. "New Jersey Laws and the Negro." *Journal of Negro History* 28 (1943): 156−99.

Wood, W. J. "The Illegal Beginning of American Negro Slavery." *American Bar Association Journal* 56 (1970): 45−49.

Younger, Richard D. "Southern Grand Juries and Slavery." *The Journal of Negro History* 40 (1955): 166−78.

Zilversmit, A. *The First Emancipation: The Abolition of Slavery in the North*. Chicago, 1967.

——. "Quock Walker, Mumbet, and the Abolition of Slavery in Massachusetts." *William and Mary Quarterly*, 3d ser., 25 (1968): 614−24.

Index

A

Ableman, Stephen (U.S. marshal, Wis.),
119–20
Abolition of slavery, Great Britain, 20
Adams, John Quincy (U.S. president),
210, 223, 225, 227, 229, 232–39,
256, 260, 261
Adams-Onis Treaty, 235
African Repository, 169
Alberti, George F. (Pa. slave catcher),
13, 83–85
Albright, A. N. (Ill. sheriff), 128–29
Allen, Henry W. (U.S. marshal, N.Y.
State), 103, 105–6
Alligator (schooner), 218
Alton Observer, 147
American Anti-Slavery Society, 132,
166–70
American Colonization Society, 38, 44,
163–70
American Revolution, 5, 6, 15n, 22, 25,
146, 160, 186, 271
Amistad (schooner), 222–29
Andrew (fugitive slave), 71
Andrew, John A. (Mass. antislavery
lawyer/politician), 116
Anne (slave brought to Mass.), 32–33
Antelope (ship), 237
Antislavery societies, 11, 143
Armitage, Mr. (Ky. slave catcher), 68,
69
Arnold, Isaac N. (Ill. lawyer), 130
Ashmead, John W. (U.S. district
attorney, Pa.), 98, 100–101
Augusta (ship), 285–89
Aves Case (*Commonwealth* v. *Aves*
[1836]), 10, 25–29, 31–33, 57,
69, 76, 77, 114, 154
Aves, Thomas (defendant in Mass. case),
25

B

Bacon, John (Ky. slaveholder), 124
Bailey, Gamaliel (antislavery editor),
181, 182
Baldwin, Henry (U.S. Supreme Court
justice), 34
Baldwin, Roger S. (Conn. antislavery
lawyer), 224–25, 229–31, 233,
237–39
Bellinger, Edmund (S.C. lawyer), 245
Bennett, Ned (slave), 203–4
Bennett, Thomas (S.C. governor), 204
Benton, Thomas Hart (U.S. senator),
50, 51
Bigler, William (Pa. governor), 85
Bill of Rights, 31, 75
Birney, James Gillespie (abolitionist),
29–31, 36–38
Blackstone, Sir William (English jurist),
5, 6, 24, 66, 77
Blair, Montgomery (Md. lawyer), 46, 48
Bland, Richard (Va. slaveholder), 28
Booth, Sherman (Wis. abolitionist),
119–23
Boston Female Antislavery Society, 28
Boston Vigilance Committee, 111, 190
Bowditch, Henry I. (Mass. abolitionist),
65
Bowditch, William I. (Mass. abolitionist),
113–15
Boynton, Lewis (Ohio farmer), 124
Bradley, J. H. (Washington, D.C.,
attorney), 165
Brent, Robert (Md. attorney general), 8,
13, 98, 100–102
British and Foreign Anti-Slavery Society,
285, 288–89
British Guiana, 272–73, 276
Broad, Amos (N.Y. slaveholder),
253–55

Broad, Demis (N.Y. slaveholder), 253–55

Brougham, Henry (British antislavery M.P.), 275, 277

Brown, Isaac (fugitive slave), 77, 78

Brown, John (abolitionist), 7, 109, 111, 156, 157, 188–95

Brown, Mason (Ky. judge), 68–69

Brown, P. A. (proslavery author), 84

Brown, Thomas (abolitionist in Ky.), 157, 174, 186–87

Brown, Watson (abolitionist), 191

Bryant, William Cullen (author/editor), 54

Buchanan, James (U.S. president), 46, 120

Buckley, Theodore (Ga. ship captain), 75, 76

Burns, Anthony (fugitive slave), 89, 107–19

Burt, William L. (Mass. antislavery lawyer), 116

Burton, Mary (indentured servant), 200

Bushnell, Simeon (Ohio abolitionist), 124–26

Butler, John (fugitive slave), 127

Butler, Pierce (S.C. delegate to Constitutional Convention), 59

Butler, Zebulon (Miss. minister), 267

C

Calhoun, John C. (U.S. senator), 51, 242

Cannon, Arthur (Pa. court reporter), 13

Carlisle, J. M. (Washington, D.C., attorney), 165

Cartwright, Dr. Samuel A. (proslavery writer and physician), 14, 53

Caton, John D. (Ill. chief justice), 129–30

Chaplin, William L. (Mass. abolitionist), 182–86

Charge to the Grand Jury, 94

Charge to the Grand Jury—Treason, 95

Chase, Salmon Portland (Ohio antislavery lawyer/politician), 10, 29–32, 70–75, 181

Chilton, Samuel (Washington, D.C., antislavery lawyer), 195

Choate, Rufus (Mass. lawyer), 25, 28

Christiana Slave Rebellion, 13, 95, 98, 99, 102, 105, 107

Cinque (or Cinquez) (slave rebellion leader), 228, 238

Civil War, 12, 19, 48, 50, 56, 57, 89, 90, 96, 111, 116, 124, 135, 168, 212, 242, 258

Clark, Henry (free black), 264–66

Clarkson, Thomas (English abolitionist), 215

Clay, Cassius (Ky. antislavery editor), 175

Clay, Henry (U.S. senator), 34, 130, 132, 175, 177

Clerke, Thomas W. (N.Y. judge), 57

Cleveland, Chauncey F. (Conn. lawyer), 143

Codman, Capt. John (Mass. slaveholder), 251–52

Coke, Sir Edward (17th-century English jurist), 52, 92

Colonization movement, 36, 37, 38

Combs, Gen. Leslie (Ky. lawyer), 175

Commentaries on the Laws of England; see Blackstone

Committee to Abolish the Slave Trade (British), 278, 283

Compromise of 1820; see Missouri Compromise

Compromise of 1850, 38, 59–60, 102, 108, 183

Comstock, George F. (N.Y. lawyer), 105, 106

Connor, James (U.S. district attorney, S.C.), 242, 244, 246

Constitutional Convention, 15n, 59, 77, 123, 211, 242

Cooke, John E. (abolitionist), 192, 193

Coolidge, Nathaniel (Boston city jailer), 64, 65

Cooper, Sir Anthony Ashley (17th-century Englishman), 4

Corrie, W. C. (ship captain), 246

Corse, Barney (N.Y. abolitionist), 264–66

Covey, James (free black sailor), 227

Coxe, R. S. (Washington, D.C., attorney), 165, 167

Cranch, William (U.S. district judge, Washington, D.C.), 165

Crandal, William Lusk (N.Y. antislavery lawyer), 105, 107

Crandall, Prudence (Conn. abolitionist), 138, 139–43, 164, 227

Crandall, Reuben (Conn. physician), 164–70

Crittenden, John J. (Ky. politician), 82, 176

Crocker, E. B. (Ind. attorney and abolitionist), 81–82

Curtis, Benjamin R. (Mass. lawyer and U.S. Supreme Court justice), 25, 27, 28, 47, 48, 50, 52, 53, 115–17

Curtis, Charles P. (Mass. lawyer), 25

Curtis, George T. (U.S. commissioner, Mass.), 87, 88, 90, 91, 93, 94

D

Daggs, Ruel (Mo. slaveholder), 79, 80

Daggett, David (Conn. chief justice), 140

Darg, John P. (La. slaveholder), 263–66

Dana, Richard Henry (Mass. antislavery lawyer), 86–88, 90, 108, 118–19

Davis, Charles G. (Mass. antislavery lawyer), 86–88

Davis, Jefferson (president, Confederate States of America), 55

Davy, Serjeant William (English lawyer), 21

Declaration of Independence, 15n, 47–48, 53, 126, 131

DeTreville, [Richard?] (S.C. lawyer), 245

Demerara; see British Guiana

Denmark Vesey; see Vesey Conspiracy

Devens, Charles (U.S. marshal, Mass.), 90, 91

Devereux, Stephen (sailor), 278

Dickinson, John (Pa. delegate to Constitutional Convention), 15n, 211

Dillaye, S. D. (N.Y. lawyer), 105, 106

Dixon, Archibald (U.S. senator, Ky.), 186

Dolphin (brig), 239

Douglass, Frederick (abolitionist), 189

Dowling, Dr. Thomas (ship surgeon), 278, 280, 282

Drayton, Daniel (abolitionist ship captain), 157, 179–81, 182

Dred Scott (slave), 46, 48, 52

Dred Scott Case (*Dred Scott* v. *Sandford* [1857]), 7, 9, 10, 13, 14, 18, 19, 25, 27, 38, 43–54, 97, 151, 160, 239, 240

Drummand, Thomas (U.S. district judge, Ill.), 128–31

Duncan, Dr. Stephen (Miss. physician), 267

Durant, Henry F. (Mass. antislavery lawyer), 116

Dyer, J. J. (Iowa judge), 80

E

Eames, Mrs. Olivia (Mass. slaveholder), 32–33

Echo (brig), 239, 240, 244, 249

Eells, Samuel (Ohio antislavery lawyer), 29

Edmonds, John W. (N.Y. circuit court judge), 76, 77

Egbert, Elisha (Ind. judge), 81

Elkison, Henry (free black sailor), 256–63

Ellers, P. (English lawyer), 25

Ellis, Charles Mayo (Mass. antislavery lawyer), 109, 116

Ellsworth, William W. (Conn. lawyer), 141–43

Emeline (slave), 127

Emerson, Dr. John (Mo. slaveholder), 45

Emerson, Mrs. John (Mo. slaveholder), 45

Evarts, William M. (N.Y. lawyer), 56

F

Fairbank, Calvin (abolitionist minister), 175–77

Fillmore, Millard (U.S. president), 87, 98, 99, 104, 126, 181

Fitch, Henry S. (U.S. district attorney, Ill.), 130, 132–34

Foot, Samuel Alfred (N.Y. lawyer/jurist), 53–54

Forbes, Mr. (Ky. slave catcher), 68, 69

Fordham, Peletiah (ship captain), 222, 228

Forsyth, John (U.S. secretary of state), 234, 236

Francis (ship), 161

Frazee, George (Iowa lawyer), 80

Frazier, Elihu (Iowa abolitionist), 79

Free blacks, 37–38, 46–48, 52, 53, 62, 101, 102, 138, 139–43, 158, 163, 167–68, 202, 205–7, 256–63, 269

Free Soil party, 119, 126

Freedom of speech and press, 143–47, 147–50, 158–61, 161–64, 164–70

Freeman, Watson (U.S. marshal, Mass.), 108

Fugitive slave clause, 59, 61, 94, 106, 123, 131

Fugitive Slave Act (1793), 31, 59–62, 66, 67, 72–76, 78–82, 84, 94, 100, 105, 106, 136, 213

Fugitive Slave Act (1850), 8, 27, 38, 59–61, 85–88, 90, 94–98, 100,

Fugitive Slave Act—Continued 101, 103–8, 113, 115, 116, 121–24, 126, 128, 130–31, 135–36, 246

Fugitive slave laws, 7, 12

Fugitive slaves, 3, 7, 14, 32, 41, 58–137, 178–79, 190, 238

G

Gardner, Alexander (clerk, U.S. district court, N.Y.), 85

Garland, Benammi S. (Mo. slaveholder), 119, 120

Garner, Peter M. (Ohio abolitionist), 178–79

Garrison, William Lloyd (abolitionist), 133, 141, 152, 157, 161–64

Gedney, Lt. (Coast Guard officer), 222, 226, 228, 230, 237

George (fugitive slave), 37

Geyer, Henry S. (U.S. senator, Mo.), 46

Gibson, John (Pa. chief justice), 78

Giddings, Joshua (Ohio antislavery congressman), 181

Gilman, William S. (Ill. antislavery man), 147–50

Gilpin, Henry D. (U.S. attorney general), 34

Glover, Joshua (fugitive slave), 119, 120

Glynn, Serjeant John (English lawyer), 21

Goddard, Calvin (Conn. lawyer), 143

Goddard, John (Washington, D.C., slave catcher), 182, 185

Gordon, George (Ohio abolitionist minister), 134–36

Gorsuch, Edward (Md. slaveholder), 95, 96, 98

Graham, Christopher (Ky. slaveholder), 35, 37

Graham, James H. (Pa. judge), 127, 128

Grampus (U.S. Navy schooner), 227, 236

Gray, Horace (legal editor/post-Civil War U.S. Supreme Court justice), 51

Gray, James B. (Va. slaveholder), 64, 65, 67

Gray, Jim (fugitive slave), 128–33

Greeley, Horace (antislavery editor), 9, 10, 50

Green, Henry (ship captain), 227–28

Gregg, Col. Maxey (S.C. lawyer), 245

Grier, Robert C. (U.S. Supreme Court justice), 8, 13, 97, 98, 100, 101

Griswold, Henry (Ohio antislavery lawyer), 195

Groves, Moses (Miss. slaveholder), 32–33

Gruber, Jacob (Pa. antislavery minister), 158–61

Gullay, Jack (slave conspirator), 204

Gurley, R. R. (colonizationist minister), 169

H

Hale, John P. (U.S. senator, N.H.), 110, 116, 181

Hallett, Benjamin F. (U.S. commissioner, Mass.), 90, 116

Hamilton, James (Charleston intendant), 208, 209, 261

Hamlet, James (fugitive slave), 85, 86

Hanway, Castner (Pa. abolitionist), 8, 13, 96–100, 101

Hargrave, Francis (English antislavery lawyer), 21, 22

Harpers Ferry Raid; see John Brown

Harth, Mingo (slave rebel), 202

Harvard Law School, 112, 117, 213

Hayden, Harriet (fugitive slave), 175–76

Hayden, Lewis (fugitive slave), 175–76

Hayne, Isaac William (S.C. lawyer), 239–44

Henry (fugitive slave), 35, 37

Higginson, Thomas Wentworth (Mass. antislavery minister), 116, 188

Hodge, Arthur (West Indian slaveholder), 290–92

Holden Anti-Slavery Society, 11, 33

Holden Slave Case, 11, 32–33

Holmes, Isaac E. (S.C. lawyer), 258

Holmes, Oliver Wendell (post-Civil War U.S. Supreme Court justice), 5

Homer (ship), 258

Hopper, Isaac T. (Quaker abolitionist), 264–66

Hornblower, Joseph C. (N.J. chief justice), 152

Horsemanden, Daniel (reporter of N.Y. slave conspiracy trials), 198, 200–201

Hoskins, Edmund (English lawyer), 25

Hossack, John (Ill. abolitionist), 8, 128–34

Howard, Benjamin (U.S. Supreme Court reporter), 9, 45, 49

Howe, Dr. Samuel G. (Mass. abolitionist), 188, 190

Howe, Julia Ward (abolitionist), 190

Hoyt, George H. (Mass. antislavery lawyer), 194, 195

Huber, Ulric (17th-century Dutch legal theorist), 52

Hughes, Thomas (slave), 264–65

Hughson, John (conspirator), 198–200

Hughson, Sarah (conspirator), 198–200

Hughson, Sarah (daughter of John and Sarah), 200

Hunt, Benjamin Faneuil (S.C. lawyer), 258–63

Huntington, Elisha M. (U.S. district judge, Ind.), 82

I

Iberia College, 135

Ingraham, Edward D. (U.S. commissioner, Pa.), 96

Irwin, Thomas (U.S. district judge, Pa.), 94–95

J

Jackson, Andrew (U.S. president), 240
Jackson, Nancy (slave), 10
Jackson, Potter (free black sailor), 9
Jackson, W. Arthur (Pa. antislavery lawyer), 102
Jackson v. *Bulloch* (Conn., 1837), 10
Jamestown, Va., 153
Jane [Johnson] (slave), 39, 41, 42
Jay, John (chief justice, U.S. Supreme Court), 76
Jay, John (N.Y. antislavery lawyer), 76, 77
Jay, William (N.Y. judge), 76, 169
Jeffers, Mr. (Washington, D.C., police officer), 167–68
Jefferson, Thomas (U.S. president), 160, 211
Jenkinson, Robert (British prime minister), 275
Jennings, Anderson D. (Ky. slaveholder), 124, 125
Jennings, Thomas (British ship captain), 287
Jerry [Henry, or William Henry] (fugitive slave), 103, 104
Jerry Rescue, 104–7
La Jeune Eugénie, 218–21
Johnson, Andrew (U.S. president), 72
Johnson, Madison C. (Ky. lawyer), 175
Johnson, Reverdy (U.S. senator), 46
Johnson, Samuel (English intellectual), 16n
Johnson, William (U.S. Supreme Court justice), 257–61
Johnston, William (Ohio lawyer), 69
Joliffe, John (Ohio antislavery lawyer), 134–36
Jones, Wharton (Ky. slaveholder), 71–74
Judson, Andrew T. (Conn. lawyer and U.S. district judge), 142, 143, 226–30, 234

K

Kane, Judge John K. (U.S. district judge, Pa.), 13, 39–43, 95, 98, 99
Kansas-Nebraska debates, 108
Kennedy, Lionel (S.C. magistrate), 205, 206, 208
Kent, James (N.Y. jurist/legal scholar), 77
Ker, John (Miss. state senator), 10, 268–69
Key, Francis Scott (Washington, D.C., district attorney), 165, 167, 169–70
Kimber, Capt. John (British slave trader/ sea captain), 277–83
King v. *Inhabitants of Thames Ditton* (England, 1785), 24
King, Henry, 164, 165
King, Rufus (N.Y. congressman), 203
Kirk, George (fugitive slave), 75, 77
Kline, Henry H. (U.S. marshal, Pa.), 96, 98, 99
Knapp, Isaac (Mass. abolitionist), 141
Knox, John C. (Pa. supreme court judge), 41–42
Knox, Joseph (Ill. lawyer), 130
Knowles, John (ship captain), 20, 21
Krum, John (mayor, Alton, Ill.), 147

L

Lamar, Charles A. L. (slave trader), 246, 248
Lamar, Gazaway Bugg (slave trader), 246–48
Langston, Charles (Ohio abolitionist), 124–26
Larned, E. C. (Ill. lawyer), 130
Latimer Case, 64–68
Latimer, George (fugitive slave), 64, 65, 67
Lawrence, Larkin (Mo. slaveholder), 29

Law Reporter; see *Monthly Law Reporter*

Leavitt, Humphrey H. (U.S. district judge, Ohio), 73

Leavitt, Joshua (abolitionist), 226

Lee, Robert E. (military officer), 190

Lemmon Case (*Lemmon* v. *The People* [N.Y.: 1852, 1857, 1860]), 9, 10, 54–57, 114

Lemmon, Jonathan, and Juliet (Va. slaveholders), 9, 54, 56

Lewis, Elijah (Pa. abolitionist), 98, 99

Lewis, Joseph J. (Pa. antislavery lawyer), 42

Liberator (Boston antislavery newspaper), 162, 163

Liberia, 38, 267

Liberty party, 36, 37, 103, 152

Lincoln, Abraham (U.S. president), 30, 46, 48, 56, 72, 111, 134, 135, 136, 242

Lincoln-Douglas debates, 45

Linder, U. F. (Ill. lawyer), 149

List, Charles (Mass. antislavery lawyer), 86, 87

Locke, John (English philosopher), 4, 5

Loguen, Jermain (abolitionist minister, Syracuse, N.Y.), 103

London Missionary Society, 272, 274–77

Long, Mrs. (Ky. slaveholder), 68, 69

Lord Stanley Guineaman (ship), 283

Loring, Charles G. (Mass. antislavery lawyer), 90–94

Loring, Edward G. (U.S. commissioner, Mass.), 108, 109, 111–13, 116–19

Loring, Ellis Gray (abolitionist lawyer), 10, 25, 28, 29, 86, 87, 225, 234

Lovejoy, Elijah P. (Ill. antislavery minister/publisher), 147–50

Lovejoy, Owen (Ill. antislavery politician), 150

Lowell, John, Jr. (legal editor/post-Civil War U.S. district judge), 51

Lundy, Benjamin (antislavery editor), 161

Lunt, George (U.S. district attorney, Mass.), 87, 88

M

Mackintosh, Sir James (British M.P.), 275

McGrath, Andrew Gordon (U.S. district judge, S.C.), 239, 241–43

McLean, John (U.S. Supreme Court justice), 34, 47, 48, 61, 73, 81–83

Madison, James (U.S. president), 77, 123, 211

Mann, Horace (Mass. antislavery congressman), 181

Mansfield, William Murray, 1st earl of (chief justice, Court of King's Bench), 6, 20, 21, 22, 24

Marbury v. *Madison* (U.S., 1803), 43, 260

Mark (colonial Mass. slave), 251–52

Marshall, John (chief justice, U.S. Supreme Court), 237, 260

Martin, David (Md. attorney), 158–61

Martin, Grandison (fugitive slave), 134

Martin, William (Ill. judge), 148

Marvin, R. P. (N.Y. judge), 105–7

Maryland House of Delgates, 7, 63

Mason, James (U.S. senator, Va.), 195

Matilda (slave), 10, 29–32

May, Samuel J. (abolitionist minister), 103, 104

Mayflower Compact, 14, 153

Med (slave), 25, 28, 29

Merritt, Henry W. (N.Y. policeman), 264

Merwin, Elias (Mass. lawyer), 116

Mexican-American War, 102

Miller, Andrew G. (U.S. district judge, Wis.), 120

Mitchell, James (Md. slaveholder), 83

Mitchell, William (N.Y. judge), 56

Missouri Compromise, 45–47, 51, 97, 102, 160, 203
Mobile (brig), 75, 76
Monday (slave conspirator), 203, 204
Montes, Pedro (Cuban slaveholder), 222, 223, 226, 230, 232
Monthly Law Reporter, 51–52, 66, 67, 77
Morgan, Margaret (fugitive slave), 60–61
Morgan, Shebel (nom de guerre); *see* Brown, John
Morris, Robert (Mass. antislavery lawyer), 87
Morsell, James S. (U.S. circuit judge, Washington, D.C.), 165
Murdock, B. F. (city attorney, Alton, Ill.), 149
Murray, William; *see* Mansfield, William Murray, 1st earl of
Myers, Emanuel (Md. slave catcher), 127–28

N

Napoleon, Lewis (N.Y. abolitionist), 56, 76
Nat Turner Rebellion, 195, 197, 273
National Era, 181, 182
Negro Seamen's Act, 256–63
Nelson, Samuel (U.S. Supreme Court justice), 47, 97
Newton, Leander (Ind. abolitionist), 81
New York gradual emancipation statute, 255
New York Legal Observer, 77
New York Manumission Society, 253–55
New York slave conspiracy, 196–202, 273
New York Tribune, 9, 50
New York-Virginia Controversy (1841), 63, 72
New York Yacht Club, 246

Norris, John (Ky. slaveholder), 80–82
Northwest Ordinance of 1787, 31, 37, 38, 59, 75, 179

O

Oberlin-Wellington Rescue, 124–26
O'Conor, Charles (N.Y. proslavery lawyer), 55, 56
Owsley, William (Ky. governor), 175

P

Paine, Byron (Wis. antislavery lawyer/jurist), 120, 122, 123
Paine, Elijah (N.Y. judge), 56
Parker, Daniel (Va. judge), 194
Parker, Thomas (S.C. magistrate), 205–8
Parker, Theodore (Mass. abolitionist minister), 89, 109, 112, 115–17, 188–89
Parker, William (fugitive slave), 96, 98
Parsons, Anson V. (Pa. judge), 78, 84, 85
Paul, William (slave rebel), 202
Pearl (schooner), 179, 180
Peck, Henry (Ohio abolitionist), 126
Pennsylvania Abolition Society, 39
Pennsylvania Anti-Slavery Society, 42
Peters, Richard (U.S. Supreme Court reporter), 9, 62, 210, 229, 233, 238
Personal liberty laws, 62, 63, 65, 85, 112
Phelps, Samuel S. (U.S. senator, Vt.), 175
Phillipps, Richard (Mo. slaveholder), 128–33
Phillips, Capt. Thomas (British slave trader), 280

Phillips, Wendell (Mass. abolitionist), 89, 116–19, 133, 149

Phillis (colonial Mass. slave), 251–52

Phinney, Jerry (fugitive slave), 68, 69

Pierce, Franklin (U.S. president), 71, 116, 242

Pierpont, Rev. John (Mass. antislavery minister), 66

Pinckney, Gen. Charles (S.C. delegate to Constitutional Convention), 242

Pitt, William (British politician), 221

Plattsburgh (schooner), 221

Plumb, Ralph (Ohio abolitionist), 126

Post, John A. (N.J. slaveholder), 151, 154

Potter, James (Ga. slaveholder), 94

Powell, David (fugitive slave), 81

Powell, Lucy (fugitive slave), 81

Poyas, Peter (slave rebel), 202, 203, 204, 209

Prigg Case (*Prigg* v. *Pennsylvania* [U.S., 1842]), 7, 9, 38, 44, 60–64, 65, 74, 76, 77, 84, 92, 123, 127, 135, 178, 213, 217

Prigg, Edward (slave catcher), 60–61, 63

Prince (slave conspirator), 206

Prosper (West Indian slave), 290–92

Punch, John (fugitive slave), 3

R

Rantoul, Robert (Mass. antislavery lawyer/U.S. senator), 90–94, 123

Reed, Enoch (abolitionist, Syracuse, N.Y.), 103

Reed, Margaret A. (Miss. slaveholder), 267, 268

Reigart, J. Franklin (Lancaster, Pa., alderman), 13, 99, 102

Republican party, 9, 41, 74, 120, 126, 149, 243, 244

Reuben (fugitive slave), 35, 37

Riley, John W. (slave catcher), 29–31

Robbins, James J. (Pa. court reporter), 99

Rolfe, Sir John (17th-century Va. leader), 3

Rolla (slave conspirator), 204, 209

Ross, Capt. Isaac (Miss. slaveholder), 267–68

Royal Africa Company, 271

Ruggles, David (abolitionist), 264–66

Ruiz, José (Cuban slaveholder), 222, 223, 230, 232

Runaways; *see* Fugitive slaves

Rycraft, John (Wis. abolitionist), 120

S

Sabine, Joseph F. (U.S. commissioner, N.Y. State), 103

Salem Witch Trials, 146, 202

Sanborn, Franklin B. (Mass. abolitionist), 189

Sanford, John F. A. (defendant in Dred Scott case), 45, 46, 48

Sandys, Sir Edwin (secretary, Virginia Company), 3

Sayers, Mr. (antislavery shipowner), 180–81

Scott, Dred; *see* Dred Scott

Scott, William, Baron Stowall (chief justice, High Court of Admiralty), 278–90

Scott, William (chief justice, Mo. supreme court), 45

Sedgwick, Charles B. (N.Y. antislavery lawyer), 105, 106

Sedgwick, Theodore (N.Y. antislavery lawyer), 225, 230

Sewall, Samuel E. (Boston antislavery lawyer), 25, 28, 86, 87, 90

Seward, William Henry (N.Y. antislavery lawyer/politician), 10, 63, 72, 73, 75, 181, 243

Shadrach (fugitive slave), 86–90, 104, 107

Sharp, Granville (English abolitionist), 20

Sharpstein, J. R. (U.S. district attorney, Wis.), 122

Shaw, Lemuel (chief justice, Mass. Supreme Judicial Court), 10, 25, 26, 29, 31, 64–66, 89, 90, 123, 154

Shipherd, Jacob R. (Ohio abolitionist), 125, 126

Sierre Leone, 259, 285

Sims Case, 89–94, 123

Sims, Thomas (fugitive slave), 88–94

Slade, William (Vt. governor), 175

Slater, Mary (Mass. slaveholder), 25

Slaughter, Robert (slave trader, domestic), 34–35

The Slave, Grace (England, 1827), 46

Slave trade (African), 12, 211–49, 271, 277–89

Slave trade (domestic), 33–35, 161–64, 250

Slave Trade Prohibition Act, 211, 212, 213, 214, 217, 242, 245

Smith, A. D. (Wis. supreme court judge), 121

Smith, Gerrit (N.Y. State abolitionist lawyer/congressman), 10, 103, 105, 106, 188

Smith, Rev. John (Demerara missionary), 272, 274–77

Somerset Case (*Somerset* v. *Stewart* [G. B., 1772]), 6, 7, 18, 19–25, 31, 52, 57, 76, 77, 153, 154, 186, 271

Somerset, James (slave), 20, 22

South Bend Fugitive Slave Case, 80–83

South Carolina Association, 258, 261

Spooner, Lysander (Mass. antislavery lawyer), 106

Sprague, Peleg (U.S. district judge, Mass.), 90, 247, 248

Spratt, Leonidas (S.C. lawyer), 245

St. Jocelyn, Simeon (abolitionist), 226

Staples, Seth P. (N.Y. antislavery lawyer), 225, 230, 231

Stearns, George L. (Mass. abolitionist), 188

Stephen, Sir George (British abolitionist), 285

Stephen, Sir James (British abolitionist), 285, 289

Stephens, Alexander (Ga. congressman), 182, 184

Stevens, Thaddeus (Pa. congressman), 96, 98, 99

Stewart, Alvan (N.Y. abolitionist lawyer), 151–55

Stewart, Charles (colonial slaveholder), 20, 21

Stockton, Robert F. (naval officer), 218

Stono Rebellion, 197, 208, 209, 273

Storrs, George (N.H. abolitionist minister), 143–47

Story, Joseph (U.S. Supreme Court justice), 29, 52, 61–63, 65, 66, 77, 92, 117, 212–17, 219–21, 228, 233, 234

Stout, Joseph (Ill. abolitionist), 129, 130, 132

Stowall, Baron; *see* Scott, William

Stowell, Martin (Mass. abolitionist), 116

Strange, John (English lawyer), 25

Stratton, Samuel (Mass. abolitionist), 32, 33

Strader, Jacob (Ohio steamship owner), 37

Strader v. *Graham* (U.S., 1850), 35–38, 46

Stuart, J. E. B. (military officer), 190

Sullivan, William (Mass. lawyer), 218

Sumner, Charles (Mass. antislavery lawyer/U.S. senator), 65, 89, 181

Suttle, Charles F. (Va. slaveholder), 108, 109, 113–15

T

Tallmadge, Benjamin H. (U.S. deputy
    marshal, N.Y.), 85
Tallmadge, James (congressman, N.Y.),
    160
Taney, Roger B. (chief justice, U.S.
    Supreme Court), 13, 37, 38,
    44–48, 50–54, 62, 63, 120,
    151, 158–61, 240
Tappan, Arthur (abolitionist), 163, 169
Tappan, Lewis (abolitionist), 10, 86,
    224, 225, 226, 229, 233
Texas annexation, 102
Thompson, Joel (Pa. free black),
    83–84
Thompson, Mrs. (fugitive slave),
    83–84
Thompson, Smith (U.S. Supreme Court
    justice), 34, 226, 229, 230, 231,
    232
Thoreau, Henry David (antislavery poet),
    191–92
Thruston, Buckner (U.S. circuit judge,
    Washington, D.C.), 165, 168
Todd, Francis (Mass. shipowner),
    161–64
Toombs, Robert (congressman, Ga.),
    182, 183
Tortola, 290
Townsend, E. C. (ship captain), 239
Treason, 95–102, 251–53
Tubman, Harriet (abolitionist), 157
Turner, Nat (slave rebellion leader);
    see Nat Turner Rebellion

U

Ury, John (N.Y. conspirator),
    200–202

V

Valladingham, Clement (Ohio
    congressman), 195

Van Beuren, Edward (N.J. slaveholder),
    151, 154
Van Buren, Martin (U.S. president),
    227, 234, 236, 237
Van Evrie, Dr. J. H. (proslavery
    racial theorist), 53
Van Ness, Peter (U.S. district
    judge, N.Y.), 221
Van Zandt Case (*Jones* v.
    Van Zandt [1847]), 10, 30,
    70–75
Van Zandt, John (Ohio abolitionist),
    70, 72–74
Vattel, Emmerich de (legal theorist),
    15, 262
Vesey Conspiracy, 202–10, 256, 261
Vesey, Denmark, 202–10
Vinton, Samuel F. (Ohio lawyer),
    178–79
Virginia Colony, 3, 153

W

Wade, Edward (Ohio antislavery
    lawyer/politician), 126
Walker, Jonathan, "The Man with the
    Branded Hand" (abolitionist),
    12, 157, 170–75
Walker, Robert J. (U.S. senator, Miss.),
    34, 35
Wanderer (schooner), 212, 246–49
Ward, Samuel Ringgold (abolitionist
    minister), 103
Warfield, Elizabeth (Md. slaveholder),
    127
War of Jenkins' Ear, 198
Washington (brig), 222
Washington, George (U.S. president),
    2, 130
Wayne, James M. (U.S. Supreme
    Court justice), 239, 240, 244, 246
Webster, Daniel (U.S. senator), 27, 34,
    123, 130, 132, 241
Webster, Delia A. (Vt. teacher), 175,
    177

Weed, Thurlow (N.Y. politician), 243, 244

Weld, Theodore Dwight (abolitionist), 10, 77

Wells, Nathan (N.H. justice of the peace), 144

Wells, Robert (U.S. district judge, Mo.), 46

Wilberforce, William (British antislavery M.P.), 215, 277, 278, 280, 282

Williamson, Passmore (Pa. abolitionist), 13, 39–43

Willison, Hiram V. (U.S. district judge, Ohio), 126

Wilson, Henry (U.S. vice president), 168

Wheeler, John H. (diplomat and slave-holder), 39–43

Whiton, Edward V. (Wis. chief justice), 121–22

Whittier, John Greenleaf (abolitionist poet), 174, 192

Woodbury, C. L. (U.S. district attorney, Mass.), 248

Woodbury, Levi (U.S. Supreme Court justice), 71, 73

Wright, Elizur (abolitionist), 87

Y

Yale University, 226

Yorke, Sir Joseph (British antislavery M.P.), 277

Yorke, Sir Philip (English attorney general), 24

Z

Zulueta, Pedro de (London merchant, accused slave trader), 285–89

About the Author

Paul Finkelman is an assistant professor of history at the State University of New York at Binghamton. He received his Ph.D. from the University of Chicago in 1976 and was the J. Franklin Jameson Fellow at the Library of Congress in 1978–79. He has also been a Mellon Fellow at Washington University, St. Louis, and a Liberal Arts Fellow in Law and History at Harvard Law School, 1982–83.